CW01022817

The Cambridge Companion to
the Philosophy of Law

What is the nature of law as a form of social order? What bearing do values like justice, human rights, and the rule of law have on law? Which values should law serve, and what limits must it respect in serving them? Are we always morally bound to obey the law? What are the philosophical problems that arise in specific areas of law, from criminal and tort law to contract law and public international law?

The book provides an accessible, comprehensive, and high quality introduction to the major themes of legal philosophy written by a stellar international cast of contributors, including John Finnis, Martha Nussaum, Fred Schauer, Onora O'Neill and Antony Duff. The volume is an exceptional teaching tool that provides a critical introduction to cutting-edge work in the philosophy of law.

John Tasioulas is the inaugural Yeoh Chair of Politics, Philosophy & Law and Director of the Yeoh Tiong Lay Centre for Politics, Philosophy & Law, The Dickson Poon School of Law, King's College London, England.

Cambridge Companions to Law

Cambridge Companions to Law offer thought-provoking introductions to different legal disciplines, invaluable to both the student and the scholar. Edited by world-leading academics, each offers a collection of essays which both map out the subject and allow the reader to delve deeper. Critical and enlightening, the Companions library represents legal scholarship at its best.

The Cambridge Companion to European Private Law
Edited by Christian Twigg-Flesner

The Cambridge Companion to International Law
Edited by James Crawford and Martti Koskenniemi

The Cambridge Companion to Comparative Law
Edited by Mauro Bussani and Ugo Mattei

The Cambridge Companion to Human Rights Law
Edited by Conor Gearty and Costas Douzinas

The Cambridge Companion to Public Law
Edited by Mark Elliott and David Feldman

The Cambridge Companion to International Criminal Law
Edited by William A. Schabas

The Cambridge Companion to Natural Law Jurisprudence
Edited by George Duke and Robert P. George

The Cambridge Companion to Comparative Family Law
Edited by Shazia Choudhry and Jonathan Herring

The Cambridge Companion to Comparative Constitutional Law
Edited by Roger Masterman and Robert Schütze

The Cambridge Companion to the First Amendment and Religious Liberty
Edited by Michael D. Breidenbach and Owen Anderson

The Cambridge Companion to the Philosophy of Law
Edited by John Tasioulas

The Cambridge Companion to the Philosophy of Law

Edited by

John Tasioulas
King's College London

CAMBRIDGE
UNIVERSITY PRESS

University Printing House, Cambridge CB2 8BS, United Kingdom

One Liberty Plaza, 20th Floor, New York, NY 10006, USA

477 Williamstown Road, Port Melbourne, VIC 3207, Australia

314–321, 3rd Floor, Plot 3, Splendor Forum, Jasola District Centre, New Delhi – 110025, India

79 Anson Road, #06–04/06, Singapore 079906

Cambridge University Press is part of the University of Cambridge.

It furthers the University's mission by disseminating knowledge in the pursuit of education, learning, and research at the highest international levels of excellence.

www.cambridge.org
Information on this title: www.cambridge.org/9781107087965
DOI: 10.1017/9781316104439

First published 2020

Printed in the United Kingdom by TJ International Ltd. Padstow Cornwall

A catalogue record for this publication is available from the British Library.

Library of Congress Cataloging-in-Publication Data
Names: Tasioulas, John, editor.
Title: The Cambridge companion to the philosophy of law / edited by John Tasioulas, King's College London.
Description: Cambridge, United Kingdom ; New York, NY, USA : Cambridge University Press, 2020. | Includes index.
Identifiers: LCCN 2020007143 (print) | LCCN 2020007144 (ebook) | ISBN 9781107087965 (hardback) | ISBN 9781107458222 (paperback) | ISBN 9781316104439 (epub)
Subjects: LCSH: Law–Philosophy.
Classification: LCC K235 . C36 2020 (print) | LCC K235 (ebook) | DDC 340/.1–dc23
LC record available at https://lccn.loc.gov/2020007143
LC ebook record available at https://lccn.loc.gov/2020007144

ISBN 978-1-107-08796-5 Hardback
ISBN 978-1-107-45822-2 Paperback

In memory of John Gardner (1965–2019)

Contents

Contributors

Christopher Bennett is Professor of Philosophy, Department of Philosophy, University of Sheffield, UK.

Mitchell N. Berman is Leon Meltzer Professor of Law and Professor of Philosophy, School of Law, University of Pennsylvania, USA.

Kimberley Brownlee is Professor of Philosophy, Department of Philosophy, University of Warwick, UK.

R.A. Duff is Emeritus Professor of Philosophy, Department of Philosophy, University of Stirling, UK.

John Finnis is Emeritus Professor of Law and Legal Philosophy, University of Oxford, UK, and Biolchini Family Professor of Law, University of Notre Dame, USA.

The late John Gardner was a Senior Research Fellow, All Souls College, Oxford and Professor of Law and Philosophy at the University of Oxford, UK.

Robert P. George is McCormick Professor of Jurisprudence and Director of the James Madison Program in American Ideals and Institutions at Princeton University, USA.

Sherif Girgis is a PhD student, Department of Philosophy, Princeton University, USA.

Richard Holton is Professor of Philosophy, Faculty of Philosophy, University of Cambridge and a Fellow of Peterhouse, Cambridge, UK.

Larissa Katz is Associate Professor and Canada Research Chair in Private Law Theory, School of Law, University of Toronto, Canada.

Christoph Kletzer is Reader in Law, Dickson Poon School of Law, King's College London, UK.

Grant Lamond is University Lecturer in Legal Philosophy, Faculty of Law, University of Oxford and Felix Frankfurter Fellow in Law, Balliol College, Oxford, UK.

Timothy Macklem is Professor of Law and Philosophy, Queen Mary University London, UK.

Daniel Markovits is Guido Calabresi Professor of Law, Yale Law School and Founding Director of the Center for the Study of Private Law, Yale University, USA.

Sophia Moreau is Professor of Law and Philosophy, Faculty of Law and Department of Philosophy, University of Toronto, Canada.

Martha C. Nussbaum is Ernst Freund Distinguished Service Professor of Law and Ethics, Department of Philosophy and Law School, University of Chicago, USA.

Onora O'Neill is Emeritus Professor of Philosophy, Faculty of Philosophy, University of Cambridge and a member of the House of Lords, UK.

Massimo Renzo is Professor of Politics, Philosophy and Law, Dickson Poon School of Law, King's College London, UK.

Frederick Schauer is David and Mary Harrison Distinguished Professor of Law, School of Law, University of Virginia, USA.

John Stanton-Ife is Reader in Law, Dickson Poon School of Law, King's College London, UK.

John Tasioulas is Yeoh Professor of Politics, Philosophy and Law and the Director of the Centre for Politics, Philosophy and Law, Dickson Poon School of Law, King's College London, UK.

Guglielmo Verdirame is Professor of International Law, Department of War Studies, King's College London, UK.

Jeremy Waldron is University Professor, School of Law, New York University, USA.

Introduction

John Tasioulas

Inquiry into the nature of law as a form of social ordering, including the values it ought to serve, threads a long and complex path through the great classics of Western philosophy. Plato's *Republic* and *Laws*, Aristotle's *Nicomachean Ethics* and *Politics*, Cicero's *De Officiis*, St Thomas Aquinas' *Summa Theologiae*, Thomas Hobbes' *Leviathan*, Immanuel Kant's *The Metaphysics of Morals*, and G.W.F. Hegel's *The Philosophy of Right*, all engage with questions that form part of such an inquiry. But even though many of the chapters in this volume display an acute sensitivity to this history, with some authors explicitly situating themselves in a specific tradition of philosophical thought, they all share a determinedly contemporary focus. The contributors to this volume were not invited to provide overviews of the history of ideas, but rather to identify what they judge to be the key questions for us today, and the most compelling lines of approach to those questions, in relation to topics such as the aims and limits of law; what makes for sound legal adjudication; the scope of justice and the place of human rights; the concepts, institutional structures, and values that unify individual departments of law such as crime, contract, and tort; and the prospects for transnational legal order. This contemporary focus is neither a mere accident nor an instance of sheer parochialism.

Partly this focus is a matter of our special moment in the history of legal philosophy. Since the middle of the twentieth century, legal philosophy in the English language has experienced a bright Silver Age – we can leave it as a matter of speculation when the Golden Age of the subject occurred. There were twin engines powering this development. The first was the emergence of legal philosophy as a serious strand within what is broadly known as 'analytic philosophy' after the Second World War, a development associated to a considerable extent with the pioneering work of H.L.A. Hart, Professor of Jurisprudence at the University of Oxford from 1952 to 1969, especially his seminal 1961 text

The Concept of Law,[1] and that of his pupils and interlocutors who became leading figures, such as Ronald Dworkin, Joseph Raz and John Finnis. The second was the re-emergence of political philosophy as a flourishing discipline after a long period of torpor during which scepticism about objective inquiry into matters of value, largely associated with the logical positivist school, had seemed to consign it to obsolescence. Here the dominant figure was the Harvard philosopher John Rawls, whose great treatise *A Theory of Justice* (1971)[2] resuscitated political justice as a topic of philosophical investigation, one that was in turn to be taken up by the legal philosophers already mentioned in addition to political philosophers such as Robert Nozick, Michael Walzer, Susan Moller Okin, G.A. Cohen, Amartya Sen and Elizabeth Anderson. The relevance of this second development is due to the intimate connection between the legal and the political, insofar as the former constitutes one manifestation of the latter, taken in a broad sense. These works stand behind, and are the indispensable reference points for, the essays in this volume.

Partly, however, the focus on the contemporary reflects the inevitable responsiveness of a healthy philosophical culture to the changing circumstances and needs of its own times. Legal philosophy's dominant preoccupations, methods and doctrines evolve in relation to developments in philosophy more generally, but also in relation to new ideas, challenges and opportunities sparked by the continual processes of cultural, political, scientific and technological transformation. As a result, the questions we judge to be pressing today – such as the legitimacy of comprehensive forms of transnational legal governance, the impact of digital technology on the rule of law, the tendency of the language of human rights to swallow whole fields of political discourse, and so on – could hardly have arisen with the same urgency in 1971 (the publication date of *A Theory of Justice*), let alone ten years earlier (the publication date of *The Concept of Law*).

Rather than engage in the daunting task of giving a detailed introduction to the rich variety of insights offered by all of the chapters in this book, the rest of this Introduction will instead pick out, and elaborate on, three major themes that this volume exemplifies, each of them emblematic

[1] H.L.A. Hart, *The Concept of Law*, 3rd ed. (with Intro. by L. Green) (Oxford University Press, 2012).

[2] J. Rawls, *A Theory of Justice*, rev. ed. (Harvard University Press, 1999).

of ways in which legal philosophy has evolved in recent decades. These three themes are: (1) the diminishing significance within the field of the traditional rivalry between legal positivists and natural law theorists; (2) the increasing engagement with ethical/political questions regarding the values law should serve, and in terms of which it should be judged, reflecting both the influence of moral and political philosophy and the (potentially conflicting) need to draw upon a plurality of values; and (3) the rise of 'special' or 'particular' legal philosophy, focused on conceptual and normative issues regarding specific domains of law, such as contract law or public international law, and specific legal ideas, such as punishment or responsibility, as opposed to 'general' legal philosophy, which concerns itself with the phenomenon of law as such.

The first theme is the downgrading of the clash between 'legal positivist' and 'natural law' theories that has occurred in the last few decades. Many students in the recent past were taught legal philosophy largely through the prism afforded by this supposedly decisively important philosophical rivalry. One of the most distinguished legal philosophers of the last fifty years, Tony Honoré, captured this view of the subject in a vivid image:

> Decade after decade Positivists and Natural Lawyers face one another in the final of the World Cup ... Victory goes now to one side, now to the other, but the enthusiasm of players and spectators alike ensures that the losing side will take its revenge.[3]

But just over a decade after these words were originally published (in an essay of 1973), they had already begun to lose the ring of truth. To some extent, the downgrading of the significance of this debate was the upshot of a process of disaggregation. As Hart had already observed in *The Concept of Law*, legal positivism is not historically a label given to a single doctrine, but to a multiplicity of quite distinct theses.[4] By the same token, those usually described as 'legal positivists' and 'natural lawyers' did not simply address a single question, but rather an array of quite different, loosely related questions. These questions focused very broadly on law, morality and their relations, and included the following: (1) are there any objective moral values discoverable by the use of reason? (2) Does a law or

[3] A.M. Honoré, *Making Law Bind: Essays Legal and Philosophical* (Oxford University Press, 1987), 33.

[4] Hart, *Concept of Law*, 302.

legal system, simply in virtue of its status as a law or legal system, possess some moral value? (3) What makes for a good law, either in general or with respect to a particular department of law, such as criminal law? (4) When, if ever, is there a genuine reason to obey the law, one that rises to the level of imposing a moral obligation of obedience? (5) What are the respective roles of legal and moral considerations in good legal adjudication? And (6) how is the existence and content of a valid law to be determined, and does moral judgement inevitably play a role in this process of identification?

Once these distinct questions – and others besides – were clearly disentangled, it emerged that self-styled legal positivists increasingly came to regard their self-defining doctrine as predominantly, if not exclusively, an answer only to question (6).[5] The positivist view held that the existence and content of law was exclusively, or at least ultimately, a matter of social fact, so that its identification as valid law did not require the making of a moral judgement. Law was *posited*, a social creation, a matter of what had been duly enacted by a properly constituted legislature, or a decision laid down by a court, or a customary practice within a community, and so on. All of these are matters of social fact that require no moral judgement in their discernment. The 'natural law theorist', by contrast, contested this claim, insisting that moral judgement is indispensable in some manner to the identification of the existence of laws and the specification of their content.

These moves deflated the significance of the legal positivist/natural law debate for a number of reasons. First, in terms of scope, legal positivism now manifestly addressed only one out of the myriad questions arising within the philosophy of law – question (6) – and not obviously the most momentous question. To that extent, legal positivism could not purport to be 'complete' as a theory of law, in contrast to the more comprehensive ambitions of most natural law theorists. Moreover, even with respect to question (6), both positivists and their natural law opponents have tended to accept some version of the hermeneutical thesis, powerfully articulated by H.L.A. Hart, that a theory of the nature of law must be duly sensitive to the 'internal' point of view of those who accept legal standards as genuine reasons for action. In this way, the methodology of legal philosophy is

[5] See, for example, J. Gardner, 'Legal positivism: 5½ myths', *American Journal of Jurisprudence* 46 (2001), 199–227 and L. Green, 'Legal positivism' in E.N. Zalta (ed.), *The Stanford Encyclopedia of Philosophy* (Stanford University, 2003), https://plato.stanford.edu/entries/legal-positivism/.

radically distinct from that of the natural sciences, since atoms or quarks (for example) do not have a point of view that needs to be taken into account in explaining their behaviour. Indeed, many critics of legal positivism, such as Dworkin and Finnis, have presented their anti-positivist views as flowing from a more thoroughgoing effort to take seriously this 'internal' point of view on the very point of legal ordering. Second, insofar as legal positivists did address questions such as (1)–(5) listed above, they frequently found themselves allied with self-described natural law theorists, for example, on whether moral values are objective or on the qualities that make for a good law or morally binding law. Finally, the positivist thesis that law is a matter of social fact was not only championed in (often subtly) different versions by legal positivists, but at a very general level – the idea that law depends for its existence on social fact, such as enactments of legislatures or decisions by courts, and in that sense cannot be grounded on value judgements alone – it was also affirmed by leading natural lawyers from Aquinas to Finnis. In light of this situation, it is perhaps not surprising to find the most influential 'legal positivist' today responding to yet another attempt to 'refute' that doctrine by suggesting that '[p]erhaps it is not time to refute legal positivism, but to forget the label and consider the views of various writers within that tradition on their own terms'.[6]

Intersecting in complex ways with the de-emphasis of the legal positivism/natural law debate in recent decades has been scepticism about the idea that inquiries into the nature of law should be framed, either exclusively or predominantly, as exercises in 'conceptual analysis', a theme taken up in the chapter by Grant Lamond. The privileging of conceptual analysis is itself a legacy of the language-focused approach of the school of analytical philosophy. Thus, leading legal positivists, such as Joseph Raz, have presented their investigation of the nature of law as a form of conceptual analysis, aiming to limn the essential features of our concept of law and, as a result, to identify those features all legal systems necessarily possess. Their claim is that some version of the legal positivist thesis – that law's existence and content is identifiable independently of moral judgement – constitutes one of the necessary features of law.[7] Some critics

[6] J. Raz, *The Authority of Law*, 2nd ed. (Oxford University Press, 2009), 335.

[7] J. Raz, *Between Authority and Interpretation: On the Theory of Law and Practical Reason* (Oxford University Press, 2009), chs. 2–3.

have questioned, in the name of a naturalistic approach to legal philosophy continuous with the methods of natural science, the very idea of an objective inquiry into the concept of law.[8] Others, who conceive of law as an inherently value-laden, interpretive concept, have questioned the utility of conceptual analysis.[9] Still other, more moderate critics, have argued that conceptual analysis is only one strand of inquiry into the nature of law, and that it either needs to be subordinated to, or at least supplemented by, a substantive account of the moral value of law[10] or an empirical investigation into culturally and historically variable facts about how law operates.[11]

The second general theme foreshadowed above is an increased engagement with questions about the ethical values law should serve, and in terms of which it should be judged, rather than with any purely conceptual or descriptive enterprise. There is no doubt that an important influence here has been the revival of moral and political philosophy addressing *normative* questions – what is morally right and wrong, as a general matter, and in relation to specific ethical conundrums such as abortion or capital punishment – as opposed to *meta-ethical* questions addressing the metaphysics, epistemology or semantics of moral claims or else purely conceptual questions. One factor explaining the lively state of normative ethics and political philosophy in recent decades is the revival since the 1970s of broadly objectivist views of moral judgements, according to which they can be true, in some mind-independent sense, and also capable of being known. It is a striking fact, in this connection, that the most prominent 'legal positivist' of our day, Joseph Raz, and the most prominent 'natural lawyer', John Finnis, are both squarely in the objectivist camp in meta-ethics, even if they differ quite markedly on some of the normative questions they have addressed. This objectivist revival came after a long period of dominance of subjectivist views of ethics, most notably those of the logical positivist school, which largely limited the domain of objective truth to that of empirical investigation, paradigmatically in the natural sciences.

It is worth noting, however, that embracing ethical objectivism is something that both Hart and Rawls, in different ways, sought to avoid. Hart

[8] B. Leiter, *Naturalizing Jurisprudence* (Oxford University Press, 2007).

[9] R. Dworkin, *Justice in Robes* (Harvard University Press, 2009), chs. 6–8.

[10] J. Finnis, 'The nature of law', in this volume.

[11] F. Schauer, 'Social science', in this volume.

was throughout his career drawn to a broadly Humean, subjectivist view of the ethical, which he combined with the belief that in articulating a general theory about the nature of law one should remain studiously agnostic as to meta-ethical questions.[12] Rawls, meanwhile, came in the latter phase of his career to argue that political justification is an exercise in public reason, drawing on values and ideas implicit in the liberal democratic tradition, but scrupulously avoiding entanglement with 'comprehensive' ethical, philosophical or religious doctrines, such as those relating to the objectivity of value, on which reasonable persons inevitably differ.[13] Obviously, the non-objectivist and non-committal stances, respectively, of Hart and Rawls did not prevent either of them from engaging with some of the deepest moral questions relating to law, from the obligation to obedience to the justification of punishment. Whether these stances benefited their engagement with those questions, however, is another matter.

Another feature worth noting under this heading is a growing sensitivity to the plurality of values that need to be considered in the evaluation of law. Part of the context here is that Rawls' *A Theory of Justice* was crucial in rehabilitating broadly deontological approaches to moral and political philosophy. Unlike the previously dominant utilitarian approaches, which conceived of morality as essentially concerned with the maximisation of overall welfare, deontological approaches sought to elucidate norms of justice, equality, obligation and rights whose basis did not lie in welfare or its maximisation. Ronald Dworkin fused these two strands of thought by famously characterising rights as 'trumps' against the pursuit of general utility. A beautiful statement of the dialectic between these two views is Hart's essay 'Between utility and rights', first published in 1973.[14] But since that time we have seen the emergence of moral theories that transcend the utilitarian/deontological divide, including the development, by philosophers such as Philippa Foot and Alasdair MacIntyre, of virtue ethics, which draws inspiration from Plato and Aristotle in according

[12] Hart's endorsement of an official stance of meta-ethical neutrality in general philosophy of law can be found in Hart, *Concept of Law*, 168. His anti-objectivist sympathies in moral philosophy are evident in H.L.A. Hart, 'Who can tell right from wrong?', *New York Review of Books*, July 17 (1986).

[13] J. Rawls, *Political Liberalism* (1993); see also the discussion in J. Stanton-Ife, 'The ends and limits of law', in this volume.

[14] H.L.A. Hart, 'Between utility and rights' in H.L.A. Hart, *Essays in Jurisprudence and Philosophy* (Oxford University Press, 1983).

centrality to the virtues of character needed for a flourishing life. Martha Nussbaum's discussion of legal adjudication in this volume is largely structured around a contrast between utilitarian and common law approaches, where the latter is taken as a form of 'Aristotelian rationalism' that stresses the importance of case-by-case judgement against the background of a tradition that embodies the accumulated wisdom of past generations. Additionally, more thoroughgoing forms of pluralism have been advanced that recognise a variety of moral values, often with a basis in deep human interests or needs, but which are not amenable to complete subsumption under a utilitarian, deontological or virtue-ethical framework. A version of this sort of pluralism, one that conceives of values such as knowledge, friendship and health, as incommensurable, hence as not amenable to maximisation, is advocated in the chapter on civil rights and liberties by Sherif Girgis and Robert P. George in this volume.[15]

Part II of this volume is concerned with articulating specific ethical and political values relevant to the assessment of law, such as justice, legitimacy, autonomy, rights and the rule of law. Central here is the value of justice, which has long been thought to be intimately connected with law. Yet, assuming that justice is not synonymous with the whole of interpersonal morality, the question as to which subset of moral norms it encompasses is a difficult one. Onora O'Neill's chapter gives an account of justice as largely comprising those moral obligations that are appropriately enforced through law, supplemented by the idea that the core standards of justice are those 'perfect' obligations that are owed to some determinate right-holder. The fact that the revival of political philosophy has taken place under the stimulus of Rawls' *A Theory of Justice* has not prevented ongoing obscurity as to the boundaries of the concept of justice. However, commanding a clear-sighted view of those boundaries is vital to two key concerns. The first is that of identifying the extent to which justice conflicts with other values, such as mercy or economic prosperity, and may have to be compromised in order to make room for their demands.[16] The second is the extent to which justice itself may depend, both for the

[15] Philosophers such as John Finnis, James Griffin, Amartya Sen, Bernard Williams and Susan Wolf are also notable exponents of this pluralist tendency.

[16] Notable here is G.A. Cohen's critique of Rawls' difference principle as not truly a principle of justice, since it involves compromising the egalitarianism required by justice in order to take on board other considerations, such as prosperity; see G.A. Cohen, *Rescuing Justice and Equality* (Oxford University Press, 2008), ch. 7.

formulation and successful realisation of its demands, on a broader spectrum of obligations and ethical ideals that are not themselves matters of justice, such as norms of civility or public service. The second theme features prominently in O'Neill's chapter.

The concern with plotting the boundaries of ethical concepts relevant to law is perhaps especially important in relation to rights (including, notably, human rights). When Hart wrote *The Concept of Law*, the idea of an individual right had only a liminal presence in his elucidation of the conceptions of justice and morality. Today, the discourse of human rights has become the dominant vehicle for formulating politically resonant moral demands in the wider public culture, to the point of sparking worries about the debasement of the language of human rights as a result of this unruly proliferation of human rights claims. In Chapter 8, Jeremy Waldron seeks to inject some rigour into this domain by elucidating rights in terms of obligations that are justified by some valuable feature (e.g. an interest) of an individual taken by itself (rather than as part of an aggregate with other individuals),[17] while human rights are those rights that are possessed by all in virtue of their humanity and should in principle find expression in law.

A similar issue of expansionism arises in relation to the rule of law. My chapter on that topic addresses the rivalry between 'thick' and 'thin' conceptions of that ideal. Hart himself was a proponent of a thin view, according to which the rule of law consists in certain formal and procedural standards, such as clarity, publicity and non-retrospectivity, which are nonetheless compatible with a law's grave injustice in other respects. But in the intervening period, 'thick' accounts of the rule of law, which portray it as encompassing virtually all of the values manifested by good law, have gained widespread currency. All three of these chapters bring into focus the question of the price of this expansionism, of what may be lost when we try to incorporate a near-comprehensive legal ethic into a single concept such as justice, human rights or the rule of law.

By contrast, the topic of the legitimacy of law suffers not so much from the challenge of stemming undue expansion, but from systematic ambiguity regarding what 'legitimacy' means in a given context. Its various

[17] For a discussion of the pros and cons of the rival 'interest' and 'will' theories of rights, and for the thesis that rights are grounded ultimately in the common good rather than individual choices or interests, see Sherif Girgis and Robert P. George, 'Civil rights and liberties', in this volume.

meanings vary from simple empirical readings of the notion as referring to a general belief in, or acceptance of, the moral acceptability or bindingness of the law among a given populace, to normative readings that include, for example, the compliance of the law with certain formal and procedural norms (such as the rule of law) or the existence of good reasons for creating and maintaining in existence a certain law or legal system or for not obstructing its workings. In their historically informed chapter, Christoph Kletzer and Massimo Renzo engage with the recent debates on this topic, focusing on legitimacy as a right to rule that imposes an obligation of obedience on those over whom the authority purports to rule. A notable feature of these debates is that the familiar idea that an authority's right to rule has its source in the consent of subjects is rejected by many of the dominant theories of legitimacy today.

Whether we are bound to obey the law, of course, hardly exhausts the questions of ethical evaluation that the law poses. Even if we are obliged to obey a given law, it does not follow that the law is not defective in some way in achieving its proper ends, such as justice or the promotion of individual well-being. Whether we are ordinary citizens or officials, we need ethical principles to guide us on which domains of activity may be subject to legal regulation, and how to improve the quality of the laws that govern those domains. Here there is a longstanding philosophical concern with the ethical limits on the law's interference with individual choice, especially through forms of coercion, including, at the limit, criminal punishment. This has been one of the liveliest areas of debate in recent decades, and its contours are traced in John Stanton-Ife's chapter. Again, the theme of value pluralism is notable. The chapter shows how John Stuart Mill's famous 'harm principle' is open to multiple interpretations, depending in part on whether its focus is on harm prevention or the promotion of independence. Moreover, legal moralist approaches have arisen which contend that the implementation of morality through law can be reconciled with the Millian emphasis on individual freedom. The more radical of these embrace a radical pluralism that abandons the search for a master principle to govern the limits of coercive legal intervention, and place great stress on sensitivity to real-world conditions that justifiably limit the use of law to promote certain moral goals.[18] Inevitably, the

[18] See also the discussion of the harm principle as a basis for criminalisation in R.A. Duff, 'Criminal law', in this volume.

question will arise whether the increased complexity and intuitive plausibility of such pluralist views is secured at the price of excessive indeterminacy in its practical implications.

The third broad theme I wish to highlight is the increasing prominence of 'special' legal philosophy, which addresses conceptual and normative issues that relate to specific departments of law, such as contract law or international law, or particular legal concepts, such as causation and responsibility. Engagement with 'special' legal philosophy has risen sharply in recent decades. Now, of course, H.L.A. Hart was himself a pioneer in 'special' legal philosophy, with important writings on causation, punishment, responsibility and the limits of the criminal law. However, since the 1980s there has been a flowering of activity in this area, especially in relation to departments of private law, such as tort and contract, and now increasingly in international law, a discipline that had until very recently been philosophically dormant despite – or, perhaps, in part because of – the attention it received in the rather downbeat concluding chapter of *The Concept of Law*.

One might conjecture about the explanation for the rise of special legal philosophy. Partly, no doubt, it bears a complex relationship to the shift of focus away from the natural law/legal positivism debate, and perhaps from general legal philosophy more generally. Partly, it may be a product of the fact that increasing numbers of scholars have competence in both doctrinal law and philosophy. Finally, the general revival of moral and political philosophy no doubt also plays a role, since many of the questions that occupy special legal philosophy – such as whether contract law is best conceived of as an instrument of well-maximisation or a legal means of upholding duties to fulfil certain categories of promise – are fundamentally normative in character. This last feature of special jurisprudence raises the important question of its relationship to moral philosophy. Crudely, for those in the grip of an abstract moral theory, such as utilitarianism, the temptation will be to adopt a top-down approach in which particular departments of law, insofar as they are justifiable, are interpreted as distinctive institutional means for promoting the overarching goal of welfare maximisation. Those who are sceptical about the prospects of such a general moral theory, although not sceptical about morality, will be more inclined to adopt a 'bottom-up' approach which regards each department of law as acquiring its distinctive significance and coherence through a characteristic way of engaging with a certain value or combination of values.

Some of the richest work in special legal philosophy today is of this latter, 'bottom-up' variety. It typically pays very close attention to the contours of legal doctrine. And while leaving open the possibility that large areas of legal principle are seriously morally deficient, it tends to proceed on the basis of the presumption that this is not so in general, and that most departments of law embody a kernel of wisdom regarding some dimension of the legal regulation of social life, even if there are areas of doctrine in need of significant revision. Indeed, some of the revisions contemplated may challenge the deep significance of our familiar divisions between departments of law, such as contract, property and tort.[19] But even for such 'bottom-up' approaches, important questions remain as to the extent to which a given area of law can be understood by reference to a single organising concern or else a plurality of concerns and, if the latter, how this value pluralism can be integrated into a coherent whole that provides effective guidance for the development of doctrine, especially if the values are prone to address disparate problems or else to conflict among themselves.

Sophia Moreau's chapter on discrimination law illustrates many of the issues at play here. She highlights the way in which different theorists have sought to explain and justify discrimination law by reference to some key consideration – such as respect for equal social standing, the protection of freedom, or enhancing well-being (especially that of the worst off) – and moots the possibility of a pluralist theory that acknowledges all of them as good reasons for prohibiting discrimination. On a pluralist view, some of these considerations play a greater role with respect to some kinds of discrimination than others or generate different moral consequences as compared to others. As an example of the latter phenomenon, protecting people from discrimination that attacks equal social standing or individual freedom seems to be a matter of upholding duties owed to them as a matter of right, whereas the aim of eliminating discrimination so as to improve the position of the worst off may not generate such personal, rights-based duties. Similarly, John Gardner urges the merits of a theory of tort law that can overcome the stand-off between economic approaches, which view it as dealing with allocation problems thrown up by activities competing for

[19] See, for example, Daniel Markovits, 'Contract' and Larissa Katz, 'Property law', in this volume, which discuss theories that tend to assimilate contract and property, respectively, to a tort-like duty of non-harm.

scarce resources, and moral approaches, which regard it as focused on certain wrongful acts, by encompassing important truths captured by both approaches. But, as Moreau also notes, a pluralist theory risks appearing 'arbitrary', since there is no overarching value that ties together the other values into a coherent package and helps structure relations among them in guiding the development of legal doctrine. Can such coherence and guidance be achieved through more detailed examination of the values involved, the relations between them, and the problems they engage with, without resorting to a master value? Or must we temper any strong ambitions of theory guiding practice, resorting instead to an Aristotelian emphasis on uncodifiable practical wisdom?

Finally, it is worth mentioning the much more recent resurgence of philosophy of international law after a long period of hibernation since Hart's concluding chapter in *The Concept of Law*, as well as Hans Kelsen's voluminous writings on the subject. Engagement with the philosophy of international law may have suffered from a double impediment. On the one hand, there is a longstanding tradition of scepticism about whether it truly counts as law, at least in a central sense. For John Austin it was the absence of a global sovereign whose commands are backed up with sanctions that was the decisive factor, whereas Hart's subtler scepticism focused on the supposed absence of secondary rules for identifying, changing and adjudicating upon primary rules. On the other hand, there is longstanding scepticism, associated with various 'realist' schools in international relations, about the possibility of subjecting international relations, of which international law would necessarily form a part, to any really robust form of moral evaluation.[20] As Guglielmo Verdirame's chapter in this volume shows, the debate has largely moved beyond both of these obstacles. There is now more philosophical work being done on general theoretical questions, as well as particular areas within international law, such as human rights, the law of armed conflict, international environmental law and international criminal law, and also specific legal principles, such as sovereignty and self-determination. Partly this reflects the escalating degree of economic and other forms of globalisation, and the consequent deeper intermingling of domestic and international legal orders, especially as the latter penetrates more and more areas of our lives

[20] See 'Introduction' in S. Besson and J. Tasioulas (eds.), *The Philosophy of International Law* (Oxford University Press, 2010).

previously left to the sovereign discretion of individual states. A key question that confronts us is to what extent ideas about the nature and ends of municipal legal systems can be simply extended globally, or whether a more bespoke approach is required. As Verdirame points out, the most fundamental difference between international and domestic legal systems is the absence of a court with compulsory jurisdiction, and effective enforcement mechanisms, in the case of the former. Ronald Dworkin, in his last published article, attempted to overcome this difficulty by elaborating a theory of law premised on what he called the 'fantasy' that such an international court exists.[21] But this is a rather drastic move. On the question of the ends of international law, Verdirame plausibly denies that international law should be interpreted as subservient to any one master value, but he also highlights the deeper issue confronting us today: how should international law respond to the radical de facto ideological pluralism that exists in the world, and what is the role that the institution of state sovereignty should play in this response? Can international law, as a mechanism of globalisation, increasingly encroach upon sovereignty without risking its own legitimacy? We are still at a fairly early stage in addressing that large question, and recent political developments such as widespread discontent with the economic consequences of globalisation in mature democracies and the rise of authoritarianism across the globe, will make it even more pressing in the years to come.

I have had to be ruthlessly selective in focusing on these three main themes. Readers of this book will find in it many more questions and trends of thought that are worth pondering. In so doing, they will hopefully be inspired to join in the bigger conversation to which the chapters in this volume are contributions.

[21] R.M. Dworkin, 'A new philosophy of international law', *Philosophy and Public Affairs* (2013).

Part I

General Theory

Methodology 1

Grant Lamond

Introduction

Reflection on the law gives rise to many methodological questions. Some relate to legal doctrines – how best to understand, rationalise and potentially justify areas such as contract law or administrative law or criminal procedure. This chapter, by contrast, will focus on the question of how to understand 'law in general', or the 'nature of law'. Law in this sense is standardly regarded as a particular type of social practice with two dimensions: an institutional dimension involving bodies such as legislatures and courts, and a normative dimension involving the standards and other considerations created and applied by those bodies ('*the* law'). How should we go about making sense of this social practice? In what way should it be approached? There are three prominent features of our contemporary understanding of law that feed into the methodological debate: (a) the idea that law is a *general* type of social practice, found in different cultures at different times; (b) the idea that law is a social *construction*, whose existence depends upon the combined beliefs and actions of a variety of social actors; and (c) the idea that law is a *hermeneutic* practice, that is, a practice that we self-consciously understand as a distinctive sort of social practice, and in terms of which we understand and structure features of our social world.

A number of methodological approaches are evident in current philosophical discussions: (1) conceptual analysis, (2) theory construction, (3) central case method, (4) interpretivism and (5) naturalism. Three issues run through these different approaches: (i) whether law is best characterised in terms of its possessing necessary features; (ii) whether a characterisation of law must involve a moral evaluation of it; and (iii) how universal a theory of law should be.

1 Conceptual Analysis

Conceptual analysis takes as its starting point our current conception of law: what do we take law to be, and how do we distinguish law from other social practices? Conceptual analysis should not be equated, as it sometimes is, with linguistic analysis – that is, with an analysis of the use of the *word* 'law'. There are three main reasons why this is a mistake. First, the social practice that is the focus of inquiry can be referred to by terms other than 'law' (e.g. by 'legal practice', or 'legal systems'), and it can be referred to in languages other than English (e.g. by *droit*, or *Recht*). Secondly, the word 'law' refers to many things other than the social practice that is the focus of legal philosophy, for example, the laws of nature, or logic, or cricket. Finally, even if we restrict our attention to (what might be called) the 'juridical' sense of 'law', we are not primarily interested in what can or cannot be said with linguistic propriety about law: instead we are interested in understanding the nature of the practice that we refer to when we speak of 'law'.[1]

Conceptual analysis in legal philosophy generally proceeds along the lines described by Frank Jackson for philosophy generally, that is, as 'modest conceptual analysis'.[2] In a philosophical investigation, we must start with some question or issue that concerns us and that can be described in some way. The subject of the investigation (X) has to be identified in the terms in which we understand X, that is, in terms of our conception of X. So if we want to investigate the possibility of free will, we have to first understand what we ordinarily think we are designating by 'free will', and why we think it is significant. The way we do this is by reflecting on our intuitive judgements of when it would be appropriate to consider various real or hypothetical cases as involving X. When is X present or absent? Would something still be an instance of X if it lacked feature Y? To the extent that our intuitions about these cases generally coincide, we have a shared conception of X, and if there is sufficient convergence we can construct what might be called our 'folk theory' of X, that is, what we understand X to be, how we understand X to be related

[1] In writing of the 'nature' of law throughout this chapter, I mean simply the set of features that characterise the practice (or at least characterise paradigmatic instances of the practice).

[2] F. Jackson, *From Metaphysics to Ethics: A Defence of Conceptual Analysis* (Oxford University Press, 1998).

to other aspects of the world, and why we think X matters. On this approach, any theory of X must *start* with modest conceptual analysis, because any theory must identify the object of investigation. A theory of X which is based on an account that deviates too far from our folk theory of X is simply not a theory of X at all. Instead it is a theory of something else that bears some relationship or affinity to X. Conceptual analysis aims, therefore, to make explicit what is already implicit in our collective understanding of some subject matter.

There are three major objections to conceptual analysis as a method in legal philosophy: problems of (i) pluralism; (ii) indeterminacy; and (iii) parochialism. The first objection argues that even if we restrict our attention to law in its juridical sense, there is more diversity in the range of phenomena referred to by the term 'law' than conceptual analysis recognises. Legal pluralists point out that there are a wide variety of legal practices: for example, customary law, religious law, state law, international law, transnational law (such as *lex mercatoria*), and natural law.[3] The most influential contemporary theories of law neglect this diversity by focusing on state law as the paradigm of law. As a consequence they struggle to account for the other types of legal practices manifested in human history. To this objection it may be said that the type of law found in modern states seems to be a distinctive type of practice, different from though related to the others enumerated above.[4] The fact that there may be a higher-order category of 'law' to which this type of law belongs does not rule out developing a theory of (what we might call) municipal law, as well as a theory of the higher-order category. There seems to be no reason why one cannot develop theories of both, neither of which has a claim to be the single correct theory of law, or to have priority over the other.

The second objection to conceptual analysis is the concern that we do not, in fact, have a sufficiently determinate conception of law to allow for the construction of a robust 'folk theory', even if we limit ourselves to the

[3] B.Z. Tamanaha, *A General Jurisprudence of Law and Society* (Oxford University Press, 2001); W. Twining, *General Jurisprudence: Understanding Law from a Global Perspective* (Cambridge University Press, 2008).

[4] I say 'the type of law found in modern states' advisedly, because it is not clear that this type of law is limited to states (and thus it is not clear that it should be described as 'state law'): it may be that other stateless political communities also possess this type of law (e.g. European Union law, international law).

legal systems of political communities. It is argued that our understanding of law is extremely vague and open-ended, and any folk theory we might extract is correspondingly thin and indeterminate. It is not even clear that the variety of things we believe about the law are internally coherent. Any theory of law we construct, therefore, will have to go well beyond any shared understanding and make choices as to which parts of our ordinary understanding to foreground (and supplement), and which parts to relegate or reject. Conceptual analysis, on this view, is *so* modest that it does little more than vaguely identify an area of social life. To construct a theory of law we will have to turn to other resources.[5] To this it might be replied that legal philosophy is not, in fact, concerned with the 'folk' understanding of law. Law is an intricate social practice that can be understood properly only by those who are experts in the field, viz. those who either practise law or have studied it in detail (i.e. 'lawyers'). Just as we would not rely on the lay understanding of 'species' or 'evolution' in the philosophy of biology, so we do not base the philosophy of law on the views of the 'folk'. The philosophy of law works (primarily) from the views of lawyers, just as the philosophy of biology works from the views of biologists.[6] This is only a partial defence, however. It might be said that biologists are assumed to have the current state of biological knowledge at their disposal, that is, the best current understanding of the variety of life forms that exist. Lawyers, by contrast, are only experts on their own legal systems. They have no special expertise about the variety of forms of legal practice that have existed at different times and in different places. Their expertise is thus far more local than biologists.[7]

The third line of objection is based on the fact that modest conceptual analysis is limited to revealing *our* conception of X, that is, what *we* understand X to be, as elicited through our collective judgements about various real and hypothetical cases.[8] Even if we restrict ourselves to the

[5] J.M. Finnis, *Natural Law and Natural Rights*, 2nd ed. (Oxford University Press, 2011), 278–9; L. Murphy, 'Concepts of law', *Australian Journal of Legal Philosophy*, 30 (2005), 1, 7–8; and R.M. Dworkin, *Justice in Robes* (Harvard University Press, 2006), 228.

[6] Legal philosophy differs from the philosophy of biology inasmuch as some of the views of non-lawyers still matter, though to a lesser extent than the views of lawyers.

[7] One response to these concerns is found in 'theory construction', Section 2 below.

[8] This of course prompts the question: who are 'we' for the sake of this inquiry? I will assume that there is sufficient similarity in the views of contemporary lawyers, i.e. those trained in or practising in present-day municipal legal systems. This is not, of course, an uncontroversial assumption.

views of lawyers, it does not claim to show that the world is as lawyers might think it to be. Our concepts can be mistaken, since the world may fail to correspond to them. So, it can be argued, the aim of legal philosophy should not be to understand our *concept* of law, but to understand the social practice referred to by 'law'. Our concept of law might be flawed and misrepresent this practice. The only role for our understanding is in the initial identification of certain social practices as 'legal' practices. What makes those practices legal practices must be determined by an examination of the practices themselves, not our conception of the practices.

To this objection it may be replied that law differs from many other parts of the world in an important way. Law is a social construction: it is constituted by the concerted and coordinated actions and beliefs of many agents. This line of thought importantly underlies Hart's influential approach in *The Concept of Law*.[9] The aim of legal philosophy, for Hart, is to understand law from the point of view of those who participate in the practice, that is, to understand what those participants characteristically think, say and do when engaged in the practice. In particular, the aim is to understand the 'internal point of view', that is, the point of view of those participants who accept the practice, and are willing to be guided by it. In saying this, the assumption is that the internal point of view is the best *explanation* for what lawyers do, and why they do what they do. The way that committed lawyers understand their own actions as part of a particular social practice with a distinctive structure and method is the best explanation, on the whole, for the way the practice operates. So the practice 'itself' just is the practice as understood by the participants in it. In deepening our understanding of our conception of the practice we are at the same time deepening our understanding of the practice itself. This line of thought has proved extremely influential with later legal philosophers,[10] but it has not been without its critics. Some more sociologically minded theorists have doubted the significance attached to the internal point of view.[11] Others, inspired by the naturalistic turn in contemporary analytic

[9] H.L.A. Hart, *The Concept of Law*, 3rd ed. (Oxford University Press, 2012).

[10] See, for example, Raz's detailed elaboration of this line of thought: 'Can there be a theory of law?' in J. Raz, ed., *Between Authority and Interpretation* (Oxford University Press, 2009).

[11] E.g. N. Luhmann, *Law as a Social System*, trans K. Ziegert (Oxford University Press, 2004).

philosophy, have questioned the methodological attachment to the internal point of view.[12]

2 Theory Construction

Although Hart and many other legal philosophers are often thought to be engaged in the type of conceptual analysis described above, this is not the only way to understand their approach. Instead, conceptual analysis may be regarded as simply the starting point for the development of a theory of the social practice in question. To avoid confusion, I will refer to this alternative as 'theory construction', though it could just as easily be entitled 'rational reconstruction', or 'conceptual explanation'.[13] Many legal philosophers see something like modest conceptual analysis as doing no more than roughly identifying the object of theoretical investigation. Shapiro, for instance, presents this approach in terms of there being a variety of 'truisms' about law, that is, things that seem obviously true about law in general, for example, that some laws create rules, and that courts can make mistakes in applying the law.[14] A wide variety of truisms are available to the theorist who is seeking to construct a theory that makes sense of the truisms, that is, that explains why they are thought to be true. Although for Shapiro the theorist is seeking to understand what is necessary for a practice to be a legal practice, the truisms themselves are not necessarily true. They are instead (though Shapiro does not put it in these terms) the best evidence for the nature of law, but evidence that is provisional and may be rebuttable. Like evidence, some truisms are more easily rebutted than others, and some truisms may be – in a sense – irrebuttable. The truisms that courts are part of the legal system, or that legislatures can change the law, for example, are so central to our understanding of the law that a theory of law could not reject them. Or, to be more precise, a theory could not reject them without turning into a theory

[12] See Section 5 below.

[13] A distinction with some similarities to that drawn here between conceptual analysis and theory construction is very interestingly developed (in terms of conceptual analysis versus descriptive analysis) in N. Stoljar, 'What do we want law to be? Philosophical analysis and the concept of law' in W. Waluchow and S. Sciaraffa (eds.), *Philosophical Foundations of the Nature of Law* (Oxford University Press, 2013). See also M. Guidice, *Understanding the Nature of Law* (Edward Elgar Publishing, 2015).

[14] S. Shapiro, *Legality* (Harvard University Press, 2011), 15.

of something else, other than law. A theory of *law* has to be an account of a social practice that is (as Jackson puts it) suitably close to our ordinary conception of law.[15] Otherwise there is little point in regarding it as a theory of law.[16]

So there are two things going on with truisms. Some truisms may be so central to our current understanding of law that we would regard a theory that rejected any of them as no longer a theory of law. But there are, in addition, other truisms that matter to our conception of law, and are relatively central to our understanding of it, though we could abandon some of them and still regard a theory as a theory of law. The more of these truisms that a theory can account for – other things being equal – the better the theory. This naturally raises the question of what makes some truisms more 'central' to the law than others. Generally speaking, it is because they are either (a) regarded by the participants in the practice as fundamental or important aspects of legal practice, or (b) that they provide a deeper explanation for a significant range of the other truisms. Various truisms can be central to participants for a range of reasons, for example, because they bear on the operation and function(s) of the practice, or its social significance, or its evaluative importance.[17] In brief, central truisms relate to the basic operation and structural features of the practice, and to the fundamental evaluative significance of aspects of the practice in the eyes of its participants. Since law is a social practice, a theory of law is interested in both how it works and what it means (to the participants) in its social setting.

The theorist, then, is seeking not just to construct a theory that makes sense of enough of the truisms, but a theory that seeks to provide an explanation for the truisms and show how they fit together. What is involved is the construction of a theory of the object of study. As Marmor has argued, such theories are often constitutively reductive, in the sense that they attempt to explain legal phenomena in terms of non-legal

[15] Jackson, *From Metaphysics to Ethics*, 31.

[16] Though it is always possible to argue that there just is not a satisfactory theory that is 'suitably close' to our ordinary conception, in which case we may need to 'change the subject' of our theoretical inquiries. Some naturalists take this view in other branches of philosophy. See Section 5 below, and for further discussion B. Leiter, 'The demarcation problem in jurisprudence: a new case for scepticism', *Oxford Journal of Legal Studies* 31 (2011), 663–77.

[17] See J. Dickson, *Evaluation in Legal Theory* (Hart Publishing, 2001), ch. 2.

phenomena, and thus help us to better understand the nature of law.[18] So Hart's theory explains law in terms of the existence of a fundamental 'social rule' (the rule of recognition) that accounts for the nature of legal validity and explains the special role of officials in modern legal systems.[19] Raz in his earlier work explains legal norms in terms of 'exclusionary reasons' and legal systems in terms of the distinctive role of 'primary norm-applying institutions'.[20] Shapiro presents the law as a form of structured social plans.[21] All of these and many other theories attempt to construct an illuminating model of law out of components drawn from other aspects of social life. Such theoretical constructions, therefore, go beyond conceptual analysis. They are potentially revisionary, in two ways. First of all, they do not seek to preserve all of our pre-theoretical truisms about the law, and they may even involve the rejection of a few relatively central truisms. They seek instead to preserve sufficient truisms for the theory to still be recognisable as a theory of law. Secondly, they seek to provide a theoretical understanding that is itself cogent, that is, that is grounded in a plausible account of the social world. But theories differ in terms of the type of model that is provided, and the degree to which they seek to vindicate the beliefs of participants in the practice. These differences are reflected in the ways in which the truisms associated with law are revised by the theory.[22] Because of these complexities, comparing the merits of different theories can be very challenging, involving an overall assessment of both how convincingly they account for the truisms about law and how convincing an account they provide of the structure and functions of law.

From the perspective of theory construction, questions about which features of law are 'necessary' or 'essential' to law's existence are not the

[18] A. Marmor, 'Farewell to conceptual analysis (in jurisprudence)' in W. Waluchow and S. Sciaraffa (eds.), *Philosophical Foundations of the Nature of Law* (Oxford University Press, 2013), 214–17.

[19] Hart, *Concept*, chs. 5 and 6.

[20] J. Raz, *Practical Reason and Norms*, 2nd ed. (Princeton University Press, 1990), 73–84, 132–7.

[21] Shapiro, *Legality*, chs 5–7.

[22] This is one way to understand Stephen Perry's claim that an account of 'legal obligation' must be an internal claim that addresses whether, and under what conditions, people do have such obligations, and what sorts of reasons for action they create: S. Perry, 'Hart's methodological positivism', *Legal Theory* 4 (1998), 427, 446–50. It is not that a theory of law *must* be committed to doing this, but that it is a possible ambition of a theory.

key concern. Instead the emphasis is on the theoretical model that best accounts for the truisms associated with law. The model provides the paradigmatic case of a legal system, that is, the legal system that possesses all of the features accounted for by the theory. But the model is invariably a complicated one, with many components, and just as some of the truisms associated with law are more important than others, some of the components of a theoretical model are more fundamental than others. Consequently, there can be social practices that lack some of the components (e.g. having no 'legislative' body) that are still appropriately regarded as legal systems. Theorists tend to be less interested both in where the (rather indeterminate) borderline lies between law and non-law, and in which components are completely indispensable for a practice to be regarded as law.[23] Instead of the focus being on the minimum necessary features of law, the focus is on the paradigmatic case which possesses all of the characteristic features of law accounted for by the theoretical model.[24]

An important area of dispute in theory construction concerns the desiderata for assessing the success of the models. It is generally agreed that the desiderata include those that apply to all other theoretical endeavours, that is, considerations such as simplicity, clarity, comprehensiveness, coherence, explanatory consilience (which could be describe as 'meta-theoretic considerations',[25] or 'epistemic values'[26]). Such desiderata also include the importance of preserving enough of the participants' point of view, either as an additional constraint[27] or as part of the existing considerations (e.g. the epistemic value of 'evidentiary adequacy'[28]). Views divide, however, over the relevance of moral considerations to theory construction. Given that the methodology of theory construction allows for revisions to our pre-theoretical views, should the fact that a theory presents law as having some moral value or some moral point count in favour of that theory? Some theorists argue that a theory of law is seeking simply to understand the nature of law as it is, and so the moral

[23] Theorists often say that they are seeking the necessary features for a social practice to be a legal practice, but their theories normally go well beyond such an account.

[24] The paradigmatic can also be described as the 'central case' of law, but in a different sense to that discussed below in Section 3.

[25] Dickson, *Evaluation*, ch. 2.

[26] B. Leiter, *Naturalizing Jurisprudence* (Oxford University Press, 2007), 167–8.

[27] Dickson, *Evaluation*, ch. 2.

[28] Leiter, *Naturalizing Jurisprudence*, 172–5, 194–6.

character of the model endorsed by a theory is irrelevant to its success.[29] Other theorists regard taking into account a moral dimension as a legitimate consideration (albeit in different ways).[30]

It is worth emphasising that the view taken at this methodological level does not foreclose the type of substantive theory of law supported by it. MacCormick for example uses moral considerations to support a positivistic understanding of law.[31] On the other hand, a theory attributing moral value, purpose or content to the paradigmatic instances of law is not ruled out on the basis of non-moral desiderata.[32] There are, after all, a wide range of truisms about law that support a moralised account of its nature, for example, the commendatory sense of 'law' found in many European languages (*ius*, *droit*, *Recht*[33]), the law's use of the concepts of rights, duties and wrongs, the close association between law and justice, the law's claims on our allegiance, etc. So theory construction is compatible with many different types of substantive theories of law, and it would be a mistake to think that the use of moral considerations at a methodological level leads inevitably to a non-positivistic theory of law, or that the rejection of moral considerations at the methodological level is correlated with a positivistic theory of law.

3 Central Case Analysis

A very different approach can be found in the work of John Finnis.[34] Finnis rejects a methodology grounded in conceptual

[29] Dickson, *Evaluation*; A. Marmor, *Philosophy of Law* (Princeton University Press, 2011), ch. 5; Shapiro, *Legality*, ch. 1.

[30] E.g. N. MacCormick, 'A moralistic case for a-moralistic law?' *Valparaiso University Law Review*, 20 (1985), 1–41; Perry, 'Hart's methodological positivism'; J. Coleman, *The Practice of Principle* (Oxford University Press, 2001), 210; and Murphy, 'Concepts of law', 9. An alternative view is that the use of moral considerations involves a different project to theory construction, viz. the creation of an 'ameliorative' concept of law: see Stoljar, 'What do we want law to be?', 237–9, 247–51.

[31] MacCormick, 'A moralistic case'. Similarly, Coleman's philosophical pragmatism leads to a positivistic theory of law: Coleman, *Practice of Principle*, part 2.

[32] It will be suggested in Section 4 below that Dworkin's interpretive theory of law might be understood in this way.

[33] Cf. *lex*, *loi*, *Gesetz*.

[34] See *Natural Law and Natural Rights*, 3–22, 278–9, 417–19, 426–36; 'Describing law normatively' in *Philosophy of Law: Collected Essays Volume 4* (Oxford University Press,

analysis,[35] and proposes instead an analysis in terms of the 'central case' of a social or cultural practice. For Finnis, there is no one concept of law, but different concepts depending upon the type of inquiry that is being pursued. An historian may legitimately use a different concept of law to that used by a legal philosopher.[36] Legal philosophy, as a branch of social theory or social science,[37] is interested in developing a theory of law that is *general*, that is, that applies to different cultures and different times.[38] It aims to develop a concept for use in a general descriptive-explanatory account of human affairs.[39] And in moving from particular instances of legal practices to a general theory of law it necessarily uses *morally* evaluative judgement.[40]

The central case method has the following features. It begins with the assortment of phenomena that are routinely treated as instances of legal practices.[41] It then considers what the *point* of such practices is, that is, why there is a human social need (if there is) for something along the lines of these practices.[42] This is not simply a question of what the participants in those practices *believe* are the point of the practices, or what needs they *believe* those practices address. A theorist must determine what are the *genuine* human needs served by such practices, that is, what human goods and values are served by their existence, and could not be adequately served without them.[43] The next step is to develop an account of the form of the practice that most fully and adequately addresses the needs that the practices serve. This account constitutes the *focal meaning* of the general concept, and it refers to those instances of the practice that constitute its *central cases*. The general concept, however, also has a *secondary meaning*,

2011); 'Grounds of law and legal theory: a response', *Legal Theory* 13 (2007), 315–21; 'Introduction' in *Philosophy of Law*, 1–9. For discussion see Dickson, *Evaluation*, ch. 4; Leiter, *Naturalizing*, ch. 6; J. Gardner, 'Nearly natural law' in *Law as a Leap of Faith* (Oxford University Press, 2012); and V. Rodriguez-Blanco, 'Is Finnis wrong? Understanding normative jurisprudence', *Legal Theory* 13 (2007), 257–83.

35 Finnis, *Natural Law*, 278–9.

36 Finnis, 'Grounds of law', 318; *Natural Law*, 430.

37 See *Natural Law*, 3, 4, 16, 17, 18, 19, 417, 418, 426, 428–9, 430–1, 434, 435.

38 *Natural Law*, 4, 9, 18, 426, 428–9, 431, 434 n. 14, 436.

39 *Natural Law*, 428–9, 430–1; 'Grounds of law', 319.

40 Strictly speaking for Finnis it involves the use of judgements of 'practical reasonableness', of which morality is the most important form: see *Natural Law*, ch. 5.

41 *Natural Law*, 3–4, 278–9, 428.

42 *Natural Law*, 3, 14, 16, 278–9, 432 n. 13, 434.

43 *Natural Law*, 3, 11–18 (especially 15, 16, 18), 433.

which refers to those instances of the practice that are (to a lesser or greater extent) *peripheral cases*, that is, those forms of the practice where some of the features found in the central cases are less well instantiated (or even absent altogether).[44]

The inspiration for this type of analysis of social and cultural practices goes back to Aristotle's discussion of homonymy.[45] Aristotle's account of friendship, for instance, distinguishes true (complete) friendship from other forms of friendship, such as those that are merely useful (e.g. business friendships), or merely for pleasure.[46] The claim is that social and cultural relationships and practices display a common pattern in which some forms of the relationship or practice are core forms, with other forms being dependent on the core in the sense that they are similar to the core, but do not fully possess all of its features. To properly understand the relationships or practices we must focus on the core case, since that is the case where the relationship or practice is fully instantiated, and understand dependent cases as derivative, and less complete, versions of the central case.

To understand law, therefore, a theorist must determine what human needs law truly serves, and that could not be adequately served without it. The form of legal system that most fully and adequately meets those needs is the central case of law, and the focal meaning of the concept of law is the account that properly explains the need for a social practice with the type of internal structure and mode of operating found in the central case. Finnis himself proposes that in any complex society there will be a need for a system of authority for social decision-making, that is, for decisions to be made in the name of the community and to be binding on the members of the community.[47] Such a system is necessary to protect and promote the 'common good' of the community, that is, the set of conditions which enable all of the members of the community to lead morally worthwhile lives, both individually and in partnership with others, and enable the community as a whole to flourish.[48] It is the need for a system of authority that is in accord with and that promotes the common good that gives the central case of law its particular structure and modes of operation.[49]

[44] *Natural Law*, 9–11, 429–30, 431–2.
[45] *Natural Law*, 9–11.
[46] Aristotle, *Nicomachean Ethics*, VIII.3.
[47] *Natural Law*, ch. 9.
[48] *Natural Law*, ch. 6, especially 154–6.
[49] *Natural Law*, ch. 10.

A number of questions can be raised about this methodological approach. One concerns whether it always delivers a central case of complex social practices. Consider systems of property. Every society needs some rules over who can use resources, and how and when. This is because there are needs such as reducing conflict over the control and benefits of resources, ensuring sufficient productive use of them, and conserving scarce but valuable resources. So there are a variety of functions that any system of property serves. Now it may be that every society needs *some* system of property, but such systems vary greatly, and which type of system is desirable depends on the historical circumstances facing a society: what would work well in medieval Europe might not in the digital age in India. So every society needs to have rules on the use of resources, and similarly every complex society needs to have rules on social decision-making, but the preferable form of law may well vary greatly from one social context to another. It may be, then, that there is no central case of a practice in the sense of a form of the practice (even one at a very high level of abstraction) that is suited to the varying circumstances of different societies. There are, instead, just a variety of functions that the practice serves, and a basic set of components from which different practices can be assembled to serve them. Which form of the practice best serves the common good of the community is a highly variable matter, and there is no higher-order form under which all of these can be subsumed. So the central case method may not, in fact, be able to deliver a unitary central case of the practice: rather, the method may simply explain the social needs which the practice addresses, and the elements which can be useful for addressing those needs successfully.

A separate issue is whether the central case method need be committed to a complete account of human goods and values, that is, a highly precise and detailed specification of what the human good consists in. An alternative would be to develop the central case of a social practice on the basis of a far weaker account of human goods, that is, an account that relied on widely endorsed and relatively uncontroversial views about what things were valuable for humans – a broadly ecumenical perspective. This might then provide common ground for theorists to develop accounts of the morally preferable form of law.[50] This weaker approach would still rely

[50] See N.E. Simmonds, 'Philosophy of law' in N. Bunnin and E.P. Tsui-James (eds.), *The Blackwell Companion to Philosophy*, 2nd ed. (Blackwell, 2002), 417–18.

on moral evaluation to develop a general account of law, but it would not claim to provide a complete account of the central case of law. It might be argued, for instance, that this is what Hart was really doing in *The Concept of Law* in explaining the existence of certain common features of legal systems, despite his own protestations of value-neutrality.[51] It is just that the assumptions are so weak and widely held that the fact that they are evaluations of the human good goes unnoticed in the discussion.

Finally, the need for *any* moral evaluation might be challenged in the following way. It is always possible that in considering the various instances of a social practice that are categorised together at the initial stage of inquiry, we might find a consensus (or at least widespread agreement) among the participants in those practices over the point or functions of the practice, or widespread agreement on a subset of functions served by the law, despite variation in other functions attributed to it. If these functions provide a rationale for identifying certain features of legal practice as key features then it would be possible to have a general characterisation of the practice that did not require moral evaluation of the genuine human goods and values served by the practice. It could be based instead simply on what was generally believed about the practice by the participants in the practice.

4 Interpretivism

Another approach that also regards moral evaluation as indispensable to understanding the nature of law is Dworkin's interpretivism as presented in *Law's Empire*.[52] According to Dworkin, law is an 'interpretive' social practice, and it follows from this that any account of the practice must seek to provide a justification for it. Why is this? An 'interpretive' social

[51] See Hart, *Concept*, 239–41, though here Hart is eschewing the aim of *justifying* legal institutions. A theory that relies on moral evaluation need not be seeking to *justify* law as a social institution: it may simply be pointing to those features that, *pro tanto*, make the practice humanly valuable and explain its existence, even if, all things considered, it is not morally justified.

[52] Harvard University Press, 1986. Dworkin's later views depart from the account in *Law's Empire*, as will be noted below: see *Justice in Robes*, Introduction and ch. 8. On the methodology of *Law's Empire* see J.M. Finnis, 'Reason and authority in *Law's Empire*' in *Philosophy of Law*; Raz, 'Two views of the nature of the theory of law' in *Between Authority*; and Dickson, *Evaluation*, ch. 6.

practice is one in which the participants manifest an 'interpretive attitude', that is, (a) they regard the practice as having some point (or purpose or value) that can be described independently of the standards that make up the practice, and (b) they regard what is required according to the practice as not being necessarily or exclusively what it is presently taken to be but as being instead sensitive to its point, so that the requirements must be understood or applied or extended or modified or qualified or limited by that point.[53] Furthermore, an interpretive practice is characteristically capable of bearing more than one account of its point or purpose, so it allows for competing accounts of these.[54] Consequently, the participants in an interpretive practice can engage in meaningful disagreements over what the practice really requires: it depends upon which account of the point of the practice is the best account, all things considered.

Dworkin argues that law is an interpretive practice in this sense.[55] Accordingly, a theorist cannot provide a morally value-neutral account of the practice, because in attributing some point or value to the practice, the theorist is taking sides in the inherently controversial debate over what gives the practice value. Nor can a theorist provide an account of the practice's essential or necessary features. Every interpretive practice is particular to its cultural context. The content of an interpretive practice is given simply by whatever the participants in the practice generally regard as being part of the practice. It is the totality of the practice that is the subject of participants' interpretations.[56] The content of the practice is susceptible to change over time, and there are no essential features that preserve its identity over time.[57] So when we speak of a certain 'type' of social practice, we are simply extrapolating from the immediate practice and judging some other practice(s) to be sufficiently similar to be described in the same terms. But the relationship between the different practices is merely one of overlapping similarities: there is no 'essence' of the practice that they all share.

Even if we allow for the sake of argument that law is an interpretive practice in Dworkin's sense, does it follow that there cannot be a non-morally evaluative account of the practice, and that the practice has no

[53] *Law's Empire*, 47.
[54] *Law's Empire*, 52–3.
[55] *Law' Empire*, 87.
[56] *Law's Empire*, 65–6.
[57] *Law's Empire*, 69–70.

essential features? It clearly does follow that a theorist cannot provide a non-committed account of what the practice requires of those to whom it applies (i.e. a non-committed account of 'the law'), but that in itself does not rule out understanding the practice itself in non-justificatory terms. A theorist can still say, for example, that a community has a social practice 'X': (i) which has (roughly) a certain content (i.e. the content that the members of the community generally regard it as having); (ii) which is an 'interpretive' practice due to the attitudes of the members toward X; (iii) (at present) the members either (a) generally agree that the point of X is *y*, or (b) each has their own view as to the point of X, or (c) some variation between (a) and (b) (e.g. there are two or three dominant views, or one dominant view and three influential alternatives, etc.); and (iv) that views over the point of X are susceptible to change over time. The practice could be understood in terms (i)–(iv), then, without the theorist herself proposing some value or point to the practice.

A more interesting claim is that interpretive practices do not have essential features. This stems from Dworkin's view that there is a primary referent for an interpretive practice X, and that other instances of X are identified by their (differing) similarities to that primary referent. Since, over time, the practice that is the primary referent could itself change radically, it would be a mistake to think that it has any defining features, and that other practices (including earlier and later stages of the primary referent) are referred to as 'X' because they share those features.[58] In itself, however, this argument does not rule out the possibility that *at a particular point in time* the participants in a practice may regard it as having certain essential features, and treat practices in other cultures as being of the same kind because they share those features. If a particular practice can be the primary referent for X, then that practice at a certain period of time can equally well be the primary referent. Nonetheless, this makes the question of whether practice X is regarded by its participants as having essential features a contingent question at a particular point in X's history. It is possible that the participants in a practice may not regard X in this way: they may simply regard a number of social practices as obvious cases of X without there being a set of features that they all share. This raises a more general question of whether we should regard legal practices as

[58] *Law's Empire*, 69–70.

connected through a set of necessary and sufficient features that they all share (with there being some marginal or borderline cases that do not possess all of the features), or whether legal practices are related in terms of their family resemblance to one another.[59] On the latter view, we regard our own practice as a paradigmatic case of law, and recognise other clear cases of law, but we do not do so on the basis of a shared set of essential features. There is just a range of features that overlap between some of the instances. There may be some necessary features shared by all legal practices, but the set of these necessary features is not sufficient to distinguish law from other (non-legal) practices. This view of law is an interesting possibility. It does not however show that a theory of law must be morally evaluative: whether law is a family resemblance concept does not depend on moral evaluation.

At some points Dworkin suggests that determining whether a practice is interpretive is itself an interpretive question, that is, that the characterisation of the practice depends upon which view shows the practice in its 'best' light, and is thus inherently moralised.[60] But this claim seems to cash out in terms of which view makes best *sense* of what the participants in the practice think, say and do.[61] To say that the best interpretation of a practice is that it is an interpretive practice is not to say that this is the view of the practice that shows it in its morally best light; it is just to say that it shows the participants' conduct to be more coherently intelligible and meaningful than characterising the practice in any other way. After all, for Dworkin a practice may be best understood as an interpretive practice despite there *not* being a good interpretation of the practice, that is, in spite of the fact that there is no value in the practice sufficient to show that it is worth carrying on.[62] The fact that the best interpretation of an interpretive practice is what Dworkin calls a 'sceptical' one[63] does not prevent the practice itself from being an interpretive one.

[59] See L. Wittgenstein, *Philosophical Investigations*, 4th ed. (Wiley-Blackwell, 2009), §§65–77, and for discussion R.J. Fogelin, *Wittgenstein*, 2nd ed. (Routledge & Kegan Paul, 1987), 133–8 and M. Forster, 'Wittgenstein on family resemblance concepts' in A. Ahmed (ed.), *Wittgenstein's Philosophical Investigations: A Critical Guide* (Cambridge University Press, 2010).

[60] See, e.g. R.M. Dworkin, *Justice for Hedgehogs* (Harvard University Press, 2011), 160–3.

[61] E.g. Dworkin, *Justice in Robes*, 12.

[62] *Law's Empire*, 66.

[63] *Law's Empire*, 78–9.

In Dworkin's later work his focus shifts exclusively to understanding 'the law', that is, the legal rights and duties that exist under the social practice of law.[64] Arguably, this no longer involves a distinctive methodology, but rather a distinctive substantive view of the nature of legal practice. The argument for characterising law as interpretive, after all, is that it better accommodates certain fundamental features of legal practice, particularly substantive disagreements over the grounds of law and the moral force of legal claims.[65] If law is best characterised as an interpretive practice, this entails that how to determine legal rights and duties (and how to determine which aspects of the social practice count (and in what way) toward determining those rights and duties) is always in part a moral question.[66] But the argument that law *is* an interpretive practice in the first place need not rely on the moral attractiveness of this characterisation. It may rely instead on its making better sense of the practice than any rival characterisation. In this case it may be understood as a form of theory construction that produces a moralised account of the nature of law on the basis of non-moral criteria.

5 Naturalism

Naturalism in legal philosophy is inspired by work in general analytic philosophy that is sceptical of both the use of 'intuitions' by philosophers in their arguments, and by the idea that philosophical methods can determine the necessary features of phenomena.[67] On the issue of intuitions, naturalism is agnostic on the debate noted in Section 1 as to whether we have a coherent and determinate set of intuitions about law. Instead, it

[64] In *Justice in Robes*, for instance, Dworkin seems to abandon some of the claims in *Law's Empire* about interpretive practices by introducing the idea that there is a 'sociological' concept of law – law in the sense of a social practice – that is 'imprecisely criterial', as opposed to a 'doctrinal' concept of law, i.e. 'the law' of a jurisdiction, which is interpretive: 2–4.

[65] *Law's Empire*, 1–44, 108–13.

[66] See N. Stavropoulos, 'Interpretivism' in E.N. Zalta (ed.), *Stanford Encyclopedia of Philosophy* (Summer 2014 ed.).

[67] Leiter, *Naturalizing Jurisprudence*, 175–81. See *Naturalizing Jurisprudence*, part II, which contains the most sustained discussion of the possible relevance of philosophical naturalism for legal philosophy. For discussion see Finnis, 'Describing law'; J. Dickson, 'On naturalizing jurisprudence', *Law and Philosophy*, 30 (2011), 477–97; and B. Leiter, 'Naturalized jurisprudence and American legal realism revisited', *Law and Philosophy*, 30 (2011), 499–516.

points out that the question whether either view is correct is an empirical one, and none of the participants in the debate have undertaken any proper empirical research to establish their views. So we should abstain from drawing any strong conclusions about what we would 'intuitively' think about law, at least beyond the most obvious points, which are probably insufficient to establish any sort of theory. On the issue of our 'concept' of law, the point is this. At best, conceptual analysis will tell us what 'our' concept of law is, that is, what we take law to be. But concepts are not set in stone; they can change, and do change, in response to related changes in our understanding of the world. So even if some aspect of 'our' concept of law is currently understood as a necessary condition for a practice to be a legal practice, that could change in time. At best conceptual analysis can give us local ethnographic information about the content of our current concepts: it cannot deliver timeless truths about the nature of the world.

Of course, as noted above, some legal philosophers would concede the point that our concept of law is parochial. But, they would continue, it is an important task to better comprehend how we understand our social world.[68] We are not seeking 'timeless' truths, but truths about our own self-understanding. We are also seeking to understand what is central to our current conception of law in order to evaluate that understanding, and see whether or not it is flawed. Other theorists might argue that the significance of our current concept of law is simply that it places some constraints on constructing a theory if that theory is to be, in any meaningful sense, a theory of *law*.

But there is a deeper point embedded in the naturalistic critique. As noted earlier, one of Hart's most influential contributions to legal philosophy was his emphasis on understanding the 'internal point of view' – understanding law from the point of view of those participants in legal practice who accept the practice. But this was not simply an exercise in self-understanding. The assumption in Hart's work was that the internal point of view had explanatory priority: the conduct of the participants in the practice was best explained in terms of their beliefs about how they should act within the practice. It is this assumption that is called into question. Again, this is not because it is necessarily false, but because

[68] Raz, 'Can there be a theory of law?', 31.

whether it is correct needs to be vindicated by empirical research, rather than intuitive judgements based on anecdotal evidence that this is how law operates. Empirical research might, for example, show that official behaviour is better predicted and explained by factors other than the legal standards that officials claim to be following.

Naturalism proposes that instead of relying on our intuitive judgements and our conceptual understanding of law, we should turn to the social sciences to see whether law earns its keep. What does the best science say about the place of law in society? Indeed, does the best science *have* a place for law in its account of how society functions? And if it does, what conception of law does that science utilise? On this approach, legal philosophy should respond to the social sciences, just as the philosophy of biology responds to the natural sciences. Both law and biology are aspects of the world, and the role for philosophy is to work in partnership with the best empirical theories to enrich our understanding of these parts of the world.

Against this it may be noted that the social sciences have nothing like the explanatory power and theoretical depth of the natural sciences.[69] Physics, chemistry and biology are immensely successful research programmes with great predictive power. The social sciences tend, by contrast, to have piecemeal value and pockets of depth. Understanding humans as cultural subjects has so far proved an elusive task. It is not clear that the social sciences need theorists to abandon their own methodologies: instead, it may be that the social sciences can benefit from alternative approaches.

Still, the point remains that our current conception of law may be mistaken. It is vulnerable to empirical research undermining the explanatory significance of participants' own beliefs about why they do what they do, and why they attribute certain value to the practice. It may be that our self-understanding is flawed. But it might be said that given the highly self-conscious type of activity that legal practice is, it would be surprising if the participants' perspective was *systematically* flawed. Social scientific research could, of course, surprise us and undermine the legal view, but absent such evidence it is a reasonable presumption that this is not the case, and so legal philosophers need not yet abandon their various *modi operandi*.

[69] As Leiter himself recognises: *Naturalizing Jurisprudence*, 192.

Having said all this, the philosophical naturalist (like the central case theorist) might press the following question: if a theory of law is based (even loosely) on 'our current conception of law', why is this an apt subject of philosophical study? It may be a subject of considerable anthropological and cultural interest – particularly to us – but why is it of any *philosophical* interest?[70] One possible line of response might be this. Our contemporary conception of law is heavily conditioned by the practices of modern municipal legal systems, since these are the systems under which we live, and with which we are most familiar. Furthermore, modern municipal legal systems are fairly similar to each other, due to the historical circumstances that led to the export of European legal practice throughout the world (often by conquest and colonisation) from the fifteenth century on. And one of the key features of modern municipal law is its hermeneutic nature, that is, that it is partly constituted by our self-conscious conception of it as a distinctive social practice. To understand modern law, therefore, is in part to understand our conception of law. Now it may be that our concept of law relates primarily to a particular kind of social construction with a specific historical genealogy. But philosophy is not restricted to the study of the timeless and the universal features of the world and of human existence. Instead, philosophical inquiry can be appropriate to help us understand any area of human experience which puzzles us, and where the puzzles resist other methods of investigation. Given the enormous importance of law in modern life, and the perplexities over its nature, philosophical study might be said to be entirely apt.

[70] Leiter, *Naturalizing Jurisprudence*, 177.

2 The Nature of Law

John Finnis

Recent work in philosophy of law includes many discussions of law's 'nature or essence', understood as those properties of law that are necessary, or at least important and typical or characteristic of 'law as such, wherever it may be found'[1] (or that help explain how and why law can be considered a *kind*, and laws or legal systems its *instances* or instantiations). Some hold that law has no nature; only natural objects have a nature, and law is artefactual, not natural. Others reply that there are *kinds* of artefacts: paper clips differ in nature from printer drivers, and being a soft cheese blob excludes being a paper clip – excludes being something of that kind or nature. Attention is shifting promisingly to paradigms of artefact more relevant to law than paper clips are: assertions, for example.[2]

Discussions of law's nature need a better inventory of the kinds and paradigms of description(s), explanation(s), and *kind(s)* (natures). Consider the inventory (still improvable) with which Aquinas began his *Commentary on Aristotle's Ethics*.[3] It identifies four kinds, or domains, of pattern (*ordo*)

[1] J. Gardner, 'Law in general' in J. Gardner, *Law as a Leap of Faith: and Other Essays on Law in General* (Oxford University Press, 2012) 270, 279, 301.

[2] Exemplars besides Gardner include Raz, 'The problem about the nature of law' (1983) in J. Raz, *Ethics in the Public Domain* (Oxford University Press, paperback ed. 1995); Raz, 'On the nature of law' (1994/6) and 'About morality and the nature of law' (2003) in J. Raz, *Between Authority and Interpretation* (Oxford University Press, 2009); F. Schauer, 'On the nature of the nature of law', *Archiv für Rechts- und Sozialphilosophie*, 98/4 (2012), 457–67; B. Leiter, 'The demarcation problem in jurisprudence: a new case for skepticism', *Oxford Journal of Legal Studies* 1 (2011) 663–77; essays by Murphy, Flores and Marmor in W. Waluchow and S. Sciaraffa (eds.), *Philosophical Foundations of the Nature of Law* (Oxford University Press, 2013); M. Murphy, 'Two unhappy dilemmas for natural law jurisprudence', *American Journal of Jurisprudence* 60 (2015) 121–41; and L. Burazin, 'Can there be an Artefactual Theory of Law?', *Ratio Juris* 29 (2016) 385–401.

[3] Finnis, *Aquinas* (1998), 20–3; *Natural Law and Natural Rights*, 2nd ed. (2011), 136–8, 457; J. Finnis, 'Reflections and responses' in J. Keown and R.P. George (eds.), *Reason, Morality, and Law: The Philosophy of John Finnis* (Oxford University Press, 2013), 459–584, 462 n. 14.

and correspondingly of explanatory (analytical and synthesising) description (*scientia*), each irreducibly distinct though all found in the life and nature of human persons and their groups.

First domain: patterns (and patterned things or subjects of inquiry) and systems that are what they are quite independently of our thinking – the domain of **nature**, investigated by the natural sciences, in which natural kinds and natural laws (such as the Second Law of Thermodynamics) are discerned and experiments are accordingly expected to be replicable in many times and places.

Second domain: patterns or systems of thought by which we make our thinking coherent and fruitfully non-fallacious: logical. This is **logic**, not just formal or symbolic. Aquinas put linguistic skills and language here, but they belong more to the fourth domain, artefacts. Assertions, for example: as linguistic acts of communication, they are artefacts, and could each have been constructed differently in every detail. Still, they belong to the very logic of rationality's and discourse's intrinsic structures, moving from questions about givens, through insights as hypotheses about why the givens are as they are (and thus about *what* they amount to, or are evidence of), to judgements asserting that *such and such is* (or is not) *the case*.

Third domain: the order (pattern) one can bring into one's deliberating toward acting to attain ends by means in the open horizon of one's life (as individual or group). This practical rationality, in its developed forms, amounts to a **morality** or ethics of conduct, identifying kinds of choice, disposition and action as good or bad, right, acceptable or wrong by virtue of their reasonableness or unreasonableness in that open horizon.

Fourth domain: the kind of pattern one can impose upon matter (stuff, materials, including one's bodily parts and operations) with the kind of means–end practical rationality that concerns making (and working with) **artefacts** in the widest usual sense, including arts, crafts and technologies or techniques including, as just noted, language and its use.

Each of the terms 'nature' ('of this nature'), 'essence' ('essentially', . . .), 'kind' ('of a different kind'), 'identity' ('identical', 'similar', . . .), and so forth, is correctly usable in each of the four domains. But the precise meaning of each shifts, more or less systematically, as its use shifts between domains: they are **analogical** terms, neither univocal nor merely equivocal.

Law (understood not as in 'the Second Law of Thermodynamics' but as in this *Cambridge Companion*'s title, and matching 'legal/legally') belongs within each of the four domains. Thought about its nature must attend to this complexity, and avoid describing and explaining law *reductively*, as if it pertained essentially to only one (or two, or three) of these domains. The properties necessary – needed – to constitute law and fully instantiate its nature include properties in each of the four domains. Deficiencies in a property in (say) one domain but not the others need not entail that the law or legal order is so deficient that it is simply not law: loss of limbs does not leave one non-human; enthymematic argument is argument (albeit weak and problematic); cowardice need not eliminate all practical reasonableness and virtue; a vessel unable to tack is still a sailing ship; citizenship conferring rights to vote but not to be elected is citizenship, but (as with the other examples) is not a **central case** of that reality nor the **focal meaning** of that term. Deficient, mutant, borderline instances leave intact the theses that law has a nature, which theories of law describe and explain, correctly or deficiently and more or less erroneously. Theories should focus on the central (kinds of) cases of law, which embody its nature most fully or adequately, and should locate non-central cases in the subject matter's analogical structure, a location settled not by *statistical* 'typicality', but by each relevant domain's criteria of good (true) explanation.

This chapter considers law as involved essentially with each of the four domains. What best explains the features law has, taking all four domains together, proves to be its (third-domain) character as a response to human communities' morally significant need for the kind of access to justice that only law systematically provides.

1 Law, Nature and History

Laws of nature (such as the Second Law of Thermodynamics, among countless examples) share some kinds of property with legal philosophy's subject matter: they are articulable in general ('universal') propositions about patterns of activity of a kind of physical–biological entity that are to be expected[4] in specifiable kinds of circumstance. Lacking properties of a legal system that pertain to the other three domains of reality and explanation, however, they are only weakly analogous to the law in this volume's title.

[4] Here 'to be expected' is predictive, not optative, directive or normative (directly action-*guiding*).

But before leaving this first domain, we should note that Aquinas' account again needs amendment, to accommodate historical or sociological knowledge: of facts that are what they are independently of whether and how we think about them, yet not with the natural necessity of laws of nature or the replicability of instances of natural kinds, but with the different necessity which everything that *was so* in the past has – that it *cannot* now be the case that it *was not so* – and therefore just awaits discovery, description and explanation. And any account of law's nature must attend to this aspect of the first domain. Why?

For one thing, laws must belong to some legal system that exists, in the sense that it is by and large 'efficacious', that is, acknowledged and applied in practice among very many of those to whom its laws are addressed. The present tense 'is' here implies a reference to the past – the recent past, at least, and in many cases the past of the decades or centuries of a stable legal system's continuous existence as the legal order of a more or less stably self-constituted people distinct from other peoples. Though the Roman law promulgated by Justinian in 529–34, and the legal system of Tsarist Russia, are instances of *law*, richly illustrative of its nature – and are discussed today as containing solutions to articulable legal problems just *as if* they were efficacious today – they no longer have the nature of law, in one decisive respect: they in fact no longer are available to secure justice for anyone.

For another thing, a legal system needs to include many rules and institutions that belong to it only because they *were instituted* by some lawmaking event or process in the past.

Both these properties of law are necessary (needed), in senses and ways involving the other three domains.

2 Law and the Logic of its Propositions

Law is by its nature the law of a group (community) ruled more or less by law. *The law* of a group can be called the community's legal system or legal order. In a primary respect, such a system or order is a set of laws, each a universal proposition. The law, in this respect, is *a set of propositions* of law, each stating what legally, according to the group's law, may not be done (is prohibited, a duty not to . . .), or may be done (is permitted), or must be done (is mandatory, required, a duty to . . .); or what, according to law, certain or all persons have power (authority, faculty) to do in order to affect the way the law's propositions apply to or bear upon what those persons or others may or may not or must do, or have power to do. Propositions of law are universal in that they apply to all persons and acts in the class of persons and class of acts specified by the proposition, however wide or narrow the classes. A valid legal proposition that picks out not classes of person (such as 'the President') but a particular person (William K. Brown born 16 September 1943) and particular acts of that person (his will made 26 June 2011 and codicil made 27 April 2013) is not a central case of 'a law'.

In a secondary respect, a legal system is a *set of persons, institutions and practices*. Though a legal system as set of propositions can hardly be said to be (say) flourishing or corrupt, legal systems in this secondary respect do have such temporal and morally relevant historical properties.

Central to law as a set of propositions is the logic first fully analysed by Hohfeld.[5] A proposition of law specifying that persons of class Y have a duty *not to do* acts of class/type A – or a duty *to do* acts of class/type B – and either making this specification for the benefit of each person of class/type X, or specifying that each person of class X (or representative of those persons) has power to enforce or waive that duty, *entails* that each X *has* (by virtue of that same proposition of law) *a right* correlative to the relevant duty – the right that each Y so act/refrain from acting. This exemplifies the correlativity that, in one kind of way or another, is entailed by each duty or power specified by a proposition of law valid in a given legal system. But besides the rights (of X) correlative to the duties (of Y), there are other rights that (members of class) X might have (by virtue of some other proposition(s) of law): rights to, or over, things – rights of property and possession. Of course, such rights to/over things go along with (not by entailment but by virtue of legal rules) powers (of X) to transfer those rights to Z, to impose or waive duties (of Y), to refrain from use of the things, and so forth. And, somewhat similarly, there are rights of (members of class) X that are neither correlatives nor negations of any duty, but are (say) 'to life' or 'to private life' or 'to free assembly' and so on.

[5] W.N. Hohfeld, *Fundamental Legal Conceptions as Applied in Judicial Reasoning*, Ed. W.W. Cook (Yale University Press, 1923); J. Finnis, 'Rights: their logic restated' in J. Finnis, *Collected Essays of John Finnis [CEJF]* (Oxford University Press, 2011, paperback ed. 2013), Vol. IV (*Philosophy of Law*), 18.

Such 'two-term' rights are linked to duties not by logic but by rules and decisions of this legal system's law.

The technical, artefactual, fourth-domain postulate that a legal system is complete and gapless, in containing a legally correct answer to every question of conduct within its jurisdiction, makes plausible the thought that every two-term right can 'in principle' be exhaustively stated in the (vast) set of three-term rights it legally entails. On that postulate, a two-term right such as to freedom of speech 'must' be capable of being exhaustively stated, for purposes of law, in terms of three-term rights such as A's right that B, C, D, . . . not intercept his telephone conversations; A's liberty to make telephone calls and B's, C's . . . lack of right that he not make them; A's power to grant B a contractual liberty to listen to A's phone conversations; A's immunity from B's acquiring that liberty by any other source of power . . .; etc., etc.

One specific kind of two-term right is the public power/authority to make law, primarily to make rules of law, secondarily to make particular legal rights and duties by issuing a judicial or similar order; comparably, there are private powers to create rights and duties by contract or other private law assumptions of obligation. The idea of **validity** implicit in statements about the validity of propositions of law draws upon the idea of logical validity (of argumentation or proof in logic, geometry, etc.). But its legal sense adds the idea that a proposition *has been made* true by the exercise of a public power/authority of lawmaking, or by the exercise of a private power of contracting, appointment (of agents), creation (of a trust), and so forth. This legal sense of validity extends further to include other valid ways of introducing new laws and/or propositions of law into the legal system by processes of custom formation, estoppel, prescription and so forth – authoritative processes which do not depend upon or include any person's exercise of *authority* or *power to* introduce them.[6]

When propositions of law are made true by such acts or processes, the validating operation of power-conferring or other rules of recognition bears, in the first instance, not on the proposition as such but on the *statements* uttered in legislative *texts* authoritatively settled and adopted. The distinction between a statement, its utterance in a speech or text, and

[6] See further M. Köpcke, *Legal Validity: The Fabric of Justice* (Hart Publishing, 2019); and *A Short History of Legal Validity: Foundations of Private and Public Law* (Hart Publishing, 2019).

the proposition(s) that it expresses (or in some other way conveys), is not peculiar to legal texts, but is a general feature of the second domain and of its relationship to the fourth (to which belong languages, as modes of expression, and other conventional forms, like other artefacts as such). In legal systems, however, the distinctions, and the problems of **interpretation** to which they give rise, are of special importance. For legal systems seek indirectly and directly – by making true certain very generic propositions of law about how to interpret legal texts – to regulate both the processes by which (say) legislative texts *become* authoritative and the processes and techniques whereby they thereafter are lawfully interpreted and the resulting propositions of law applied. Law by its nature is reflexive – seeks to regulate its own creation, application and interpretation.[7]

Why that is so, and why the other second-domain features of law above-mentioned are characteristic of law, becomes clearer when we examine its third-domain characteristics. But the ineliminable gap between textual statement and proposition of law is a resultant of the first-domain fact that human persons cannot communicate with each other by thought alone ('mind-reading' of a non-metaphorical kind), but must share their thoughts, so far as these can be shared, by more or less *bodily* signs and acts of communication. And those acts deploy, and depend almost entirely, upon the artefacts we call language and its utterance in the further artefacts and artifices of speech and text. Law by its nature needs to be published ('promulgated'), and its publication can always be incomplete or in some other way incompletely successful in communicating what was intended and meant to be made true as a matter of law.

3 Law and Pursuing Human Good(s) Reasonably

As actual, law can be understood by asking why existing specimens or instantiations of it have the kinds of stuff and shape they do. As achievable kind of reality, law can be understood by considering the features of the human predicament that make evidently reasonable a kind of response-to-predicament that has or produces that sort of stuff and shape. Both these methods of inquiry converge upon a common result (already mentioned): it

[7] This was fundamental to H. Kelsen, *General Theory of Law and State* (Harvard University Press, 1945), 124, 126, 132, 198, 354.

is law's third-domain features or elements that most explain the other-domain features and elements characteristic of it.

For the flourishing of individuals and groups is weakened, damaged or destroyed by various kinds of danger, and these threats or perils may often be alleviated or overcome by positive or negative coordination intended to avert them, coordination and cooperation which in turn can also make available various kinds of elements in human flourishing that are otherwise unavailable. Plans for and modalities of cooperation can be brought into operation and made effective by rules and institutions of law which make them authoritative and compulsory. Defections from the authoritatively required modes of cooperation can be ascertained, assessed and rectified by legal rules for compensation or punishment, rules applied after trial according to law. Trial according to law is itself a form of cooperation oriented toward averting the menace and harm that consists in unjust deprivation of liberty, property or opportunity, whether by simple lawless private force and oppression, or by public orders predicated not on true facts of guilt or liability but on false claims and/or false public adjudications induced by fear, bribery or other favour.

Recognising with clarity that law's nature must be described/explained as a system of institutions and rules **for meeting human needs**, the central chapters of Hart's *The Concept of Law* (1961) strove nonetheless to present as *non-moral* the evaluations implicit in identifying a 'need' (or 'remedying a defect'). (Hart doubted whether moral propositions can be true.[8]) Thus he presented rules and institutions of adjudication as needed for 'efficiency' in resolution of disputes; and presented lawmaking institutions and rules of change as needed for efficiency in responding to change of circumstances and/or of ideas about ends and/or means. And in another phase of his explanation of law, he argued that the only basic need (or basic value or ultimate end) that such an explanation should postulate is *survival* (whether of me or our group, he left in shadow). Although these needs were presented as the de facto content of an attitude or viewpoint observable among those whose possession of this 'internal attitude/viewpoint' makes a set of rules exist, and exist as law, Hart nonetheless plainly expected readers to share the viewpoint, in relation to whatever legal system they happened to be (or could realistically imagine being) subjects

[8] See *Collected Essays, CEJF* IV, 254; Raz, *Between Authority and Interpretation*, 52.

or officials of. That the philosopher's account 'reproduces'[9] this internal attitude (as an attitude of acceptance of rules in the combination of them distinctive of legal systems) was thus, for Hart, a primary criterion of sound legal–philosophical/theoretical description and explanation. And this was indeed progress in the theory of law (Jurisprudence). For it located law explicitly in the life of practical reason, understanding legal rules as a distinctive kind of *reason for action.*

And reasons for action are the matter of the third and fourth domains – but more fundamentally of the third, since the reasons for being *concerned with* that sort of arrangement of means to an end that constitutes a fourth-domain artefact (technique/technology) are always, in the last analysis, third-order reasons – reasons to *deploy* that technique or *use* that artefact in some conduct chosen for its contribution to one's (or one's group's) open-ended life as a whole: that is, morally significant reasons for action. So Hart's methodology systematically opened up the inquiry about the nature of law to that philosophy of practical reasonableness which we call ethics or moral philosophy or rational morality.

No one is rationally obliged to accept Hart's implicit proposal to reduce or limit the explanation of adjudication to considerations of efficiency in 'dispute-resolution', as distinct from concern to require impartial ('judicial') attention to finding the *truth* about what wrongs were or were not done, and *fidelity-in-application* of the law(s) defining the obligations and rights of the parties at the time the cause of action (tort or crime or breach of trust . . .) arose. Such values as truth, honesty and fidelity to past commitments and expectations cannot be fully explained in terms of promoting survival, but instead need to be reported as aspects of a concern for practical reasonableness for its own sake, as an intrinsic human good just as intrinsic or 'basic' as survival in life and health, knowledge for its own sake, friendship and interpersonal harmony, and the handing on of life and education in maritally committed procreation and parental nurture. *The Concept of Law* has a chapter on Justice as willingness to treat like cases alike and different cases differently, and this justice is obviously a central aspect or implication of the good of being practically reasonable, and the good of interpersonal harmony, and the truth about all basic human goods: that they are *as intelligibly good* in the lives of other persons

[9] H.L.A. Hart, *The Concept of Law*, 3rd ed. (Oxford University Press, 2012, orig. published 1961), 90.

as in my own. Morality is just another name for a fully reasonable concern for human flourishing in all its basic aspects, integrally considered (without arbitrary cutting back in attention to basic goods, or to the persons in whose lives they might be instantiated). So, though Hart's own study of law's nature remained, by restriction, amoral or incompletely moral, his method invited the unrestricted exploration of the bearing of reasons for action, as a set, on the making and maintaining of laws, law and legal systems. That is, his method invited a thorough exploration of law as a reality or potential reality in the third domain.[10]

And those third-domain reasons which give law its characteristic shape and nature are reasons for making it have the character it has as participating in the first, second and fourth domains of explanation, as a natural reality governing natural realities (human persons), as a logical-propositional realm of validity and correlativities of duty, power and right, and as a complex artefact and technique of signs, institutions and activities – a *positing* yielding *positive* law.

Central to law's nature is that law links – because a society needs, in justice, to link – present decisions not simply to achieving future benefits (as any rational plan does) but also to doing so by honouring *past* commitments both public *and private*. Legislation is a form of public commitment: to deal with certain matters *henceforth* in the way that *was* specified in the law-making act (constitution, statute, etc.). Adjudication by application of law is a complex, thorough public acknowledgement (and following through) of those and comparable (customary, precedential) commitments. Private acts of undertaking obligations are commitments to act in the ambulatory present with fidelity to those past acts even when one's future well-being might in other respects be enhanced by neglecting those commitments.

So law and the rule of law cannot be reduced to the model of planning.[11] For that model includes, perhaps paradigmatically, the activities of soldiers, architects and engineers, whose sole concern quite reasonably is future well-being as it may be enhanced or protected *starting from now* with what *now* lies to hand. Law is planning in (reformable) fidelity to past

[10] On these issues in Hart, see J. Finnis, 'How persistent are Hart's "persistent questions"?' in L.D. d'Almeida, J. Edwards and A. Dolcetti (eds.), *Reading H.L.A. Hart's The Concept of Law* (Hart Publishing, 2013), 227–36 ; *CEJF* IV, essays 10 and 11.

[11] Cf. S. Shapiro, *Legality* (Harvard University Press, 2011), 194: 'the law is simply a sophisticated apparatus for planning in very complex, contentious, and arbitrary communal settings'.

enactments and other historical ('social fact') *sources* of law and obligation or entitlement (acquired rights); the plan was adopted *then*, and is (presumptively) to be applied *now* not so much for its promise of benefit as for its validity as **positive (posited) law** (and therefore as political commitment of the community). The fully reasonable premise for acknowledging positive law as a reason for action now (as judge, administrator or other subject) is a moral premise: justice as a fundamental aspect of promoting the common good of my political community presumptively requires me, in reason, to respect the commitments articulated in the rules, and by the institutions, of our law.

The principles directing this needed willingness (or summons) to act justly are traditionally called **natural law** (synonymously, 'natural right'). Principles of natural law – that is, of practical reasonableness uncorrupted by sub-rational bias or inattention – direct us not only to make all our choices consistent with various specific principles and norms of justice, but also to promote and protect these by establishing positive laws and law, and then by recognising, maintaining and applying the rules of this positive law according to their tenor – that is, in the meaning established by their own content and by the content of rules of validity and principles of interpretation and requirements of coherence with other positive rules of the system considered as a whole that ought (according to the same foundational, natural law principles of justice) to be coherent, capable of application and compliance (and so not retroactive), relatively stable, intelligible to those whom they concern, and actually adhered to by those whom this legal system designates as its officers. Where a legal system's rules, institutions and practices conform sufficiently to these morally desirable structural/procedural features, the political community[12] they govern can be said (in the wake of Aristotle's debate about the matter) to instantiate the **rule of law**,[13] the *primauté de droit*.

[12] A non-state community can have a legal system in a near focal sense. So Pope Paul III's commission of inquiry into the Reformation's causes reported that some popes (misadvised, it said, by ecclesiastical lawyers) ruled like private owners rule over their property, setting aside the Rule of Law commended in Aristotle's *Politics*, and governing the Church *just as they pleased*, whence (as from a Trojan horse) came the desperate illnesses infecting the Church of 1537: *Consilium de Emendanda Ecclesia* (Rome, Anthony Bladus, 1538), Aii–iv.

[13] See N. Simmonds, *Law as a Moral Idea* (Oxford University Press, 2007), s.v. 'rule of law'; J. Finnis, 'Law as idea, ideal, and duty: a comment on Simmonds, *Law as a Moral Idea*', *Jurisprudence* 1 (2010) 247–53.

What about the content of these legally structured rules? The specific norms of justice which, just as a sound ethics identifies them, need to be included in any legal system are now often called *jus cogens*. These rules (*jus*), peremptory (*cogens*) by virtue of their content – their inherent reasonableness – rather than merely by virtue of their enactment or their adoption in custom and/or judicial precedent, forbid choices, private or public, to kill or harm with intent precisely to terminate life or damage bodily integrity; or to rape; or to deceive by asserting a proposition believed by the asserter to be false. As well as such exceptionless negative norms, natural law's foundational substantive principles include affirmative directions whose application is dependent on appropriate circumstances (including the reasonable content of other parts of the particular legal system). Given what a sound ethics and a sound political philosophy establish, and the experience of lawyers and comparativists across many centuries confirms, about these 'appropriate circumstances', the main affirmative principles mandate, and give broad guidance in establishing, not only (i) constitutional and other institutions of **legislation** and **adjudication** but also (ii) rights of **property** (whether ownership or lesser possessory or beneficiary rights) in portions of the world's resources (excluding human persons), with appurtenant powers such as sale and rights such as inheritance, all subject to responsibilities of distribution of holdings in excess of the owner's reasonable needs; and (iii) rights to make and enforce **contractual** and other voluntarily assumed obligations, such as the **marriage** of two persons who together can be the father and mother of these spouses' own children, a relationship important to law for the sake of justice to the child(ren) and of sustaining the people itself whose law this all is; and (iv) entitlements **to compensation** for losses imposed by another's fault; and (v) liabilities to **punishment** for defined offences against the law; and (vi) conditional entitlements to sustenance in circumstances of extreme or undeserving indigence; and so forth. Such natural law principles, precepts (negative or affirmative) and institutions, adopted concretely into all or many legal systems, have traditionally been called the ***jus gentium*, the law of peoples.**[14]

[14] See *CEJF* IV at 182 n. 37, 183 nn. 40–1; *CEJF* II at 101–3. International law, as the law regulating relations between peoples, is quite a different matter (and see Section 5 below), even though it too *contains* an important natural law element, which can therefore be called *ius gentium*.

The generic, underdetermined character of these wide-ranging responsibilities of lawmakers and other persons responsible for the well-being of their community and all its members – that is, for its **common good** – entails that there should be positive rules of law created to crystallise these principles as fully legal obligations, rights, powers, etc. Such crystallising or concretising has been called *determinatio* ('concretisation'), to distinguish it from the more deductive process of acknowledging – and deciding to give positive-law legal effect to – the moral truth of the principles (and precepts, especially the negative precepts) of natural moral law. But within a positive law system, even these last-mentioned natural law, *jus cogens* principles and precepts need some *determinatio*: the moral goods of fairness, like the technical goods of craftsmanship, in application of law call for stability, clarity and transparency, and predictability in their application – rule of law – so that their applicability's precise terms are made common, and coherent with the system's vocabulary and institutions. So, for example, murder can be defined so as to distinguish it as a 'degree' of criminal homicide, and can be declared (say) a felony, susceptible to (say) whole-of-life imprisonment, a disqualification from office or vote, and so forth – but in all these details murder could reasonably have been defined somewhat differently with somewhat different legal incidents or consequences.[15]

In short, a legal system adequate to human needs will be of complex nature: *all positive*, yet partly a matter of natural law ('*jus gentium*') and partly (indeed largely) a matter of 'purely positive' rules. Rules of this latter kind appropriately have a relation to their justifying principles that is too indefinite or disputable for the rules to be describable as declarations (or even applications) of the principles or as deductions from them.

Everything said in the last four paragraphs could be accurately and sufficiently stated without speaking of 'natural law' or 'natural right' (or *jus gentium*). That traditional language has always been exposed to misunderstanding, and is perhaps particularly exposed today, when the history of philosophy is not widely known and the success of the natural sciences arouses or reinforces the thought that explanation and description, and the very idea of 'the nature of X', are all properly located in the first domain and its models of reality and explanation. But the principles of

[15] As to what positive law adds in (say) *mala in se* offences, see J. Finnis, *Natural Law and Natural Rights* (Oxford University Press, 1980, 2nd ed. 2011), 282–3.

natural law relevant to the understanding and justification of authority and the laws of legally ordered societies are principles in the third domain (though presupposing certain truths in the first and second). Knowledge of them is the fruit of a search to bring order and reasonableness into one's own and one's groups' choices and actions. They are moral (= ethical) principles, and those among them that are directly relevant to and properly directive of lawmaking and compliance with law are principles of justice – that is, of practical reasonableness' requirements for those of one's choices that directly or indirectly affect the good of other human beings.

Despite the doubts of Hart and countless others, there are indeed such principles and norms of practical right reason. Unfortunately, philosophical understanding and vindication of them has suffered many vicissitudes. Notable among these setbacks are the utilitarianism that Bentham laboured but failed to make coherent, let alone reasonable, and the alternative to it proposed by Kant to rescue morality from utilitarianism's reduction of third-domain rationality to fourth-domain, technological reasoning. For Kant's rescue effort made the analogous mistake of seeking moral rationality's paradigm in the *second* domain (retaining from the third domain little save the idea of bringing order into one's free choices – 'autonomy'), and modelling all ethical argument on logic's mission to eliminate contradiction. He failed to acknowledge any of the first principles of practical reason (each in truth directing us to a substantive human good such as life, knowledge, friendship, etc.), save the good of practical reasonableness itself, a good which, since he had deprived it of subject matter, he took to be the reasonableness of coherence. Dominated by these failed reductions of ethics to inappropriate domains, modern moral philosophy as actually expounded has been of little assistance to philosophers of law.[16]

A sound moral philosophy, developing Plato's, Aristotle's and Aquinas', can be articulated not as 'natural' or 'law', but as principles and norms (precepts, rules) of reason(ableness) that direct us to understand and pursue, coherently, the flourishing of all human persons and communities with reasonable prioritising and essential respect for persons in each basic

[16] Dworkin's philosophy of law (e.g. in R. Dworkin, *Law's Empire* (Harvard University Press, 1986)) is essentially Kantian in its reduction of the goods for which law is needed to equality and autonomy, and consequent focus on coercion and adjudication (rather than on the substantive just common good that is the primary concern of lawmakers).

aspect of their flourishing – each basic human good. Still, by understanding human flourishing in the only way it can be adequately understood (namely, from within practical understanding and reasoning), we also understand human nature adequately. For (as Aquinas stresses, but many would-be successors have overlooked) the **nature** of any dynamic reality can be understood only by understanding that kind of thing's **capacities** (potentialities), and these we can understand only by understanding the **activities** that make them manifest, and activities cannot be well understood except by understanding what they are heading for – their '**objects**'. And the objects of *human* acts are first the basic goods (needs; ends; elements of human flourishing) and then the means (kinds of action) that, considered integrally, they call for.

Adequate third-domain understanding of law's nature thus relates law in all its features to human needs, both as intrinsic ends (basic human goods, intrinsic elements or aspects of human flourishing) and as empirically effective and morally respectful means of realising those intrinsic ends/goods/basic elements of well-being. We need common good and justice, and for that we need the moral judgements and legal institutions needed to make those very complex ends (and the principles directing us about and to them) actual in the life of an ongoing community that is in (or can be got into) shape for political existence and action.

But what about laws that, in manner of positing or in content, are made without concern, or (knowingly or not) without respect, for common good and/or for justice? Well, they lack an essential precondition for the claim to authoritativeness that is part of law's nature, an authoritativeness (more simply, authority) that from the side of the law's subjects entails an obligatoriness that is both strictly and purely legal (like the predicate 'legally valid') and, presumptively but defeasibly, also moral obligatoriness. (The obligation is owed not to the bearers of lawmaking or executive authority, but to other subjects of the law.) It may still be morally wrong to do what they purport to (and as a matter of legal validity do) prohibit; for such behaviour may as a side-effect have effects that it is unfair to impose on one's fellow subjects. But from a moral point of view which includes but is not limited to the legal system's own criteria of validity and interpretation, these are laws that are (each in itself) unsupported by law's most basic organising *point* (rationale, purpose). So it is an implication of law's positivity, adequately understood in terms of its justifying purposes, that a seriously unjust positive law is so radically defective that, just as a persuasive but logically fallacious argument is 'no argument' and an old friend who turns out to be one's betrayer is 'no friend', so too 'an unjust law is not a law'. Or, as Aquinas always preferred to say, 'is not a central case of law', or 'is not without qualification a law' (but rather a kind of corruption of law – deficient as law). The idioms are various, but the propositions at stake should not be controversial. They involve no denial of or inattention to the sad facts of human immorality and wicked law. Rather, they draw attention to such immorality's (injustice's) significance as depriving an act of human governance of all just title to be regarded as changing the moral obligations of its subjects *in the way* law – by its nature – is to be regarded as changing them, namely, in just the way and (presumptively, defeasibly) to just the extent that it changes those subjects' legal obligations.[17]

Some recent work in legal philosophy contends that, while 'unjust law is not law' is false, 'law not claiming moral legitimacy is not law' is true: the very 'concept of law' is said to entail, 'conceptually', that all laws claim (often falsely) to be morally legitimate/obligatory.[18] Philosophy of law, we should reply, is a study not primarily of concepts and 'conceptual necessities', but of what law needs to be in each of the four domains in which it can be understood, acknowledged and posited; and it is the understanding of these natural preconditions, logical necessities, morally significant needs, and need (as we shall see) for kinds of technique and artefactual institutions, etc., that yields concepts – in the first instance, (i) the concepts excogitated and used by the persons and societies that have more or less unphilosophically (or with common-sense's philosophy) understood those needs and responded to that understanding by creating and maintaining legal systems (whether under the terminology of 'law' and its foreign language cognates or not); and then, secondarily, (ii) the more adequate, coherent and explanatory concepts of a philosophy of law, usually but not exclusively framed in terminology borrowed from the practical life of lawmakers, judges, legal advisers and citizens. So we should understand both 'unjust laws are not law' and 'laws not claiming to be just are not law'

[17] See J. Finnis, 'Law as fact and as reason for action: a response to Robert Alexy on law's "Ideal Dimension"', *American Journal of Jurisprudence*, 59 (2014) 100–9.

[18] Raz, *Between Authority and Interpretation*, 180; R. Alexy, *The Argument from Injustice: A Reply to Legal Positivism* (Oxford University Press, 2002), 36; Gardner, *Law as a Leap of Faith*, 125–45; contrast *CEJF* IV, 8 n. 18; Finnis, 'Reflections and responses', 538, 553–6; 'Law as fact and as reason for action . . .', 91–3.

as items in a philosophical reflection on what law needs to be. Morally (that is, integrally reasonably), law ought to *aspire* to be just (morally legitimate, etc.), ought to *claim* to be just (morally obligatory, etc.), and ought, most importantly, to *be just*. Laws that are defective in aspiration, form or content are so seriously defective that, in a decisive respect, they fail to be law(s). But of course, they remain law(s) insofar as they are being promulgated and enforced and historically efficacious in a given time and place, as artefacts available, like other tools, for abuse as well as appropriate use.

In these respects, law is no different from many other realities and concepts with which social (political, legal, etc.) philosophy must come to terms, and on which it should seek to shed the light of nuanced, supple, undogmatic explanation.

4 Law as an Artefact of Artefacts

In order to be a just and effective form, and source for forms and instances, of social coordination effective in promoting human flourishing within a framework of respect for natural (= human) rights, law needs to have the stability of a publicly accessible **craft** working within (and as) the framework of **institutions** for lawmaking, law-administering and law-adjudicating/enforcing. The idea of validity characteristic of positive law (and as such distinct from logical/argumentative validity as such) is a primary manifestation and instrument of law's operations and nature as a fourth-domain, artefactual kind of reality and aspiration responsive to that need.

Institutions as various as a constitution, a legislature, a judicature and judiciary, a common law, a law of property and within it a law of real property and a law of entails, or a law of contract and within it a law of mistake in formation and a doctrine of interpretation . . . are all artefactual instruments of a legal logic (see Section 2) and of a historically effective (Section 1) legally ordered moral enterprise (Section 3). Many of these have been mentioned in Section 3's sketch of moral needs justifying and demanding legal rules and institutions. As was also mentioned, they are like other artefacts, in having significant intelligibility and reality simply as artefacts, or techniques, or plans, which can also be deployed, even successfully (and therefore also unsuccessfully), for more or less amoral objectives or immoral purposes.

That is, they can be studied precisely as techniques, detached from their (or any) moral rationale. They can be imitated more or less closely for non-moral rationales, such as the wealth or power of their inventors, designers, or master (or more lowly) users. This gives an opening for philosophies of '(legal) positivism', claiming that law's nature had best be defined amorally, *before* any investigation of the moral purposes to which it may be put or the moral criteria by which particular laws may be assessed, or by which, if positive laws happen so to provide, rules may be granted validity by reason of their moral soundness. But there is no reason to try to define law (other than stipulatively, or lexicographically) before understanding the reasons for having law at all, and some of those reasons are third-domain reasons – reasons that when fully teased out as reasons are of the kind we call moral: attentive to intrinsic human goods, and to the fundamental equality of human beings, all of us benefited by the instantiation of those goods, and none of us *a priori* entitled to identity-based, as distinct from reasons- and responsibilities-based, priority in the private or public distribution of those goods. Vocabulary (lexicographical definition)[19] assists us to see that we are discoursing about broadly the same sort of subject matter,[20] but any explanatory definition[21] should express the results of reflection on that subject matter's nature, a nature understood as what is articulated in a sufficient answer to 'What is . . .?' questions

[19] Most recently, Gardner, *Law as a Leap of Faith*, 275–7 (in the idiom of 'classification' rather than 'definition'); contrast ibid., 175: 'the study of the nature of law can and must begin, in a certain sense, with the central case of law as morally successful law'.

[20] See for example, the first sentence of the penultimate paragraph of the introductory section, p. 39.

[21] That is, 'real definition' (definition that *sums up an explanation* of the thing [*res*] in question, rather than reporting or stipulating usage of the word): R. Robinson, *Definition* (Oxford University Press, 1952); Hart, *Concept of Law*, 279. An example: Aquinas proposes and argues for a definition of law: an ordinance of reason for the common good of a [complete] community, promulgated by the person or body responsible for looking after that community [*Summa Theologiae* I–II, q. 90 a. 4c]. But in supplementing and explicating that definition, Aquinas immediately stresses that law – a law – is 'simply a sort of prescription (*dictamen*) of practical reason *in the ruler* governing a complete community', and that 'prescriptions' are simply universal propositions of practical reason which prescribe and direct to action.

Finnis, *Aquinas*, 255–6. For an expansion of that definition (and commentary on definition) in light of subsequent work in the philosophy of law, see Finnis, *Natural Law and Natural Rights*, 276–9, 472; J. Finnis, 'Aquinas and natural law jurisprudence' in G. Duke and R.P. George (eds.), *Cambridge Companion to Natural Law Jurisprudence* (Cambridge University Press, 2017), 17–55.

arising in all the four domains in which human life (as distinct from sub-rational forms of life and existence) is lived.

So: self-styled 'positivist' definitions of law are more or less arbitrary to the extent that they genuinely precede a moral assessment of the need for law and legal institutions, and try to describe law's nature and characteristic institutions without the benefit of understanding that set of needs – that set of reasons foundational for the articulated reasons (propositions) about action that we reasonably call laws.[22] Nothing philosophically sufficient or explanatorily satisfying can be said about law without understanding it as – by its nature, though not adequately (and therefore centrally) so in its many defective forms and instances – responsive to morally weighty purposes of fair dealing between the members of a community across time. And the truths, welcome or unwelcome, about law in its defective forms and evil instances, truths which legal positivists rightly resolve to face and explore, are all just as well, or better, disclosed (and are unconfusedly describable and explicable) within the framework of moral inquiry that historically generated the philosophical idea of 'positive law',[23] a framework continuous with the third-domain practical thinking

[22] Raz rightly deprecates labeling legal *theories* 'positivist' or 'non-positivist'; his theory of law's nature is in this and some other respects not a 'self-styled "positivist" theory'. But in 'The problem about the nature of law' (1983) he applies the term 'positivist' to any source-based *standard*; he defines as *positivist* any standard or consideration the existence and content of which 'can be ascertained without resort to moral [or any other evaluative] argument' – standards which the present essay, like most theorists, calls *positive* or posited law). And he holds (in that essay and in 'Authority, law, and morality' (1985)) that, while a 'doctrine of the nature of law' must be evaluative ('of the relative importance of various features of social organizations'), its point and upshot is not to show that (or to what extent) law is morally needed or appropriate, but rather to 'elaborate and explain' 'the concept of law' as 'part of our culture', by 'pick[ing] on those [ideas] which are central and significant to the way the concept plays its role in people's understanding of society': *Ethics in the Public Domain* 205–9, 211–12, 237; his 1994/6 essay on the nature of law ('On the nature of law') does not depart from this position. So – though his 2003 essay ('About morality and the nature of law') makes some movement toward accepting a 'Thomist' 'moral case for having legal authorities' (*Between Authority and Interpretation*, 173) – his 'doctrine of the nature of law', unlike other parts of his philosophy of law (including parts as proximate to that doctrine as his 'service conception of authority'), has deliberately proceeded without incorporating or presupposing a systematic *moral* assessment of the need for law and legal institutions; his account of the evaluations involved in the 'doctrine' truncates the nature of third-domain investigations of practical reason, and remains too limited to describing culture *qua* first-domain fact of a 'historical or sociological' kind.

[23] Finnis, 'The truth in legal positivism', in *CEJF* IV, 174–88.

of those who have constructed the systems of normative coordination and direction called by them, and then by us all, legal.

5 Law and the Nature of Persons and Groups

Law has the nature it has because human persons have the nature they have, and beings of that nature need for their nature's full or even adequate instantiation the assistance of many, the respect of all, and the love, in varying measure, of some. Law has its existence primarily in the mind (conceptions and assent) of the person or persons who accept responsibility for serving the common good of a community capable in principle of meeting all the kinds of this-worldly needs. It has its existence secondarily but most importantly in the minds of all who understand and assent to what propositions of law the lawmaker(s) intended to introduce into the set of propositions constituting that community's law (its legal system). Many of those may regret and even resent one or more laws, yet comply with them for the sake of upholding the legal ordering of their community, an ordering which depends for its fairness, and even its existence, on excluding all picking-and-choosing save that which a serious, authentic competing moral responsibility mandates. Some members of any community, and some (perhaps many) persons in other communities, or in stateless piracy/brigandage, will willingly defy the law's requirements. So the responsibility of the lawmakers includes a very serious duty to provide for the forceful application of the law to such people, and for their punishment, and the deterrence and suppression of future offences. Entrusting to rulers this power of applying force is reasonable, though also very risky.

Within a well-ordered political community substantially united by common history, memory, culture and reciprocal trust, the constitutionally stipulated rule of law can often ensure that abuse of legal and de facto power by rulers is kept to tolerable levels. But as between states, which must share the Earth with each other and respect the common good of mankind, many of those preconditions do not obtain. So it is reasonable to judge that public international law, though obviously needed (as a matter of moral responsibility), does not fully participate, and for the foreseeable future should not be conceived as fully participating, in the nature of law as one of law's central forms. International law, as morally needed, is positive law, but made directly or indirectly by agreements rather than by rulers entrusted with the power to compel obedience to law and punish disobedience. Here as elsewhere in these reflections, sound judgement about the nature of the subject matter has as one[24] of its necessary conditions sound evaluations and judgements about moral responsibilities and entitlements: a sound, historically informed ethics and political philosophy.

[24] Another necessary condition (as in all practical reasoning) is accurate understanding of and attentiveness to the facts about the circumstances in which (including likely consequences with which) these responsibilities will be carried out, entitlements granted (or acknowledged) and respected, and so forth.

Legal Reasoning 3

Martha C. Nussbaum*

Legal reasoning is a vast topic. In principle, it includes the reasoning of lawyers, judges, and even lawmakers, in every area of law, from family law to contracts, from criminal law to constitutional adjudication. And it is thoroughly global, encompassing enormously different national and regional understandings. Bringing the topic down to a size compatible with saying anything useful means leaving out most of it. Accordingly, this chapter will be confined to countries with a common law legal system, and its primary focus will be judicial reasoning. Most of its examples will be drawn from just two areas of law, criminal and constitutional law. Its argument will focus on the philosophical underpinnings of an ongoing debate between defenders of common law legal reasoning and a variety of utilitarian challengers.

Legal reasoning, in my view (as in that of Joseph Raz[1]) is not a distinct **type** of reasoning; instead it is practical reasoning with a distinctive subject matter. It is a species of normative reasoning that makes ample room for moral reasoning, although at times it involves special technical and institutional considerations.

1 The Common Law

Legal reasoning in the common law tradition is typically incremental and traditionalist. It uses a framework of principles and precedents established by past generations, building on these and departing from them relatively rarely. But what is the deeper rationale for common law judging? Some

* I am grateful to David Strauss, Cass Sunstein and John Tasioulas for invaluable advice and to Nicole Briody and Ruth Thomson for excellent research assistance.

[1] J. Raz, *Ethics in the Public Domain: Essays in the Morality of Law and Politics* (Clarendon Press, 1995).

statements by Burke and early defenders of the common law (such as Sir Matthew Hale) suggest that the basis of the common law is a form of irrationalism: the common law is valuable because it is very old, because it is a legacy or patrimony from our ancestors, and because it is 'ours', a way in which the English define their identity. Burke also at times speaks of a wisdom of nature, as though there are forces working within the system at a preconscious level.

This sort of grandiose mysticism encourages scepticism. Why should something be good just because it is old and part of our national identity? Especially as regards the eighteenth century, a time when entrenched injustices of the past were being challenged in the name of human rights, a naked appeal to custom does not look very persuasive. More generally, in any age there is an urgent need to challenge unjust hierarchies of power, and judges are among those who have the job (or so many believe) of breaking with wrongful conventions and righting old wrongs.

A far stronger case for the common law is made in other passages by Burke, and given an elegant philosophical elaboration in the work of contemporary theorist David Strauss.[2] Following Strauss' lucid account, we may say that common law reasoning is not a form of irrationalism, it is a form of Aristotelian rationalism. It has two aspects: a type of open-eyed and not uncritical traditionalism; and conventionalism. Traditionalism is defended on the grounds that the common law embodies the wisdom of many minds confronting, in good faith and with intelligence, many situations of different types over a long period of time. Its ideas have weathered many tests (or have been revised when they did not withstand challenge). On the whole, this type of cumulative wisdom is more trustworthy than any single mind; judges should on the whole rely on the past rather than making abstract pronouncements, not out of sheer deference to the past as such, but out of humility and a sense of each person's bounded rationality.

The other element of the common law, according to Strauss, is conventionalism: once some things have been settled, it is useful to follow the solution laid down, rather than to see everything as up for grabs at every moment.

Common law judges, Strauss emphasises, retain and use their own critical moral judgement. A departure from tradition should not be

[2] D.A. Strauss, 'Common law constitutional interpretation', *University of Chicago Law Review*, 63 (1996), 877–935; D.A. Strauss, 'Does the Constitution mean what it says?', Supreme Court Foreword, *Harvard Law Review*, 129 (2015), 1–61.

undertaken lightly, but at times an obvious wrong may require it. The common law is thus an ongoing evolutionary process, in which tradition plays a major role, but a sense of present circumstances and the judge's own reflective awareness of moral norms also figure. Although theorists of the common law tradition often focus on the views of judges, it is also part of that tradition to look beyond judicial precedents to both statutes and larger developments in society.

Strauss' version of the common law is thus not hostile to the natural law tradition, often contrasted with it, and implicitly contrasted with it by Burke,[3] with his attack on the abstractions of the French Revolution. The natural law tradition (which has roots in the thought of Cicero, Aquinas and Grotius, among others) asks judges to become aware of, and to hold laws up against, independent objective moral truths. Grotius emphasises that where there are gaps in positive law (as in the realm between states) there is no gap in morality, and moral norms bind us wherever we are. Although Burke's version of the common law was profoundly opposed to eighteenth-century natural law abstractions, there is no reason why the common law as such must be so opposed. Particularly in the USA, where the Constitution, and especially the Bill of Rights, itself contains many moral abstractions, the common law judge has no choice but to make the best sense of them, usually in the light of a tradition of interpretation and precedent, but at times creatively departing from that tradition in order to realise the abstract value more completely. It is no surprise to one who views the common law in this way that the thought of Blackstone, the great British jurist, contains both common law and natural law elements.

Nor is it surprising that Ronald Dworkin,[4] who might easily be classified as a natural law theorist for the role that objective moral norms play in his account of judicial reasoning, is also a common law theorist, situating moral reasoning within an ongoing evolutionary process. In his view, legal claims are interpretive judgements that combine backward-looking and forward-looking elements. In a famous metaphor, he compares the good judge to someone who continues a chain novel. The author of the next chapter of such a novel must endeavour to fit his or her chapter to what has gone before. In order to do this, she must first interpret what has gone before. Fit

[3] J.G.A. Pocock, 'Burke and the ancient constitution: a problem in the history of ideas' in J.G.A. Pocock (ed.), *Politics, Language, and Time: Essays on Political Thought and History* (University of Chicago Press, 1960), 202–32.

[4] R. Dworkin, *Law's Empire* (Harvard University Press, 1986); R. Dworkin, 'Darwin's new bulldog', *Harvard Law Review* 111 (1998), 1718-38.

need not be exact, but it ought to have general explanatory power. At the same time, she should also try to make the work the best it can be, preferring, among the possible continuations, those that realise appropriate norms (in the judicial case, typically norms involving principles of justice, fairness and due process that are themselves inherent in the nation's tradition).

The difficulty with even the most attractive versions of common law judicial reasoning is that the common law, on such accounts (Strauss' account, for example), gives the judge such broad discretion that it is difficult to say which of two diametrically opposed opinions exhibits 'good' common law judging. Let us consider two pairs of cases, one from each of our legal areas. The constitutional jurisprudence of the Fourteenth Amendment frequently generates contradictory results, depending on the level of generality chosen by the judge for the adjudication of the rights claims. Thus, in *Bowers* v. *Hardwick* (478 US 186), which upheld the sodomy law of the state of Georgia against a challenge from a gay man, the majority and concurring opinions understood the legal question to be whether the Due Process Clause of the Fourteenth Amendment protects a right to 'homosexual sodomy'. (Although the Georgia law actually included opposite-sex as well as same-sex sodomy, a heterosexual couple who also challenged the law were dismissed for lack of standing on the ground that they were in no danger of prosecution.) Reasoning that our traditions give no basis for the recognition of such a right, a majority upheld the Georgia law. In *Lawrence* v. *Texas* 539 US 558 (2003), the Court overruled *Bowers* and struck down the Texas sodomy law (and similar laws in thirteen other states), arguing that *Bowers* had understood the liberty interest too narrowly: it is rightly understood to be an interest in intimate consensual sexual activity, and that interest is protected by the Due Process Clause (and by a long tradition limiting government interference into adult intimacy). By now most Americans feel that it was mistaken to segment 'homosexual sodomy' from other consensual sex acts, and mean-spirited to recognise rights unevenly. But is there anything in the theoretical account of common law judging that tells us that, or why, one opinion is a good piece of common law judging and the other is not so good? Common law judges use their own judgement: that is both the strength of the method and its great weakness in the eyes of those who think that rationality demands something more in a legal methodology.

When we turn to the criminal law, the same sort of conflict can easily be found, and sometimes common law theorists themselves appear to apply similar insights differently. David Strauss, illustrating the progressive potential of the common law, cites the gradual evolution of criminal defendants' rights, particularly the right of indigent defendants to legal counsel (*Gideon* v. *Wainwright* 372 US 335 (1963)). Strauss uses this case to illustrate the way in which only the thinnest and most incidental hook to a constitutional text may sometimes, through intelligent common law judging, give rise to a new and very important tradition of rights-recognition. Edward Levi,[5] another major defender of common law reasoning, illustrates its creative potential, in the criminal law area, in quite a different way, citing the incremental jurisprudence of the Mann Act. The Mann Act was a statute passed by Congress in 1910 to address a widespread panic about 'white slavery', the (alleged) kidnapping and enslavement of white women in prostitution. It made it a crime to transport someone across state lines for the purposes of 'prostitution or debauchery, or for any other immoral purpose'. Of course the progressive common law judge would very likely be appalled by the racism of the statute itself (which was clearly inspired by worries about white women only, and which was very likely specifically inspired by outrage over the interracial marriage of African American boxer Jack Johnson, who was convicted under the Act in 1912 for travelling with his wife). The progressive judge would certainly seek to interpret the statute in the narrowest possible way, as a prohibition on kidnapping and human trafficking. The unsavoury history of the Act is not mentioned in Levi's account. Levi then goes on to show how common law judges extended the idea of 'immoral purpose', in *Caminetti* v. *US* 242 US 470 (1917), to include a variety of consensual sexual activities, including interracial, premarital and extra-marital sex between consenting adults. Although the Court found that Caminetti's actions with consenting women fell within the 'plain meaning' of the statute, a progressive judge would probably disagree. This disturbing sequence of events, in which the USA gradually saw a widening net of governmental control over the sex lives of people disliked and stigmatised by the majority, shows the common law deferring to American traditions of the most unsavoury kind: racism, sexism (the woman's consent is ignored), intrusive puritanism. The statute itself is already disturbing, but its extension by courts made it do far more damage to many American

[5] E. Levi, *An Introduction to Legal Reasoning* (University of Chicago Press, 1948).

lives. Here we find Levi himself holding up the judicial extension of the Mann Act, apparently with approval and certainly without disapproval, as a typical example of common law judging at work. What is one to think? It is tempting to conclude that what is appealing about Strauss' reasoning and disturbing about Levi's has nothing to do, per se, with the methodology of the common law, and far more to do with the quality of moral judgement displayed by each.

How can the common lawyer reply to this critique? One very promising avenue of defence involves offering a more structured and prescriptive account of analogical reasoning, an important part of common law methodology. Opponents of the common law argue that analogical reasoning is just an invitation to whim and caprice: anything can be compared to anything. Scott Brewer,[6] drawing on Aristotle, constructs a very helpful model of such reasoning, involving abduction (movement from examples to a rule), confirmation or disconfirmation by reflective adjustment, and application to the case. Moreover, he finds that common law judges actually follow this process.

Another avenue of defence would be to return to Dworkin[7] and natural law. Dworkin's Hercules is constrained not only by the chain of past narratives, but also by 'substantive political morality', and especially 'the two constituent virtues of political morality ... justice and fairness'. Dworkin's complex and in many ways appealing view requires a far more detailed treatment than can be given here. We should ask, however, whether the view is in the end materially different from traditional views of the common law, which certainly invite judges to consult moral values as part of the fabric of experience, either following them or using them to criticise precedents deemed unjust. Does the appeal to abstract moral values (which is also open to a common law judge) really reduce or substantially constrain the indeterminacy inherent in the common law?

2 The Utilitarian Challenge

For the early utilitarians, the common law is a mess. Not implausibly, they think standard accounts of common law judging give no clear or

[6] S. Brewer, 'Exemplary reasoning: semantics, pragmatics, and the rational force of legal arguments by analogy', *Harvard Law Review*, 109 (1996), 923–1028.

[7] Dworkin, *Law's Empire*; Dworkin, 'Darwin's new bulldog'.

determinate guidance, and are thus simply invitations to judges to do whatever they please. They also see this irrational mess as not especially benign: they are typically highly sceptical of tradition, which they see as riddled with prejudice and arbitrary privileging of some groups and people over others. It is important to bear in mind that the three leading utilitarian philosophers were all radicals in several domains. Jeremy Bentham[8] (1748–1832) defended the decriminalisation of sodomy and the rights of non-human animals; John Stuart Mill[9] (1806–73) wrote one of the best philosophical works on women's equality ever, and introduced the first bill for women's suffrage in the British Parliament; he also defended animal rights and left his fortune to that cause. Henry Sidgwick[10] (1838–1900), though in some respects more conventional than his predecessors, waged a highly successful campaign for women's higher education and (with his wife Eleanor) established Newnham College (1871), the second women's college in Cambridge. Recent scholarship has revealed that Sidgwick was a closeted and probably celibate gay man whose contorted positions on issues of sexual morality emerge from an agonised inner life. Instead of seeing the common law as wisdom emerging from the confluence of many minds independently working in good faith, all these men more often see it as the product of minds in bad faith, bent on denying the just moral claims of others. And the fact that the common law is such an irrational mess makes things much worse, making the bad faith harder to expose. Summarises Mill: 'For the apotheosis of Reason we have substituted that of Instinct; and we call everything instinct which we find in ourselves and for which we cannot trace any rational foundation'. Mill's indictment of his era, though general, might also serve to encapsulate the utilitarian response to the common law.

In place of that mess, utilitarians propose a scientific rational approach. Bentham first argues that the appropriate end of conduct (and thence of law and policy) is the maximisation of net pleasure. Although each person naturally seeks to maximise personal pleasure, the rational end of human conduct in general is the maximisation of total (or average) pleasure.

[8] J. Bentham, *Introduction to the Principles of Morals and Legislation* (Hafner Press, 1948 (original publication 1789)).

[9] J.S. Mill, *The Subjection of Women*, Ed. S.M. Okin (Hackett, 1988 (original publication 1869)).

[10] H. Sidgwick, *The Methods of Ethics*, 7th ed. (Dover Publications, 1966 (original publication 1902)).

Bentham clearly believes that law supplies the coordination necessary to achieve this goal. Thus law should promote the welfare of all society's members, using an unbiased and clear-eyed calculus in which 'each [is] to count for one, none for more than one'. Law's job is constructive, forward-looking, and resolutely critical. It was clear to the utilitarians that most people do not treat the pleasures of all society's members equally, even if one confines oneself to human members (and Bentham and Mill would include animals as well, although they do not tell us how). Bentham was so determined to get rid of the common law in favour of a clear and complete legal code that he tried, without success, to convince President James Madison in 1811 to allow him to create a complete codified legal code for the United States. Although Bentham himself preferred comprehensive legislation to judicial discretion, the codes he envisaged have not materialised; moreover, any code leaves room for interpretation, which means, unavoidably, a role for judicial decision. So a utilitarian needs a theory of adjudication; and judges have in many cases taken up the task of judging in a utilitarian spirit.

The primary focus of the early utilitarians was the criminal law. All the utilitarian thinkers find that society has long been dominated by ideas of retribution and revenge. These ideas are irrational, since inflicting pain on the wrongdoer does not undo the crime. And they escalate in ways that are extremely harsh and counterproductive, causing societies to lose valuable human capital. Punishment of crime is best understood not in retributive but in forward-looking terms. Its legitimate goals are incapacitation of offenders, specific deterrence, general deterrence, and reform. If we look at punishments with these practical purposes in mind, we may sometimes choose harsh punishments, but with a rational justification, not just because it satisfies irrational vindictive sentiments. And the utilitarians agree that the harshest of punishments, torture and capital punishment, cannot be justified by reason.

Even before Bentham, Cesare Beccaria[11] (1737–93) had already advocated penal reform along utilitarian lines. In *On Crimes and Punishments* (1764), Beccaria argues that the appropriate aim of punishment is not retribution, but the creation of a better society. In order to ensure rationality in punishments, these must be promulgated in clear legislative rules,

[11] C. Beccaria, *On Crimes and Punishments and Other Writings*, Ed. R. Bellamy (Cambridge University Press, 1995).

not created by judicial discretion. (Thus he agrees with Bentham in his distrust of judges.) Notably he discusses torture at length, concluding that it is not useful and does not promote truthfulness. He also argues that the death penalty is inefficient.

All of these issues are taken up at greater length and with greater rigour by Bentham, both in the early *Rationale of Punishment* (1775) and *Introduction to the Principles of Morals and Legislation* (1789) and in later works such as *On Death Punishment* (1831). Bentham's general argument is that it is stupid for societies to focus most of their attention on punishment **ex post**, rather than on prevention of crime **ex ante**. The latter task should occupy most of a utilitarian's attention, since social happiness is much more effectively promoted by making people less likely to choose a life of crime than by inflicting 'mischief' on them after, often due to poverty and neglect, they have offended. Thus the primary job of dealing with crime belongs not to the legal system at all, but to social welfare policies promoting nutrition, health, education and employment. Nonetheless, Bentham, deeply engaged with the legal order and scathingly critical of it, does devote considerable attention to punishment, since he thinks reform in this area should not await the decision of societies to treat deprived people well. Nor should reform await societies' adoption of codified rules: judges, faute de mieux, can implement utilitarian recommendations.

The details of Bentham's elaborate scheme of punishments need not concern us, only its general rationale. Judges should refuse to be guided by the irrational retributive feelings of the populace; here as elsewhere Bentham scoffs at the idea that tradition embodies ethical wisdom. Instead, their punishments should be future-directed and calculated by reason to achieve a specific result. All punishment is painful, so the question must always be what happiness for society will be gained thereby. In general, this means that greater pain should be reserved for the most damaging offences, since in that way deterrence will be maximised: if people are punished equally severely for crimes large and small, they will be likely to opt for the more serious offence. This observation is important in Bentham's complicated arguments against the death penalty, which he restates and changes throughout his career – since the death penalty in Britain in his time was used for crimes large and small. His argument against the death penalty for homicide is never clearly stated, but the primary consideration seems to be its irrevocability and the consequent likelihood that innocents will be punished. (Bentham concedes that the death penalty serves incapacitation and specific deterrence extremely well!)

Concerning topics that are treated today (especially in the USA) as belonging to constitutional law, Bentham has a lot to say, and he is once again scathingly critical of tradition. A fine example of his approach is given by his treatment of a topic we have already addressed, the decriminalisation of homosexual sodomy. In four works published between 1785 and 1818, but especially in the remarkable book *Not Paul, But Jesus*, (part of which was published during Bentham's lifetime under a pseudonym, but of which the all-important third book was published only in 2013 by the Bentham Project at University College London), he produces a barrage of fascinating and often cogent arguments in favour of decriminalisation.

Bentham adduces many types of arguments, some involving radical biblical exegesis (he argues with considerable philological sophistication that Jesus approved same-sex conduct and even practised it himself!). Let us focus on the core arguments concerning harm to society. Do same-sex acts cause harm by decreasing reproduction? Here Bentham argues that homosexual individuals have often married and produced children, and he notes that reproduction does not take up much time, leaving a lot of time free for non-reproductive pursuits, some of them sexual (as we readily grant when heterosexual acts are in question). Moreover, Malthus has shown that we ought to be worried about population growth, not population decline. A more serious worry might be that male–male couples would deprive women of children and companionship. (Although Bentham recognises the existence of female homosexuality, never illegal in Britain, he apparently assumes that the number of lesbians may turn out to be smaller than the number of gay men.) Here Bentham makes a remarkable response. What harms women, he says, is their legal subordination, the 'afflictiveness of the yoke to which they are subjected'. This yoke, in turn, is certainly not caused by homosexuality, and is often caused by heterosexuality, 'the magnitude of the value set upon their charms by their barbarian masters'. Indeed, he continues, women in general do better in nations that have a larger proportion of open homosexuals: thus better in Italy than in Britain, with France somewhere in the middle.

More generally, throughout his work, Bentham lays siege to the entire Victorian ideology of 'higher' and 'lower' pleasures: pleasure is pleasure, and the bodily orifice used makes no rational difference at all.

Utilitarian legal rationalism can seem like a ray of light, illuminating the smug and frequently repressive darkness of the Victorian (and pre-Victorian) era. And yet the view has many difficulties. The first is the implausibility of its proposed end. Pleasure, conceived as Bentham conceives it, as a feeling varying only in intensity and duration, is not a good candidate for the appropriate end of all human conduct, as the more philosophical Mill immediately saw. We can see why Bentham chose it, since British morality seemed determined to deny the goodness of the body and its pleasant experiences; and yet its promotion to the status of sole good seems myopic. Even if one likes Bentham's proposal, it creates problems as yet insuperable of how to make the requisite interpersonal comparisons of welfare (problems made all the worse by Bentham's salient concern for non-human animals). But it is difficult to like Bentham's solution, once one realises that human flourishing consists of activity as well as feeling – and, moreover, of activities of many different types, differing in quality and not simply in quantity. Even one who largely agrees with the utilitarian critique of the common law is likely to wonder whether that messy system, with all its evident defects, does not more closely track the variety of genuine goods that human beings have typically found worth promoting.

It is worthy of note that Bentham's actual policy arguments, concerning both crime and sex, display greater flexibility than does his official theory. Thus he considers the happiness of poor people and of women in a way not limited to consideration of a quality of physical feeling (though he probably thought the reduction could ultimately be made).

One attempt to retain utilitarianism's commitment to commensurability (a single maximand) while removing the problem of interpersonal comparisons is Judge Richard Posner's proposal[12] to see wealth-maximisation as the goal of the legal system. In some areas Posner maintains that the legal system, and judicial reasoning in particular, actually does promote wealth-maximisation. In the area of constitutional law, however, he criticises it for departing from this norm. He never applies his idea to the criminal law.

The utilitarian critique of the common law has a number of distinct aspects. One may seek an approach to law that is forward-looking, critical and pragmatic without espousing Bentham's commitment to hedonism

[12] R.A. Posner, *The Economics of Justice* (Harvard University Press, 1981); R.A. Posner, 'The problematics of moral and legal theory', *Harvard Law Review* 111 (1998), 1637–710.

and to commensurability – thus following Bentham's policy arguments rather than his official theory. Posner, for example, has increasingly departed from wealth-maximisation and espoused a type of pragmatism. His approach has a great deal in common with the way in which Bentham actually deals with bad laws: in an acidic spirit of disdain for hypocrisy and special pleading, and with an emphasis on clear-eyed argument aimed at social happiness. One instructive instance is the recent *Baskin* v. *Bogan* 766 F.3d 648 (2014), the case overturning the laws in Indiana and Wisconsin that banned same-sex marriage. To each of the states' arguments that the welfare of children is promoted by the ban in question, Posner offers a witty and devastating rebuttal. Indeed, comparing his opinion in this case with Justice Kennedy's opinion in *Obergefell* v. *Hodges* 576 US (2015), the case that legalised same-sex marriage nationwide, is a good way of seeing the difference between the reasoning of a utilitarian judge and a common law judge (with liberal dollops of natural law), where both address the same question within the same legal and constitutional framework. Posner's tone is sceptical, caustic, intolerant of cant; Kennedy's is solemn and lofty. Posner addresses concrete issues of welfare; Kennedy adduces high ethical abstractions, dignity and equality. Posner is punctilious in matters of argument, Kennedy loose and impressionistic. It may seem unfair to cast Kennedy as the archetype of the common law judge, since he is hardly known for clarity or close argument. I do not suggest that common law judging can offer nothing more. Still, since Posner so obviously channels Bentham (without even having read *Not Paul, But Jesus* until after he wrote the opinion!), the parallel is not without interest. (Posner's judicial pragmatism, much in the spirit of Holmes, is more disciplined and appealing than his Holmes Lectures' theory of relativism and subjectivism, which has been rightly criticised as inconsistent and underdeveloped by Dworkin, Nussbaum[13] and others.)

3 Mixed Views

Since both utilitarianism and the common law have distinctive merits, it is not surprising that jurists and philosophers alike have tried to combine

[13] M.C. Nussbaum, 'Still worthy of praise: comments on Richard Posner', *Harvard Law Review* 111 (1998), 1776–95.

them. On the side of moral philosophy, Henry Sidgwick,[14] more deferential to custom than Bentham, recognises in philosophical intuitionism – the sifted and articulated form of shared moral beliefs – a legitimate method of ethics. Albeit not without some unease, he validates most of its holdings, including those relating to sexual propriety and retribution. His primary objection to ordinary belief (hence, were he to address our topic, to the common law) is lack of order and system: there are no principles for resolving conflicts between the different virtues, or even between different claims within each. Sidgwick thus argues that the intuitionist (the common lawyer) is forced by rationality itself to move on to utilitarianism, to find in it the complete form of the wisdom embodied in ordinary belief. Thus he credits the traditionalist rationale for the common law, objecting only to its formal inadequacy.

A related mixed view is Oliver Wendell Holmes' view of the common law.[15] Holmes rejects the claim that the common law is superior on account of tradition or the wisdom of time: 'it is revolting to have no better reason for a rule of law than that it was laid down in the time of Henry IV'. Judges should take the materials of the common law as a starting point for pragmatic reasons, but should own up to their responsibility to look forward, not back, and to fill gaps in the law with an eye to what is best for society. Like Sidgwick, then, he sees the past as a starting point, but one that needs to be completed by a future-directed pragmatism. Holmes' pragmatism, however, is looser than Sidgwick's, lacking the emphasis on commensurability and conflict-resolution. Holmes' views[16] were a leading precursor of legal realism, which cannot be discussed here because of limits of space.

A resolution distinctly more friendly to the common law is that of Justice Benjamin Cardozo[17] in *The Nature of the Judicial Process*. Cardozo emphasises that the judge operates within an ongoing framework of precedents and statutes. If there is a clear statute governing the case, the judge applies it; if not, precedent must be consulted, and if the precedent is clear, once again the judge is to apply it. But often it is not clear, and then

[14] Sidgwick, *Methods of Ethics*.

[15] O.W. Holmes Jr, *The Common Law* (Dover Publications, 1991 (original publication 1881)).

[16] O.W. Holmes Jr, *The Essential Holmes*, Ed. R.A. Posner (University of Chicago Press, 1997); O.W. Holmes Jr, *The Path of the Law* (Martino Publishing, 2012 (originally published in *Harvard Law Review* 10 (1897)).

[17] B.N. Cardozo, *The Nature of the Judicial Process* (Dover Publications, 2005 (original publication 1921)).

the judge must extract the underlying principle from the precedent(s) and determine the direction in which the principle is to develop. This is difficult, and the judge must consider issues such as logical progression, historical development, social welfare, and also justice and morality. Often, the welfare of society must 'fix the path' of a principle's development. Uniformity is usually good, but not when it is 'uniformity of oppression'. In such cases, judges must consult moral norms and even depart from precedent. All of this must be decided by the judge's own judgement. Judges legislate only interstitially, but '[t]he process in its highest reaches is not discovery, but creation'. Here we have arrived back at the attractive David Strauss portrait of the common law judge, but with a distinctively (albeit loosely) utilitarian cast. To which Bentham would surely reply, 'Precisely: and why should we trust you?'

4 Current Questions

The debate between the common law and utilitarianism will long continue, with natural law playing a speaking role in moderate versions of both. And as we have seen, the common law and utilitarianism overlap in many ways. But two questions plague the whole debate as we go forward.

a The Limits of the Judicial Role

The first is a question about the judicial role. Many, including leading US common law and utilitarian theorists, defend a large role for judges as constitutional interpreters, and, *ipso facto*, as arbiters of crucial matters in criminal law (and every other major area of law). But numerous theorists of varied views are troubled by the fact that judges, though indirectly accountable to the people, and a large part of most modern constitutional democracies, have somewhat questionable democratic credentials; some would simply assert that they are undemocratic (using, presumably, a majoritarian conception of democracy). Jeremy Waldron[18] has long argued energetically against judicial review on such grounds, albeit relying on assumptions (particularly 'a commitment on the part of most members of

[18] J. Waldron, 'The core of the case against judicial review', *Yale Law Journal* 115 (2006), 1346–406.

the society and most of its officials to the idea of individual and minority rights') that suit a somewhat idealised Britain better than they do either the United States, where the opposition of whole states to basic human rights caused not only the Civil War but, more recently, the upheaval of the Civil Rights Movement, or India, where majoritarian politics have turned power over to a group complicit in genocidal crimes against an ethnic minority, and the Supreme Court frequently seems the last bastion of the fundamental rights of citizens.

Another complaint against judicial review points out that judges are not (or at least not always) objective arbiters, but are highly political, often reflecting the positions of the party of the President who appointed them. (Obviously there are limits to this, since the positions of the parties may change considerably during a judge's long tenure, and so too may the positions of the judge. Thus it surprises most Americans to hear that the famous liberal Justices Harry A. Blackmun and John Paul Stevens were Republican appointees.) Finally, one might mention Bentham's objection: judges are often messy thinkers, and incapable of precise delineation of social welfare.

Some critics, for example Waldron, would prefer to avoid judicial review of a written constitution and to confine the role of the judge to a more humble common law role. Others go further, with Bentham recommending that we jettison the common law judge altogether, in favour of codified statutes. Even in the USA, where such a position would be very radical, a powerful challenge of this sort has been issued by Adrian Vermeule.[19] Reviving the views of James Bradley Thayer (1831–1902), Vermeule urges judicial humility and deference to legislative majorities. His critique is especially valuable because he confronts the strongest arguments advanced in favour of common law constitutionalism.

Vermeule makes the valuable point that 'many minds' arguments of the sort used to defend the common law do not have robust credentials, especially when, as here, one cannot show that each judge is an independent contributor to the evolving view. He suggests that it would be better to defer to legislators because they appear to have superior epistemic credentials. Thus the very arguments used to support common law constitutionalism, in his view, actually turn against it.

[19] A. Vermeule, *Law and the Limits of Reason* (Oxford University Press, 2009).

Such arguments cannot be answered in the abstract. Clearly each country must assess its own political situation and the epistemic credentials of its judges and legislators. But critics of judicial review must beware of comparing actual judges, with all their flaws, to an idealised conception of legislative politics. Vermeule, though writing in the USA in 2009, describes legislative debate in a way that seems to have little connection to current reality. Most appellate judges are at least likely to believe in reason and the conclusions of science, desirable traits that legislators may lack. Moreover, they respect the slowly evolving traditions of our democracy in a way that many current legislators, inspired by radical anti-government views, surely do not. Perhaps that very untimeliness gives us a reason to keep judges around a little longer.

It is surely true that in this science-dependent era judges cannot be expected to understand all they need to know in order to judge well in complicated matters involving the environment, or even the economy. But that leads us in a direction very different from Vermeule's. The constitutional principle of deference to administrative agencies' interpretations of statutes in their domain (famously known as *Chevron* deference) is wise. It leads away from deference to legislatures and toward a greater reliance on informed scientific expertise.

A more nuanced Vermeule-like position has been advanced by Cass Sunstein.[20] Sunstein, a serious defender of the administrative state (and former head of the Office of Information and Regulatory Affairs during the Obama administration) has energetically defended scientifically grounded cost–benefit analysis, conducted by administrative agencies, as superior to the unreliable judgements of the public about matters of risk. His defence of 'judicial minimalism' is limited to the sphere of core constitutional law. He holds that judges deciding complicated cases involving contested values ought to proceed incrementally and 'one case at a time', rather than making bold statements about abstract values. He is thus especially opposed to the part of common law practice that overlaps with natural law, bringing large moral concepts to bear on tradition and precedent. Sunstein's rationale for his judicial minimalism, however, is not Vermeule's epistemic argument; it appears to be above all a form of cautious

[20] C.R. Sunstein, *One Case at a Time: Judicial Minimalism on the Supreme Court* (Harvard University Press, 2001); C.R. Sunstein, *Risk and Reason: Safety, Law, and the Environment* (Cambridge University Press, 2004).

pragmatism. Seeing that their democratic credentials are contested, judges ought to proceed incrementally and case by case, lest they set off a popular backlash, as has undoubtedly happened in the area of abortion rights.

Still other critics of common law judging favour originalism or textualism as ways of introducing fixity and limit into the process of judicial reasoning. Thus Justice Antonin Scalia[21] first develops a very general critique of the common law in favour of a jurisprudence of general rules and principles: we have the rule of law only to the extent that we have a 'Law of Rules', since predictability and uniformity are hallmarks of the rule of law. He then goes on to defend a textual approach as the best way of establishing the requisite fixity. In response to the general Scalia critique we should turn to the elegant treatment of rules in Herbert Hart's *The Concept of Law*.[22] Hart argues that there is no way to avoid judicial discretion, since our rules always have an open texture. This role for discretion, however, does not entail that society will be lawless and subject to the whims of the judiciary.

As for Scalia's preferred alternative, text-based views have numerous problems. Texts always need interpretation, and neither the intentions of the Founders (originalism) nor the common meaning of a term in the year of the drafting of the relevant text (textualism) seem well positioned to trump the responsible judgement of a living person, particularly concerning abstract concepts such as 'liberty' and 'equality'. As Strauss remarks, text is most powerful when it is highly concrete, and in such cases the stakes are usually pretty low: thus nobody favours creative interpretation of the Constitution's statements about the age of the president. But most provisions of the Constitution are not like this: they have been extensively altered by years of precedents, and few originalists really want to throw all this history away. (Thus it is a rare extreme position to reject the incorporation of the Bill of Rights, meaning its application to acts of state and local government as well as the federal government – even though the Founders explicitly rejected incorporation when Madison proposed it, and the textual rationale for holding that the post-Civil War Fourteenth Amendment entails it is murky and uncertain.) Finally, originalism and textualism may

[21] A. Scalia, 'The rule of law as the law of rules', *University of Chicago Law Review*, 56 (1989), 1175–88.

[22] H.L.A. Hart, *The Concept of Law* (Oxford University Press, 2012 (original publication 1961)).

well be self-undermining: for there is much evidence that the intention of the framers was to create an open text that could be reinterpreted by successive generations, and the meaning of key abstract terms at the time of drafting was also very open, in the sense that thousands of years of philosophical debate about these notions had already made them contested concepts.

b The Use of Foreign Cases as Precedents

When, if at all, should common law judges look to the law and the holdings of other nations? In our increasingly interlocking world, this question can hardly be ignored. Oddly, some aspects of the question are uncontested: thus US courts routinely draw on the British common law as a source of both principle and precedent. But, whereas many nations feel free to draw liberally on the judgments of courts of other nations, as well as international law and human rights instruments (appellate courts in India are especially notable in this regard), the USA has been very cautious, refusing to grant precedential status to foreign holdings. Even with regard to a more general use of foreign judgments, to illuminate the issue and set it in a larger context, there is deep controversy. On today's US Supreme Court, Justices Ginsburg and Breyer[23] are well known for their interest in non-US law, and the late Justice Scalia was a dogged opponent of this practice. He repeatedly argued that this practice opens the door to arbitrary and wilful judicial reasoning, since judges are bound to cherry-pick those foreign practices that agree with what they would like to say and to ignore others they do not like. Obviously this is a real problem.

Supporters of the practice of appealing to foreign law, however, do not defend the practice indiscriminately. Thus in *Roper* v. *Simmons*,[24] concerning the juvenile death penalty, the examination of international treaty law took place in a determinate legal context. Eighth Amendment jurisprudence already instructs judges to refer to 'the evolving standards of decency that mark the progress of a maturing society' in order to determine which punishments are 'cruel and unusual'. The Court must use its own independent judgement, but it is appropriate to take note of social

[23] S.J. Breyer, *The Court and the World: American Law and New Global Realities* (Knopf, 2015).
[24] *Roper* v. *Simmons* 543 U.S. 551 (2005).

evolution. The Court reasoned that 30 states already prohibited the execution of juveniles and that juries in other states assigned this penalty very rarely. Thus the reference to international treaties was icing on the cake, further confirmation of the Court's judgment. Foreign law was not used as binding precedent, but rather as an extra piece of evidence for a social evolution that was amply evident also in the USA. As Justice Stevens emphasised in his concurring opinion, the main point is that the Eighth Amendment must be seen not as having its meaning fixed in all detail at the time of drafting (in which case a seven-year-old might legally be executed), but rather as a work-in-progress, its abstract concepts deriving changing meaning from evolving judgments. The Court is on firm ground here: used modestly in the course of such an inquiry, selected foreign materials are helpful.

In his 2015 book *The Court and the World,*[25] Justice Stephen Breyer makes a far more wide-ranging case for not just the wisdom but also the necessity of dealing with foreign law in an interconnected world. Breyer is less concerned with the large human abstractions involved in the Eighth Amendment than with a host of issues, sometimes quite technical, ranging from national security to intellectual property to the conduct of international trade, that require US courts to learn and deal with the legal judgments of other nations. Globalisation, he argues, has made engagement with foreign law unavoidable. Breyer's rich menu of cases shows that an interest in the foreign is not simply a way of gaining an illicit advantage for one's own moral views (that is in essence Scalia's critique); it simply cannot be avoided in a world in which technical developments have caused us to share a world. The common law judge of the future, he argued, cannot afford to be an isolationist.

[25] Breyer, *The Court and the World.*

4 Law and Living Well

Timothy Macklem

1 Good Lives and How to Lead Them

As human beings we seek to live well, to lead lives that are rich, meaningful, genuinely worth living (as we sometimes put it). We are bound to do so by the very terms of our existence. This sense of basic purpose, of what fundamentally animates us, is not some function of the human condition, or of its capacity for reflection and action, though it may sometimes seem that way, but on the contrary, extends to everything that can be said to have an existence, whether that be other animals, other living organisms, or even those features of the world, such as rocks and waterfalls, that flourish or fail to flourish, have worth or fail to have worth, despite the fact that they themselves play no active role, whether deliberative or otherwise, in securing either their flourishing or their worth.[1] That said, as human beings we have a distinctive, some might call it a special, relationship to this shared purpose, one that is born of our distinctive capacity to perceive and to discharge the many and complex responsibilities of living well. So living well is a human project but not merely a human project.

The combination of these facts, and the further fact that they are in tension with one another, gives rise to two distinct and familiar demands upon each of us in the conduct of our lives. First, whatever might be true of a particular moment, over the course of a life we can live well only in concert with the world and with one another. A good life is the product of success in all the varied shadings of our existence as agents, those that are distinctive to us and those that we share with others, and so can be achieved only in full recognition of, respect for and collaboration with all else that is involved in its pursuit.[2]

[1] See T. Macklem and J. Gardner, 'Human disability', *King's Law Journal* 25 (2014), 60.

[2] That is not to say that a good life need otherwise be multidimensional. It is perfectly possible to live well by focusing on a narrow set of values. See J. Gardner and T. Macklem, 'Value, interest and well-being', *Utilitas* 18 (2006), 362.

It is not something that we can master on our own, or something that we can achieve either at the expense of others or in neglect of ourselves. Second, as human beings, and hence as creatures with a heightened capacity for reasoning and reflection (or so it would seem), we have an unusually complex, often conflicted, set of responsibilities to the shared project of living well. A good life is a matter of managing these twin demands successfully: that of living well in a way that is at once distinctive and non-distinctive, in terms of one's condition as a human being and as the particular human being that each of us happens to be from time to time; that of giving full credence to all the various shadings of existence, rather than assigning priority to one over the other, or searching for a resolution among them.

With this in mind, we have brought into the world, consciously and unconsciously, a vast range of social forms and practices, ever fluid, always various, to guide and support us in the achievement of good lives for us and our fellows. Some of these social forms and practices have proved to be extremely fruitful, others less so. Sadly, a great many more than we care to admit have proven to be perverse, undermining rather than furthering even human flourishing, let alone all else in the world that values or is valued.

Among the most prominent of our social practices, at least in the world we now live in, is that of the law. The scheme of law, in its forms and institutions, helps to structure our pursuit of good lives, both individually and communally. Where then does it stand in terms of fruitfulness? Why do we need it? In just what ways does it help us to live well? What role does this unusually self-aware aspect of the everyday play in the realisation of the ideal, that is, in the project of making our lives genuinely good ones? More broadly, to step a little further back, just what is the nature of the relationship between the everyday and the ideal? We know something, perhaps quite a lot, of what the ideal has to teach the everyday, because that much is built into the very concept of the ideal. What, if anything, does the everyday have to teach the ideal in return? Is there a genuine sense in which each has something to learn from the other? If so, what might that tell us about the law? Do we need to know the law in order to know what the law ought to be, in some respects at least?

The questions raised here are perhaps more familiarly rendered in terms of the relationship between law and morality, rather than in terms of law and living well. There is nothing wrong with speaking in that familiar way, or at least there ought not to be. Yet it seems to me that one needs to be a little cautious about doing so, because the idea of the moral is frequently identified with a particular vision of what it means to live well, sometimes with a particular set of doctrines, often though not inevitably religious ones, sometimes with a particular concern for the flourishing of one's fellows rather than oneself, so as to contrast the moral to the prudential, sometimes with a concern for the ethical as opposed, say, to the aesthetic. As I see it, all of these things are inescapable features of a good life, and therefore, in speaking of living well, I am adopting a view of the moral that embraces and transcends such ways of narrowing or focusing the idea of a good life, so as to be open to all that can make a life go well, and to the kinds of contribution that law might have to such a project.[3]

I will also assume, without seeking to demonstrate, that the moral world, the world the resources of which we draw upon in order to live well, is fundamentally diverse, so that the demands it makes upon us, and the resources that it offers to us, are not only complex but often contradictory, perhaps characteristically so. Some of the issues that confront us are ones that can be settled by reference to the weight of reasons, to the fact that one course of action has more to be said for it than does another, but a good many others can be settled only by the fact of decision. Reasons always tell us what to do and what not to do, but on the whole they do not tell us which of their claims to prefer to another. Reasons not only differ in kind as well as degree, just because and to the extent that they are distinctive, but, a few special cases aside, they do not embody any resource that would tell us which kind to prefer to another. We must simply decide, so that it is the fact of decision that confers whatever priority one reason has over another in the shaping of our lives. That is because it is the fact of our lives that places these reasons, and the values that give rise to them, in collision with one another. In and of themselves, and as long as they are not engaged with, they can be at odds with one another without ever coming into conflict. Indeed the many possibilities for their prioritising are part of the richness of the resource they offer us. The practical conflict between them, whatever costs and rewards it may give rise to, is born of the fact that our lives are actual and limited, concrete and specific, so as to make commitment to one form of living well rather than another

[3] On the absence of any deep divide between the prudential and the moral see J. Raz, 'The central conflict: morality and self-interest' in his *Engaging Reason* (Oxford University Press, 1999), 303.

incumbent upon us, and upon our many fellow travellers in the cause of living well. That conflict is our special creation, as finite and temporal beings, and it is our special burden to resolve.

2 Idealism and Scepticism

For some, most notably Ronald Dworkin, law is not to be identified with the form that it apparently takes in the particular legal doctrines of particular legal jurisdictions. Those doctrines are in fact but the unreliable shadows of an ideal that legal officials have sought to trace, inevitably rather imperfectly. If we were to take law as it is so identified for what law really is we would mistake the everyday for the ideal, mistake moral practice and moral aspiration. It makes no more sense to do this than to identify any other aspect of morality with what people from time to time take it to be. We do not identify honesty with what is practised as honesty, integrity with what is regarded as integrity, justice with what is meted out as justice, and we should no more identify law with what is practised as law.[4] On the contrary, law is rightly understood as the collective morality of a particular political community. It is a shared aspiration, toward which all citizens rightly strive, always just out of reach, calling us on. Its ongoing delineation, imperfect as that may be, is a matter of moral philosophy writ small. We can never be entirely confident in our knowledge of it, or assured of our achievement of it, yet we can become well enough versed in it to be able to rely upon it as our guide.

The attractions of this view are obvious, particularly to the self-understanding of lawyers and judges, whose role it becomes to use their moral wisdom to articulate the proper aspirations of their community. Yet the prominence that it assigns to law in our collective life has obscure foundations. Some of this obscurity is internal to the account. How can we hope to distinguish the law from other aspects of what it means to lead a good life in common with our fellows without the assistance of a theory of the state, one that is sufficiently fine-grained to pick out our legal responsibilities and distinguish them from our wider social mores, the shared commitments that tell us, for example, how courtesy is to be practised among us? How can we ever be guided by law if its identification, even by

[4] See R. Dworkin, *Law's Empire* (Harvard University Press, 1986) at 47ff.

those who are recognised as official experts, is not something to be relied upon? If we are each to identify law for ourselves, in the moral manner, as apparently follows from the fact that we lack adequate reason to rely on the judgement of legal officials, what basis do we have for giving our personal identification any particular credence, and how can we hope to share what we have so identified with others who have made different identifications, as we must if law is to be able to articulate a common framework for the shared project of living well? Some of the obscurity is external to the account. Why do we preserve and continue to engage with the forms and practices of law if they have no significance for us other than as pre-interpretive data? Why do we not deal with the moral directly, in the manner of a pre-legal community? If the answer is that it is not possible to do so in the circumstances of a large, complex, modern society, then law must possess a life that is sufficiently independent of direct moral perception to do the work that is expected of it in such a complex society, a level of autonomy that Dworkin's account denies to it. And more profoundly, how can the everyday be equated with the ideal, so that we should understand our lives as the things they ought to be? The problem of moral failings aside, are the resources of the ideal adequate to the articulation of the everyday? Or does the ideal depend on the resources of the everyday for its instantiation?

For others, most notably Hans Kelsen and Herbert Hart, a form of moral scepticism appears to obviate these difficulties, albeit at a significant price.[5] Both Kelsen and Hart distinguish, surely correctly, the project of law, which they see as a social practice, from the fact of morality, which is the standard to which practices are held for their excellence. Like all other artefacts, social and natural, or more broadly as I have put it, all other existences, law operates in the realm of goodness, the realm in which we seek to instantiate value as part of the project of living well, a realm that is inevitably, one is bound to admit, as morally fallible as those who practice within it, thereby make it what it is, and so impress it with their frailty. On this view of the matter, law is one thing and morality another. Or so it has often been said.

Yet like many such ways of expressing ideas in overly striking terms this view is one that is liable to be, and indeed has widely been, misunderstood.

[5] In describing Kelsen and Hart as moral sceptics, here and in what follows, I mean that they are sceptical of moral realism, not that they are sceptical of the very possibility of the moral.

Law is not in any real sense separate from morality, of course, any more than is any other artefact that has been created or called upon with the project of living well in mind. It is simply that they are not to be identified with one another. Law is a moral project, and the point of distinguishing the project and its moral inspiration is in part to recognise that the project is one that can easily miscarry and commonly does. Yet that straightforward point, at least as so expressed, needs to be taken on board carefully. As frequent and as profound as miscarriages of justice can be, it is difficult, perhaps close to impossible, to imagine a legal system without at least some moral worth. Even were there a legal system without moral worth, it would not be enough to establish the separation of law and morals. It would simply establish the existence of an immoral legal system.

Yet it seems to me that there is a reason for the misapprehension, and that it is to be found in the distinctive view of obligation, or more broadly, of normativity, that is at work in this view of law. Both Kelsen and Hart, in their rather different ways, regard the normativity of law as a species of normativity quite distinct from that which is constitutive of morality. As moral sceptics, they are committed to the idea that there are many normativities in the world, just as many as there are moral observers and participants. What we speak of as the moral outlook is, for them, but a point of view that is accountable only to the viewer. As many people put it, it is a matter of opinion, albeit a very special kind of opinion, one that is accountable to the person who holds it rather than to its object. The difference between Hart's scepticism and Kelsen's, and it is an important one, is this.[6] For Kelsen there can be only one point of view in relation to any object for any person at any given moment. So when we possess or accept a point of view we consequently possess or accept its attendant normativity. As he sees things, legal normativity is a rational postulate, to which one may or may not be personally committed, depending on one's moral outlook. In one's capacity as a legal official, say, one may be committed to the normativity of law in general or of laws in particular, while in the next moment and in one's capacity as a lay person one might reject law in general or in particular. One puts one's legal hat on, and from that point of view concludes that speed limits ought to be observed and prohibited drugs ought not to be taken, but then

[6] For a helpful presentation and analysis of Kelsen's account see J. Raz, 'Legal validity' in *The Authority of Law* (Clarendon Press, 1979) 146.

takes one's legal hat off and from that point of view may reach the opposite conclusions. There is only one species of normativity, namely moral normativity, just as there is only one point of view that a person can adopt at any given moment. Yet the claims of normativity are ever dependent upon a point of view, though that will vary from person to person and time to time. There are many hats that one can wear but it is only possible to wear one hat at a time.

For Hart, however, legal normativity is not a function of moral normativity but rather a species of normativity in its own right, albeit one that is ultimately answerable to one's moral outlook. It follows that it is possible for a person to subscribe to more than one species of normativity in relation to the same object at the same moment, so as to be legally committed but morally uncommitted to a particular legal provision. From there it is an easy step to the idea that law and its normativity are separate from morality and its normativity. Easy but mistaken, for Hart, like everybody else, thought that law was infused by and answerable to morality, albeit a morality that he himself understood in sceptical terms. Yet that qualification makes clear why the step to the idea of the separation of law and morals is an understandable one. The mistake in it arises from interpreting a morally sceptical picture in morally realistic terms, so as to speak of the separation of law from that which is genuinely normative. Hart did not believe in such a separation, and neither should anyone else.

Yet there are deep difficulties in the attempt to understand legal normativity, and normativity more generally, in sceptical terms, despite the fact that valuable things have been learned from it, at least in the case of Kelsen's work in the hands of Joseph Raz. Most obviously, the sceptic no more explains than Dworkin does why those who seek to live well should turn to the law for guidance rather than engaging with the moral directly.

3 The Limits of Moral Guidance

The disagreement between idealists and sceptics over the identification of law and the nature of its normativity has been most famously, some would say tiresomely, played out in terms of the possibility of bad laws. Is an unjust law really law? For an idealist, clearly not. Practices that do not succeed in living up to their moral inspiration are simply not cases of what they purport to be. Legal practice that falls short of what law should be is not law to the extent of the shortfall, which may be partial or complete, any more than a practice that fails to be honest is a case of honesty, a practice that fails to display integrity is a case of integrity, a meting out of justice that fails to be just is a case of justice. The very concept of a practice is impressed with the aspiration that it seeks to realise. Put most dramatically, an immoral act is not an act, or in more intelligible terms, an irrational act is not an act. Ideas and ideals become one. For a moral sceptic, of course, none of this holds. The world is something that exists in advance of any ideals, to be invested with the attitudes of those who engage with it, as and to the extent that they see fit. From the sceptical point of view, if a practice could exist only in terms of an ideal, then much, perhaps all of the world would come into existence only as each one of us imagined it in imagining goodness as we see it, so that different people would necessarily inhabit different actual worlds. Moral scepticism would slide into solipsism.

It sometimes seems to me that there is more than a little of the tempest in the teapot about this particular way of capturing the disagreement between idealists and sceptics. Special cases aside, both parties agree that we should uphold morally sound laws and reject morally unsound laws. That being the case, both parties are liable to respond to the law in the same way for the same reason, namely its moral worth or lack thereof, whether that worth is ideally or sceptically rendered. In what sense, then, does it matter whether in so doing they are or are not acting under the description of law? Both sides are silent on this question. Why not just do the good thing, whatever that is, *qua* good thing, and so regard other normative demands either as superfluous and potentially distracting (when they function to reinforce what goodness calls upon us to do or not do), or as corrupt and capable of only prudential significance (when they contradict the claims of goodness)? Why go through the law at all?[7]

Idealists about law wear the habit of law in implicit recognition of the benefits that the habit and its possible wearings are capable of giving rise to, without taking the existence of the habit sufficiently seriously to offer any account of it, and without offering any explanation of the value that may arise from its wearing. In fairness of course, they could not do so

[7] For similar concerns see D. Enoch, 'Is general jurisprudence interesting?' (2015) ssrn.com/abstract=2601537.

without undermining the premises of their own account, yet that fact surely tells us only that the premises need revisiting, on the grounds of inconsistency with their practice. Sceptics in turn offer no explanation of the priority of morality that they typically acknowledge or of the alternative significance of legal normativity. Why isn't one species of normativity as good as the other to the sceptic, at least in principle, that is, unless one of them happens to be the sceptic's personal view, in which case it is the only view that could matter, rendering legal normativity oxymoronic? It would seem that for the sceptic legal normativity either is some other person's normativity or exists only in theory, that is, as long as and to the extent that the sceptic has no views on the matter in question.

These issues have been to some extent resolved by more probing views of the law that might be said to be broadly intermediate between those of the idealist and the sceptic. For John Finnis law is at once both idealising and non-idealising. Law exists only because and to the extent that it fulfils a moral purpose, but the fact of its existence, including the crucial, non-idealising fact that law can be identified without invoking the answers to the problems of living well that it exists to resolve, means that law is able to fulfil two functions that are essential to living well but that morality, as directly apprehended, has no capacity of its own to fulfil. Morality cannot help us to live well without a degree of specification that it is incapable of providing on its own, for morality is typically general in its terms, while life is fine-grained. Law can help bring morality to earth, so as to render it both in sufficient detail to make it practical as a guide for daily living and in terms that are sufficiently recognisable to make them intelligible to their intended audience and broadly consonant with rival renderings of moral obligation in the community in question, so helping to constitute a reasonably harmonious and sustainable moral culture. Second, morality has no capacity to resolve the many conflicts of reasons that its instantiation gives rise to. It needs the support of decision to fully determine its application, and the operation of a legal system is one particularly self-conscious, deliberative way of embodying social decision. In these ways law first distils and then selects among moral expectations. It does so in ways that are guided but not determined by morality. That is the service that it can perform for morality, but it performs that service only if and as long as its purpose is a genuinely moral one.

For Joseph Raz, the role of law is more open-ended and morally ambiguous. Law as he sees it is quintessentially authoritative, and authority, of whatever kind, is an aid to our rational life if and when it enables us to do better in the project of living well than we would be able to do simply through the exercise of our own judgement. Of course, we may nevertheless decide to exercise our own judgement, despite its limitations, and would be warranted in doing so, just because the autonomous exercise of judgement is itself an aspect of living well, one that is incommensurable with the better judgement that it may displace. Yet if and to the extent that we are prepared to yield aspects of our autonomy, in certain settings at certain times, to a social practice that, taken overall, is compatible with our condition as autonomous beings, law offers us a way of resolving difficulties of many different kinds. The coordination of our lives with the lives of others is often assisted by the presence of a norm that is in many respects morally arbitrary, a norm that tells us which side of the road to drive on, for example, or just what speed it is safe to drive at. Law may also embody expertise that is difficult or impossible for us to acquire on our own, both technical expertise, such as is embodied in health and safety standards, and moral expertise, such as is embodied in laws that prohibit certain kinds of insider trading.

It seems clear that these two views are more promising than their predecessors because they suggest ways in which law may assist the project of living well by offering guidance of a kind that morality is incapable of offering itself. Yet both views stop short of answering the correlative and more profound question of whether law (and indeed human experience generally) has any capacity to enhance the content of morality, to enlarge its domain, to give rise to new values or shades of value that can serve as aspirations to other moral agents. In the case of Finnis this is perhaps for reasons of principle, to do with what he takes to be the conceptual subordination of the everyday to the ideal. In the case of Raz it is for reasons of intellectual circumspection: it is not his purpose to demonstrate anything beyond the ways in which the authority of law is compatible with the project of living well in a culture that, as it happens in much of the world as we know it, is committed to autonomy.

Yet circumspection leaves more subtle possibilities on the table than much of the literature has drawn attention to. In particular, the extremely fruitful idea of a point of view, first proposed by Kelsen, with its sceptically inspired implication that a point of view might have a role to play in the construction as well as the realisation of value, is given no weight in

Finnis' account, understandably, yet has a central place in that of Raz.[8] For Raz, the idea of a point of view is embedded in the service conception of authority, which regards authority as justified as and when it enables us to comply better with the reasons that otherwise apply to us.[9] Yet what are those reasons exactly, and just what accounts for their present form? To what extent, if any, does authority and the point of view that it embodies have the capacity to reshape the reasons that otherwise apply to us? Raz makes clear that the law's claim to have created valid reasons is to be understood as a statement from a point of view. Is that point of view no more than the perspective from which the law is regarded as successful in creating justified authority, or does it sometimes help to contribute to that success? The former possibility lends support to a practice of mild scepticism, that which asks whether something really is the case. The latter possibility lends support to something more like radical forms of scepticism, in which point of view helps to make something the case, so that the everyday may have a significant role to play in the construction of the ideal, if not the truly radical role, characteristic of deep moral scepticism, of being its entire ground.

4 Creativity and Existence

In setting out the idea of a statement from a point of view, Raz offers a helpful everyday illustration.[10] A Catholic scholar of Jewish doctrine reminds his weakly observant Jewish friend to do or not to do something in accordance with Jewish doctrine. The reminder is to be understood, Raz explains, as a detached normative statement, a statement from a point of view from which the Catholic scholar is detached by reason of his or her Catholic faith but to which the Jewish friend is correspondingly committed. So far, so good. Yet what is it that makes Jewish doctrine, in all its intricacy, much of which is historically derived and so dependent on the

[8] See Raz, 'On the autonomy of legal reasoning' in *Ethics in the Public Domain* (Clarendon Press, 1994) 326.

[9] For Raz's most recent rendering of that account see J. Raz, 'The problem of authority: revisiting the service conception' in *Between Authority and Interpretation* (Oxford Scholarship Online, 2009) 126.

[10] See his 'Legal validity' in *Authority of Law* 146 at 156–9.

existence of those whose lives gave rise to it, something that it is possible to be rationally committed to?

For Raz, one concludes by extrapolation from his position on authority generally and on the authority of law in particular, it must be something like the fact that Jewish doctrine enables believers to do better in terms of the reasons that otherwise apply to them than they would do by thinking for themselves. But what are those reasons exactly, what shapes their content and their application, and how do they consequently come to embrace both the Catholic and the Jewish faiths, that is, come to be the standards against which the authority of those faiths and what they require is to be tested for its rationality? Are they the same reasons that existed before either Judaism or Catholicism came into being?

The point here is not one that has anything to do with the special character of religion; it applies with equal force to the secular commitments of a lay culture. Any assessment of whether one course of conduct would enable us to do better than another is bound to take full account of the possibilities for value in either course, and full account can be taken only by registering each course in all its richness, much of which has been established by human beings in ways that, as Finnis has emphasised, were compatible with, yet not fully determined by, the very general and conflicting requirements of morality, and that consequently owe much of their present form, and possibilities for value, to the fact of our lives, or more precisely, to the facts of the lives of those who were responsible for their present shape.

Let me step back a little further. One may consider the idea of a point of view sceptically, in the manner of Kelsen, or agnostically, in the manner of Raz. What matters is that each consideration depends for its rationality, at least in part, on the possibility that a point of view, and the existence that gives rise to it, is capable of moral significance. That is the crux of the service conception of authority. What the service conception does not draw attention to, however, yet the normal justification of authority is bound to invoke, is that the moral significance in question may or may not be one that existed in advance of the culture, the allied point of view, and the consequent commitment that is being assessed in terms of it. The service conception of authority is silent on this issue, and correspondingly accommodating of either possibility. As I see it, that is because both possibilities are morally realistic.

Any point of view that claims to be in some sense pre-emptive, and to that extent claims to be authoritative, is bound to be assessed according to the terms of Raz's normal justification of authority if it is to pass rational muster. Yet the reason under which much of human experience is bound to be assessed in that way is one that would not have existed in the form that it does but for the presence of some religion, culture, social practice, legal system or other artefact of human experience. It follows that many of the reasons by which we are to be judged are ones that we have had some hand in making. Clearly one should tread carefully here. Reasons do not, despite what many have maintained, in any sense mark out value and disvalue, what it means to live well and to fail to live well, do not have the shape they have, simply because we would have them do so. They are not functions of our will, or of whatever is the corresponding quality in any of the other forms of being to which reasons and value apply. Nonetheless the value they mark out would not have possessed quite the contours it does but for the fact of our being. Morality inescapably bears the imprint of the existences of those who have practised it.

The claim can be expressed rather more accessibly in terms of the everyday, for the simple reason that what it describes is a feature born of the everyday. When we go through the daily business of living well, or more accurately, of attempting to live well, we make artefacts of our lives and of the various goods and practices that we live through. Our realisation of aesthetic value, for example, takes the form of music, dance, painting, sculpture, literature, film, photography and much else, together with their associated practices. In this way we have developed jazz, ballet, cubism, conceptual art, novels, poetry and so on, all of which have their roots in attention to the abstract demands of aesthetic value yet all of which have depended for their instantiation, as Finnis points out, on forms of grounding that are inspired by value but not fully determined by value. Once they are in existence, however, proper appreciation of them is appreciation of the fusion of what is morally derivable and what is not, so that appreciation of their moral achievement, and the legacy of that achievement, is a function of both the moral values that inspired them and the facts of circumstance that brought them into existence, without which they would not look quite the way they do, or possess quite the value that they possess.[11]

[11] See Raz, 'Moral change and social relativism' and 'The value of practice' in his *Engaging Reason* (1999) 161, 202. See also, more radically and since my writing this, 'Can moral principles change?' at ssrn.com/abstract=3024030.

What is true of the aesthetic dimensions of living well is no less true of the other dimensions of living well. I emphasised from the outset that living well is a shared project, one that inescapably draws upon social practices and institutions, some of them informal and intuitive, such as those that give rise to a sense of community and communal norms, some of them self-conscious and deliberative, such as the law. Law has given rise to a wide range of practices that have become part of our vocabulary of living, practices such as contract and trust, and those practices have then reflected their possibilities for value, some of which they have brought into existence, back into the realm of moral possibility generally. We make, as well as discover, new ways of living well, and law helps us to do that. Once made, these ways of living well become part of the moral universe, which consequently expands, changes shape, acquires detail, thanks to us. Living well is thus a fundamentally creative project, not merely a perceptive, decisive or interpretive one. Were it otherwise the various ways of being that characterise the human condition, the social forms and practices that define particular cultural movements, would be (at their best) morally permissible but not morally significant, just because we could do no better by pursuing one rather than another. Life would be a matter of discovering instantiations of and accommodations among existing moral possibilities. Yet in fact our ways of being further matter because they give rise to a prospect that we may do better in developing and pursuing them than the content of morality would have enabled us to do otherwise. All of this is ancient and familiar, consistent with what Aristotle maintained, that we understand virtue by learning from its practice. Once it is recognised that morality is very often, perhaps characteristically, artefactually imbued, it becomes clear that to understand morality fully one must understand its instantiations, so that to know how to live well one must know what living well looks like: hence to know how to practice law well (whether by making, applying or following it) one must first grasp the practice(s) of law.

An analogy might be drawn to biological diversity. Some believe that this diversity was in some sense present from the start, whether in the eye of a creator or otherwise. More commonly, it is thought that this diversity developed over time as a result of mutations that persisted because they were compatible with survival, and indeed with a degree of flourishing, compatible, that is, with living well. The biological diversity present in the world today can, in principle at least, be traced back to one or more biological starting points, yet the details of that diversity are not ones that were fully determinable from the terms of that starting point. Once they came into being, however, they were as much a part of biological possibility, and the consequent possibilities for living well, as anything else.

What does that tell us about the law and the part it has to play in the project of living well? Many speak of natural law in a way that makes clear that they have a moral nature in mind, one that human beings seek to instantiate as part of their social practices, and one against which what is practised as law is to be assessed not merely for its success as an aid to living well but ultimately for its very existence. Yet this is to misapprehend the relationship between morality and existence, between the ideal and the everyday, which inevitably and for the better as well as for the worse is influential in both directions. One can speak of all this as natural, in the same way that one speaks of the natural world, but in both cases the content of the natural is one in which existence past and present helps to constitute the possibilities for existence future, both positively and negatively. Those who are idealistic or even semi-idealistic about law neglect this crucial fact and correspondingly neglect much of the significance of law, and indeed of the endeavour of humans and other participants in the project of living well. The fact that law is laid down by human beings, however imperfectly, helps over time, in and through the success of its accumulated layerings, to constitute just what law ought to be, and more broadly, what we ought to be. This is part of what it means to say that there is no separation of law and morals.

I have sought to describe elsewhere[12] some of the ways in which the law supplements its rational pull with arational forces, and to identify the chief resources that it calls upon in order to do so, most prominently the will, which enables us to fasten upon conclusions that are rationally eligible but not rationally determined, and the imagination, which enables us to generate new practices and fresh ways of pursuing familiar practices, and further, enables us to invest a rationally eligible option with an arational pull that makes that option seem rationally pre-eminent

[12] T. Macklem, *Law and Life in Common* (Oxford University Press, 2015).

and indeed, once the option has been committed to, helps to secure the rational pre-eminence it once merely pretended to. I have also sought to acknowledge the ways in which arational forces such as these may also operate in place of the law or alongside it, in a tacit partnership between cultural authority and legal authority, a partnership the balance among whose constituents varies, sometimes arbitrarily and sometimes non-arbitrarily, from culture to culture, so helping to characterise societies and their eras.

5 Concepts of Law

What does this tell us about the concept of law? Plainly law is not unique in its ability to render the requirements of living well in genuinely liveable form, in its capacity to help reason become genuinely practical. There are many largely unselfconscious social practices that do similar work as well as a few conscious ones. There are yet others, no doubt, of which we are unaware simply because they form no part of our cultural history. Whether those others are nearby, so to speak, so as to be recognisable to us as law, is unclear, since our ignorance of them means that they are by definition beyond our present contemplation. Law is our idea, where the word 'our' refers to a certain cultural tradition. There might well be cultures (whether in the world, without our being aware of it, or in some past or future world) that are either without law or with phenomena that are in some ways law-like and in some ways not, and that may think of those phenomena as law or not. The genuine alternatives are surely interesting, the cases of vagueness, of where imprecision can be argued to be more illuminatingly understood as difference, are surely less so.

That said, a proposal for an understanding of law that fails to take on board the ways in which the practice of living feeds back into the idea of living well will fail to capture much of the richness of that idea, and in the setting of the law, much of the significance of the law as a collective practice that helps us to structure the shared enterprise of living well. Put from the opposite perspective, such a proposal will fail to take fully on board the fact that the nature of morality, as ideally understood, is in most cases such as to prevent its coalescence into law. More profoundly, it neglects the significance of creation, in particular the significance of the human condition and others like it, as unpredictable instantiations of moral possibility that themselves give rise to their own consequent, unpredictable instantiations of moral possibility, in law and elsewhere, so making the moral universe ever greater than could be contemplated in advance, whether by some divine creator or by the power of reason.[13]

[13] Notice that this is a reason for humans (and other moral agents and patients) to exist and (for those who think that way) to have been created. A universe of infinite wisdom, infinite goodness, and eternal life, or a divine creator that is understood in those terms, is cut off from all those dimensions of goodness that depend for their existence on the circumstances of finitude, to the extent of the dependency. Somewhat disconcertingly, the divine can be as good as it is thanks only to the presence in the world of limited creatures like us. That calls upon us to be morally self-reliant in ways that we might rather not be. In doing so, however, we are by definition not playing God. On the contrary.

5 Social Science and the Philosophy of Law

Frederick Schauer

Introduction

Is social science a large part, a small part or no part of the philosophy of law? The question is important, and its importance is highlighted, perhaps ironically, in a strong, unqualified and prominent assertion by Joseph Raz. 'The sociology of law', Raz says, 'provides a wealth of detailed information and analysis of the functions of law in some particular societies. Legal philosophy has to be content with those few features which all legal systems necessarily possess.'[1]

Raz's pronouncement might be understood as simply marking a distinction between two different forms of legal theory, or, if you will, jurisprudence.[2] One form would be the entire domain of social scientific study of the phenomenon of law, including not only that which is informed by and located within the domain of sociology, but also by perspectives and methods from political science, psychology,[3] anthropology, empirical economics[4] and history, among others. But even if we bracket disputes over

[1] J. Raz, *The Authority of Law: Essays on Law and Morality* (Clarendon Press, 1979), 104–5.

[2] The word 'jurisprudence' is often used these days as a synonym for 'philosophy of law'. But given the longstanding existence of fields known as historical jurisprudence, sociological jurisprudence, and so on, and given the common use of the word 'jurisprudence' simply to refer to a domain of legal doctrine, as in, for example, equity jurisprudence or even dental jurisprudence, the word 'jurisprudence' remains ambiguous. Nevertheless, it remains important to resist the notion that any theoretical inquiry designated as jurisprudential is or must necessarily be philosophical in method or focus.

[3] Including that form of psychology that scholars in law and economics are fond of referring to as 'behavioral economics'. But although the leading figure working in that domain, Daniel Kahneman (T. Gilovich, D. Griffin and D. Kahneman, *Heuristics and Biases: The Psychology of Intuitive Judgment* (Cambridge University Press, 2002) did indeed win a Nobel Prize in economics, his training, his methods and his publications are well-situated in the centre of the experimental psychology tradition.

[4] Modern law and economics, like economics generally, has its formal side, using techniques of formal and sometimes mathematical modelling to explore the implications of one or

which theoretical approaches are deserving of the title 'jurisprudence', a host of issues remain. One is the distinction, recognised by Raz, between conclusions about some or even all actual legal systems, an inquiry often characterised as *particular* jurisprudence, and *general* jurisprudence, which seeks to offer explanatory statements that are not only contingently true about all actual legal systems, but that are also necessarily true about all possible legal systems in all possible worlds. For Raz[5] and others (e.g. Coleman, Dickson, Marmor, Shapiro, Tur[6]), general jurisprudence aims to identify truths about the *concept* of law, and thus focuses on locating and analysing necessary truths about law itself, whenever and wherever law may appear.

The key issue, however, is not merely the distinction between particular and general jurisprudence. Equally important is the related question about the role of contingent empirical facts in identifying the deep truths about law and in explaining the more contingent – culturally and historically dependent – aspects of how law operates. Insofar as such contingent empirical facts are important in analysing the concept and operation of

another initial assumption. This approach is to be distinguished from more overtly empirical economics, which employs the tools of statistics and econometrics to explain, with particular attention to issues of causation, the extant phenomena of the world. The demarcation between the two is not always sharp, nor should it be, but in this entry it should be understood that references to empirical enquiries undoubtedly include those performed by economists using the techniques of economics as well as those performed within the other social sciences.

A somewhat different branch of law and economics seeks to explain the rise, existence and operation of law itself (or sometimes its particular branches, such as property, contract or tort) from the incentive-based perspectives of game theory, decision theory and political economy (G.K. Hadfield and B. Weingast, 'A coordination model of the characteristics of legal order', *Journal of Legal Analysis* 4 (2012), 471–515). There is no question but that such inquiries are jurisprudential in the widest understanding of jurisprudence, and even philosophical in the widest understanding of philosophy, but because law and economics has become such a self-standing domain of inquiry, and because it is dealt with extensively elsewhere in this volume, references to this form of economic analysis of law and its component parts will be treated here only in passing.

[5] J. Raz, 'On the nature of law', *Archiv für Rechts- und Sozialphilosophie* 82 (1996), 1–25; J. Raz, 'Can there be a theory of law?' in M.P. Golding and W.A. Edmundson (eds.), *The Blackwell Guide to the Philosophy of Law and Legal Theory* (Basil Blackwell, 2005), 324–42.

[6] J.L. Coleman, *The Practice of Principle: In Defence of a Pragmatist Approach to Legal Theory* (Oxford University Press, 2001); J. Dickson, *Evaluation and Legal Theory* (Hart Publishing, 2001); A. Marmor, *Interpretation and Legal Theory*, 2nd ed. (Oxford University Press, 2005); S. Shapiro, *Legality* (Harvard University Press, 2011); R.H.S. Tur, 'What is jurisprudence?', *The Philosophical Quarterly* 28 (1978), 149–61.

law, there follows the further question of the role of social science in locating and explaining those empirical facts. For Raz and others with similar methodological orientation, what makes the philosophy of law philosophical is precisely its non-dependence on the kinds of spatially and temporally contingent empirical information about different legal systems that might be obtained by sociologists, psychologists, political scientists, anthropologists, economists and others of related empirical bent.[7] And thus a pervasive question, and one of the topics of this entry, is the relationship between empirical social science and the sorts of inquiries associated these days with an analytic jurisprudential tradition going back as least as far as H.L.A. Hart,[8] and perhaps even further back to the contributions of Jeremy Bentham[9] and John Austin.[10] So although few doubt that there is much to learn from what social scientists can tell us about particular legal systems (or families of legal systems) in particular places at particular times or time periods, one persistent question is whether such learning is relevant or necessary to one branch of contemporary philosophy of law.

1 '... an essay in descriptive sociology ...'

In the Preface to *The Concept of Law*, the work widely understood to mark the beginning of the modern tradition in the philosophy of law, H.L.A. Hart described his project as 'an essay in descriptive sociology'.[11] The statement has long been controversial, in large part because little in Hart's book resembles academic sociology even as it was practised in 1961, and much less as it is practised now. Nor does the book seem to bear much affinity with any of the other social sciences, again either then or now.

[7] Raz acknowledges that concepts themselves are dependent on contingent empirical facts about the individuals and cultures who use the concepts. And thus different people or different societies might have different concepts of law. But any individual's or society's concept of law is, for Raz, a concept that applies to all possible legal systems in all possible worlds.

[8] H.L.A. Hart, *The Concept of Law*, 3rd ed., Eds. P.A. Bulloch, J. Raz and L. Green (Clarendon Press, 2012, orig. published 1961).

[9] J. Bentham, *Of the Limits of the Penal Branch of Jurisprudence*, Ed. P. Schofield (Clarendon Press, 2010), 1780–2.

[10] J. Austin, *The Province of Jurisprudence Determined*, Ed. W.E. Rumble (Cambridge University Press, 1995, originally published 1832).

[11] Hart, *The Concept of Law*, v.

Despite the seeming oddity of using such a statement to introduce a book that was then and still remains so explicitly philosophical, there are three possible interpretations of what was plainly a carefully considered claim. First, and the interpretation most consistent with Hart's method and with what he himself appeared to say about the claim, is that careful reflection on ordinary language is itself a sociological method, insofar as both the language and reflection upon it can tell us things about the world within which the language is situated. Hart[12] quotes J.L. Austin, the doyen of the ordinary language approach to philosophy, in saying that we can use 'a sharpened awareness of words to sharpen our awareness of the phenomena'.[13] Insofar as this assumption is sound,[14] ordinary language philosophy just *is* descriptive sociology, because, like other forms of sociological or social science inquiry, it seeks to discover empirical truths about the world. Examination of language, for the ordinary language philosopher, is the method, but the object is to offer conclusions about the world and not (merely) about language.

The influence of ordinary language philosophy has waned since it flourished in Oxford and its intellectual environs in the 1940s and 1950s, but in any event we should not make too much of Hart's claims for (J.L.) Austinian methodology. For although Hart acknowledges his debts to Austin by quoting him, the analysis of ordinary language as philosophical method (as opposed to Austin- and Wittgenstein-inspired philosophy of language[15]) makes only an infrequent appearance in *The Concept of Law*. The method is most prominent when Hart uses a supposed distinction between *being obliged* and *having an obligation*[16] to discuss the idea of legal obligation and the concept of the internal point of view, but the method rarely appears

[12] Ibid., vii.

[13] Hart's not quite accurate quotation is from J.L. Austin, 'A plea for excuses', *Proceedings of the Aristotelian Society* 57 (1957) 1–30, 8. In the original, Austin's statement is more qualified, and he talks about 'perceptions' rather than 'awareness' of actual phenomena.

[14] An interesting contemporaneous challenge to this assumption is F. Waismann, 'The linguistic technique' in B. McGuinness (ed.), *Philosophical Papers* (Reidel, 1977), 150–65.

[15] The distinction is important. Ordinary language philosophy uses the analysis of ordinary language to address a host of questions in the philosophy of mind, philosophy of action, epistemology, and much else. But many ordinary language philosophers also contributed important ideas *about* language, some of which are part of a larger anti-essentialist understanding of words and concepts. Many of these ideas in the philosophy of language, although often contested, have more contemporary viability than does ordinary language analysis as a method of general philosophical inquiry.

[16] Hart, *Concept of Law*, 82–3.

elsewhere, may have been misused even in this case,[17] and is hardly necessary to support Hart's valuable point. It is thus useful, even if somewhat removed from Hart's likely intentions, to consider what else Hart might have meant in making his claim to be doing descriptive sociology.

A second possible interpretation of Hart's claim to be doing descriptive sociology is thus that Hart was engaged in an approach that often these days goes by the name of participant observation. Unlike most legal theorists, who tend to have between no and limited experience actually in the law, Hart spent nine years as a practising equity barrister before entering full-time academic life.[18] Consequently, his claim to be doing descriptive sociology might be understood, albeit less obviously, as a claim to be making empirical assertions about law, and more particularly about legal rules, the internal point of view and the idea of a rule of recognition, on the basis of his own relatively lengthy practice experience and the perceptions that came from it. It is an argument from the epistemological advantages of the first-person or insider perspective.

As sociological method, this approach too is open to challenge. Insiders do often know and see things that outsiders do not, but the insider perspective is still a perspective, and outsiders often see things that insiders, for various complex reasons, ignore, mischaracterise, overestimate or underestimate. Insiders (the Justices and their law clerks, most obviously) to decisions of the United States Supreme Court, for example, often stress the importance of legal doctrine – constitutional text, precedents and rules derived from them – in determining outcomes, but a longstanding body of serious social science research about the determinants of such outcomes has concluded that the causal role of such sources in determining outcomes is much less than commonly supposed.[19] This is not to say that one perspective is necessarily better than another, but only that it is hardly clear that first-person accounts qualify as social science, or

[17] That is, it is hardly clear that ordinary language actually does draw a distinction between being obliged and having an obligation, as opposed to treating the two as roughly equivalent. For examples that undercut Hart's claim about usage, see F. Schauer, 'Was Austin right after all? On the role of sanctions in a theory of law', *Ratio Juris* 23 (2010), 1–21.

[18] N. Lacey, *A Life of H.L.A. Hart: The Nightmare and the Noble Dream* (Oxford University Press, 2004).

[19] S. Brenner and H.J. Spaeth, *Stare Indecisis: The Alteration of Precedent on the Supreme Court, 1946–1992* (Cambridge University Press, 2006); J.A. Segal and H.J. Spaeth, *The Supreme Court and the Attitudinal Model Revisited* (Cambridge University Press, 2002).

that, even if they do, such accounts are in some way uniquely or perhaps even comparatively reliable.[20]

As argued by Hart's biographer Nicola Lacey,[21] still a third sense of the 'descriptive sociology' claim, while perhaps least derivable from Hart's text, is that the kind of conceptual analysis that Hart, and even more his successors, offered is best understood as a necessary precursor, or at least an important adjunct of, more systematic empirical inquiry into the phenomenon of law, its characteristic features and its causes and consequences. In order truly to understand the phenomenon of law, we need to understand what law is, how law operates, what its purposes are and how people understand it, with all of these being the kind of empirical inquiries that require, so it might be said, initial conceptual analysis in the Hartian tradition in order to get the empirical enterprise off the ground. In order to look, we first need a good and well-analysed account of what we are looking for and what we are looking at (Green;[22] compare Schauer[23]). This understanding of the descriptive sociology claim seems consistent with Lacey's, although she laments that Hart, who earlier in his academic career may well have thought something along these lines, soon lost interest in the empirical project and became increasingly narrower in his understanding of how the idea of law might be explained.

Lacey's speculations about Hart's earlier but then aborted interests in social science are reinforced by other language in *The Concept of Law*, especially Hart's complaint that Austin's account of the nature of law did not 'fit the facts'.[24,25] The questions then, are, first, what *are* the facts that

[20] The unreliability of first-person accounts has been the subject of literary theory – W.C. Booth, *The Rhetoric of Fiction* (University of Chicago Press, 1961); philosophy – F.J. Varela and J. Shear, 'First-person methodologies: what, why, and how?', *Journal of Consciousness Studies* 6 (1999), 1–14; and psychology – T. Gilovich, *How We Know What Isn't So: The Fallibility of Human Reason in Everyday Life* (Free Press, 1991), among others, with each, in different ways, asking us to question the widespread assumption that an account coming from someone who was 'there' is in some way epistemologically superior.

[21] N. Lacey, 'Analytical jurisprudence versus descriptive sociology revisited', *Texas Law Review* 84 (2006), 945–82; N. Lacey, 'The path not taken: H.L.A. Hart's Harvard essay on Discretion', *Harvard Law Review* 127 (2013), 636–51; D. Sugarman, 'Hart interviewed: H.L.A. Hart in conversation with David Sugarman', *Journal of Law and Society* 32 (2005), 267–93; W. Twining, 'Schauer on Hart', *Harvard Law Review Forum* 119 (2006), 122–30.

[22] L. Green, 'The forces of law: duty, coercion, and power', *Ratio Juris* 29 (2016), 164–81.

[23] F. Schauer, *The Force of Law* (Harvard University Press, 2015).

[24] Hart, *The Concept of Law*, 78.

[25] See also Hart, *The Concept of Law*, 91, where Hart charges Austin and others with offering accounts that do not do justice to the 'complexity of facts' about modern legal systems.

a theory of law must fit, and, second, just how are we to go about ascertaining those facts. But in order to pursue these issues, it will be necessary to take leave of Hart and look more broadly at the enterprise of developing a theory of law itself.

2 The Empirical Dimensions of Conceptual Analysis

Many philosophers of law who support or engage in conceptual analysis of the concept of law distinguish their enterprise from social science inquiry about law, as the initial quote from Joseph Raz in this entry illustrates, but the empirical dimensions of conceptual analysis itself remain contested. Some philosophers insist that conceptual analysis is the prime philosophical task,[26] while others with equal fervour argue that the form of conceptual analysis defended by Jackson and McGinn and others is, if not futile, then at the very least more dependent on contingent empirical facts than conceptual analysis' most fervent proponents are willing to admit.[27] And these debates are replicated in the philosophy of law. Raz and some of the others cited above (e.g. Coleman, Dickson, Marmor and Shapiro) have either defended or in their work presupposed the enterprise of conceptual analysis of the concept of law, while others[28] have insisted either that such an approach masks what is in fact a collection of contingent empirical assertions, or that searching for the necessary or essential properties of a contingent human artefact such as law is for all practical purposes an impossibility.[29]

This debate about the importance, possibility and empirical dependence of conceptual analysis of the concept of law is important, but we should not lose sight of the fact that even the proponents of conceptual analysis acknowledge that contingent empirical assumptions underlie even the seemingly most abstract of conceptual analyses. When Raz, for example,

[26] F. Jackson, *From Metaphysics to Ethics: A Defence of Conceptual Analysis* (Oxford University Press, 1998); C. McGinn, *Truth by Analysis: Games, Names, and Philosophy* (Oxford University Press, 2012).

[27] G. Harman, 'Doubts about conceptual analysis', *Philosophy in Mind – Philosophical Studies Series* 60 (1994), 43–8.

[28] B. Leiter, 'The naturalistic turn in legal philosophy', *APA Newsletter on Philosophy of Law* (Spring 2001), 142–6; B. Leiter, *Naturalizing Jurisprudence: Essays on American Legal Realism and Naturalism in Legal Philosophy* (Oxford University Press, 2007).

[29] R. Dworkin, 'Thirty years on', *Harvard Law Review* 115 (2002), 1655–87.

argues that a claim of authority (but not necessarily actual authority) is among the necessary and important[30] features of the concept of law[31]), he bases that conclusion on his own perception of law, or his own perception of how the culture in which he is located perceives law. Similarly, when Hart talks of law as necessarily involving the union of primary and secondary rules,[32] he tells us that rule by the fiat of an absolute ruler constrained by no secondary rules would not in fact count as a legal system at all. But these conclusions are contingent, and although they might be true of *our* concept of law, as Raz puts it, and thus of *our* concept of all law wherever and whenever it may appear, it may not be true of another culture's concept of law wherever and whenever it may appear. Raz would thus likely take issue with those (e.g. Tamanaha, Twining[33]) who maintain that the diversity of legal systems makes it impossible to analyse a single concept of law. Other societies might have other concepts of law, he says, but our society has a single concept of law, one with essential properties, and one that enables us to assess whether what other societies think of as law is or is not consistent with our concept of law.

Even if Raz is correct, however, his approach still presupposes the theorist's irreducibly empirical assessment of just how people in some culture understand the very idea – or concept – of law. And on this question, genuine social science inquiry can be of some assistance. Such an inquiry might be partly linguistic, but it need not be entirely or even substantially so. And it might be partly psychological, attempting by experimental or other methods to determine just how people understand the idea of law and not just the meaning of the word 'law'. But once we understand that the conceptual analyst is attempting to do much the same

[30] Those who defend the enterprise of conceptual analysis of the concept of law properly maintain that they are looking for those properties that are not only essential, but also important, given that there are essential but unimportant properties of law, Dickson, *Evaluation*. And for the view, resisted by those philosophers of law most committed to conceptual analysis, that the philosophy of law should also include the analysis of those properties that are important but not essential, see F. Schauer, 'On the nature of the nature of law', *Archiv für Rechts- und Sozialphilosophie* 98 (2012), 457–67; Schauer, *The Force of Law*.

[31] Raz, *Authority of Law;* J. Raz, *The Morality of Freedom* (Clarendon Press, 1986).

[32] Hart, *The Concept of Law*, 77–9.

[33] B.Z. Tamanaha, 'Understanding legal pluralism: past to present, local to global', *Sydney Law Review* (2008), 375–411; W. Twining, *Globalisation and Legal Theory* (Cambridge University Press, 2000).

thing about the culture in which she lives, we can understand that there is no reason to believe that genuine social science inquiry might not be a useful adjunct to conceptual analysis as widely understood even by its supporters and practitioners.

3 Beyond Conceptual Analysis

The foregoing discussion focused on the empirical dimensions of conceptual analysis, a project for which there may be more room for social science than has traditionally been acknowledged by contemporary practitioners of conceptual analysis. But the role of social science in the philosophy of law is not restricted to the enterprise of conceptual analysis. If we understand the philosophy of law more broadly, the place of social science broadens commensurately.

Consider, for example, the perspective broadly known as legal pluralism.[34] Legal pluralists avoid conceptual analysis, and disdain searching for the necessary or essential features of law or the concept of it. Instead they tend to adopt expansive and fuzzy-edged understandings of what is to count as law. Law might have different dimensions and even different defining characteristics in different systems, they argue, and law might include various forms of rule-based social ordering and social control only loosely connected with the state, or even not connected with the state at all. For the legal pluralist, these law-like entities are properly the subject of theoretical inquiry, an inquiry that is as empirical as it is philosophical.

Examining the various forms of what diverse cultures think of as the law can itself form part of the philosophy of law. To examine these forms requires the analytic tools of the philosopher, but is also dependent on understanding the different societies themselves. Here the inquiry is necessarily empirical, and it is the kind of empirical inquiry that has a home in social science, or at least that relies heavily on social science. Indeed, just as comparative law is itself an important enterprise, then so too might be comparative legal theory, an inquiry seeking to investigate the normative and conceptual foundations of law in different times and places, and

[34] U. Baxi, C. McCrudden and A. Paliwala, *Law's Ethical, Global and Theoretical Contexts* (Cambridge University Press, 2015); B.Z. Tamanaha, *A General Jurisprudence of Law and Society* (Oxford University Press, 2001); Twining, 2000.

seeking as well to see what might be learned from what both practitioners and theorists see as the important theoretical and philosophical issues within their particular societies. And once again, engaging in just this inquiry without the benefit of serious social science seems a mistake. The relevant social science might be qualitative, examining particular legal cultures and their philosophical roots, in depth, or might instead (or also) be quantitative, attempting to categorise the normative foundations and conceptual understandings by types of legal system, and attempting to examine the relationships between types of law and legal systems and the philosophical assumptions that those types generate or reflect.

Even legal pluralism far from exhausts the types of empirical questions that might attach to theoretical inquiries about the nature and effects of law. Consider, for example, the range of perspectives seeking to explain the need for (and operation of) law in terms of the purposes that law is designed to serve. For some, especially those coming out of modern law and economics, law is an efficiency- or welfare-maximising institution.[35] For others, again often (but not necessarily[36]) from an economic or political economy perspective, law is a way of achieving social cooperation and solving prisoners' dilemma and other coordination problems.[37] For others, Lon Fuller most prominently,[38] law is the embodiment of the pursuit of human reason. And for still others, such as Scott Shapiro most recently,[39] law is the way in which a community can make and carry out its plans.

This is not the place to discuss in any depth each of these perspectives, except to note that they are all about the phenomenon of law and not just about law here or there, and that they all both rest on and call for empirical research. This is perhaps most apparent with respect to Fuller,[40] who claimed, while acknowledging the empirical nature of the claim, that

[35] D.D. Friedman, *Law's Order: An Economic Account* (Princeton University Press, 2000); S. Shavell, *Foundations of Economic Analysis of Law* (Harvard University Press, 2004).

[36] See G. Postema, 'Coordination and convention at the foundations of law', *Journal of Legal Studies* 11 (1982), 165–202.

[37] D.G. Baird, R.H. Gertner and R.C. Picker, *Game Theory and the Law* (Harvard University Press, 1994); R.H. McAdams, 'Beyond the prisoners' dilemma: coordination, game theory, and law', *Southern California Law Review* 82 (2009), 209–58.

[38] Fuller, 1969; K. Rundle, *Forms Liberate: Reclaiming the Jurisprudence of Lon L Fuller* (Hart Publishing, 2012).

[39] Shapiro, 2010.

[40] L.L. Fuller, 'Positivism and fidelity to law – a reply to Professor Hart', *Harvard Law Review* 71 (1958), 630–72, 636.

institutions established in accordance with his (procedural) desiderata for legality would be more inclined to 'goodness' than 'evil'. But is this true? If we think of law itself or the narrower idea of the rule of law as the independent variable, and some first-order conception of the good as the dependent variable, then does more of law or the rule of law produce more good? Little if any research has focused on the question in exactly this way, but one can imagine natural experiments, or laboratory experiments, that might focus on this question. Or consider the same independent variable but instead with efficiency or economic growth as the dependent variable. Here there is some research focused on considering the extent to which, if at all, law inclines toward economic growth or other economically desirable outcomes,[41] but much more needs to be done.

The philosophy of law as it now exists is replete with claims about the purpose or point or function of law. But most of these claims are instrumental, thus positing an inevitably empirical relationship between law as the independent variable (or cause) and some state of affairs as the dependent variable (or effect). In some areas we have seen efforts to use social science to test and measure these claims, but in extant philosophy of law what we see most are simple assertions with little empirical support. Here, as elsewhere, social science might usefully examine the empirical claims that even now pervade the practice of the philosophy of law.

4 The Role of Law in Decision-Making

A prominent feature of much of modern legal philosophy is a claim about the role of law *qua* law in making judgements and reaching conclusions. As part of his argument against John Austin's coercion-based account of law and legal obligation, for example, H.L.A. Hart famously made reference to the 'puzzled man'.[42] The locution is presented in contrast to Oliver Wendell Holmes' 'bad man',[43] whose interest in law is reducible to a prediction of what will happen to him if he engages in this or that course of conduct. But although Hart's wording plays off that of Holmes, Hart's

[41] T. Ginsburg, 'Does law matter for economic development', *Law & Society Review* 34 (2000), 829–56; S. Haggard and L. Tiede, 'The rule of law and economic growth: where are we?', *World Development* 39 (2011), 673–85.

[42] Hart, *The Concept of Law*, 40.

[43] O.W. Holmes Jr, 'The path of the law', *Harvard Law Review* 10 (1897), 457–78, 459.

target in talking about the puzzled man is not Holmes as much as Austin, and Hart, in contrast to Austin, suggests that a satisfactory account of the nature of law – one that would 'fit the facts' – is one that recognises the existence of the puzzled man, who is motivated (and not by the threat of sanctions) to do the lawful thing, if only he can know what the lawful thing is. To assume the non-existence of such puzzled people, Hart tells us, is to offer an (empirically) inaccurate account of the nature of law and of the role that law plays in human societies and human deliberations.

Hart does not tell us what quantity of puzzled people in just this sense there must be in a society in order for their law-dependent deliberations to figure in a satisfactory account of the nature of law, but other theorists have been more explicit. Scott Shapiro, for example, expressly presupposes that there are 'many' such people in actual societies,[44] and thus that it is an important datum that a satisfactory theory must account for the fact that many people take the existence of law *qua* law as a reason for action and a reason for decision.

For Hart, for Shapiro, and for others, therefore, part of what they want to explain, and part of what they believe that Austin and Holmes, most prominently, did not explain, is the empirical role of law as an actual motivation for human behaviour. This might not be especially important if the only goal was to explain how law *might* motivate. But Hart and Shapiro, along with others, make claims about law's actual and not just potential motivating force. Hart, after all, argued that Austin's account was not true to the facts, and Shapiro goes even further in claiming that 'many' people treat the law *qua* law as actually motivating. But these are claims that can be and should be tested empirically, even though for both Hart and Shapiro they are presented more as undeniable fact rather than as testable and potentially false hypotheses.

In order to make sense of the claim, however, and to connect it with the idea of a theory of *law*, it is important to distinguish law-motivated behaviour from morality-motivated behaviour. It is of course true that many people often do things solely for reasons of self-interest, and these are the kinds of people to whom Holmes was referring in using his somewhat hyperbolic image of the bad man. But even if we put the bad man aside, and even if, more broadly, we put pure self-interest aside, we

[44] Shapiro, *Legality*, 69.

discover from a great deal of serious social psychology research, most of it experimental, that many people often act altruistically – that is, they do what they think is the right thing to do for others or for the society in which they live even if it is not the best thing to do for their own interests.[45]

Because the phenomenon of altruistic behaviour is by all accounts real and widespread, the task of identifying the role of law becomes more complex. To take an extreme example, the people who refrain from selfish murder or self-interested larceny, for example, even under circumstances in which the possibility of legal sanctions is effectively non-existent, might be doing so because murder and larceny are against the law, but might instead be doing so because they believe murder and larceny to be wrong, regardless of what the law says or does not say. The challenging empirical task, then, is to distinguish morality-motivated behaviour from law-motivated behaviour, or, more accurately, moral reasons from legal reasons, because only if the latter are important components of human action, sanctions apart, does law occupy a role in human decision-making that cannot be explained in law-independent terms.

We have here an important example of the intersection between social science and the philosophy of law, because we now see that at least one of the central claims of some legal philosophers is dependent on the existence of some appreciable quantity of law-motivated human behaviour. It turns out, however, that there is little social science research directly on the topic. Some of what research there is, most prominently that of the social psychologist Tom Tyler, is less helpful than it might be, because Tyler does not distinguish the non-self-serving behaviour that is motivated by law from the non-self-serving behaviour that is motivated by moral sense. Now of course much non-self-serving behaviour is both moral and consistent with the law – avoiding murder and larceny, again – but without distinguishing morally motivated behaviour that happens to be consistent with the law from law-motivated behaviour, Tyler[46] and others wind up saying very little about the causal or (actual) reason-giving effect of the

[45] R.C. Barragan and C.S. Dweck, 'Rethinking natural altruism: simple reciprocal interactions trigger children's benevolence', *Proceedings of the National Academy of Sciences* 111:48 (2014), 17071–4; C.D. Batson, *The Altruism Question: Toward a Social Psychological Answer* (Erlbaum, 1991).

[46] T.R. Tyler, *Why People Obey the Law*, revised ed. (Princeton University Press, 2006).

law, and thus about the extent to which legal motivation *qua* legal motivation in fact exists.

Although Tyler's methods are based primarily on surveys, other social science research relevant to the question of the role of law in providing reasons for action is experimental. Here again, there is less carefully focused and jurisprudentially informed research than might be desired, but in at least some experimental contexts subjects who believed that moral or altruistic or pro-social or policy considerations pointed in one direction and positive law in another tended, in the absence of sanctions, to make the decisions they thought right on all-things-other-than-the-law-considered grounds rather than the decisions that were indicated by the positive law.[47]

This is not the place to examine in detail all of the research that has been or might be conducted on the question of law-based motivation, or, more broadly, on the empirical realities of legal obligation. Still, given that the question whether there is a *prima facie* obligation to obey the law has been dealt with as a normative matter from the time of Socrates to the present,[48] it is surprising that so little research has been pursued on whether people actually behave as Socrates and successor believers in the existence of such an obligation have argued they should behave, or whether they behave as John Simmons[49] and other so-called philosophical anarchists have argued, and thus make what they think is the right decision, the law aside. This is the issue to which Hart was alluding with his puzzled man metaphor, but as of now we remain uncertain, at best, whether there are very many of the puzzled men whom Hart thought important in offering a realistic philosophical account of the phenomenon of law. Good social science research might tell us more than we now know about law's causal effect on human decision-making, and thus can tell us whether, and to what extent, what many legal philosophers have simply assumed or asserted in fact exists.

[47] J. Furgeson, L. Babcock and P.M. Shane, 'Behind the mask of method: political orientation and constitutional interpretive method', *Law and Human Behavior* 32 (2008a), 502–10; J. Furgeson, L. Babcock and P.M. Shane, 'Do a law's policy implications affect belief about its constitutionality?', *Law and Human Behavior* 32 (2008b), 219–27. Other studies are cited and described in Schauer 2015, 200–1.

[48] W.A. Edmundson, 'State of the art: the duty to obey the law', *Legal Theory* 10 (2004), 215–59.

[49] A.J. Simmons, *Moral Principles and Political Obligations* (Princeton University Press, 1981).

5 The Question of Legal Compliance

Much of the foregoing can be understood as inquiry into the question of legal compliance. Do people, or officials, comply with the law, and, if so, how much, and under what conditions? The question is partly philosophical, or conceptual, in that we cannot examine the extent and circumstances of legal compliance without first being clear about just what it is to comply with a law. And thus much of the discussion above can be understood as directed not only to clarifying the nature of legal compliance, but also to distinguishing compliance from consistency, a crucial distinction if we are interested in the causal consequences of law.

The distinction between compliance – or obedience – and consistency has in recent years been a subject of considerable controversy among scholars of international law. A common view, often explained using the tools of modern game theory, has been that international actors – principally states – may have good reasons to comply with international law, and in fact do so with some frequency. But others have insisted that states act consistently with the requirements of international law only when they have a law-independent motivation to engage in the relevant behaviour, thus making the motivating force of international law *qua* law far less than it appears at first glance.

The debate in international law is replicated in numerous domestic contexts, but in both domestic and international settings the conceptual clarification is only the first step. Once the conceptual groundwork has been laid, there must be an empirical inquiry into the extent to which law actually has the causal or motivating force just described. Such an inquiry might use the tools of modern econometrics to isolate the causal effect of law, or it might search for natural experiments in which the law varies while other factors remain constant, or it might use experiments with 'artificial' subjects to try again to isolate the effect of law. Or it might even use case studies or other qualitative approaches that might indicate, even if not establish conclusively, the effect of law.

As things now stand, the literature on legal compliance is largely unconnected with the literature on jurisprudence. But there is no reason why this state of affairs need be accepted. Once we understand jurisprudence as being properly concerned with far more than conceptual analysis, or even with far more than searching for the definition or nature of law, then many aspects of the phenomenon of law are open for both philosophical and empirical inquiry. Compliance is no doubt among these, and indeed the question of compliance may be among the most fruitful domains in which some combination of conceptual clarification and empirical inquiry will help to reveal important truths about the operation of law.

6 The Social Science of Adjudication

Closely related to the puzzled man question is the issue of the role that positive law plays in judicial decisions and legal argument. Insofar as some – but decidedly not all[50] – legal philosophers have believed that giving a philosophical account of adjudication is an important task of legal philosophy, then the empirical dimensions become more salient, and the role of social science more obvious.

Although the American Legal Realists were at best impatient with the idea of exploring the nature of law as a conceptual or even more broadly philosophical matter, it is to them, principally, that we owe a series of hypotheses about the role of positive law – of rule of recognition-recognised law – in legal decision-making. And so although many legal philosophers have taken pains to insist that not all disputes could be settled by appeal to existing law, and that judicial discretion was an inevitable part of legal life, they often assert as well, as Hart did, that such discretion is epiphenomenal. Many legal philosophers believe that in the ordinary course of things legal questions are relatively straightforwardly answerable by reference to moderately clear legal rules recognised as such by a rule of recognition validated in turn by an ultimate rule of recognition.[51]

But is this true? The American Legal Realists, often flamboyantly, argued to the contrary, believing that a panoply of non-legal factors were far more important, especially in contested cases, in determining legal outcomes than many legal theorists have long maintained.[52] For the

[50] Thus Joseph Raz (*The Authority of Law*; *The Morality of Freedom*) distinguishes law from legal reasoning, believing that the task of the legal philosopher is to give an account of the former, but not principally to explain – philosophically or empirically – the role of the former within the latter.

[51] B. Leiter, 'Explaining theoretical disagreement', *University of Chicago Law Review* 76 (2009), 1215–50, 1228.

[52] The statement in the text is plainly anachronistic, insofar as Jerome Frank, Karl Llewellyn, Herman Oliphant and the other most prominent Realists wrote and flourished from the late 1920s to the late 1940s, well before Hart embarked on the project that culminated with *The*

Realists, a judge's personality, politics and policy views, and the particular facts of particular cases, were far more important in determining outcomes than were the statutes, decided cases and legal doctrines that Llewellyn dismissed collectively as 'paper rules'.[53,54]

These opposed views, both lying along a spectrum of just how much positive law mattered in the process of argument and decision, appear to present a testable empirical hypothesis, but that hypothesis is only interesting and testable under a particular view about the nature of law as such. To the extent that we understand law capaciously, whether with Dworkin's view[55] about the role of moral and political principles as part of law rather than as distinguished from it, or with more traditional natural law views, or even with some modern perspectives that see politics and policy as part of law, it becomes difficult, if not impossible to determine the role that narrowly conceived positive law – the official acts of legislatures and other official bodies, and the decisions of courts – plays in legal argument and legal decision-making. Perhaps, of course, we do not care, but such a view is counterintuitive, for the things that look like law in a narrow and conventional sense – Ruth Gavison[56] usefully refers to this as 'first stage' law – seem to have a certain kind of salience that makes examining their comparative importance a useful task. Perhaps the result of this examination will be that such materials have relatively little causal effect, or at least less than the standard picture assumes, and that is what many of the Realists and some others – Lon Fuller (Fuller and Ronald Dworkin[57]), in different ways, for example – believed. Or perhaps the examination will show that statutes, decided cases and strictly legal principles of

Concept of Law. Nevertheless, at least for present purposes, it is useful to see Hart, especially the Hart of ch. 7 of *The Concept of Law*, and the Legal Realists as representing two importantly opposed positions on the causal importance of rule-of-recognition recognised positive law in determining legal outcomes.

[53] Leiter, *Naturalizing Jurisprudence*; F. Schauer, *Thinking like a Lawyer: A New Introduction to Legal Reasoning* (Harvard University Press, 2009), ch. 7; F. Schauer, 'Legal realism untamed', *Texas Law Review*, 92 (2013), 749–80; W. Twining, *Karl Llewellyn and the Realist Movement*, 2nd ed. (Cambridge University Press, 2014).

[54] K. Llewellyn, *The Theory of Rules*, Ed. F. Schauer (University of Chicago Press, 2011), 11–14, 17–23.

[55] R. Dworkin, *Taking Rights Seriously* (Duckworth, 1977); R. Dworkin, *Law's Empire* (Harvard University Press, 1986).

[56] R. Gavison, 'Comment' in R. Gavison (ed.), *Issues in Contemporary Legal Philosophy: The Influence of H.L.A. Hart* (Oxford University Press, 1987), 16–21.

[57] Dworkin, *Taking Rights Seriously*, 1986.

interpretation and construction are the dominant force in legal decision-making, as many lawyers, many judges and most law schools believe. But without a somewhat non-capacious understanding of law, one somewhat consistent with the view of the so-called exclusive positivists, it will be impossible to even attempt to examine the question.[58]

This is not the place to survey all of the actual social science research that has been done on this question. The Realists recognised the issue, urging more social science research on the determinants of judicial and other legal decisions. And although some – Underhill Moore, perhaps most notably[59] – did pursue such inquiries, their methods were crude by today's standards. But now that empirical methodology has become far more rigorous and sophisticated, the role of the social sciences in examining the effect of positive law has become greater. Some of this research is directed to determining the relative contribution of law compared to policy, politics, ideology and morality, often but not exclusively in the context of constitutional courts.[60] Other research focuses on the relationship between legal change and behavioural change, because it is far from self-evident that changes in the law will produce commensurate changes in the behaviour that the law seeks to regulate. And still other research is focused more directly on the psychology of judging and legal decision-making, often using experimental methods to determine the thinking and reasoning processes of judges and jurors, and to see how much, and under what circumstances, law figures in that process.[61]

7 A Note on the Selection Effect

Judges are important figures in the law. But they are not the only important figures in the law. Consequently, if we are interested in law's reason-giving reality and in law's effect on human behaviour, then it is important

[58] Leiter, *Naturalizing Jurisprudence*; F. Schauer, 'Official obedience and the politics of defining "law"', *Southern California Law Review* 86 (2013), 1165–94.

[59] J.H. Schlegel, *American Legal Realism and Empirical Social Science* (University of North Carolina Press, 1995).

[60] Brenner and Spaeth, *Stare Indecisis*; Segal and Spaeth, *The Supreme Court and the Attitudinal Model Revisited*.

[61] A.J. Wistrich, C. Guthrie and J.J. Rachlinski, 'Can judges ignore inadmissible information: the difficulty of deliberately disregarding', *University of Pennsylvania Law Review* 153 (2005), 1251–325.

to recognise that there is more to examine than just how judges make decisions. Indeed, Hart recognised this when he criticised the Realists for exaggerating the role of judging hard cases in assessing the determinacy and importance of law, chapter 7).[62] Hart's reading of the Realists has been properly criticised, not because he was wrong but because a careful reading of the Realists, even the ones that Hart specifically referenced, shows beyond question that they fully recognised what Hart claimed they had ignored – that judging in general, and judging of hard cases in particular – is but a small and skewed sample of law in action precisely because almost all of the straightforward applications of law, the so-called easy cases, and more, will never wind up in court at all.

This observation, recognised by Karl Llewellyn in the very same article that Hart used to accuse him of ignoring it,[63] has generated a social science literature of its own, much of it conducted by economists, and going by the name of the 'selection effect'.[64] When there are events about which one party to a dispute will clearly win as a matter of settled law and the other party clearly lose, the party with no chance of winning will, normally, have no incentive to litigate, and the matter will accordingly be either conceded or settled. The profoundly important corollary of this fact is that the cases that do wind up in the courts – the disputes that are neither conceded nor settled – constitute an unrepresentative sample of legal events, a set of events in which the opposing parties to a dispute, each holding mutually exclusive views about the law or about the effect of the law on the facts of the dispute, each believe they have a plausible chance of winning. Because this will rarely be the case – self-delusion aside – when the facts are clear and the law is clear, the cases that are litigated will overwhelmingly be ones in which the law is unclear, or the facts are unclear, or both. The same phenomenon exists, and even more so, as disputes progress through the courts and up the appellate ladder, and thus it should be hardly surprising that cases decided by the Supreme Court of the United States – approximately seventy a year out of the approximately eight thousand the Court is asked to decide – are ones in which the effect of positive law, or hard law, is disproportionately small. This consequence of

[62] Hart, *The Concept of Law*, ch. 7.

[63] K. Llewellyn, *The Bramble Bush – On Law and Its Study* (Columbia University Press, 1930).

[64] G.L. Priest and B. Klein, 'The selection of disputes for litigation', *Journal of Legal Studies* 13 (1984), 1–55.

the selection effect is important, but it is perhaps not nearly as important as the consequence that such cases tell us far less about law in its day-to-day operation than many have supposed. And thus if we are interested, as we should be, in serious social science research about the effect of positive law on human behaviour, the decisions of apex courts are not only *not* the first places we should look, but possibly should be the last.

Part II

Values

6 The Rule of Law

John Tasioulas

1 The Many Faces of the Rule of Law

An ideal called 'the rule of law' has won praise since ancient times from a diverse band of enthusiasts ranging from Aristotle and John Locke to the former UN Secretary-General, Kofi Annan. This apparent consensus, one that impressively bridges temporal, cultural and ideological divides, partly reflects the obvious fact that the phrase 'the rule of law' means different things to different people.[1] One can, without linguistic impropriety, use this expression to refer to a number of significant though distinct ideas, or indeed to no clear idea whatsoever. To make progress, we must disentangle some of these ideas before trying to identify and elaborate the most compelling or fruitful version(s) of the rule of law.

On the broadest interpretation, 'the rule of law' refers to the rule of *good law*. This encompasses all of the goods, running the gamut from justice through charity to efficiency, that law should ideally embody or promote. Presumably, not everything we rightly prize will fall within the legitimate ambit of legal concern. Some goods are not properly the law's business, either because there are decisive reasons of principle for this exclusion (e.g. considerations of personal autonomy may preclude the law addressing the just division of domestic labour) or because the law is a blunt or counterproductive instrument for advancing them. On a somewhat less broad construal, the rule of law may be thought to comprehend all the conditions that law must meet in order to be *legitimate*, that is, actually

[1] For the sceptical claim that the expression 'has become meaningless thanks to ideological abuse and general over-use', see J.N. Shklar, 'Political theory and the rule of law' in A.C. Hutchinson and P. Monahan (eds.), *The Rule of Law: Ideal or Ideology* (Carswell, 1987), 1. For a more upbeat take on the contestability of the rule of law idea, see J. Waldron, 'Is the rule of law an essentially contested concept (in Florida)?', *Law and Philosophy* 21 (2002), 137–64. For a helpful general survey of evolving ideas of the Rule of Law, see B.Z. Tamahana, *On the Rule of Law: History, Politics, Theory* (Cambridge University Press, 2004).

morally binding on its purported subjects. These conditions might include conformity with democratic procedure or basic human rights.[2] This allows for the possibility that a legal system complies with the rule of law yet is deficient in certain other vital respects. It is arguably something approximating this broad sense of the rule of law, in either of these two variants, that has found favour among a large number of international institutions, such as the United Nations,[3] the International Commission of Jurists,[4] and the European Commission for Democracy through Law (the Venice Commission),[5] as well as among influential writers, such as Lord Bingham.[6]

However, broad interpretations face serious objections. The first variant – the rule of *good* law – loses its grip on the widely credited idea that the rule of law is only one legally relevant value among others. The error here is analogous to the World Health Organization's widely criticised definition of health as 'a state of complete physical, mental and social well-being and not merely the absence of disease or infirmity'.[7] This bloated definition mistakenly equates an *element* of well-being (health) with the *totality* of well-being. It thereby loses sight of the distinctive character of health as just one element of well-being, alongside other elements (e.g. knowledge, accomplishment, friendship) and the potential for conflicts among these elements of well-being (e.g. when confronting the question whether to sacrifice one's health in order to accomplish some

[2] D. Beyleveld and R. Brownsword, *Law as a Moral Judgment* (Sweet & Maxwell, 1986), chs. 7–9.

[3] The Report of the Secretary-General on the Rule of Law and Transitional Justice in Conflict and Post-Conflict Societies, UN Doc. S/2004/616 (2004) para. 6 includes consistency with 'international human rights norms and standards' as part of the rule of law.

[4] Its 1959 Declaration of Delhi describes the rule of law as a concept that should be used not only to safeguard and advance 'the civil and political rights of the individual in a free society, but also to establish social, economic, educational and cultural conditions under which his legitimate aspirations and dignity may be realized' http://icj.wpengine.netdna-cdn.com/wp-content/uploads/1959/01/Rule-of-law-in-a-free-society-conference-report-1959-eng.pdf.

[5] European Commission for Democracy through Law (Venice Commission), Report on the Rule of Law, adopted at its 86th plenary session (Venice, March 2011) http://www.venice.coe.int/webforms/documents/?pdf=CDL-AD(2011)003rev-e, which includes democratic lawmaking and respect for human rights as elements of the rule of law.

[6] His eight rule of law principles include 'adequate protection of fundamental human rights' and compliance with international legal obligations. T. Bingham, *The Rule of Law* (Allen Lane, 2010).

[7] Constitution of the World Health Organization, 1946, preamble.

valuable goal). Similarly, the objection goes, the rule of law encapsulates one important value bearing on law and legal institutions, but it does not encompass anything like the total sum of those values. Organisations charged with promoting the rule of law, or health, might be tempted to adopt all-encompassing interpretations of those values – whether through an anxiety to cover all bases or as camouflage for bureaucratic mission creep, etc. – but this is something that, as critical thinkers and citizens, we should guard against.

Now, this is a point conceded by the second variant of the broad interpretation, according to which the rule of law is the rule of *legitimate* law. But this variant begs the question of why we need to refer specifically to the rule of law given that we already have the notion of legitimacy on hand. Rather than being a robustly independent value, the rule of law becomes just another way of referring to the legitimacy of law and, to this extent, it seems redundant. A further problem with the legitimacy interpretation is that its proponents typically fail to establish the precise nature of the relationship between those requirements we typically think of as part of the rule of law and the status of legitimacy. Are these requirements, taken together, a sufficient condition of legitimacy, or a necessary condition, or both?

It is not surprising, therefore, that many philosophers who have seriously meditated on the rule of law had something different in mind from an all-encompassing concern with the rule of good or legitimate law. They have typically sought to articulate the ideal of the rule of law in a way that satisfies two methodological constraints. First, a constraint of *pluralism*: the rule of law is only one evaluative standard, among various others, for assessing laws and legal institutions. It does not amount to anything approximating a comprehensive normative theory of law, nor is it to be equated with some independent political concept, such as legitimacy. Second, a constraint of *coherence*: the various demands of the rule of law must be the expression of an underlying ethical concern or coherent set of concerns and not simply an arbitrarily assembled schedule of desiderata. Given the pluralism constraint, that underlying concern cannot consist merely in the ultra-minimal one of relevance to the ethical assessment of law in general or of its legitimacy in particular.

Notoriously, jurisprudential thinkers have developed 'thicker' and 'thinner' conceptions of the rule of law, the former often called 'substantive', the latter 'formal/procedural'. But, despite significant differences among these conceptions, they all typically seek to satisfy the desiderata of pluralism and coherence.

Ronald Dworkin, an influential proponent of the thick approach, characterises the rule of law as 'rule by an accurate public conception of individual [moral] rights'.[8] Since not all of the values relevant to the assessment of law, such as economic prosperity, environmental protection or animal welfare, are a matter of securing individual moral rights, the pluralist constraint seems to be satisfied by this view. Meanwhile, coherence is secured through the organising idea of moral rights that are appropriately advanced by means of law. Yet Dworkin's view nonetheless seems overly expansive insofar as it equates the rule of law with justice generally, at least to the extent that the latter bears on law. This is because a venerable tradition of thought – one that includes Grotius, Hume, Kant and Mill – construes the concept of justice as picking out just those moral duties that have associated moral rights and that, at least ideally, ought to be legally enshrined or enforceable. The Dworkinian analysis comes to grief at a hurdle similar to the one that toppled the idea of the rule of law as the rule of *legitimate law*: it threatens to make the rule of law ideal redundant to another ideal, in this case, justice, therefore failing to satisfy adequately the pluralism constraint. The rule of law as the rule of *just law* can thus be set aside for our purposes in this chapter, just as we earlier set aside the rule of law as the rule of *good law* or *legitimate law*.

We can now begin to appreciate the motivation to adopt a 'thin' account of the rule of law, one constituted by a series of formal and procedural requirements. There is no definitive list of these requirements, but the following are usually accepted as figuring among them: (1) that laws are prospective, rather than retroactive, in their effect, (2) that they are generally possible for their addressees to comply with; (3) that they are promulgated in advance to those addressees; (4) that their meaning is tolerably clear; (5) that they are consistent with one another, in that compliance with one law does not preclude compliance with others; (6) that they are sufficiently stable over time so that people may be reliably guided by their knowledge of them; (7) that any legal orders addressed to specific individuals or situations be controlled and justified by laws cast in general terms which meet the foregoing requirements; and (8) that officials charged with

[8] R.M. Dworkin, *A Matter of Principle* (Harvard University Press, 1985), 11–12.

making, adjudicating upon, and implementing laws do so in accordance with the meaning of the latter and also with any other laws that govern their activities.[9]

The tightly circumscribed scope of the rule of law, thinly understood, means that a legal system can in principle satisfy its demands in spite of deficiencies with respect to other values, such as justice, human rights or democracy. Indeed, this is a consequence of the way in which the constraint of pluralism is met by 'thin' accounts. On the other hand, the coherence of the thin view consists in the fact that its formal and procedural requirements pay tribute to the rational autonomy of those subject to the law, which is a vital dimension of the dignity, or intrinsic moral worth, of human beings. This is because the rule of law respects the capacity of the individuals who are subject to the law to choose and pursue pathways through life by weighing up reasons and by anticipating how the law is liable to impinge upon their potential decisions through grasping the content of legal rules. In Lon Fuller's dramatic formulation: 'Every deviation from [the rule of law] is an affront to man's dignity as a responsible agent',[10] although it is important to recognise on this view that some affronts to human dignity – such as poverty or torture – are not proscribed by the rule of law. The latter excludes only those affronts that violate the formal and procedural requirements that enable the law to perform its role of guiding rational agents.

Other requirements may be added to the list in the previous paragraph, provided they are consistent with its general tenor: the specification of procedural and formal requirements on a legal system out of respect for its subjects' rational autonomy. However, it is worth distinguishing between the abstract normative requirements themselves and particular institutional arrangements that may be found useful, or even necessary, at any given time and place to ensure their fulfilment. One such

[9] Influential formulations of rule of law standards along these lines are to be found in L.L. Fuller, *The Morality of Law*, rev. ed. (Yale University Press, 1965), ch. 2; J. Raz, 'The rule of law and its virtue' in *The Authority of Law* (Oxford University Press, 1979), 214–8; J.M. Finnis, *Natural Law and Natural Rights*, 2nd ed. (Oxford University Press, 2011), 270–1; C. Sunstein, *Legal Reasoning and Political Conflict*, 2nd ed. (Oxford University Press, 2018), 119–22); M.J. Radin, 'Reconsidering the rule of law', *Boston University Law Review* 69 (1989) 781.

[10] Fuller, *The Morality of Law*, 162; See also Raz, 'The rule of law and its virtue', 221 and Finnis, *Natural Law and Natural Rights*, 273.

institution, in contemporary societies, is an independent legal profession, and some provision of legal aid to litigants in order ensure adequate access to the expert services of its members. Given the huge volume of law that is evidently needed to regulate large, complex and technologically advanced societies, it is highly unrealistic to suppose that ordinary citizens will have the opportunity or ability to acquire knowledge of all the detailed legal provisions that potentially apply to them. This seems to imperil the fulfilment of desiderata such as those listed above, which appear to be premised on the possibility of ordinary, law-abiding citizens applying such knowledge in exercising their practical reason to order their lives. However, the difficulty may be ameliorated in various ways. One is by ensuring that the content of laws, especially those whose breach would incur criminal sanctions, does not deviate excessively from common-sense standards of reasonable behaviour. But another, equally important, method is to maintain a corps of legal professionals upon whose advice ordinary citizens may draw without incurring prohibitive financial or other burdens. Other institutional arrangements may also be found recurrently necessary or valuable in securing the rule of law, such as an independent judiciary,[11] a separation of governmental powers,[12] or, rather more controversially, a robust institution of private property that delimits a domain of objects over which individuals have the right to exert control and to exclude all others.[13] Some of the liveliest debates surrounding the rule of law concern the kinds of legal institutions and practices that best fulfil its demands, for instance, whether this is to be primarily achieved through the enactment of comprehensive regimes of statutory rules or the evolution of legal doctrine through the gradual accumulation of judicial decisions that crystallise generally held beliefs about what is just (Bentham famously endorsed the former, whereas F.A. Hayek shifted view between *The Road to Serfdom* and *Law, Legislation and Liberty*).[14] It is worth adding that there is no *a priori* reason to suppose that there is a single best institutional arrangement for securing

[11] A.V. Dicey, *Introduction to the Study of the Law of the Constitution* (1885) (Macmillan, 1982), 114.

[12] C. Montesquieu, *The Spirit of the Laws* (1748) (Cambridge University Press, 1989), Bk II, ch. 6.

[13] F.A. Hayek, *Law, Legislation and Liberty*, Vol. 1 (University of Chicago Press, 1973), 108–9.

[14] F.A. Hayek, *The Road to Serfdom* (1944) (University of Chicago Press, 1972) and F.A. Hayek, *Law, Legislation and Liberty*, Vol. 1, 116.

the rule of law. Failure to register these points can lead to the rule of law ideal being parochially equated with the detailed arrangements in place in a specific jurisdiction, such as the United States or the European Union, which are then to be simply 'exported' to jurisdictions that currently lack those precise arrangements.[15]

As presented above, the rule of law primarily imposes requirements on the organs of government ensuring that their operations are not above the law. Given the massive disparity in power that typically exists between the state and its subjects, this focus on curbing arbitrary government power is perfectly understandable. However, the demands of the rule of law extend beyond the institutions of government. The rule of law can also be flouted by private individuals, for example, when they engage in vigilantism that pre-empts the workings of the criminal justice system, or by corporations, for example, when they bribe officials in order to depart from the law, but also when such agents fail to comply with a legal system that is itself compliant with rule of law requirements. This enhanced scope of the rule of law underlines the fact that securing it is not merely a task for a narrowly political morality, aimed exclusively at officials and institutions, but also for the wider ethos animating the attitudes and conduct of individuals and groups within society more generally.

2 The Virtue of the Rule of Law

Proponents of 'thick' conceptions of the rule of law complain that the thin, formal–procedural conception is simply too meagre to warrant endorsement. Thus, Lord Bingham:

> A state which savagely represses or persecutes sections of its people cannot in my view be regarded as observing the rule of law, even if the transport of the persecuted minority to the concentration camp or the compulsory exposure of female children on the mountainside is the subject of detailed laws duly enacted and scrupulously observed. So to hold would, I think, strip 'the existing constitutional principle of the rule of law'. . . of much of its virtue.[16]

[15] On perils in the idea of 'exporting' the rule of law more generally, see T. Ginsburg, 'In defence of imperialism? The rule of law and the state-building project' in J. Fleming (ed.), *Getting to the Rule of Law* (New York University Press, 2011).

[16] Bingham, *The Rule of Law*, 67.

To proponents of the thin conception, however, Bingham's objection seems akin to insisting that being in good health is stripped of much of its virtue unless one also has knowledge, friendship, accomplishment, and various other elements of a good human life. There is a significant value to being healthy – in a state without disease or various kinds of physical or psychological malfunction – even if this does not necessarily bring other aspects of well-being with it. What reason has Bingham given us to suppose the thin account of the rule of law is too meagre, apart from the question-begging reason that it could be made even more attractive by subsuming other values within it? After all, so long as we accept the rule of law as one legal virtue among others, it can always be 'improved' by conjoining with it some other value, but that would not justify us in concluding that the latter value is really an aspect of the rule of law. A principled basis needs to be offered for drawing the line between those values encompassed by the rule of law and those that are not, a basis that respects the desiderata of pluralism and coherence.[17] In the absence of such an account, we risk losing the significant advantages of the thin view: on the one hand, the theoretical coherence of a unifying explanation of why only the listed formal–procedural requirements fall under the rule of law; on the other hand, the practical benefit of being able to make the case for the rule of law – especially to those societies that do not already accept it or that are mistrustful of it – without thereby also being lumbered with defending additional, more demanding, values, such as human rights or democracy, as part of a single liberal democratic package deal.

Still, one might concede that some defenders of the thin view have been somewhat over-enthusiastic in insisting upon the compatibility of the rule of law with grave moral defects in a legal system. Indeed, some regard the rule of law not as a moral virtue but rather as a morally neutral instrument for achieving a variety of goals – akin to a sharp knife, which can be turned to both moral and immoral purposes[18] – and one that is no less liable to serve the ends of oppressive legal systems than of decent ones. On this view, the rule of law is a virtue of the law – indeed, it is the specific

[17] Tellingly, in this regard, Bingham described the rule of law as the 'nearest we're likely to come to a universal secular religion', which suggests a comprehensive legal ideal, rather than one that satisfies the constraint of pluralism. Lord Bingham – The Rule of Law https://www.youtube.com/watch?time_continue=9&v=XlMCCGD2TeM

[18] Raz, 'The rule of law and its virtue', 225–6.

excellence of the law, since compliance with it enables law to fulfil its essential action-guiding function – but it is not an inherently *moral* virtue.[19] But this arguably goes too far and naturally invites the sort of backlash exemplified by the passage from Bingham. A more nuanced elaboration of the thin account of the rule of law would stress that it possesses significant moral value in its own right and that it has intimate connections with other important values, such as human rights and democracy, and is therefore not properly conceived of as a mere regulatory tool that is equally at home in decent and oppressive regimes. Such an approach promises to take much of the steam out of Bingham's objection.

As indicated earlier, the core value secured by the formal–procedural requirements of the rule of law is a due respect for the rational autonomy of human beings. Humans possess the capacity to grasp the normative reasons for and against various courses of conduct and to reach, and act upon, decisions in light of their assessment of the overall balance of these reasons. This is a capacity uniquely found among humans, certainly in its upper reaches where it involves deliberation about entire modes of life and conceptions of the good, and one that is heavily dependent on the ability, enabled by the acquisition of language, to draw upon a storehouse of concepts in formulating, communicating and contesting ideas about reasons for action. In seeking to regulate the decision-making of its subjects, a legal system should respect our capacity for rational deliberation by adhering to the rule of law's procedural and formal requirements, since by doing so it addresses those subjects as rational agents in advance of their moment of decision, providing them with the additional input of further reasons – cast in the form of legal rules – that they can factor into their deliberation.

The value of such respect for rational autonomy can be further elaborated in terms of the value of liberty or the security afforded by a predictable social environment, although caution needs to be exercised in making both extensions. So, for example, although the rule of law certainly erects a barrier to certain kinds of arbitrary interference by the state in the lives

[19] Hence Raz: 'A non-democratic legal system, based on the denial of human rights, on extensive poverty, on racial segregation, sexual inequalities, and religious persecution may, in principle, conform to the requirements of the rule of law better than any of the legal systems of the more enlightened Western democracies', 'The rule of law and its virtue', 211.

of its subjects – a form of respect for negative liberty – it by no means exhausts all aspects of the legal–political dimensions of liberty, among them other protections of negative liberty, such as prohibitions on torture, as well as the positive measures that a state should take to foster personal autonomy, including the provision of education, health care or valuable cultural pursuits.[20] By contrast, predictability can too easily be interpreted as an unduly exiguous grounding of the rule of law, for what the latter requires is not simply that the law's intervention into our lives be predictable, but that it be predictable *in a certain way*, that is, one that exemplifies the respect for our rational nature shown by adherence to its formal–procedural requirements. Predictions of the legal consequences of acting on our decisions, made on the basis of the law's compliance with the rule of law, are thus very different from a dog's ability to predict when it is liable to be beaten by its owner.[21] When officials act on the basis of their rational apprehension of legal rules, and ordinary citizens are able to anticipate how officials are liable to impinge upon their activities by means of a comparable grasp of those same rules, a distinctively valuable form of predictability is secured, one grounded in the reciprocal operation of the rational nature possessed by both officials and citizens.

The inherent value of the rule of law, as a way of respecting rational autonomy, shows the error of conceiving of it in purely instrumental terms, with its moral value being entirely a function of the value of the legal ends that it is made to serve. This allows for the possibility that rule of law requirements may be deployed by a wicked legal system as an effective means of achieving its goals. To this extent, we may think of the rule of law as analogous to the personal virtue of courage. Arguably both good and bad individuals can be courageous, but this is not to deny that courage is a moral virtue, or that the value of exhibiting it is sensitive to the worth of the goals it is used to pursue on any particular occasion. Given a sufficiently heinous goal, such as perpetrating a terrorist attack, we may

[20] Hayek's claim that 'any policy aiming at a substantive ideal of distributive justice must lead to the destruction of the Rule of Law' seems guilty of importing a complete (and contestable) account of liberty into the rule of law, one that goes beyond the eight listed formal desiderata to insist that the content of legal rules should also be 'formal', i.e. not embodying a choice among particular ends or people, see *The Road to Serfdom*, 78, 82. For criticism, see Sunstein, *Legal Reasoning and Political Conflict*, 136–8.

[21] The reference here is to Jeremy Bentham's critique of 'dog law' made by 'Judge & Co', see J. Bentham, *Of Laws in General*, Ed. H.L.A. Hart (Athlone Press, 1970), 152–3 and 184ff.

be unwilling to speak of courage or to ascribe any moral worth to the facing down of danger that is manifested in achieving such a goal. Equally, it may well be that scrupulous compliance with the rule of law in a death camp context, if we are willing to entertain such an utterly fanciful example, lacks any redeeming moral value whatsoever. In short, the rule of law has intrinsic moral value that is in complex ways conditional on the value of the goals that a law or legal system seeks to pursue; it is not simply a morally neutral instrument for achieving those goals.[22]

These points about the inherent moral value of the rule of law may be reinforced by tracing some of the connections it bears to further values, such as human rights and democracy. There is little point, for example, in enshrining human rights in law, or in creating laws by democratic means generally, if legal officials regularly fail to apply those laws impartially according to their true meaning. Aside from this largely instrumental point, the rule of law bears more constitutive connections to human rights and democracy. As is well known, human rights as a matter of morality are often not fully determinate as to both the content of their associated duties and the assignment of those duties to specific duty-bearers. Law is often needed to fill in such gaps left by pure moral reasoning about human rights. Compliance with the rule of law's requirements helps the law in specifying the content of human rights duties and allocating them to duty-bearers in an effective and morally defensible way. Among the laws to which this point applies are those intended to secure the right to democratic political participation, such as the laws specifying the conditions of eligibility to vote or stand for election. Moreover, some rule of law demands constitute human rights, pre-eminent among them the right not to be punished for an act that was not criminally prohibited at the time the accused acted. To this extent, although the rule of law is compatible with many human rights abuses, it is incorrect to assert that it is compatible with *all* of them.

With these observations in place, it is doubtful that generally decent or just regimes have no more affinity for adherence to the rule of law than do tyrannies. Given the rule of law is not merely a list of desiderata that are effective techniques for pursuing governmental objectives of whatever kind

[22] For one defence of the claim that the rule of law has conditional intrinsic value, as well as instrumental value, see C.M. Murphy, 'Lon Fuller and the moral value of the rule of law', *Law and Philosophy* 24 (2005), 239–62.

but, instead, embody one strand of respect for human dignity, it seems that a state attuned to those considerations will, *ceteris paribus*, be more likely to adhere to the rule of law, to extend its operation in appropriate ways, and to uphold its demands when other, more expedient, means of achieving the state's goals are available. As John Finnis has observed:

> A tyranny devoted to pernicious ends has no self-sufficient *reason* to submit itself to the discipline of operating consistently through the demanding processes of law, granted that the rational point of such self-discipline is the very value of reciprocity, fairness, and respect for persons which the tyrant, *ex hypothesi*, holds in contempt.[23]

Now, some have advanced beyond this point to make the claim that any legal system, insofar as it is truly a legal system, necessarily complies with the rule of law in some measure, and in virtue of that compliance has some moral value, even if not full-blown legitimacy.[24] Although not without interest, it is doubtful that a conceptual investigation into the nature of law is the best framework for articulating a complete understanding of the rule of law as a legal value. We can therefore leave this speculation to one side and conclude this section with two observations. First, compliance with the rule of law is a matter of degree rather than an all-or-nothing question. Often a legal system, or an individual law, will fall short of what can be reasonably achieved in terms of compliance, but it is important also to recognise that the rule of law necessitates trade-offs, both trade-offs among its eight desiderata when they conflict, such as between stability and possibility of compliance, and also trade-offs of those desiderata against other considerations, such as democracy or justice.[25] Such trade-offs may be unavoidable and hence justifiably necessitate less than maximal compliance with the rule of law. The extent to which this is so will naturally differ from one society to another, depending on their individual circumstances. Second, the moral reasons to comply with the rule of law vary significantly in character. Although the rule of law is standardly cast as a demand of justice,[26] if we take a strict interpretation of justice as a

[23] Finnis, *Natural Law and Natural Rights*, 273.

[24] A key issue in the Hart/Fuller debate: H.L.A. Hart, 'Positivism and the separation of law and morals', *Harvard Law Review* 71 (1958), 593–629 and L.L. Fuller, 'Positivism and fidelity to law – a reply to Professor Hart', *Harvard Law Review* 71 (1958), 630–72.

[25] Fuller, *The Morality of Law*, 44–6.

[26] Finnis, *Natural Law and Natural Rights*, 273.

matter of individual rights, then not all deviations from the rule of law will be rights violations. Some may be violations of imperfect duties directed at fostering and preserving common goods to which no one can claim to have an individual right. And some, perhaps most,[27] may be fallings-short from ideal aspirations that the rule of law embodies. So, for example, it is admirable for legislators to strive for levels of clarity and accessibility in statutory language that exceed anything citizens have a right to demand, or anything that the legislators are duty-bound to secure, in the sense that they would be properly blameable where they to fail to do so. In this way, the rule of law is a supererogatory *ideal* to which we may aspire and not only a matter of justice or duty.

3 Challenges and Limits

We began by observing that the rule of law has attracted considerable support from diverse ideological quarters throughout history. But it also has implacable foes, such as Marxists, who view its formal and procedural demands as a façade behind which class-based exploitation and oppression can flourish undisturbed. The differences here run deep, but one reply that a proponent of the thin conception can make is that the rule of law is just one legal virtue among others, so that compliance with it should never be treated as generally *sufficient* to confer good moral standing on the law. Still, the objection may persist that no set of legal rules promulgated in advance, framed in general terms and consistently applied in line with their meaning can ever be fashioned in such a way as to reliably secure morally acceptable outcomes. Instead, what is ideally needed is a highly contextualised practice of case-by-case judgement that draws on an inherently uncodifiable virtue of practical wisdom. Variants of this criticism can be discerned all the way from Plato to contemporary feminist critics who are sceptical about rule-based moral and legal reasoning.

The most historically significant attempt to address this concern about the limitations of law-based rule is made by Aristotle. He advocated a form of the rule of law while acknowledging its limitations: the strict application of general legal rules promulgated in advance can yield injustices in particular cases, either through silence or indeterminacy on the matter at

[27] According to Fuller, *The Morality of Law*, 42–3.

hand or by positively requiring a morally flawed outcome. Thus, even a generally morally sound legal rule, such as one requiring the closure of the city gates at midnight, will work an injustice if strictly applied in all circumstances, for example, so as to require closing the gates in the face of a retreating army defending the city.[28] For Aristotle, this phenomenon was endemic to any legal order framed in terms of general rules promulgated in advance and consistently applied according to their meaning.[29] This is because no legislator, no matter how powerfully motivated to advance the common good, can anticipate by means of legal rules all future contingencies that might bear on the morally sound regulation of particular cases. This inability is primarily attributable to two factors. First, the unforeseeability of innumerable future developments, for example, in technology, economic organisation, patterns of social life, etc. and hence the vast range of morally significant circumstances that may arise. Second, even if some of these future contingencies are foreseeable, there is a limit to the extent to which they can be addressed legally without creating rules so laboriously detailed that they would be highly inefficient guides to action, flouting the rule of law requirements of generality and accessibility. For Aristotle, however, this did not mean rejecting the rule of law, but rather tempering it through the operation of *equity*, whereby an adjudicator is licensed to depart from the strict application of a general legal rule in order to avoid a sufficiently grave injustice in particular cases.[30]

The result is an attempt to hold both the rule of law and equity in balance, founded on the idea that they are both means for the attainment of justice (in the broad sense of the moral goals appropriate to law), with judgement needing to be deployed as to when equitable departures from the application of law (as mandated by requirement (8)) are warranted.[31] The equity tradition, in both philosophy and legal doctrine, discloses some

[28] Aquinas, *Summa Theologiae*, IaIIae.96.6.

[29] The extent to which it is endemic, of course, will depend on which theory of legal interpretation we adopt, and these range from those that are narrowly positivistic in permitting no moral judgment to influence the determination of the existence and content of a legal standard (Raz) to those that hold that any such determination must ultimately heavily implicate such judgement (Dworkin).

[30] Aristotle, *Nicomachean Ethics*, 1137b26–27.

[31] For discussions of a topic rather neglected in contemporary legal philosophy, see J.R. Lucas, *The Principles of Politics* (Oxford University Press, 1966), 139–43, 212–22; M.C. Nussbaum, 'Equity and mercy', *Philosophy and Public Affairs* 22 (1993), 83–125; and F. Schauer, *Profiles, Probabilities, and Stereotypes* (Harvard University Press, 2006), ch. 1.

considerations bearing on how the rule of law and equity should be balanced against each other, including the following:[32] (i) equity will generally only be legitimately exercised by formally authorised adjudicators and enforcement agencies rather than through individuals acting unilaterally; (ii) equity should seek to realise the legal rule's true underlying purpose even as it departs from its strict terms; (iii) equitable judgments should track the objective moral reasons for departing from the law, rather than simply reflecting the adjudicator's subjective preferences; (iv) the injustice remedied by equity should be sufficiently grave to warrant deviation from the rule of law requirement to apply existing law according to its strict terms; (v) equity is less readily justified in areas of law and social life where the values served by the rule of law, such as predictability, carry especially great weight and variations in salient facts tend to be less frequent, for example, commercial and criminal contexts, as opposed to other areas that may not exemplify these features to the same extent, such as disputes among family members; and (vi) equitable deviations from law that are lenient in effect, especially in a criminal law context, are more readily justifiable than those that aggravate the situation of the parties under existing law.[33]

But even leaving aside generalised attacks on the rule of law, to which the equity tradition offers resources for a response, we may conclude by noting two major challenges that confront the rule of law in the contemporary world: technological innovation and internationalisation in governance.[34]

The first challenge arises from the advent of increasingly sophisticated forms of technology, especially computer technology allied to developments

[32] J. Tasioulas, 'The paradox of equity', *Cambridge Law Journal* 55:3 (1996), 463–6.

[33] Equitable discretion, as discussed here, is a form of non-legislative decision-making; the ethical judgement correcting existing law does not itself become a new law that adds to or modifies existing law. However, historically, the exercise of equity has led to the formulation of maxims and doctrines that themselves came to acquire legal force. But, in casting these equitable considerations in the form of legal rules, a risk is created of their being applied inflexibly in a way that yields injustice in the particular case – a phenomenon dubbed 'the decadence of equity', see H. Maine, *Ancient Law*, new. ed. (London, 1930), 73–5 and R. Pound, 'The decadence of equity', *Columbia Law Review* (1905) 25.

[34] Of course, there are many more challenges than can be discussed here, including squaring the rule of law with the high levels of bureaucratic discretion implicit in the modern administrative state, see e.g. R.A. Epstein, *Design for Liberty: Private Property, Public Administration, and the Rule of Law* (Harvard University Press, 2011).

in artificial intelligence and robotics. There is an understandable temptation to harness these ever-increasing technological capacities to advance not only the rule of law but also other valuable social goals, such as economic prosperity, democracy, public health and security. Humans are after all fallible creatures, and this fallibility extends to compliance with the rule of law. For example, research has found that length of sentences imposed by judges depends on the time of day and whether they are hungry.[35] Yet these technological solutions may seriously damage those same values.

One problem with these technologies is that they are often defective in their operation. For example, artificial intelligence systems used in decision-making in various domains, from insurance to policing, have been found to operate on the basis of algorithms that replicate and magnify existing human biases against women and minority groups. More fundamentally, there is a serious question whether legal rules can be adequately translated into code for use by artificial intelligence. Even if one could do so, the resulting algorithm may still be incapable of registering adequately all of the unpredictable and context-dependent considerations that arise in a given case, especially those that would ground a case in equity for departing from the strict application of existing law.[36] But even if we bracket operational bugs and limitations serious challenges remain.

Consider, for example, forms of technological governance that 'crowd out' the scope for an individual's freedom to choose whether or not to behave in certain ways. This may be either because they render those forms of conduct physically impossible or else because they drastically curtail an individual's effective freedom to choose them through the imposition of techniques such as facial recognition, digital surveillance and various modes of 'predictive' policing. Such an intrusion by technology into governance threatens to corrode the very value of human dignity that is at the core of the rule of law, the idea of human beings as rational agents autonomously shaping their lives through successive choices. Alternatively, consider the use of artificial intelligence to replace official decision-making by humans on matters such as the custody of suspects

[35] S. Danziger, J. Levav and L. Avanim-Pesso, 'Extraneous factors in judicial decisions', *Proceedings of the National Academy of Science* 108 (2010), 6889–92.

[36] F. Pasquale, 'A rule of persons, not machines: the limits of legal automation', University of Maryland Francis King Carey School of Law, Legal Studies Research Paper No. 2018-08 http://ssrn.com/abstract=3135549.

and the sentencing of convicted criminals. Perhaps Judge Robot would outperform ordinary human judges in the consistent application of relevant law thanks to its immunity from the biases and frailties, such as tiredness or ignorance, that afflict ordinary human beings. To this extent, the rule of law requirement of congruence between the existing law and official action will be better secured. But is not something vitally important also lost – the kind of reciprocity among officials and ordinary citizens characteristic of a society that respects the rule of law – when human beings are subject to algorithm-generated 'decisions' made by machines that do not share their autonomous rational nature? Is it enough to give those subject to automated decision-making a 'right to an explanation' by guaranteeing transparency regarding the algorithmic basis of decision? Or does a deeper realisation of the rule of law require a fellow human being, exercising their powers of rational autonomy, to take responsibility for the judgment rendered in a particular case, with artificial intelligence limited to the role of assisting a human decision-maker?

An important question we need to confront is how technological innovations can be integrated into a legal system in a way that enhances or at least respects, rather than undermines, the rule of law. More radically, we will have to face up to the question whether the benefits promised by new technologies – for example, enhanced security against epidemics or terrorist attacks – warrant sacrificing our commitment to the rule of law and, if so, to what extent and under which conditions.[37]

Another pressing challenge concerns the extent to which the rule of law has application in relation to the proliferating forms of international governance that have emerged in the last half century or so, largely in response to the increasingly global character of many of the problems that confront human beings. Some have denied that the rule of law applies internationally in any way strongly comparable to its salience in domestic contests. Sometimes this scepticism stems from an overly demanding conception of the rule of law, for example, as embodying requirements of democratic governance.[38] Such scepticism may inadvertently attest to the merits of the thin theory of the rule of law in identifying an important

[37] For a helpful discussion of such concerns, see R. Brownsword, 'Technological management and the rule of law', *Law, Innovation and Technology* 8 (2016), 100–40.

[38] J. Crawford, *Chance, Order, Change: The Course of International Law* (AIL-Pocket, 2014), chs. XI–XII.

value bearing on international law that is distinct from other values, including democracy. Others have pointed to the fact that the application of the rule of law to international law is impaired by the fact that states are both the subjects and the officials (including, the creators) of international law and that, unlike individual human beings, their dignity and freedom does not have ultimate moral worth.[39] Finally, some argue that tremendous disparities of power in the international domain, combined with the absence of centralised and effective enforcement mechanisms, pose a systemic obstacle to the realisation of the rule of law.[40] Perhaps one of the most egregious illustrations of this concern is that defendants who stand trial for international crimes overwhelmingly come from the Global South rather than from the powerful North Atlantic democracies. Like cases are decidedly not treated alike.[41]

A more moderate form of scepticism holds that even if rule of law desiderata apply to international law, the weight they bear is nowhere near as great as that which they possess domestically. So, for example, with respect to international criminal law, at least in the case of trials for crimes against humanity, one theorist has conjectured that rule of law considerations have diminished weight for two reasons. First, unlike the domestic context, there is no centralised global state whose arbitrary exercise of massive power urgently needs to be reined in by law. And, second, because crimes against humanity are so manifestly evil that there is little need for would-be perpetrators to be given advance notice of the potential for criminal trial and punishment.[42] Complex questions arise here both about trading off compliance with the rule of law against the achievement of substantive justice and about the possibility that the realisation in the long term of an international legal order that shows greater respect for the rule of law may require some willingness to transgress its demands in the short term.

[39] J. Waldron, 'Are sovereigns entitled to the benefit of the international rule of law', *European Journal of International Law* 22 (2011), 315–43.
[40] E. Posner, *The Perils of Global Legalism* (University of Chicago Press, 2009).
[41] M. Osiel, 'The demise of international criminal law', *Humanity Journal* (10 June 2014).
[42] D. Luban, 'Fairness to rightness: jurisdiction, legality, and the legitimacy of international criminal law' in S. Besson and J. Tasioulas (eds.), *The Philosophy of International Law* (Oxford University Press, 2010), 583–7.

7 Justice without Ethics: A Twentieth-Century Innovation?

Onora O'Neill

For centuries discussions of justice and ethics were closely linked in European thought and culture, but they have now diverged in marked, interesting and unsettling ways. European traditions had seen them as contributing distinct but parallel answers to the classic question 'what ought we to do?'[1] *Duties of justice* were widely seen as requirements both on individuals and on institutions that could, and in many cases should, be backed by legal sanctions, and could in some cases also define counterpart rights. *Ethical duties* were widely seen as requirements on individuals and certain institutions that did not need to be, and indeed on many views should not be, backed by legal sanctions and did not define counterpart rights. Yet by the start of the twenty-first century claims that justice and ethics were complementary and linked domains of duty – although still deeply embedded in European languages and culture – were often questioned, ignored or even explicitly rejected.

These have been momentous changes, and their implications are not obvious. So I begin with a sketchy reminder of some changes that have led many now to think of certain standards of justice as fundamental and universal, but ethical standards as the creatures of specific cultures or of individual choice or preference. I shall then comment on the widening gap between the justifications now proposed for duties of justice and for ethical duties, ask how complete and convincing the separation is, and consider whether justice can in fact be realised without taking ethical duties and their justification seriously.

[1] Duties of justice and ethical duties have been distinguished in differing ways at various times. Many of the classical distinctions (e.g. narrow or strict vs wide duties; perfect vs imperfect duties; duties to self vs duties to others) are still useful. However, in this paper I shall say little about the various formulations of these distinctions or about supererogatory action (action that goes beyond duty).

1 Duties and Rights

Both philosophical and popular conceptions of justice and ethics traditionally focused on what we should do, rather than on what we should receive, hence on duties or requirements rather than on rights or entitlements to others' action. In Europe duties had been central to normative debate since antiquity, and had played a large part in shaping religious, philosophical and popular discussions of how institutions should be constituted and how lives should be lived.

Duties of justice were formulated from the perspective of agents, and specified what they ought to do in (relatively) strict or narrow terms that were in principle enforceable. Some duties of justice also specified others' rights to just action of certain sorts (typically where that action formed part of a defined relationship or transaction); others were silent about rights.[2] Using a modern idiom, we might characterise duties of justice as stating what it is right to do, without necessarily asserting that some right-holder has a right to its being done. *Ethical duties* – such as beneficence, loyalty, civility, courage and many others – were seen as wide rather than strict duties, which left agents greater discretion in judging when and whether they should act, and how much they should do. Ethical duties therefore did not define counterpart rights, and were sometimes characterised as *duties of virtue* because they depended on character and culture, rather than on compliance with enforceable requirements.

So it was a momentous shift in the late twentieth century when rights rather than duties came to be seen as basic to justice. For rights *must* have counterpart duties, whereas duties *need not* have counterpart rights. Traditional practical reasoning that focused on duties had offered a *wider* perspective than can be reached by taking rights as fundamental. Indeed, once rights were taken as fundamental, both those duties of justice that lacked counterpart rights and wider ethical duties were marginalised, creating a temptation to favour expansive interpretations of rights which could cover some of what would previously have been covered in an account of duties.

[2] For example, duties to self cannot have counterpart rights, but some are strict or narrow duties (a classical example was the duty not to commit suicide), and on some accounts there can be duties of justice that are not owed to and cannot be claimed by individuals because they do not have counterpart rights. For some examples see my 'Enactable and enforceable: Kant's criteria for right and virtue', *Kant-Studien* 107:1 (2016), 111–25.

Contemporary human rights discourse typically allows for an account of those duties of justice that are matched by others' rights, but is silent about other aspects of justice and about (the rest of) ethics. Some contemporary discussions of justice see this as unproblematic, indeed hope that a focus on rights will *extend* or *strengthen* rather than *restrict* accounts of what ought to be done. However, while treating rights as fundamental may support stronger claims about *sanctions* and *enforcement*, reasoning that treats duties as basic is likely to support a wider range of claims about what ought to be done, because it will cover not only the full range of duties of justice but also duties that lack counterpart rights, including ethical duties.

2 The Decline of Duty

In the main this momentous shift in views about duty is a twentieth-century phenomenon, but there were earlier signs of unease. Duty was still pre-eminent in discussions of what ought to be done at the start of the nineteenth century, across the spectrum from Immanuel Kant's late practical philosophy to Wordsworth's 1805 'Ode to Duty', with its confident equation of Duty with Divine demand:

> Stern Daughter of the Voice of God!
> O Duty! if that name thou love
> Who art a light to guide, a rod
> To check the erring and reprove;
> Thou, who art victory and law
> When empty terrors overawe;
> From vain temptations dost set free;
> And calm'st the weary strife of frail humanity![3]

But by the middle of the nineteenth century claims of duty evoked occasional unease, and even hostility. Some feared the undermining of moral certainties and clarity, but some were positively eager to see duty downgraded.

Fear is uppermost in Matthew Arnold's wistful sadness about the waning of Christian faith, and the ebbing of duty:

[3] Cf. William Wordsworth's 1805 'Ode to Duty'.

> The Sea of Faith
> Was once, too, at the full, and round earth's shore
> Lay like the folds of a bright girdle furl'd.
> But now I only hear
> Its melancholy, long, withdrawing roar,
> Retreating, to the breath
> Of the night-wind, down the vast edges drear
> And naked shingles of the world . . .
>
> Ah, love, let us be true
> To one another! for the world, which seems
> To lie before us like a land of dreams,
> So various, so beautiful, so new,
> Hath really neither joy, nor love, nor light,
> Nor certitude, nor peace, nor help for pain;
> And we are here as on a darkling plain
> Swept with confused alarms of struggle and flight,
> Where ignorant armies clash by night.[4]

Yet less than thirty years later Friedrich Nietzsche saw nothing but gain in doing without duty:

> What destroys a man more quickly than to work, think and feel without inner necessity, without any deep personal desire, without pleasure – as a mere automaton of duty?[5]

Although their attitudes to the decline of duty are poles apart, both Arnold and Nietzsche see the alternative as an increasing emphasis on *personal* and *subjective* standards and concerns. Claims that personal and subjective choices are successors to the claims of duty gained surprising prominence. For example, at the very start of the twentieth century, G.E. Moore's *Principia Ethica*[6] ends with a surprisingly influential chapter that endorses a privatised vision of ethics centred on individual experiences of beauty, pleasure, friendship and knowledge – but no longer on families, institutions, communities or nations or their action, and least of all on duty.

[4] M. Arnold, 'Dover Beach', 1867.
[5] F. Nietzsche, *The Antichrist* (Alfred A. Knopf, Inc., 1895), Part II.
[6] G.E. Moore, *Principia Ethica* (Cambridge University Press, 1903).

3 Interlude: Patriotic Duty

However, the decline of duty was slow and uneven. The fact that a few writers and intellectuals cast doubt on duty did not undermine the ethics of duty in day-to-day life. Indeed, appeals to duty gained new prominence for many during the First World War, in the form of widespread, sometimes enthusiastic, insistence that duty demanded readiness to serve and to kill or be killed for your country. Of course, most people saw duty to King (or Kaiser) and Country as the public face of duty, to be honoured alongside duties to God, to family and friends, to neighbours and to the poor. Yet a belief that patriotic duty had distinctive, even overriding, importance became briefly and wildly popular. It is sobering to remember the fervour with which the outbreak of war in 1914 was greeted, and how widely killing for a patriotic cause was seen as a matter not merely of duty, but of noble duty.

Some even represented (or misrepresented) patriotic duty as an ethic of sacrifice.[7] Those killed in conflict, including conscripts who had no choice but to serve, were seen as making 'the ultimate sacrifice'. The idea that *being killed for a cause* and *killing for a cause* were forms of noble 'blood sacrifice' was in the air. Some supporters of the Easter 1916 rising against British rule in Ireland described those who lost their lives in attacks that they had themselves initiated as *martyrs*.[8] And this terminology is still popular in some quarters, particularly at present in the rhetoric of so-called Islamic State. Classically martyrs defend a noble or principled cause and are killed *by others* for doing so. Something surprising is going on when those who kill themselves for a cause (e.g. hunger strikers), or who kill others who are no threat to them for a cause (e.g. suicide bombers) are described as *martyrs*. This, it seems to me, is vivid evidence of an ethical tradition in disarray.

The exaggerated emphasis on patriotic duty and sacrifice in the early years of the First World War was not universally shared, even among those

[7] Cf. the pre-war patriotic version of Cecil Spring-Rice's verse (rewritten after 1918 as the Christian hymn 'I Vow To Thee My Country'), which runs: 'I heard my country calling, away across the sea/Across the waste of waters, she calls and calls to me./Her sword is girded at her side, her helmet on her head,/And around her feet are lying the dying and the dead;/I hear the noise of battle, the thunder of her guns;/I haste to thee, my mother, a son among thy sons.'

[8] Disagreement whether the leaders of 1916 should be seen as martyrs has persisted. See recently F. Flanagan, *Remembering the Revolution: Dissent, Culture, Nationalism in the Irish Free State* (Oxford University Press, 2015) and L. Kennedy, *Unhappy the Land: The Most Oppressed People Ever, the Irish?* (Merrion Press, 2016).

close to and sympathetic to patriotic causes. W.B. Yeats explicitly rejected it in his wartime poem 'An Irish Airman Foresees His Death', but he too places personal choice to fight and to risk life above duty to do so:

> I know that I shall meet my fate
> Somewhere among the clouds above;
> Those that I fight I do not hate
> Those that I guard I do not love;
> My country is Kiltartan Cross,
> My countrymen Kiltartan's poor,
> No likely end could bring them loss
> Or leave them happier than before.
> Nor law, nor duty bade me fight,
> Nor public men, nor cheering crowds,
> A lonely impulse of delight
> Drove to this tumult in the clouds;
> I balanced all, brought all to mind,
> The years to come seemed waste of breath,
> A waste of breath the years behind
> In balance with this life, this death.[9]

The crowds who cheered in 1914 felt otherwise. But unsurprisingly enthusiasm for patriotic duty waned as the war proved more catastrophically brutal and destructive than expected, or even imagined. Hostility to a narrow conception of public duty as patriotism in wartime mounted. It became a leading theme of many poems of the First World War, and is the target of E.M. Forster's later and much-quoted aphorism: 'If I had to choose between betraying my country and betraying my friend I hope I should have the guts to betray my country.'[10] The thought that personal loyalties and preferences matter more than patriotic duty resonated and spread into wider questioning and criticism of all duties.

4 Retreat from Justification

Between the two wars, initially only in limited academic circles, a more radical retreat from duty emerged. The startling success of logical

[9] W.B. Yeats 'An Irish Airman Foresees His Death', written in 1918, but not published until after the war in 1919.

[10] E.M. Forster, *Two Cheers for Democracy.*

positivism, with its uncompromising insistence that only empirically verifiable and analytical claims were meaningful, and that ethics, aesthetics, metaphysics and theology should all consequently be jettisoned as 'literally meaningless', rejected both duties of justice and ethical duties. Logical positivism did not offer convincing arguments for these claims, and those it offered were soon questioned, rejected or dismissed. Nevertheless its influence spread from narrow philosophical circles in Berlin and Vienna, partly because all too many of its early exponents were driven into exile across the world. However, while logical positivism failed to show that claims about justice or about (the rest of) ethics were 'literally meaningless', it succeeded in spreading uncertainty about their *justification*.

Doing without an account of duty, and in particular without an account of justice, has evident costs. In the face of the further catastrophes of the Second World War it was widely agreed that universal standards of justice mattered and must be reinstated, but they were now to be formulated in terms of rights rather than of duties. The Universal Declaration of Human Rights (UDHR) was adopted by member states of the United Nations in 1948, and the European Convention on Human Rights by the Council of Europe in 1950. Both documents view rights as basic to justice, and depart from earlier accounts of justice in marked ways. Giving priority to rights does not abolish duty, since rights require *others* to carry the relevant counterpart duties. However, declarations do not need to specify those duties clearly, or to allocate them to competent agents. Declarations of rights are also silent about ethical duties, and of course say nothing about justification.

On some views UDHR is only rhetorical or hortatory, and in its early days it was sometimes described pejoratively as promoting 'manifesto rights'. However as states became signatories to the Declaration, and later to the two 1966 Covenants intended to give greater institutional backing to the UDHR rights, human rights gained the backing of an argument from authority. Arguments from authority offer conditional justifications: but only to those who accept the relevant authority.

Yet it is likely that many who accept that justice should be thought of in terms of individual rights do not view appeals to authority as adequate justification. Despite uncertainties about deeper questions of justification, many who set store by human rights and international law, and more broadly by the rule of law, by detailed regulation and by demanding standards of accountability, probably think that some deeper justification for human rights standards is needed. However, for everyday purposes they seemingly find it variously necessary, adequate (or perhaps just convenient) to appeal to authority and to ignore demands for deeper justification.[11]

5 A Partial Restoration?

What emerged after the Second World War was therefore *not* a revised or restored version of the entire ethics of duty, or even a revised and restored account of all duties of justice. It was a narrower public commitment to specified human rights. But is this enough? Although both UDHR and ECHR look superficially as if they might provide an account of certain duties of justice that is nicely shorn of metaphysical and theological presuppositions, the reality is less clear and more troubling, in several ways. Some obvious difficulties arise when an account of justice is detached both from deeper forms of justification and from any account of ethical duties.

First, since declarations and conventions are not in the business of deeper justification, it is unclear what normative weight should attach to the standards they proclaim. To be sure, treating the Universal Declaration and the European Convention as fundamental authorities meant that human rights could be supported in many, but not all, contexts by invoking these instruments and the fact that many states had ratified them. However, the downside is that these 'positive' justifications have limited weight. They cannot provide reasons for states that have not signed up to do so, and they are silent about duties that lack counterpart rights.

Secondly, the rights proclaimed in 1948 were not linked to any clear account of the allocation of the necessary counterpart duties to competent agents. That is seemingly unproblematic where counterpart duties must be held by all. Rights not to be tortured or not to be enslaved, for example,

[11] Deeper justifications of normative claims and principles, including those that are basic to justice and to ethics, are I believe feasible, and need appeal neither to subjective preferences nor to contingent or hypothetical agreement. Some broadly Aristotelian approaches appeal to conceptions of the good for man, of human interests and of flourishing; some broadly Kantian approaches appeal to the necessary conditions of the possibility of principles with universal scope. I have set out what I think can be said for the latter approach in O. O'Neill, *Constructing Authorities: Reason, Politics and Interpretation in Kant's Philosophy* (Cambridge University Press, 2016).

require *all* others to hold the counterpart *'negative' duties*. However other duties that support liberty rights – including duties to enforce or protect those rights – must be held by specified agents rather than by all agents, as must duties to 'realise' social and economic rights. Only if such duties are allocated to specified competent agents is it clear *who* ought to do *what* for *whom*.[12] Proclaiming rights without specifying the necessary counterpart duties and allocating them to competent duty-bearers leaves it unclear what action is required of whom.

The drafting of UDHR had gestured to the thought that the counterpart duties lie with *states*, but had also referred variously to *nations*, *countries* and *peoples*, which lack the integrated capacities for action and decision-making required for agency, let alone for carrying complex duties to respect or realise the proclaimed rights. It is no wonder that some complained that UDHR declared only *manifesto rights* and lacked adequately clear practical import.

These lacunae were addressed *up to a point* by the two UN Covenants of 1966, the International Covenant on Civil and Political Rights (CCPR) and the International Covenant on Economic, Social and Cultural Rights (CESCR), which aimed to assign the relevant duties to states that ratified these instruments. However, the Covenants do not in fact assign the duties that have to be met to secure the UDHR rights to the signatory states. Rather they assign to those states *second-order duties* to allocate and enforce some configuration of duties that will *ensure respect* for the rights in CCPR and that will *support the realisation* of the rights in CESCR. For example, Article 2 of CESCR runs:

> Each State Party to the present Covenant undertakes to take steps, individually and through international assistance and co-operation, especially economic and technical, to the maximum of its available resources, with a view to achieving progressively the full realisation of the rights recognised in the present Covenant by all appropriate means, including particularly the adoption of legislative measures.[13]

'Achieving progressively the full realisation of . . . rights . . . by all appropriate means' is a matter of ensuring that *unspecified others* – individuals that are not identified, and institutions who may not (yet) exist – discharge

[12] The point has been emphasised for many years. See for example H. Shue, *Basic Rights: Subsistence, Affluence, and US Foreign Policy* (Princeton University Press, 1980, second edition 1996).

[13] Article 2 CESCR at http://www.unhchr.ch/html/menu3/b/a_cescr.htm.

the complex range of duties needed to secure those rights. Article 2 simply requires states to *construct* institutions and to *delegate* and *allocate* tasks to secure *some* effective allocation of the counterpart duties.

So whereas traditional discussions of duties of justice had focused on human duties to others, the discourse of human rights was doubly indirect about duties. It pointed to second-order duties to bring about some allocation of first-order duties that would, if observed, secure the human rights that had been declared. Despite this limitation, the Covenants of 1966 – now past their 50th year – were clearly an advance on the even more indeterminate claims of UDHR, and went some way to address the accusation that human rights were only manifesto rights. Human rights were to be seen as rights for which the signatory states (but not other states) would assign second-order duties, intended to ensure that the rights were respected or realised by those to whom they were assigned.

6 States as Guarantors of Rights

Was it a good idea to assign these complex second-order duties to states? One answer might be that it was a good idea, at least at the time, because states alone had powers sufficient to secure respect for and realisation of rights by others. A second, more pessimistic, answer might be that assigning the task of ensuring that everyone and all institutions respect and realise rights to the very powerful is intrinsically problematic – it is rather like assigning the supervision of hen houses to foxes, a parallel illustrated by the fact that some states are major and persistent violators of human rights.

A third answer might be that the solution at which the Covenants aimed is obsolescent. The year 1966 was a high-water mark of state power: the Western colonial empires were being dismantled; a Westphalian world of independent states seemed to be emerging; both old and new states were taken to have – and sometimes had – well-defined boundaries, and some of them could exercise power effectively within those boundaries. Since then, however, globalisation has transformed and reconfigured power in ways that often make securing respect for and realisation of human rights harder for states. Our world not merely includes a range of rogue states and failed states that respectively will not or cannot secure rights for their inhabitants, but is a world of porous borders, in which many states find their power to secure an adequate realisation of rights constrained by powerful non-state actors. These changes suggest that it may now be *less* feasible for states that are party to international instruments to be the sole and pivotal bearers of second-order duties to ensure that others respect and realise all rights.[14]

Moreover, even where first-order duties to respect and realise human rights can be effectively allocated to competent agents, ethical duties may also be important for realising duties of justice. While declarations of rights are unavoidably silent about duties without counterpart rights, including ethical duties, it is far from clear that human rights standards can be implemented without also relying on and cultivating ethical duties. Treating rights rather than duties as fundamental may leave neither justice nor ethics unchanged: the cultural costs of prioritising recipience over action, and rights over duties, include a view of human beings as claimants or potential victims and may give undue prominence to passive and reactive responses, such as resentment, rancour and blame.[15] I will return to consider whether justice without ethics is feasible and sufficient in Section 8.

7 Deeper Justifications for Principles of Justice?

However, the contemporary landscape also has encouraging features. Most evidently, deeper justifications of principles of justice are no longer taken to be impossible, and arguments from authority do not dominate discussions of justice. In the 1950s many still assumed that logical positivism had undermined duties of justice as well as ethical duties, and claims that 'political philosophy is dead' were widely circulated and discussed.[16] But

[14] S. Caney *Justice beyond Borders: Global Political Theory* (Oxford University Press, 2005); O. O'Neill, *Justice across Boundaries: Whose Obligations?* (Cambridge University Press, 2016).

[15] Criticism of ethical writing that focuses narrowly on these and similar responses can be found in Friedrich Nietzsche, *The Genealogy of Morals*, Part III, Section 15, and more recently in Bernard Williams, *Ethics and the Limits of Philosophy*, and other work that casts people largely as victims and recipients. For historical illustration see L. Kennedy, *Unhappy the Land*, 2016.

[16] The formulation is due to Peter Laslett, who claimed that 'for the moment, anyway, political philosophy is dead' in the introduction to the first of his series of edited books *Philosophy, Politics and Society* (Basil Blackwell, 1950), vii; the theme was widely discussed for some years.

this is no longer the case. Since the 1970s political philosophy has flourished again. Accounts of justice, beginning with those proposed by John Rawls, Robert Nozick and Jürgen Habermas, and since extended and elaborated by many others, now acknowledge the importance of justifying standards of justice rather than relying on appeals to declarations and conventions.[17]

Yet while the vast body of contemporary writing in political philosophy seeks deeper justifications of duties of justice than appeals to the authority of declarations and conventions can provide, much still also ignores wider ethical questions. Unlike earlier discussions of duty, much contemporary political philosophy focuses *only* on justice, and says nothing about the many (other) ethical duties that had traditionally formed part of the normative framework of European societies. Although contemporary political philosophy addresses aspects of justice that go beyond human rights standards, much of it ignores wider ethical issues.

The thought that we can provide adequate justifications for principles of justice, but not for (other) ethical principles, is central to John Rawls' later work. His 1985 article 'Justice as fairness: political not metaphysical', his 1993 book *Political Liberalism* and a number of his later essays argue explicitly that deeper justifications can support *only* principles of justice, and cannot be extended to (other) ethical principles, as he had suggested in his earlier *A Theory of Justice.*[18] While Rawls' late work does not reduce justice to rights – there are no individual rights that correspond to the difference principle – it aims to justify only principles of justice. He rejects forms of *comprehensive liberalism* that argue for ethical standards as well as for justice, in favour of a form of *political liberalism* that is silent about ethical duties. A similar focus on justice without close links to ethics can be found in the work of some other leading contributors to contemporary political philosophy. Habermas explicitly anchors justificatory arguments in the possibility of agreement reached via inclusive public discourse, while Nozick's libertarian arguments support a maximal private sphere in which individuals' choices and preferences are seen as decisive;

[17] However, while they avoid arguments from authority, contemporary discussions of justice often assume that agreement, or at least agreement reached under specified conditions, can provide sufficient justification. This is not obvious: iniquitous arrangements sometimes receive widespread agreement.

[18] See my 'The method of *A Theory of Justice*' in O. Höffe, (ed.), *John Rawls: Eine Theorie der Gerechtigkeit* (Akademie Verlag, 1998), 27–43.

neoclassical economists have argued for similar conclusions. Much of the revived political philosophy of recent decades has left ethical duties and their justification out of scope.

8 Justifications: Ethical Principles

The thought that justifications can support political but not ethical standards fits well with *some* liberal conceptions of justice, since it evidently protects individual choice and preference. But this can hardly be the whole story. Nobody thinks that it does not matter what individuals choose, or that all choices should be protected. Yet if justifications can support *only* principles of justice, the only choices their proponents will find reason to criticise, sanction or forbid will seemingly be those that breach some requirement of justice, for example by violating some others' rights – a conclusion that libertarian liberals welcome and see as decisive. It seems to me highly implausible to think that a convincing account of justice can be indifferent to everything that is not unjust. More is at stake, and some choices are more valuable than others.

This issue is often obscured by the promiscuous use of the term 'value' to characterise whatever individuals happen to choose or prefer, which leaves it fatally obscure whether empirical or normative claims are at stake. Where empirical claims are made about individuals' choices or preferences, there will be no general reason to see anything (let alone everything) that is chosen or preferred by agents as valuable: much that is chosen or preferred may be worthless or bad. Some individuals choose self-enrichment or sadistic treatment of others, but this does not show that self-enrichment and sadism are values, and the fact that some people choose or pursue them does not make them into values. Referring to whatever individuals choose as 'values' confuses empirical claims about preferences with normative claims about what is valuable, thereby conflating subjective and ethical claims.

Three illustrations of such confusions will have to suffice. First: *individual autonomy* (variously conceived, and very different from Kant's conception of autonomy) is widely said to be an important liberal 'value'. Yet individual autonomy can be used to adopt odious as well as admirable principles and decisions, and it is less than clear why it is to be valued if there is no robust distinction between ethically valuable and ethically unacceptable uses of autonomy. Second: appeals to *individuals' choices and preferences* are central to much economic theory and consumerist ideologies. But if individuals' actual preferences are automatically counted as 'values', a covert and unsupported normative claim has been advanced on the basis of subjective claims: promoting preferences as values simply misleads. Third: appeals to *individual identity* discards the older and more precise idioms that distinguish between a person's *sense of identity* (a subjective matter) and her *identity* (not a subjective matter). This move is often used to suggest that whatever someone happens to choose defines 'who they are', and must be of value. This seems misleading. *Identity* in the older sense of the term may indeed be weighty, and may define who someone is: but it is not a matter of choice – indeed that is a commonly given reason for thinking that identity *in that older sense of the term* matters and deserves protection. However *senses of identity* that can be chosen or discarded are less weighty, and self-evidently do not define who someone is – as is shown by the very fact that they are taken to be chosen, so alterable. If individuals can choose, define and redefine 'values' and 'identities', ethical claims are replaced by subjective claims.

9 Can We Have Justice without Ethics?

Anyone who thinks that ethical standards, unlike standards of justice, are a matter of individual choice is likely to think that these standards and their justification (if any) are irrelevant to justice. Yet this seems to me a mistake. Working out how to realise justice requires us to take a view of broader ethical standards as well as of standards of justice.

Realising standards of justice, including any rights that they define, requires more than the establishment of just constitutions and laws, and more than compliance with and enforcement of their requirements. The requirements of justice will indeed constrain just action, but they provide only indeterminate guidance. Compliance with these standards is not a matter of following complete instructions for action. Even if legal instruments are reinforced with more specific regulations, supplemented by more discursive guidance and backed by specific and demanding forms of accountability, proliferating rules can never fully specify exactly what must be done – or not done – if justice is to be respected and realised. Providing more or more explicit procedures for deploying and applying rules no doubt has its place, particularly in the procedures of courts and tribunals, of arbitration and administration. Doing so can help established authorities decide how to proceed, and can show whether a decision was reached by a duly constituted authority using an appropriate procedure. But while these procedures can provide a template for showing that due process was followed, they will not be enough to determine whether the decisions made or action taken were optimal or even acceptable in actual cases.

Principles of justice, like all principles of action, are indeterminate – and indeterminacy goes 'all the way down'. This point is neither new nor trivial. Both Kant and Wittgenstein pointed out that normative rules of all sorts (principles, standards, laws, regulations, guidelines) are intrinsically incomplete, and that indeterminacy cannot be eliminated by adding more rules, more requirements, more regulations or more guidance. There is no way to extend the paraphernalia of institutional life that will define sharp boundaries between compliance and infraction for every situation. Trying to offer 'complete' rules, instructions or guidance is in principle impossible, not to mention daunting or depressing for those who are meant to live up to them, who may conclude that even compliance demands too much, and end up ignoring or flouting demands, or 'gaming' the system.

There is of course a standard response to this point. It will be said that practical judgement and good sense are needed to shape action to fit standards of justice in particular contexts. However, there can be no complete rules – no algorithms – for practical judgement. Practical judgement is a matter of combining a clear sense of what *may* and *ought* to be done – of the principles, rules and standards that must be respected – with a grasp of the situation in which action takes place, of the consequences that various sorts of action may have and of an indefinite range of further considerations that bear on action in actual circumstances. For example, in living up to standards of justice, agents may also need to take account of the *feasibility*, the *consequences*, the *affordability*, and the *social acceptability* of specific ways of implementing or living up to those standards in actual situations.

However, taking account of these considerations in particular contexts is not just a matter of relying on hunch, individual preference or subjective choice to pick one or another preferred way of acting that is not unjust. Practical judgement also draws on complex webs of cultural and other considerations, and can be informed by interaction and communication with others who are sensitive to *practical* and *cultural* factors, which themselves are shaped by ethical standards. Mere conformity with requirements of justice may ensure action that complies with 'the letter of law', but is not enough for deciding how to act justly.

Of course, neither can cultures pick out unique or wholly determinate accounts of the best way to enact requirements of justice in a given situation. Rather they provide formative disciplines that can support consideration and interrogation of ways of construing situations and proposals for action. Since cultural processes are interactive, they open practical judgement to check and challenge by others and by other considerations, and thereby, to adjustment and to moderation. Cultural norms can be used to interrogate and to come to a view about situations and about proposals for action that can respect not only the requirements of justice, but a wider range of considerations.[19] In doing so they can shape judgement that complies with but is not fully determined by principles of justice. They can support (but not guarantee) convergence on feasible, affordable and socially acceptable ways of acting that lie *within* the demands of justice, and can reject proposals for just action that are not feasible or not affordable, that will not command adequate support or that will fail in other ways. A shared culture not merely need not undermine or threaten standards of justice, the rule of law or institutional probity, but can enable convergence on specific ways of respecting principles of justice that no amount of additional proliferation of law, regulation and accountability by itself can provide.

However, there is a rub. As many proponents of justice have pointed out, some cultures and subcultures may corrode or undermine justice. They may be corrupt or destructive, divisive or dishonest, and may foster derogatory and oppressive attitudes, or damage the capacity of those who live or work within them to engage and communicate with others, including their capacities to reason and to act. But other cultures do not fail in these ways. The insouciant marginalisation of ethical standards and justification that both positivist and subjectivist views of ethics have endorsed – in some cases even celebrated – across many decades must be challenged if we are to grasp when and how cultural standards and processes should be used to shape just action – and why other cultures and processes may foster and entrench injustice.

[19] G. Tett, *The Silo Effect* (Simon & Schuster, 2015).

So attempts to divide normative claims exhaustively into those that may or must be imposed by just institutions and processes, and those that are simply matters of individual choice or preference, needs reconsideration, challenge and (as I see it) revision. Many versions of modern liberalism, including those popular among some supporters of human rights, those that follow the later writings of John Rawls and espouse forms of (merely) 'political' liberalism, those that advocate libertarianism or that rely solely on the tenets of models of 'rational' choice, have bracketed or ignored wider questions of ethical justification, and have treated ethical standards as subjective or private opinions without deeper justification.

Implementing and enforcing just laws, regulation and systems of accountability is not enough for justice. Justice also needs the support of trustworthy and effective cultures and subcultures that enable those who inhabit them to bring other standards, including ethical standards, to bear on the tasks of understanding what is at stake and working out what to do. Standards of honesty and reliability, standards of confidentiality and fairness, standards of trustworthiness and discretion, and many other ethical standards are not irrelevant to justice, and cannot be replaced by ever more detailed elaboration of law, regulation and guidance. For a century past much of the public discourse of liberal societies has turned away from ethical questions and from ethical justification, and has assumed that standards of justice as embodied in law, regulation and accountability will be sufficient for the public domain, while everything else can be seen as a matter of subjective preference or choice. I think this division of labour is inadequate. If justice matters, we cannot be indifferent to ethical standards *or* to their justification.

8 Rights and Human Rights

Jeremy Waldron

What makes a right a human right? If we were to start in the realm of positive law, we might define human rights more or less by ostension. They are rights listed in certain multilateral treaties and conventions in international law, like the International Covenant on Civil and Political Rights (ICCPR) and the International Covenant on Economic, Social and Cultural Rights (ICESCR). There is nothing wrong with definition by ostension; no other mode of definition is available for certain terms like simple colour words. But 'human rights' is a complex phrase and we should expect an account of its complexity to tell us how the terms it contains – 'human' and 'rights' – work together to constitute its meaning.

1 Rights

Human rights are *rights*: that is the first thing we have to explain. A legal right is a provision that is at one and the same time protective and constraining. It aims to protect (or promote) some individual interest and it does so by imposing duties on those whose actions or neglect are likely to threaten the interest in question. I believe the most useful elucidation of the idea of a right is provided by Joseph Raz. It is not uncontroversial; there are alternative accounts that emphasise personhood and respect rather than interests.[1] But I find Raz's account useful as a starting point, because it is the most comprehensive. 'To say that a person has a right', says Raz, 'is to say that an interest of his is sufficient ground for holding another to be subject to a duty.'[2] The interest may be important because of its material significance or because of its connection with liberty or dignity. Raz's account does not depend on any narrow conception of

[1] See, for example, F. Kamm, *Intricate Ethics: Rights, Responsibilities, and Permissible Harm* (Oxford University Press, 2006), 237ff.

[2] J. Raz, 'Legal rights', *Oxford Journal of Legal Studies* 4 (1984), 1, at 14.

interest, though it does assume that interests are individualised concerns. Equally, the element of duty may involve a requirement to take some action which will serve the interest or to avoid some action which will impact adversely upon it. Again, the formulation is open. The important thing is that talk of rights is a way of talking about the grounds of duties: 'One justifies a statement that a person has a right by pointing to an interest of his and to reasons why it is to be taken seriously.'[3]

In spite of these advantages, Raz's analysis is complicated. If we are working in the realm of legal rights, the relevant grounding or justificatory relations have to be understood as legal in character. Moral justification is not enough. They are justifications recognised within the fabric of the law and they do legal work, not just policy or moral work. Talk of legal justification can make sense if we accept that, in Raz's words, 'legal rules are sometimes hierarchically nested in justificatory structures',[4] in which some of the legal rules justify others. The justification may be direct and compelling so that one legal rule provides a decisive reason for holding another putative rule to be legally valid. But even short of that, that is, even if the legal justification does not in and of itself make the justified statement a true statement of law, still it is possible that something that can be identified as a legal justification 'provides a reason for changing the law so as to make the justified statement true'.[5] Or it can provide a compelling argument in adjudication for interpreting a given rule in a certain way or, as Raz puts it, for developing the law in certain ways.[6] After all, law comprises not only rules but also deeper principles, purposes and policies implicit in the whole fabric of a given legal system.[7] So an understanding that a certain interest is important in law and that this importance is associated with a rule imposing a duty can be useful in determining the dimensions of the duty and various possible exceptions to it. A duty grounded legally in the interests of an individual may have different parameters and interact differently with other normative considerations to a duty grounded in, say, wealth-maximisation or general utility. Such information may also be used procedurally, to determine things like *locus*

[3] Ibid., 5.
[4] Ibid., 6.
[5] Ibid., 11.
[6] Ibid.
[7] The best known account is that of R. Dworkin, 'The model of rules' in his book *Taking Rights Seriously* (Harvard University Press, 1977), 14, at 22ff.

standi in relation to duties identified in this way: we may say, for instance, that only the person whose interest is the ground of the duty has standing to bring an action for its enforcement.

So we talk of rights when duties are legally justified (in these complicated ways) by reference to certain individual interests that the law undertakes to protect. As a result, rights talk will often involve a complicated back-and-forth between formulations in terms of duties and formulations that are more like the identification of legally privileged interests. Sometimes rights (and human rights) identify duties directly. They may say, for example, 'No one shall be subjected to torture or to cruel, inhuman or degrading treatment or punishment' (ICCPR, Art. 7.1). Notice that this formulation does not use the word 'rights', unlike, for instance, 'Every human being has the inherent right to life' (ICCPR, Art. 6.1). By itself, Article 6.1 does not tell us what the relevant duties are; it really just identifies a particularly important interest – namely, the individual interest in not being killed. A few duties are, however, listed in subsequent subsections of Article 6, like 'Sentence of death shall not be . . . carried out on pregnant women' (ICCPR, Art. 6.5). But the right specified in Article 6 might be used as a basis for inferring other more specific duties as well.

In none of the provisions I have mentioned are we told explicitly who the bearers are of the duties that are implied or specified. Certain things are to happen or not happen: that is the content of the relevant duties. Often we can make a pretty straightforward inference so far as rights-bearers are concerned. The duty specified in Article 6.5 is incumbent on whoever is responsible for the operation of the system of criminal justice in a country that permits capital punishment. And the duty specified in Article 7 is presumably incumbent on anyone who might be in a position to inflict torture or other forms of forbidden treatment.

But there may be other duty-bearers as well: people who have a duty to investigate allegations of torture and bring those responsible to justice, as well as people who train police and security forces and can organise things so as to make torture less likely.[8] It is often said that rights like these are rights against the state. That makes sense: national states are formally

[8] Elsewhere I have referred to these as 'waves of duties' associated with a given right, like the right assumed in Article 7.1 of the ICCPR. See J. Waldron, 'Conflicts of rights', *Ethics* 99 (1989), 503, reprinted in *Liberal Rights: Collected Papers 1981–1991* (Cambridge University Press, 1993).

speaking the parties bound by treaties such as the ICCPR. But states have a double or triple role in regard to these rights: *first*, states or state officials are often the primary threat to the interests protected by these rights; *secondly*, states are usually regarded as having the prime responsibility to stand up for these rights and protect them against violation; and *thirdly*, states are the parties whose consent and ratification makes the treaty in question a valid source of law. There is no contradiction here: states are huge and complex things and they bear interlocking duties of multiple kinds.

Raz's conception is particularly helpful in understanding so-called positive or social-economic rights. A provision like Article 7.1 of the ICCPR is, in the first instance, negative: it says that certain things are not to be done. Other rights provisions, however, impose affirmative requirements. Consider Article 12.1 of the ICESCR, which says that '[t]he States Parties to the present Covenant recognise the right of everyone to the enjoyment of the highest attainable standard of physical and mental health'. Article 12 goes on to mention some particular things that need to be done, such as reduction of infant mortality, the improvement of industrial hygiene, the prevention of epidemic diseases, and an assurance of medical service for everyone. No doubt there are other things too, not specified, that need to be done in the way of health care and public health; Article 12.1 can provide a legal ground for arguing that they should be done as well. But whose responsibility is it to do or provide these things? The Article does not say. Nevertheless, by committing itself to the importance of the interest in health care, and by showing that that interest is important enough to justify the imposition of duties, Article 12 provides a reason for us to find out who is in a position to do these things and figure out on whom the duty to do them should normally be incumbent. In this sense the right comes before the duty; as Raz puts it, 'one may know of the existence of a right without knowing who is bound by duties based on it'.[9]

My examples have been taken from human rights covenants: I wanted to illustrate the ways in which human rights satisfy the basic logic of rights and how a grasp of that logic helps us understand the different textual forms in which human rights present themselves.[10] But everything I have

[9] J. Raz, 'On the nature of rights', *Mind* 93 (1984), 194, at 211.

[10] Here I follow J. Raz, 'Human rights in the emerging world order' in R. Cruft et al. (eds.) *Philosophical Foundations of Human Rights* (Oxford University Press, 2015), 217, at 219–23.

just said could be said about legal rights generally, not only about human rights. It applies to property rights too and rights arising out of contracts and other legal relationships. My property right in a given house generates a standard package of duties (and duty-bearers) aimed at protecting my interest in the house. And saying, of X's duty to refrain from entering this house, that it is a matter of the interests protected by my rights of property distinguishes it (and its ramifications) from similar duties grounded in other ways, such as a duty imposed as a condition of probation, for example. Justifying duties by reference to the importance of individual interests is a distinct thing that law does, in all sorts of fields – distinct from other things it does – and when we take an interest in human rights we are taking an interest in that kind of thing.

2 Individual Rights

Human rights share with rights of all kinds a commitment to the importance of certain individual interests. We expect that all legal rules will be justified by reference to social interests generally, often in a utilitarian way – looking to the greatest interests of the greatest number of people in society. Rights are in question, however, when we are prepared to say, canonically, that just one person's interest is sufficient to justify holding others to be under a duty. (It may be an interest that each person shares with all others, but still it grounds duties not as an upshot of the cumulative importance of everyone's interests, but rather – and in the same way for everyone – on account of the importance of the interest in each individual case.) Rights disaggregate the general interest: they force us to look at what the protection of individual interests may require even when protecting those interests does not advance the greater interests of all. Of course we do not treat every individual interest in this way – separating it out from the general interest and giving it dedicated protection. We pick and choose. That is why *rights* is a special category, because it demarcates the range of individual interests that we are prepared to privilege in this way.[11]

[11] Joseph Raz in his later work has sought to reconcile a concern with rights with a concern for the common good. Rights do not always have to stand in an antagonistic relation with the common good by setting up the idea of an individual interest having moral force irrespective of the effect on other interests. Sometimes this is taken care of by the fact that rights are universalisable. If X has a right to P, then Y and Z have such a right as well, even

In many areas of private law, rights can be held by entities like corporations. Formally, the structural logic is the same. We treat the corporation as an entity individuated or distinguished from the aggregate social interest and we indicate our determination to justify duties (on other corporations and on natural individuals) to satisfy or respect certain interests that the corporation holds. Human rights partake of the same structural individualism – distinguishing and privileging individuated elements of the social whole. However, I believe that in the case of human rights, the individualism is substantial not just formal. Human rights are rights held by natural persons – men, women and children – certain of whose individual interests are considered to be of the utmost importance even when they are distinguished from the social whole. The idea of human rights, in other words, is rooted in a sort of ethical or normative individualism which views the human individual as the most important entity that exists in the world.[12] By and large, then, human rights are rights held by natural individuals.

The one striking exception is the presence at the beginning of each of the human rights covenants of a right to self-determination, which seems necessarily to be held by human peoples rather than human persons.[13] It is possible that this too could be disaggregated, so that the right of self-determination held by a people is ultimately derivative from some autonomy right held by natural individuals. (Analogously one might say that the free speech rights of a corporation might be treated as ultimately just an array of the rights that natural individuals have to organise in order to speak freely and with one voice within a certain corporate framework.[14]) But that would be a strained interpretation. It is better to

if they are, for time being, duty-bearers whose interests are impacted by rights. Rights are, in that sense, a good in common as between X, and Y, and Z. But Raz takes this further by suggesting that in the normal case, the reason for holding an interest of X's to be important enough to justify holding Y and Z to be under a duty, is that Y and Z will usually benefit from X's interest being treated in this way. See J. Raz, *Ethics in the Public Domain: Essays in the Morality of Law and Politics* (Oxford University Press, 1995), 45ff. I am sure this is true in some cases. But I do not follow Raz in thinking that this is necessary or the normal case with rights. We must be prepared to defend rights one at a time when the relevant interest is sufficiently important to the person whose interest it is, irrespective of the effects of that on the interests of others.

[12] For the varieties of individualism, see S. Lukes, *Individualism* (Basil Blackwell, 1973).

[13] See ICCPR Art. 1.1 and ICESCR Art. 1.1.

[14] Compare the debate about corporate speech in US constitutional law: see *Citizens United* v. *Federal Election Commission* 558 US 310 (2010).

recognise self-determination as partaking of individualism only in the structural sense I mentioned earlier, whereby a collective is treated as a separable entity individuated from the larger society (in this case, from the world as a whole).

3 Human Rights and Constitutional Rights

May only rights that are contained in international instruments count as human rights? If so, that is a problem, because one of the obligations states have under, say, the ICCPR is to ensure that provision is made for these rights in their national law. In Article 2 of the ICCPR, each state undertakes not only 'to respect and to ensure to all individuals within its territory and subject to its jurisdiction the rights recognised in the present Covenant' but also

> Where not already provided for by existing legislative or other measures, . . . to take the necessary steps, in accordance with its constitutional processes . . . to adopt such laws or other measures as may be necessary to give effect to the rights recognised in the present Covenant.

This means we should expect to find human rights in national bodies of law as well, some of them in legislation or in new constitutional instruments adopted pursuant to Article 2(2), some of them there already perhaps pre-dating the ICCPR by many years. I suppose we might say that a right changes its character from *human* right to, say, *constitutional* right when it changes its habitat in this way. I think this would be unfortunate, however, as an approach to classification, not least because some of the statutes that make provision within a legal system for the national administration of rights that are also laid down in an international instrument have titles like 'the Human Rights Act'.[15] I do not mean that there is no difference between rights as formulated in international human rights law and rights as formulated in national constitutions. There often are significant differences even when the latter are modelled on the former.[16] But this does not

[15] I have in mind the British statute of that name, enacted in 1998.

[16] For a fine discussion of this 'dual positivisation', see G. Neuman, 'Human rights and constitutional rights: harmony and dissonance', *Stanford Law Review* 55: 203 (2003), 1863.

mean that legislators are not trying to set out human rights in what they lay down in their national charters.[17]

4 Human Bearers

We have to focus now on the 'human' in human rights. The obvious thing to say is this: wherever they are located, whatever the source of their status as legal provisions, human rights are rights that people have by virtue of their being human; they are rights supposedly held by all human beings. I think this is correct. Instruments such as the ICCPR seem to embody this understanding. The ICCPR is redolent with language like 'every human being' and 'all persons'. It says 'everyone' is entitled to this or that protection, and that 'no one' is to be treated in this or that way. Admittedly some of the rights are conditional. Article 9.3 says that:

> Anyone arrested or detained on a criminal charge shall be brought promptly before a judge . . . and shall be entitled to trial within a reasonable time or to release

But the condition of arrest or detention might be satisfied, as the provision says, by 'anyone', and the requirement applies to each and every human being who falls into this category. Not only that but the Covenant requires explicitly, in Article 2.1, that the rights it lays down are to be applied to 'all individuals . . . without distinction of any kind, such as race, colour, sex, language, religion, political or other opinion, national or social origin, property, birth or other status'.

Does this mean we made a mistake when we said there might be human rights in a national constitution or bill of rights? No it does not. A national instrument such as the US Bill of Rights usually applies to *all persons* not just to US citizens.[18] What Section 2.1 of the ICCPR envisages is that each state 'undertakes to respect and to ensure *to all individuals within its territory and subject to its jurisdiction* the rights recognised in the present

[17] For a contrary view, see J. Rawls, *The Law of Peoples*, revised ed. (Harvard University Press, 2001), 79, which distinguishes sharply between human rights, on the one hand, and 'constitutional rights or the rights of liberal democratic citizenship', on the other. The reasons for Rawls' view will become apparent in Section 6 below.

[18] In some cases, the US document uses the language of 'the right of the people' (e.g. in the Second and Fourth Amendments). But these seem to be understood as individual rights that apply to 'any person', not as rights accruing to the American people as such.

Covenant, without distinction of any kind . . .' (my emphasis). And that is what the US document does (and had done long before the framing of the ICCPR). The exception, I suppose, is that national constitutions usually restrict the democratic franchise to only their own citizens, so that in the US Constitution, for example, the Fifteenth and Nineteenth Amendments may not apply directly as human rights. But they do so indirectly. The position of the ICCPR is that anyone who is a citizen of a state has the right to participate in its government (Article 25). That is a human right; it is one that they have because they are human persons; but it applies to everyone, in respect of whatever their country of citizenship happens to be.

Is there any philosophical difficulty with the claim that human rights are rights held by all humans? Someone may offer the following objection. Humans evolved as a species hundreds of thousands of years ago. For most of that time, it hardly makes sense to think of human beings as right-holders; certainly they did not think of themselves in those terms. Moreover, if humans living, say, ten or twenty thousand years ago might be said to have had any rights, they would be quite different in character from the rights humans are now thought to have. Their ways of living – their ways of being human – are or were so different from ours.

I think this objection is important but that it can be answered. Our focus on human rights as legal rights means that our primary interest is prospective or forward-looking, from the here and now of the charters and covenants to ways in which humans might deal with one another in the future.[19] What might or might not make sense as applied to Stone Age societies is disjoined from our present normative concerns by what Bernard Williams called 'the relativism of distance'.[20] Its only relevance in this debate would be as a ground for doubting the application of human rights as we now understand them to some *current* ways of being human in the world or living in a human society. And it is true that humans live even now in so many ways and are so disparately situated in such different social, cultural, economic, political and legal environments that the task of specifying a common set of rights on the basis that 'one size fits all' can sometimes seem insuperable. But this does not mean that the human rights enterprise fails to make sense, just because it is conceived of in terms of

[19] Cf. Raz's claim in 'Human rights in the emerging world order', 225, that 'human rights are synchronically universal, meaning that all people today have them'.

[20] B. Williams, *Ethics and the Limits of Philosophy* (Harvard University Press, 1985), 160–5.

universalism. Humans are similar in many important ways, just by virtue of their humanity, as well as different in many respects by virtue of the variety of their ways of life and ways of being in community. The enterprise of human rights law is the enterprise of trying to identify key interests that all humans have that are important and need protection from certain standard threats. That there may be such interests cannot be ruled out *a priori* simply by pointing to the bewildering variety of ways of being human.

The particular way in which the candidate interests are specified may be a matter of concern: our declarations talk about 'technical and professional education', 'universal and equal suffrage', and the right to 'holidays with pay'.[21] Such terms and ideas are familiar to us, but it is part of the understood pragmatics of human rights declarations that we look beyond these particular specifications to the universal human interests that they serve.[22] It may be harder to do this in some cases than in others.[23] But the fact that we cannot always find formulations which are, so to speak, neutral as between different social, political and economic consequences does not mean that there are not important and universal interests underlying these particular expressions.

In Section 8, I shall say more about how the international community goes about identifying the individual rights that are to be privileged in this way. For a philosopher, it is tempting to say that we should first identify some master value like autonomy, dignity or equality and then derive individual human rights from that. But that involves, I think, an exaggeration of the unity of our rights declarations. They tend to be presented as lists, not theories. There may be many different considerations pertaining to the importance of individual liberty and well-being that have some claim to be taken into account in the setting up of such a list. The identification of human interests that are particularly and universally important is a work-in-progress and I think it is a mistake to insist dogmatically on a single source of rights just in order to give the list a spurious coherence or closure.

[21] Universal Declaration of Human Rights (UDHR), Articles 26.1, 21.3 and 24.

[22] For an attempt to do this in the case of the UDHR's right to holidays with pay, see J. Waldron, *Nonsense upon Stilts: Bentham, Burke, and Marx on the Rights of Man* (Methuen, 1987), 180.

[23] See the discussion of specification in D. Miller, 'Joseph Raz on human rights', in Cruft et al. (eds.) *Philosophical Foundations of Human Rights*, 232, at 239.

5 Human Responders

It is possible that the term 'human' in 'human rights' may refer not to the right-bearers (and various aspects of their humanity) but to the class of people for whom violations of these rights are properly a matter of concern. Certain rights, it may be thought, are or ought to be matters of general concern among humans: as Immanuel Kant put it, 'a violation of right on *one* place of the earth is felt in all'.[24] The idea is that there is a class of rights such that no human should be indifferent to the violation of any right in that class. These rights are called 'human rights' because humans as such are called on to support them. Kant saw this as a change in the character of global community. Writing in the 1790s, he thought the world was much more interconnected in terms of moral concern than it had been previously. And of course we think it is even more so – *much* more so – 220 years later. We are now in a position to take rights seriously together in the world, not least because of the growth of human rights institutions themselves. As Joseph Raz puts it, '[o]ne of the most important transformations brought about by the pursuit of human rights has been the empowerment of ordinary people, and the emergence of a powerful network of non-governmental as well as treaty-based institutions pressurising states and corporations . . . in the name of individual rights'.[25]

But it is probably best to regard this as a complement, not as a competitor, to the proposition that human rights are rights held by all persons in virtue of their humanity. The latter proposition is probably necessary to explain why these rights are also of universal human concern, and why these practices and institutions make sense in the context of international as well as national constitutional law.

6 Human Rights as Limits on Sovereignty

For some recent theorists, the most important thing about human rights is that they impose limits on sovereignty. The idea is that we can define a class of rights such that no government or international organisation is

[24] I. Kant, 'Toward perpetual peace', Ed. M. Gregor, *Practical Philosophy* (Cambridge University Press, 1996), 330 (8: 360).

[25] Raz, 'Human rights in the emerging world order', 226.

ever required by respect for the sovereignty of another state to acknowledge that violations of these rights are not anyone's business except the country in which the violation occurs. Humans live in separate political communities and usually the violation of their rights takes place inside those communities often at the hands of the local state. And ordinarily, the sovereignty of a state is a warrant for its rebuffing any formal criticism or denunciation of its policies by outsiders. But not in the case of violation of its citizens' human rights. Those rights trump sovereignty and they empower outsiders to interfere, in extreme cases by sanctions or by force, to uphold the rights in question. This is sometimes called a 'political' conception of human rights.

The best-known proponent of this view is John Rawls, in *The Law of Peoples*, though Rawls prefers to talk of the powers of whole peoples rather than the sovereignty of states.[26] Rawls says that the role of human rights is to specify limits to the principle of non-intervention associated with authority of a people in possession of a given territory. When certain rights are violated in such a community, the people and their government lose any standing to complain about interventions by other governments aiming to vindicate the rights in question. 'Their fulfilment [*i.e. respect for these rights*] is a necessary condition of a regime's legitimacy', and it is 'also sufficient to exclude justified and forceful intervention by other peoples, say by economic sanctions or, in grave cases, by military force'.[27]

There is something to this view, but not much. If I can put the point in the language of sovereignty, certainly human rights are sovereignty-trumping principles. They are so because they preclude a sovereignty-based rebuff of any formal *démarche* or denunciation. But if the trumping of sovereignty is supposed to go beyond that – to the prospect of sanctions or armed intervention – then an account along these lines sets the bar too high.[28] Rawls was well aware that his particular criterion of importance – or anything like it – would tend to isolate as 'human rights' only a small subset of the rights that are usually given that designation. (Rawls suggested that, of the 30 rights listed in the UDHR, only the right to life and the

[26] J. Rawls, *The Law of Peoples*, 80. (For the emphasis on peoples rather than state sovereignty, see ibid., 25–6.) See also J. Raz, 'Human rights without foundations' in S. Besson and J. Tasioulas (eds.), *The Philosophy of International Law* (Oxford University Press, 2010), 321, at 336–7.

[27] Rawls, *The Law of Peoples*, 80.

[28] Cf. R. Dworkin, *Justice for Hedgehogs* (Harvard University Press, 2011), 333.

right not to be tortured are clear instances of human rights; Articles 4 (anti-slavery), 7 (non-discrimination), 9 (protection from arbitrary arrest) and 10–11 (due process) may or may not be in this category 'pending issues of interpretation', while the remaining provisions, including the socio-economic provisions count as 'liberal aspirations' rather than human rights.[29]) People do sometimes object to the proliferation of rights claims; but I do not think it warrants this truncation of the list.

I worry too that Rawls' minimalism sells short the individualism of rights, by which I mean the trumping importance of each single individual's right, irrespective of what is happening to other individuals. Consider a particular right which almost everyone accepts should be regarded as a human right – ICCPR, Art. 7.1, the right not to be tortured. Almost all of us accept that when some individual is tortured a human right is violated. But I do not think anybody believes that when *just one person* is tortured, humanitarian intervention by outside forces is justified to stop that torture or punish it. There is never any question of humanitarian intervention to vindicate just one person's right. Does this mean that the general impression that Article 7.1 is a human right is a mistake, according to Rawls' view? I think we have to reject that. As we saw in Section 3, the distinctive advantage of human rights has always been the way they force us to focus on individual wrongs, wrongs done to individual persons, rather than evaluating societies on the basis of the way they treat their members in aggregate terms. True, the view we are discussing does not adopt the worst sort of aggregation – trading off the wrongness of rights violations against the possible advantages that may accrue to a society therefrom. It is aggregative only in the sense that it sums up a large number of rights violations as a precondition for designating them as violations of *human* rights. But the 'human' now follows the particular remedy, which is a response to the aggregate, rather than the right itself, which was always understood to be individual.

No doubt if hundreds or thousands of people were being tortured, there would be some prospect of a forceful international response. So thinking about human rights in virtue of the appropriateness of international

[29] Rawls, *The Law of Peoples*, 80n. A page or so earlier (79), Rawls offered an even more restricted list: 'a special class of urgent rights, such as freedom from slavery and serfdom, liberty (but not equal liberty) of conscience, and security of ethnic groups from mass murder and genocide'.

intervention makes most sense when it is applied to large clusters of individual rights. And probably that is a sensible limitation on what is now known as 'humanitarian intervention'. It is, in Rawls' phrase, the '*systematic* violation of these rights' that trumps sovereignty: the normal principle of non-intervention does not apply to states where 'serious violations of human rights are *endemic*'.[30] Charles Beitz says something similar: 'a society's failure to respect its people's rights *on a sufficiently large scale* may provide a reason for outside agents to do something'.[31] But these practical and sensible limits on humanitarian intervention should not be used to narrow our understanding of human rights themselves.

The final objection to the Rawlsian conception has been stated by David Miller. When the international community does intervene, either formally or forcefully, against violations in a particular state, the intervention is usually justified on the grounds that it is human rights that are being violated by the state in question. The complaint that human rights are being violated is not just a way of intimating intervention; it is characteristically a way of justifying intervention. But then there must be some distinct content that talk of human rights brings to the justificatory table. One must be able to say why human rights violations are wrong and use that account to provide a substantive justification of intervention. The former is not just a way of intimating the latter. As David Miller puts it, the argument '*begins* with human rights violations, and *ends* with reasons to infringe sovereignty'.[32] We need to know what count as human rights in order to get the political argument underway, and it must be something about the rights that makes us think intervention is appropriate. It looks like we have no alternative, then, but to countenance an understanding of human rights along the lines of that sketched out in Section 4.

7 Important Rights

Joseph Raz has remarked that there is no guarantee that human rights are important if they are understood along the lines of Section 4: 'Neither being universal, that is rights that everyone has, nor being grounded in our

[30] J. Rawls, 'The law of peoples' in the Belgrade Circle (ed.), *The Politics of Human Rights* (Verso, 1999) 32 (my emphasis) and Rawls, *The Law of Peoples*, 38 (my emphasis).

[31] C.R. Beitz, *The Idea of Human Rights* (Oxford University Press, 2009)105–6 (my emphasis).

[32] Miller, 'Joseph Raz on human rights', 235 (emphasis in the original).

humanity, guarantees that they are important'.[33] Part of our response to this should be to say that the guarantee that human rights are important comes mainly from their being *rights* – that is, it comes from the identification of individual interests whose importance is sufficient to justify holding other people to be under a duty. No trivial consideration can pass that test.

The point is not only that *duties* are justified in this way, but that they are justified on the grounds of the importance of *individual* interests, considered apart from the aggregate (e.g. utilitarian) desirability of protecting them. Indeed, the duties that are generated in this way may have priority over duties generated out of aggregate considerations. It is common to say that rights are trumps over utility: an individual has a right when some interest of his or hers is important enough to warrant imposing a duty to protect it even at the cost of what would normally be a decisive consideration of the collective interest.[34] If a right, considered as such, is important enough to do that, it is probably important enough to have a pretty powerful presence in the law that embodies it.

That said, we may agree with Raz that human rights charters do characteristically include rights that the world community regards as important. This need not be definitional, though; perhaps it is more a matter of the pragmatics of legislation and covenant-framing. We invest energy in the framing of bills of rights and in the eliciting of support from the international community in order to highlight the more urgent duties that governments are under, to bring into focus the more important individual interests that underlie these duties, and to rivet attention on the individual rights and interests that time and experience have shown are particularly vulnerable and that international and constitutional law are capable of doing something about.

Raz, I think, is wrong to see the importance of human rights as nothing more than a reflex of the momentousness of the sanctions associated with rights violations: '[H]uman rights are inevitably morally important', he says, for '[i]f they were not they would not warrant interference in state sovereignty'.[35] Their importance does have a political dimension, but it is

[33] Raz, 'Human rights without foundations', 323.

[34] This way of putting the point is adapted from R. Dworkin, *Taking Rights Seriously* (Harvard University press, 1977), 191–2.

[35] Raz, 'Human rights without foundations', 337.

the politics of the framing and ratification of rights covenants not the politics of interference with sovereignty.

8 Moral Rights?

I have proceeded throughout this chapter on the basis that human rights are a sub-class of legal rights, distinguished by the range of their application or by their importance or by the remedies associated with their violation. In all of this, is it a mistake to have neglected the view that human rights are, in the first instance, *moral* rights – rights recognised by morality?

The advantage of such a view is that it would indicate an isomorphic vantage point from which a given legal charter – like the ICCPR or the UK's Human Rights Act – can be evaluated, both for what it includes and for what it leaves out. Moral rights would have the same shape as legal rights, and so it would be easy to compare them. Thus, we could have resort to a list of moral rights and see whether our legal list 'mirrors' that in some appropriate way.[36] Or rather, since not all moral rights will be rights attributed to people on the grounds of their humanity, we will work with a list of moral *human* rights as a standard for testing the adequacy of our list of *legal* human rights. James Griffin does this in his book *On Human Rights*; he constructs a list of moral rights and then he uses that to highlight 'striking discrepancies' between his own list and the lists contained in documents like the UDHR, the ICCPR and ICESCR.[37]

We certainly need some such standard, because no body of positive law is self-justifying. Human rights law has what some jurists have described as a distinctively suprapositive aspect. Gerald Neuman puts it this way:

> Positive fundamental rights embodied in a legal system are often conceived as reflections of non-legal principles that have normative force independent of their embodiment in law, or even superior to the positive legal system . . . The alternative normative systems may include natural law, religious traditions, universal

[36] A. Buchanan talks (critically) of the 'mirroring view' in his book, *The Heart of Human Rights* (Oxford University Press, 2013), 17–23. See also A. Buchanan, 'Why international legal human rights?' in Cruft et al. (eds.) *Philosophical Foundations of Human Rights*, 244, at 245–9. For a response to this critique, see J. Tasioulas, 'Human rights' in A. Marmor (ed.), *The Routledge Companion to the Philosophy of Law* (Routledge, 2012), 348.

[37] J. Griffin, *On Human Rights* (Oxford University Press, 2008), 194.

morality, or the fundamental ethical values of a particular culture. The legal rights are sometimes described as positivisations or concretisations of pre-existing supra-positive norms, or legal provisions are explained as merely recognising pre-existing suprapositive rights. The suprapositive force of the norms provides one source of legitimation for the enforcement of the legal norms. Reference to the assumed content of the suprapositive norms may provide one source of guidance in the interpretation of the legal norms.[38]

But I wonder whether it is necessary here to posit moral human rights or even natural rights as suprapositive counterparts to legal human rights. There is no particular logical difficulty in doing so. If we can talk of moral duties, we can talk of moral rights. Nonetheless it is worth considering some of the things that were said in Jeremy Bentham's well-known diatribe against natural rights as 'nonsense upon stilts'. Bentham said:

In proportion to the want of happiness resulting from the want of rights, a reason exists for wishing that there were such things as rights. But reasons for wishing there were such things as rights, are not rights; – a reason for wishing that a certain right were established, is not that right – want is not supply – hunger is not bread.[39]

It is possible for us to develop a moral theory of human rights which consists in reasons for thinking that we should formulate and proclaim certain norms as legal human rights without necessarily thinking of those reasons as rights themselves. No doubt we should hesitate when Bentham intimates that those reasons will usually be utilitarian in character – that is, when he says that the proper task is to ask

not what are our natural rights, but what in each instance ought to be our legal ones upon the principle of utility, that is, what are the rights which, in each instance, it would be for the happiness of the community that the law should create, and what means it should employ to secure us in the possession of them.[40]

Since – as we believe, though Bentham did not – rights and human rights have trumping work to do, we will not normally be looking to justify them on the basis of utilitarian considerations. But that does not mean that the only moral considerations in play are themselves to be regarded as rights.

[38] Neuman, 'Human rights and constitutional rights: harmony and dissonance', 1868.

[39] J. Bentham, 'Anarchical fallacies' in Waldron, *Nonsense upon Stilts*, 46, at 53.

[40] J. Bentham, 'Supply without burthen or escheat *vice* taxation' in Waldron, *Nonsense upon Stilts*, 70, at 75n.

Perhaps we should say that any moral consideration that argues directly in favour of a legal human right must necessarily be a moral human right. I am not sure what I think about that. All I know is that if there are moral considerations that argue for the inclusion of a putative legal human right, which cannot itself be represented as a moral right, we should pay attention to it nonetheless. What is most important is that we include in our charters of rights those rights that there is most reason to include, not just those that can be represented as moral rights.

At the end of Section 4, I observed that philosophers are interested in the possibility that human rights can be derived from the importance of values like equality, dignity or autonomy. (James Griffin, for example, seeks to show that a full theory of human rights can be derived from the importance of human personhood and the associated principle of autonomy.)[41] There is nothing wrong with such a project: these abstract values are highly significant and it is well worthwhile tracing out their implications. But human rights, as a body of law and practice, is a matter of political argument. The propositions that figure in documents like the ICCPR and the ICESCR represent the conclusions of a variety of arguments, generally accepted in the world, about the ways in which governments can pose a threat to and/or secure protection for individual interests that we have reason to regard as important. Now, human individuals are complicated entities and so are their relations with governments. There are many different aspects to their vulnerability and many different things that they might hope for or expect from those set in authority over them. We try to set these various things out in normative arguments. Some of those arguments yield moral propositions that can be stated snappily in something like a rights format; others require paragraphs or treatises. But the latter can be as much arguments for legal human rights as the former. And our rights declarations represent in conclusory form the accumulated heritage of such arguments, which have come to us in successive phases of political concern. Sometimes the concerns are about pain; sometimes they are about property. The concerns are sometimes liberal, sometimes democratic, and sometimes socialist. There are concerns of all sorts, made articulate in our traditions in lots of different ways.

Human rights, I said earlier, come to us in the form of lists and I think we should respect that mode of presentation. There seems to be no particular

[41] Griffin, *On Human Rights*, 149ff.

reason why the right not to be tortured is Article 7 of the ICCPR and Article 5 of the UDHR; no reason either why freedom of religion is postponed until Article 8 of the UDHR whereas it is included as Article 4 of the ICCPR. Rights in our bills and covenants are just one damned thing after another. They are all rights of individuals but each represents a particular concern. And the lists on which they appear are practical documents: when we are faced with a violation or an alleged violation, it is incumbent on us to focus our concern on the particular right at stake and its particular importance to the individuals who are supposed to bear it, without prejudice to the speculative possibility of its derivation from some other overarching value that unites it with other items on the list.

9 Equality and Discrimination

Sophia Moreau*

Ever since the publication of John Rawls' *A Theory of* Justice in 1971, Anglo-American philosophers have discussed the nature of equality and its place in a theory of distributive justice.[1] They have asked whether it is equality per se that is valuable, or priority for those who are worst off, or perhaps sufficiency – that is, ensuring that each person has enough.[2] They have also asked about the 'currency' of egalitarian justice: what is it that should be distributed equally? Is it welfare, resources, opportunities, or perhaps what Amartya Sen called 'capabilities'?[3] In response, philosophers such as Elizabeth Anderson, Samuel Scheffler and Joshua Cohen have argued that it is a mistake to think of the value of equality solely in distributive terms.[4] Rather, within a democratic society, we need to aim at relational equality – that is, relationships of equal status, in which no one is unfairly subordinated to others. Relational equality requires the redistribution of certain goods; so it is not unrelated to distributive equality. But from the standpoint of relational

* For helpful comments on earlier drafts, I am grateful to audiences at Berkeley School of Law and at the University of Toronto, and especially to Joshua Cohen, Niko Kolodny, Veronique Munoz-Darde and John Tasioulas. Many thanks to Andy Yu for helpful research assistance.

[1] J. Rawls, *A Theory of Justice* (Harvard University Press, 1971).

[2] D. Parfit, 'Equality or priority?' *Ratio* 10:3 (1997), 202–21; H. Frankfurt, 'Equality as a moral ideal' in *The Importance of What We Care About* (Cambridge University Press, 1988), 134–58; M. Otsuka and A. Voorhoeve, 'Why it matters that some are worse off than others: an argument against the priority view', *Philosophy and Public Affairs* 37 (2009), 171–99.

[3] See, for example, G.A. Cohen, 'On the currency of egalitarian justice', *Ethics* 99 (1989), 906–44; R. Dworkin, 'Equality of welfare' and 'Equality of resources' in *Sovereign Virtue: Equality in Theory and Practice* (Harvard University Press, 2000); A. Sen, 'Equality of what?' in *Choice, Welfare and Measurement* (MIT Press, 1982), 353–69; A. Sen, *Inequality Reexamined* (Harvard University Press, 1992).

[4] See E. Anderson, 'What is the point of equality?', *Ethics* 109 (1999), 287–337; and Anderson, 'The fundamental disagreement between luck egalitarians and relational egalitarians', *Canadian Journal of Philosophy*, Supp. Vol. 36 (2010), 1–23; J. Cohen, 'Democratic equality', *Ethics* 99 (1989), 727–51; S. Scheffler, *Boundaries and Allegiances: Problems of Justice and Responsibility in Liberal Thought* (Oxford University Press, 2003). See also K.L. Rasmussen, *Relational Egalitarianism* (Cambridge University Press, 2018).

equality, particular distributive goals matter only insofar as they help us achieve a society in which no one is relegated to the status of a second-class citizen. And to achieve such a society, we need to pay particular attention not just to how various goods are distributed, but also to inappropriate expressions of deference toward certain groups and censure of others, and to policies and structures that inadvertently leave certain groups unable to see themselves as full and equal participants in society.

This description of relational equality sounds very much like a description of the aims of discrimination law. Most preambles to anti-discrimination statutes indicate that the purpose of such legislation is to prevent the unfair subordination of certain members of society and to create a climate in which people publicly recognise each other as deserving of equal respect. Discrimination laws apply not only to the state – through constitutional rights or statutes requiring non-discrimination by the government – but also to ordinary individuals, and in particular to those individuals who have power over other people's access to basic social institutions, such as places of employment and education, and providers of goods and services. So these laws do seem to aim at ensuring, not just that the state treats us as equals, but that we treat each other as equals, giving everyone equal access to these basic social institutions without showing undue deference to some groups or undue censure of others. Discrimination law also aims to rectify certain distributive injustices, both between individuals and between groups. Those who have been unfairly denied certain goods are given them or their monetary equivalent. The discriminator is usually required to adjust his policies so that in the future, similar injustices will not occur. And sometimes quotas are imposed, for the benefit of the broader group marked out by a particular ground of discrimination.

It may therefore seem surprising that discrimination and discrimination law have not been a part of our mainstream philosophical discussions about equality.[5] Instead, they have been treated as a specialised area that

[5] There was a moment of interest by philosophers in affirmative action in the mid 1970s – see for instance T. Nagel, 'Equal treatment and compensatory discrimination', *Philosophy and Public Affairs* 2:4 (1973), 348–63, J.J. Thomson , 'Preferential hiring', *Philosophy and Public Affairs* 2:4 (1973), 364–84 and R. Dworkin, 'Reverse discrimination', ch. 9 in *Taking Rights Seriously* (Harvard University Press, 1977), 223–39. But these articles were not preoccupied with the broader question of what discrimination is and why it is wrong. Rather, they focused on the narrower issue of whether preferential hiring is unjust because it seems to depart from equality of opportunity.

does not hold much of interest to philosophers who are working on broader debates about the nature and value of equality. It is only recently that moral and political philosophers have taken an interest in discrimination and have initiated a debate about why it is wrong or unfair and what the purpose of discrimination law is.

Why was this, and why has the situation changed? How do current debates among philosophers working on discrimination law relate to the debates about distributive and relational equality that I have just mentioned? And what are the most pressing currently unresolved issues in the philosophy of discrimination? These are the questions I shall be addressing in this chapter.

1 An Expanding Conception of Discrimination

I suspect that the main reason why there was so little philosophical interest in discrimination for so long was that most philosophers held a narrow view of what discrimination consists in. We might, following Tarunabh Khaitan, call it the 'lay' conception of discrimination, because it is a view that many members of the public still hold today.[6] It has its roots in the older discrimination laws of the 1960s and 1970s. On this view, an agent wrongfully discriminates when he disadvantages a certain group of people because he holds an objectionable attitude toward them or an objectionable belief about them. What makes discrimination wrong, on this view, is the mental state that motivates it. Some of the first accounts that philosophers offered of discrimination were essentially just a more precise articulation of this lay conception, tracing the moral wrongness of discrimination back to certain objectionable mental states.[7]

If this is all that discrimination involves, it is unsurprising that philosophers thought it had little to do with philosophical debates about equality. If discrimination is wrong because of the agent's motives, and not because of how it distributes any particular good, then it does not seem to have much

[6] T. Khaitan, *A Theory of Discrimination Law* (Oxford University Press, 2015).

[7] For Richard Arneson, it was an attitude of 'unwarranted animus or prejudice'; on Larry Alexander's view, it was 'a bias premised on the belief that some people are morally worthier than others'; for Matt Cavanagh, it was 'unwarranted contempt'. See R. Arneson, 'What is wrongful discrimination?', *San Diego Law Review* 43 (2006), 775; L. Alexander, 'What makes wrongful discrimination wrong?', *University of Pennsylvania Law Review* 141 (1992), 149–219; M. Cavanagh, *Against Equality of Opportunity* (Clarendon Press, 2002).

to do with distributive justice. Moreover, the lay conception of discrimination seems of limited relevance even to relational egalitarianism. It may capture the most heinous cases of failing to treat others as equals, such as the Jim Crow laws – cases in which people exclude others out of contempt or a belief in their inferiority. But there are many ways in which our acts and policies can work to deny others equal status, even if we have no animosity toward them and no belief that they are less worthy than others.

The lay conception of discrimination, and the early mental state accounts developed from it, are now generally regarded as inadequate – even by the philosophers who originally defended them.[8] It is worth understanding why. For the reasons tell us how much our conception of discrimination has expanded since the 1960s and 1970s, and they point to some of the difficulties facing attempts to theorise about discrimination.

First, most social scientists and lawmakers now accept that much of the discrimination that occurs in our societies involves 'implicit bias' against certain groups, rather than contempt for them or a belief in their inferiority. One can act from implicit bias even when one sincerely believes that one is showing proper respect – as judges do, for instance, when they believe they are treating all those convicted of crimes of the same level of seriousness in the same way, but give longer sentences to those African Americans who have more prominent Afro-centric features, such as darker skin, a wider nose and larger lips.[9]

A second reason why the lay conception of discrimination is inadequate is that many discriminatory acts seem to be morally troubling for reasons quite apart from the agent's mental state. Sometimes, the

[8] See L. Alexander, 'Review: *Philosophical Foundations of Discrimination Law*' in *Ethics* 125:3 (2015), 872–9, who explicitly recants his earlier view; and R. Arneson, 'Discrimination, disparate impact and theories of justice' in D. Hellman and S. Moreau (eds.) *Philosophical Foundations of Discrimination Law* (Oxford University Press, 2013). Arneson does not explicitly renounce his earlier view, but endorses a different prioritarian view in this later article.

[9] See I. Blair, C. Judd and K. Chapleau, 'The influence of Afrocentric facial features in criminal sentencing', *Psychological Science* 15:10 (October 2004), 674–9. That wrongful discrimination can result from implicit bias is recognised within many legal jurisdictions. In fact, when the UK drafted its *Equality Act* (2010, c. 15), it chose to define direct discrimination without explicit reference to intention, stipulating that someone discriminates when 'because of a protected characteristic, A treats B less favourably than A treats or would treat others' – thus allowing tribunals and judges to look at factors other than the agent's intention or sincerely avowed beliefs in determining whether he has treated another person less favourably 'because of' a certain trait.

unfairness seems instead to concern what the act expresses. A general policy of placing wheelchair-accessible entrances to public buildings out of sight at the back of the building says something about the place of people with disabilities in our society and about the worth we think they have. It expresses certain messages: that requiring people with disabilities to take extra time to go around the back of the building is not an undue imposition on them because they are less productive than the rest of us; that it is fine to prioritise aesthetics over the needs of this group; that people with disabilities are, quite literally, 'invisible'. These messages are expressed by the policy regardless of whether they reflect the intentions or beliefs of the individuals who have adopted this policy. For a policy's expressive significance depends not on the agent's mental states, but on such factors as social conventions and the material effects of particular acts and rules.[10]

Third, the lay conception of discrimination is problematic because it has very little to say about the effects of discriminatory acts on the *victims* of discrimination. No one, when asked why it is important to eliminate discrimination, would say, 'It's about those privileged Caucasians and their motives!' Our main concern is to rectify an apparent injustice to the individuals who are excluded and, more broadly, to the social groups marked out by prohibited grounds of discrimination. So to offer an account of this injustice that does not refer to any effects on these groups seems problematic. Excluding people from jobs, goods and services, or public institutions because of their race or gender or sexual orientation has very real and detrimental effects. It deprives them of equal standing in society; it lowers their well-being; it denies them certain negative freedoms; and it prevents them from achieving autonomy; it lowers their self-esteem. One of the most difficult and unresolved questions for philosophers writing on discrimination today is how we should think about

[10] That such expressive meanings are relevant to whether a policy is wrongfully discriminatory is now legally recognised in many jurisdictions. In fact, even the relatively narrow protections offered by the American Fourteenth Amendment have been interpreted as prohibiting not just exclusions that are troubling because of the state's intentions, but also classifications that are troubling because of what they stand for or express. See the discussion of the Equal Protection Clause in E. Anderson and R. Pildes, 'Expressive theories of law: a general restatement', *University of Pennsylvania Law Review* 148:5 (2000), 1504, esp. at 1533–44; and see F. Schauer, *Profiles, Probabilities and Stereotypes*, and in particular ch. 5, 'The women of the Virginia Military Institute' (Belknap Press, 2006).

the moral relevance of these different effects and how they should be incorporated into a coherent theory of why discrimination is wrong. No one now denies that they matter. The question is: how?

A fourth problem with the lay conception of discrimination concerns a further expansion in our legal understanding of discrimination. Over the past twenty years, most jurisdictions have recognised that the subordination of particular social groups is sustained not just by acts of deliberate or racial exclusion, but by a variety of institutional policies and practices, many of which have innocuous aims but end up inadvertently imposing larger disadvantages on members of these groups and reinforcing stereotypes about them. Consequently, most jurisdictions now recognise two forms of discrimination. There is the kind that I have been discussing up to this point, which is often intentional or explicit – which we call 'direct discrimination' (or, in the USA, 'disparate treatment'). In cases of direct discrimination, a person is excluded because of a certain protected trait and the exclusion is generally explicit or 'facial' (on the face of the policy) and recognised by the agent, even if it is not desired or done out of malice. But there is also a second form of discrimination that is legally recognised. It is called 'indirect discrimination', and it occurs where a person or group is indirectly disadvantaged because of a protected trait. In cases of indirect discrimination, the policy causing the disadvantage is usually adopted for unrelated and often innocuous reasons, and the fact that the policy has this disadvantageous effect on particular individuals and groups is usually not known in advance.[11] Obviously, not all policies that have indirectly

[11] I have tried in this paragraph to offer relatively clear definitions of direct and indirect discrimination; but the boundaries between them can blur, in ways that make coming up with a definition that is both legally accurate and morally compelling rather like trying to work with 'ooblek' (the substance made from cornstarch and water, which is sometimes a solid but turns to a liquid when you try to hold it tightly between your fingers). Direct discrimination usually involves a policy that explicitly or 'facially' excludes a protected group; but a policy might identify a group by a certain trait that is not itself a protected trait, but that is so closely connected with a protected trait that we treat it under the law as direct discrimination. Do we do that because in such cases we think of the exclusion as something that the agent of direct discrimination *does*, as part of his action, and does the difference between direct and indirect discrimination lie in the 'closeness' of the disadvantageous effects to what the agent has done? If it does, then the difference between the two forms of discrimination seems to be a matter of degree rather than of kind. For various attempts to make sense of the distinction between direct and indirect discrimination, see the papers in T. Khaitan and H. Collins (eds.), *Foundations of Indirect Discrimination Law* (Hart Publishing, 2018).

disadvantageous effects on protected groups are morally troubling: in some cases, the policy is necessary and what we want to say about it is not that it amounts to unfair discrimination, but that, though unfortunate, it is justifiable. Its effects on a minority group are, we might say, a misfortune rather than an injustice. Because indirect discrimination is sometimes morally justifiable, most legal systems allow that in cases of indirect discrimination, there are certain justifications available. If an alleged discriminator successfully makes out such a justification, he can continue to use the policy in question. But in order to succeed, he must show that the disadvantage is proportionate, considering all of the interests affected, and the overall aim of the policy legitimate.

This expanded conception of discrimination is much more difficult to theorise about in a coherent way. It raises a number of hard questions, questions which have fascinated philosophers currently writing on discrimination, but on which they continue to disagree.

Perhaps the most fundamental question concerns which of the morally troubling features of discriminatory acts and policies actually render them unfair. The demeaning messages they express? Their failure to show proper respect for others? Or the effects on the victims' freedom? Or on the victims' well-being? Different philosophers' answers to this fundamental question have implications for whether, on their views, discrimination is primarily a problem of distributive injustice or primarily a problem of relational inequality. Those who see discrimination as unfair because of the harms that it causes to people's well-being tend to see it as a tool of distributive justice. But others – both those who focus on the demeaning or disrespectful nature of discriminatory acts and some of those who focus on the freedom that it denies to victims – see discrimination primarily as a failure to relate to others in the right way.

This fundamental question of why discrimination is wrong is complicated because philosophers have asked it with two very different purposes in mind. Some philosophers, notably legal scholars, are looking for a special feature of discrimination that would explain the distinctive way in which discriminatory acts are wrongful or unfair and would justify at least the basic outlines of our discrimination laws. By contrast, other philosophers, notably 'desert-accommodating prioritarians', hold a general moral theory according to which any act is wrong if, and only if, it fails to maximise moral value in the world. If this is true, then there is no need for a special theory of discrimination. The aim of these philosophers is to demonstrate that we can explain the wrongness of discrimination using their more general moral theory. Insofar as their general moral theory conflicts with particular doctrines within discrimination law, this just shows, in their view, that the law does not always track the moral truth about discrimination.

Buried in these discussions of what makes discrimination wrong or unfair is also a difficult set of questions about the relationship between direct and indirect discrimination. Many philosophers initially writing on discrimination simply assumed that the relevant data set included only cases of direct discrimination – that is, exclusions that occur on the basis of a protected trait and are explicit or intentional or known about by the agent. But some of their theories also apply to at least some cases of indirect discrimination – that is, disadvantage that indirectly results from a policy and affects particular groups because they possess a protected trait. So we need to look, not just at what a theory assumes its object to be, but at what it actually implies about cases of direct and indirect discrimination. Some theories imply that, although not all cases of direct and indirect discrimination are wrongful, *when* they are wrongful, this is for the same kind of reason. Other theories apply only to direct discrimination. Proponents of these theories might maintain that indirect discrimination is unfair in a derivative or a different way – or that it is not unfair at all but is simply unfortunate, something that it might be good to rectify but not something that any individual or group has a claim of justice on others to rectify.

2 Theories of Discrimination and Discrimination Law

One prominent group of theories about why discrimination is wrongful or unfair appeals to a certain kind of failure of recognition in discriminatory acts. Some of these theories are concerned specifically with the expressive value of discriminatory acts. Anderson and Pildes, for instance, have argued that discriminatory acts impose 'expressive harms', sending messages of 'contempt, hostility, or inappropriate paternalism' about certain groups.[12] Deborah Hellman combines this focus on the expressive dimension of discriminatory acts with a requirement that the act also actually

[12] Anderson and Pildes, 'Expressive theories of law: a general restatement'.

lower a person's status: she suggests that discriminatory acts 'demean' the groups marked out by protected traits, in the special sense that they both send the message that these people are inferior and also have the actual effect of lowering their status.[13] Other theorists, such as John Gardner, focus less on the expressive value of the discriminatory act and more on the agent's failure of recognition and what this does to the relationship between the discriminator and the discriminatee.[14] Ben Eidelson has argued that discrimination is intrinsically wrongful insofar as it fails to recognise someone's full standing as a person.[15]

These philosophers present their theories as accounts of the wrongfulness or unfairness of direct discrimination only, and not as accounts of indirect discrimination; not for philosophical reasons, but because they start from the legal definition of direct discrimination and offer their account as a conception that will explain the wrongness of discrimination, so conceived. However, the particular lack of recognition that makes direct discrimination wrongful on their views is often present in cases of unfair indirect discrimination as well. Consider an example. Some national health care systems require proof of address in order for patients to register with a doctor or to register at a hospital. Suppose that such a country has just experienced a huge influx of refugees from a certain ethnic minority in a neighbouring country, and suppose it also has a large itinerant Roma population. The policy will make it much harder for these ethnic minorities to obtain health care, so this will constitute indirect racial discrimination. Does it involve a failure of recognition of an objectionable sort, according to such theories as Anderson's, Hellman's or Eidelson's? It might well. We would expect a reasonable government to be aware of the plight of such ethnic groups and to factor it into their deliberations, and a failure to do this would demonstrate a failure to take their interests and their status as people seriously.

[13] D. Hellman, *When Is Discrimination Wrong?* (Harvard University Press, 2011).

[14] J. Gardner, 'On the ground of her sex(uality)', *Oxford Journal of Legal Studies*, 18 (1998) 167–87; 'Liberals and unlawful discrimination', *Oxford Journal of Legal Studies* 9 (1989) 1–22; 'Discrimination as injustice', *Oxford Journal of Legal Studies* 16:3 (1996) 353.

[15] B. Eidelson, *Discrimination and Disrespect* (Oxford University Press, 2015). Eidelson has a complex account of what it is to recognise someone's full standing as a person – but it requires, at a minimum, that we treat them both as someone whose interests must be given their proper weight in our deliberations and also as someone whose autonomy must be respected.

And insofar as the message that such a policy sends is that these people are disposable and do not merit proper health care, it also seems to demean them and to perpetuate their lower status.

If I am right, then some (if not much) of indirect discrimination is covered by these recognition-based accounts of the wrongness of discrimination. This is not a problem, though it should be acknowledged. It accords with the practice, in our legal systems, of treating as 'direct' those instances of what would otherwise be indirect discrimination in which a group is excluded based on some trait that is very closely connected to the exclusionary trait. What proponents of recognition-based accounts ought to say about the rest of indirect discrimination – that is, those cases that do not involve a failure of recognition of the relevant kind – is not clear. They might argue, as Hellman has tried to do, that these forms of indirect discrimination involve at most a derivative injustice, which depends on 'compounding' the injustice of past instances of direct discrimination.[16] Or they might argue, as John Gardner and Ben Eidelson have done, that if an instance of discrimination does not fail to recognise others in the relevant way, then it is not wrongful or unjust; though there may still be some reason to prohibit it legally, in order to ensure that disadvantaged groups are given a larger share of resources and opportunities.[17]

All of the theories that I have grouped together here as recognition-based theories capture what I think is a key moral intuition about discrimination. This is that it involves not just a failure to give certain things to people – resources, jobs, opportunities, even increases in well-being – but a failure to recognise their equal standing as fellow members of society. I think this is what outrages us most about discriminatory acts, and it is a kind of outrage that is a quite distinctive response to acts of discrimination. There are many acts that we view as objectionable because they distribute certain goods unfairly and give some people less than others or less than they deserve. But when we see photographs of the Ku Klux Klan, or when we hear that in some legal systems a woman's testimony is worth half or one-third that of a man, we feel a distinctive kind of outrage. We

[16] D. Hellman, 'Indirect discrimination and the duty to avoid compounding injustice', ch. 5 of *Foundations of Indirect Discrimination Law*, 105–22.

[17] See Gardner, 'On the ground of her sex(uality)' and Eidelson, *Discrimination and Disrespect*.

feel that some people are failing to recognise others appropriately, failing to give them full or equal social standing.

There are, however, at least two difficulties that recognition-based accounts encounter. One is that they lack a detailed account of social subordination. If I am right that the key moral intuition underlying these theories is that discriminatory acts unfairly create or perpetuate the idea that there are different classes of people in society – then they owe us a more detailed account of what such unfair subordination consists in. It is not enough to speak in the abstract about 'lowering someone's status' – as though we can read someone's status as easily as we can tell their hair colour. We need a more detailed theory of social subordination, of what it is for individuals and groups to have a certain status in society, of how exactly this status can be lowered, and of when such lowering counts as unfair subordination.[18]

Another difficulty with recognition-based accounts is that they seem to overlook certain aspects of victims' complaints. Victims of discrimination do not just want to be recognised as equals and given equal social standing. They also want access to the goods that are at issue in particular cases of discrimination: the promotions, the pensions, the institution of marriage. And they want the freedom to be able to make choices and shape their own lives without worrying about the costs imposed on them by other people's assumptions about such traits as their ethnicity or gender. Why shouldn't we suppose that these too are genuine sources of the unfairness of discrimination, as victims think?

Another group of theories of discrimination that focus on only one aspect of discrimination are the desert-accommodating prioritarian theories that have recently been developed by Kasper Lippert-Rasmussen and Richard Arneson. These theories foreground the distributive impact of discrimination, rather than the lack of recognition that it might show. Their proponents endorse a general moral theory according to which the right action is the action that maximises moral value, and they also hold

[18] Developing a rigorous account of subordination is more difficult than it might seem. Clearly, subordination involves being treated as inferior to others. But not just any treatment of people as inferior counts as subordination: if one group is genuinely less skilled in a certain respect, then one might think that recognising this and treating them accordingly does not count as subordinating them. But perhaps it would count as subordination if the reason that they lacked this skill was that they had been unfairly denied certain resources and certain educational opportunities?

that moral value is often maximised when we raise the well-being of those who are worst off, in circumstances where they are deserving.[19] They do not usually argue for this theory in their writings on discrimination; rather, they identify themselves as proponents of this moral view and then apply it to discrimination.

It is important to note the depth of the disagreement between desert-accommodating prioritarians and recognition-based theorists. They are not disagreeing only over which aspect of discrimination is morally primary. They have adopted two very different approaches to the law and its relationship to morality. Lippert-Rasmussen and Arneson start from a general theory of moral value and suggest that our intuitions about discrimination are morally justified only insofar as they conform to this theory. By contrast, recognition-based theorists are doing something different. They offer their view of discrimination as the best interpretation of the conception of discrimination that underlies our laws. That is, they start from a rough conception of the structure and purpose of our legal rules surrounding discrimination, rules that appear to prohibit actions that are unfair in a distinctive way. They then appeal to the kind of recognition that certain acts and policies fail to involve, in order to explain what this distinctive kind of unfairness consists in.

The desert-accommodating prioritarian theories have some potential problems. The first is a methodological problem, which leads in turn to a problem in the content of the theory. I think that there is something problematic about the desert-accommodating prioritarian's approach of simply taking for granted a certain moral theory and applying it to the context of discrimination, and assuming that insofar as our laws stand in tension with the implications of this moral theory, it is our laws that must be revised. For whatever kind of injustice is involved in discrimination, it seems to me that our understanding of it has been deeply shaped by our legal regimes for regulating it. And in this respect, discrimination is arguably different from certain other moral wrongs, such as failing to keep promises, or murdering. We could imagine developing a detailed and accurate conception of what a promise is and why it is morally important to keep promises even without consulting contract law, or a deep

[19] K. Lippert-Rasmussen, *Born Free and Equal: A Philosophical Inquiry into the Nature of Discrimination* (Oxford University Press, 2014); Arneson, 'Discrimination, disparate impact and theories of justice' in *Philosophical Foundations of Discrimination Law*.

understanding of what murder is and why it is morally wrong without looking at the structure of criminal prohibitions on murder. But it is arguable that our shared public views of what discrimination is and why it is unjust have, in large part, been shaped by domestic and international discrimination laws over the past fifty years. So I am not sure how an account of discrimination and its unfairness could expect to be accurate without considering certain facts about legal prohibitions on discrimination.

One of these facts is that within the law, desert or worthiness, in any substantive moral sense, is irrelevant to an individual's or group's legal right to non-discrimination. There is no stage in the legal analysis of a claim of discrimination at which we ask whether the claimant is either a morally deserving person in general or deserving of the specific benefit at issue. Similarly, whether a trait is recognised as a 'protected' trait under the law does not depend on whether the people who possess such traits are worthy – it depends on other sorts of facts entirely, such as whether those who possess such traits are powerless to change the trait, or whether those who possess that trait have historically been subjected to social exclusion and subordination on the basis of it.

There is also something about the very idea of objectively assessing someone's worth that runs deeply against the grain of discrimination law. Whatever theory of discrimination law we endorse, I think we cannot deny that part of the point of such laws is to avoid placing some people in a position where they are officially pronouncing other people unworthy of a certain redistributive programme, because their misfortune is their own fault. It is unclear whether desert-accommodating prioritarianism could avoid doing this.

But what about the 'prioritarian' component of desert-accommodating prioritarianism? Couldn't one adopt this component as a plausible account of why the elimination of discrimination matters, while rejecting the desert component of these theories? It does seem that part of what is accomplished by prohibitions on discrimination is raising the relative level of well-being of some of the more underprivileged groups in society. However, just because something is an effect of prohibitions on discrimination does not mean this is their ultimate purpose or that it is morally primary. And if our ultimate purpose were to give priority to groups that are worse off, discrimination law would seem a rather clumsy and incomplete way to try to do this. Why single out certain groups rather than others, and protect only those who have been excluded because of certain traits? No jurisdiction recognises poverty as a prohibited ground of discrimination – wouldn't this be the obvious thing to do, if our aim were to give priority to the worst off? Why should we protect only traits such as race and gender and sexual orientation? One is tempted to answer: because these traits marks out groups that have suffered some sort of oppression or subordination. But that is obviously not an answer that is open to the prioritarian, whose sole concern is the distribution of goods, and not the way in which they came to be distributed in that way. Moreover, it is unclear on a prioritarian model why we would ever ask private individuals – employers, providers of goods or services, educational institutions – to cover the costs of discrimination. Or rather, it is unclear how we could ever be justified in doing so. Why is it my responsibility, as an employer, to bear the costs of raising your level of well-being, much less the relative well-being of your group, compared to that of other groups? Wouldn't it be more justifiable if we covered the costs together, through public funds?

This dilemma for prioritarianism emerges in Tarunabh Khaitan's new book, *A Theory of Discrimination Law*.[20] Khaitan cojoins a prioritarian account of why systemic discrimination is objectionable with a supplementary account of what makes individual acts of discrimination into personal wrongs, wrongs by one person against another of a kind that require some kind of rectification and entitle the state to require that this person bear the burden of eliminating the discrimination. Khaitan argues that at the systemic level, the purpose of discrimination law is to eliminate relative disadvantages between social groups, so that everyone has enough of certain basic goods. This account is, strictly speaking, 'sufficientarian', since it holds that discrimination law's ultimate aim is to ensure that everyone has a sufficient amount of these goods to achieve autonomy. But, as Khaitan notes, in order to ensure that everyone has a sufficient amount, we will need to focus on those groups that are worse off. So in practice, his view of systemic discrimination is quite close to prioritarianism. However, he holds that particular acts of discrimination amount to personal wrongs against particular victims not because they fail to give priority to the worst off, but because 'they impose costs on membership of groups whose membership is morally irrelevant'.[21]

[20] T. Khaitan, *A Theory of Discrimination Law* (Oxford University Press, 2015).
[21] Ibid., 168.

Khaitan does not say very much about how the supplementary account of discrimination as a personal wrong is supposed to cohere with the prioritarian account of systemic discrimination, or why the supplementary account is necessary in the first place. I wonder whether it seems necessary to him because he doubts whether the kinds of group disadvantages that the prioritarian account invokes are sufficient to generate a personal duty on the discriminator not to discriminate. But if this is correct, then the supplementary account risks occupying the entire moral space and pushing out the prioritarian account. For if it is the supplementary account that really explains why discriminators have a personal duty toward particular victims not to discriminate, then it is unclear why we need any other explanation of why discrimination is wrong or unjust.

I think the difficulty here is not just a difficulty within Khaitan's theory. I think it emerges because he is honest enough to portray accurately two strands in our thought and our laws about discrimination that pull us in different directions. It is true, as the desert-accommodating prioritarians suggest, that discrimination leads certain groups to be worse off than others, and that part of what we care about is the redistributive goal of giving certain goods to these underprivileged groups. But we also think of discrimination as a personal wrong, involving the maltreatment of one person by another. This is where the recognition theorists would argue the role of recognition comes into play. What makes discrimination a personal wrong, they would say, is that it involves a failure to give someone else an equal standing in society, without subordination.

In my view, this suggests that we may need a pluralist account of discrimination, one that appeals to a number of the different facets of discrimination that I have discussed. But any pluralist account would owe us an explanation of how these different wrong-making features of discrimination work, and of how they cohere. Perhaps it is each person's entitlement to equal standing that explains why we have a personal duty not to discriminate against others. And perhaps the need to give priority to those who are worse off provides a further moral reason for not discriminating. But if it does, how exactly do these different moral reasons interact? Is each of them weighty enough to render an action wrong, if it is present? Or must both of them be present in all cases of discrimination in order to render the act or policy wrong or unjust?

Before I turn to these questions in the final section of the paper, I want to note the role of another factor in discrimination, a factor which we have not yet considered. It is the importance of the freedoms that are denied to those who face discrimination. We have seen how recognition-based theories locate the wrong of discrimination in subordination or a lack of equal standing, whereas prioritarian theories tend to locate it in the failure to give priority to those who are 'worst off', where 'worst off' is most often understood in terms of level of welfare. But a number of philosophers writing on discrimination have understood its wrongfulness in terms of another value: freedom. Just as some political philosophers have argued that we can understand the value of equality not as a value in competition with the value of liberty but as a way of guaranteeing each citizen the freedom that they are entitled to, so some philosophers writing on discrimination have suggested that the kind of equal treatment that is at issue here is best understood in terms of the value of freedom. Khaitan is one of these. His sufficientarian-prioritarian account is unlike the other prioritarian accounts I examined earlier in that for him, the social groups that are 'worst off' in the relevant sense are those that lack the basic goods (such as self-respect and a range of valuable activities from which to choose) necessary for *autonomy*. So on Khaitan's view, discrimination law ultimately protects an equal right to the conditions necessary for autonomy.

The relevance of freedom to discrimination becomes clear, I think, when we think of the severe and pervasive ways in which members of subordinated groups are affected by discrimination. Discrimination does not just deny you a job because of your race, or deny you a chance to ride public transit because you are in a wheelchair. It places a considerable burden on you and on all of your deliberations, attaching higher costs to certain options, restricting others, and requiring you constantly to factor in the assumptions that other people and their policies make about you – that being disabled, you have time to go around to the back of the building since your work can't be terribly important anyway; that if you are black and appear at school to pick someone up, you must be a nanny; that everyone has a wife at home to take their kids to school for them when work meetings start at 8:30am. What makes living so difficult and so dispiriting for members of groups that suffer from longstanding discrimination, and what leaves them unable to see themselves as equal participants in society, is not just that they have fewer jobs and fewer resources. It is that unlike other people, their lives consist in constantly having to navigate around other people's policies and assumptions, the way a wheelchair-user must navigate around bumps on the pavement. This intuition is what underlies my own early account of discrimination as a denial of deliberative freedom.[22] On this view, discrimination is a personal wrong insofar as it prevents us from having enough 'deliberative freedom' – that is, enough freedom to deliberate about, and also act on, options that are important to us – to allow us to see ourselves as equal participants in society. I now think that this account, like the others I have canvassed here, captures only part of the truth. We do care very much about giving people deliberative freedom in certain contexts; but we also care just as deeply about eliminating social subordination and ensuring that those who are worst off have access to certain basic opportunities and institutions. So the freedom-based account, like the recognition-based and desert-accommodating prioritarian accounts, is incomplete. Each seems to focus on some of our reasons for eliminating discrimination without sufficiently attending to the others.

3 A Pluralist Theory of Discrimination?

But is it possible to offer a pluralist account of discrimination and discrimination law – one which gives some role to the absence of social subordination, some role to the protection of freedoms, and some role to the effects of discrimination on people's well-being, particularly the well-being of those who are worst off? I think this is one of the key questions for us, as we move beyond our first attempts to grapple philosophically with discrimination. And I think there is room for a coherent but pluralist theory. Instead of arguing that one of these values is morally primary and the others either irrelevant or relevant only as ways of realising the one primary value, could our account not suggest that they are all equally good reasons for eliminating discrimination, and all at least sometimes

[22] See S. Moreau, 'What is discrimination?', *Philosophy and Public Affairs* 38:2 (Spring 2010), 143–79; and 'In defense of a liberty-based account of discrimination' in *Philosophical Foundations of Discrimination Law*. In these articles, I suggested that we do not always have a right to deliberative freedom, but that there is no single explanation of when we have a right to a certain deliberative freedom and when we do not. I now think that someone has a right to a certain deliberative freedom when denying her that freedom would leave her unable to see herself as an equal participant in society. For a defence of this version of the view, as well as an attempt to develop a pluralist theory of the kind sketched in Section 3 of this chapter, see Moreau, *Faces of Inequality* (Oxford University Press, 2020).

wrong-making features of acts of discrimination? As I noted above in Section 2, they do not give us the same kinds of reasons, and so they do not work in the same way, from a moral standpoint. Freedom and equal standing seem to ground a personal duty from the discriminator to particular victims, whereas the general goal of raising the level of those groups who are worst off seems to give us a more general moral reason to perform certain actions, without necessarily generating a claim to any particular goods on the part of particular individuals. But this does not seem an incoherent mix of reasons. It simply stands in need of further explanation and clarification.

One might argue, however, that such a theory of the wrongness of discrimination would not in fact be a theory at all: it would be a mere list of intuitively undesirable effects of discrimination. I suspect that this worry is partly what has led so many philosophers to appeal to one single value or state of affairs as the source of unfairness of all cases of discrimination. But this is to assume that in order to have any explanatory power, an account of why some particular set of acts are wrong or unjust must be reductive and monistic, explaining the wrongness of those acts by tracing it in all cases to one single further value. And why should we assume this? We do not ask this of theories of political justice: a coherent theory of justice can consist, as many liberal theories of justice do, in the conjunction of different but complementary principles, principles which cannot all be traced back to one further value. Nor do we suppose that coherent accounts of particular moral virtues and vices must always be monistic. No one would think it necessary, for instance, to give an account of cruelty that is monistic. Like discrimination, some acts of cruelty are intentional and some are negligent; and like discriminatory acts, cruel acts seem to be cruel both because of the magnitude of their harmful effects on the victim and because of the kind of relationship that the agent sets up between himself and his victim. But there is no one further value that we feel obliged to invoke, in order to offer a unified account of what makes all acts of cruelty cruel. Why then should we suppose that the wrongness or unfairness of discrimination must be reducible to a single further value?

Perhaps underlying this tendency toward reductionism and monism is a worry about potential arbitrariness. Pluralistic and non-reductive theories of discrimination risk appearing arbitrary. Since there is no single further value that they invoke to tie together the different values to which they appeal, it can look as though there is really no reason to appeal to *these* values rather than any other ones. One might wonder: why should we think that discrimination is unjust because of the subordination of certain groups, the effects on the victims' freedom, and the effects on their well-being? Why not think that it is unjust simply because it makes victims lose their self-respect, or simply because it causes them so much pain? One response to this worry about arbitrariness is to point out that the sorts of effects that philosophers have invoked to explain why discrimination is wrong, and that would be a part of a pluralist theory, reflect many years of shared public thought about discrimination, as well as many years of lawmaking and of the kind of political and legal argument that goes into developing case law and statutory law. So our thoughts about discrimination are not arbitrary in the sense that they reflect one philosopher's whims or one afternoon's thought. They reflect many countries' deliberations about these issues, over many years. Is it possible that we could all be collectively wrong about the moral importance of some of these sides of discrimination? Of course it is. But out of all of our available options, a theory that tries to capture the different strands of discrimination, in all their tangled messiness, seems more likely to be true – and more likely to be helpful to us – than one that overly simplifies the phenomenon for the sake of philosophical coherence.

In order to be robust and helpful, our theory would need to be more specific than philosophers writing on discrimination have been up to this point, on several matters. First, as I argued earlier, we need a robust account of subordination: what is it to subordinate certain social groups, to fail to give them equal standing? Second, we need a clearer account of the particular freedoms that seem to be at stake in cases of discrimination. And third, we need an explanation of how these moral reasons interact with the reasons generated by the need to eliminate certain severe and persistent disparities in the resources, opportunities and welfare of those social groups that are worst off.

We also need our theory to offer a more explicit account of the relationship between direct and indirect discrimination. As I suggested earlier, many of the recognition theorists writing on discrimination simply started from the legal definition of direct discrimination and offered their accounts as theories of the wrongness of direct discrimination, without really considering their application to indirect discrimination. I argued earlier that these recognition-based theories actually imply that certain cases of indirect discrimination are wrongful for the same reasons as direct discrimination. Moreover, when we focus, as prioritarian and freedom-based theories do, on the effects of discrimination on its victims, the distinction between direct and indirect discrimination starts to seem like a legal tool that has very little moral significance: for indirect discrimination, just like direct discrimination, affects people's freedoms, and indirect discrimination perpetuates the disadvantages experienced by those who are worst off just as much as do particular acts of direct discrimination. A pluralistic account would need to explain whether this distinction really does have any moral significance, and why.

Whether such a theory can be developed remains to be seen. But we care passionately about eliminating discrimination for all of these different reasons, and it seems unlikely that a theory that foregrounds only one of these reasons and turns a blind eye to the others could capture the whole truth about discrimination and why it is unfair.

10 Authority and Legitimacy

Christoph Kletzer and Massimo Renzo

Introduction

Consider two ways in which the existence of political authorities is morally problematic. Do not think only about tyrannical or unjust authorities, for example, states that persecute minorities, unjustly expropriate property or wage unnecessary wars. These authorities are morally problematic in a number of obvious ways that will not be discussed here. Think about good political authorities: the peaceful ones that protect human rights, respect minorities and enact reasonable distributive policies. To begin with, all political authorities, good and bad ones, regularly interfere with our liberty, using coercion to prevent us from acting in certain ways and ensure that we act in others. This is obviously problematic since we value our liberty and we normally think that it can be constrained only when we exercise it in ways that are morally wrongful. But political authorities do not stop at that. In addition to using coercion, they also claim the right to impose obligations on us. Thus, they interfere not only with our liberty, but also with our autonomy, that is, with our capacity to decide for ourselves how best to respond to the reasons for action that we have. We might think that this second form of interference is even more worrisome, because it constrains not only our freedom to act in accordance with what we think is right, but our very capacity to determine for ourselves how to act by exercising our autonomy. And is this not one of the capacities we should cherish the most, and be more reluctant to abdicate?

To be sure, being able to incur new moral obligations is an important aspect of our capacity to exercise our autonomous agency: we incur them, for example, by promising to act in certain ways, by signing contracts and even simply by creating valuable relationships (for example, romantic relationships or relationships of friendship) with others. As such, incurring obligations is a product of our capacity to act autonomously, and not an obstacle to it. But the obligations that political authorities (allegedly) impose on us are different. With limited exceptions – for example, when we apply to become naturalised citizens of a state – they do not seem to depend in any way on previous exercises of our autonomous agency. These are obligations that we acquire simply by being born in a certain place at a certain time. We have no control over them and thus we might worry that they are an impediment to, rather than an expression of our capacity to exercise our autonomy. This suggests that the claims of political authorities should be carefully assessed and accepted only if they survive close scrutiny. The aim of this chapter is not to complete this task, but rather to articulate some of the main issues at stake and give the reader a sense of how philosophers have tried to address them.

1 Historical Background

Before jumping into the depths of the analytics of authority and legitimacy let us have a brief look at the intellectual hinterland of these concepts. Authority plays a prominent role in contemporary legal and political philosophy. Has this always been the case? This is doubtful. While philosophers of antiquity and the Middle Ages certainly had a lot to say about authority, anticipating some of the issues discussed today, arguably the notion of authority played a significantly differently role in their debates. The ancients and most of their scholastic heirs treated the law, including its authority and our (possible) obligation to obey it, as only one among many institutions which could contribute to a good life and which were all reflexively investigated in that regard.[1] While certainly important, the question of authority did not play any special role. Rather it was one among many questions that philosophy and the Church teachers claimed competence in addressing: from giving birth to paying interest, from bodily hygiene to eternal damnation, from diet to the authority of law. All of these issues were woven together in one big tapestry, tied ultimately to a very specific understanding of God and the good life. The task of philosophy was to create and maintain learned agreement on them.[2]

[1] Aristotle, *Nicomachean Ethics* (Hackett, 2014); Aristotle, *The Politics* (Oxford University Press, 2009); T. Aquinas, *Political Writings* (Cambridge University Press, 2002).

[2] N.E. Simmonds, 'Protestant jurisprudence and modern doctrinal scholarship', *Cambridge Law Journal* 60 (2001), 275ff.

Compared with this picture, contemporary philosophy has carved out a very prominent space for authority. Why is this the case? There are three elements that can help us understand the special role of authority, and also give us a first feel of the nature of authority. First of all, in the modern age authority has increasingly become a worldly concept. As soon as our main concern is no longer the conformity of our life with a comprehensive ideal, but rather turns to the difficulty of living together with other people in a world where both labour and life experiences are highly differentiated, authority quite naturally becomes central. The more we live together with others, interacting with and being dependent on them, the more central the problem of authority is. Moreover, and this is the second element worth stressing, authority becomes more prominent when we have to live together with people with whom we fundamentally disagree. Authority is less important when we live together with people with whom we share the same outlook on what constitutes a good life. If we are all pulled in the same direction by a shared goal, we can rely on this pull to straighten out disagreement and conflict.

Variance of opinion alone, however, is not the whole story. To understand the prominence of authority in the modern and contemporary debate we need to pay attention to the fact that in addition to living closely together with people we disagree with, we do not believe we can always convince dissenters into agreement, that is, we do not think that there is or can be a canonical narrative about what constitutes a good life.[3] This is the third reason for the centrality of authority.

The conditions of authority acquiring a central role in the philosophical debate are thus as follows: authority becomes philosophically central when we live in large groups of people on whom we depend, with whom we disagree on fundamental issues, and whom we nevertheless do not want to simply dominate, as we value their subjectivity and autonomy. An important sticking point in philosophical debates is how profound the disagreement is and how far to push the value of subjectivity. Early liberal authors like Hugo Grotius have argued that despite the absence of a shared substantive world view, determined by radically different religious, metaphysical and moral views, all humans share the human capacity for moral reasoning. There are some minimal insights which can be established and

[3] J. Rawls, *Political Liberalism* (Columbia University Press, 2005).

defended 'even if we were to suppose (what we cannot suppose without the greatest wickedness) that there is no God',[4] i.e. even if we let go of any reliance on an ultimate unitary source of metaphysical truth.

These minimal insights, Grotius argued, are based solely on claims which no rational person could possibly reject, like, for instance, the claim that everyone must have a right to self-preservation. Nobody, whatever his or her substantive metaphysical outlook, could possibly deny that. Now since, according to Grotius, each person's right to self-preservation has to end where the other's begins, the idea of such rights provides us with an underlying system of non-overlapping entitlements for each person. Within his or her little allotment each person is free to pursue his or her idea of what a good life is. The authority of the state and its laws derive from their capacity to implement this underlying system of non-overlapping entitlements. The point of authority is thus to protect a reasonable system of peace, which is in principle accessible to everyone.

Other authors had a different, less optimistic, estimation of the reach of disagreement and the role of reason. They thus came to quite different conclusions on the role of authority. Hobbes, famously, argued that disagreement reaches much further into reason than Grotius allowed. He started from assumptions similar to Grotius' assumptions: despite our different moral and metaphysical commitments, no one could possibly deny that everyone has a right to self-preservation. However, he differed from Grotius in one, crucial, respect: for Hobbes the limits of our right to self-preservation cannot be measured objectively, simply by appealing to reason, since people will inevitably disagree about them, and no firm vantage point is available to us from which to adjudicate such disagreements. Accordingly, everyone has to determine for himself where the limits of the rights of self-preservation lie. Potentially, everyone has a right to everything, 'even to one another's body',[5] if he believes that this is necessary for his self-preservation. Far from leading to peace, reason by itself leads to conflict, and ultimately to a 'war of all against all'. Thus, according to Hobbes, we need authority not to police the peaceful condition we can independently secure through reason, but rather to establish a peaceful condition in the first place. Since our capacity for reason is potentially complicit in fostering conflict and even war, only authority can guarantee peace.

[4] H. Grotius, *Rights of War and Peace* (Liberty, 2005), 1748.
[5] T. Hobbes, *Leviathan* (Cambridge University Press, 1996), 91.

Hobbes' influence can hardly be overestimated. One aspect of it that is sometimes overlooked is that it has led some strands of philosophical inquiry away from normative questions and toward a more realist analysis of authority. This tradition has its forbears in some of the ancient sophists and in Machiavelli,[6] and in its modern shape goes back at least to the incisive work of Fichte. While Kant still believed he could square Hobbesian and Grotian insights in one system of natural rights, which are at the same time socially constructed yet determined by reason, in the work of Fichte one can find for the first time the fully worked out idea that moral and political philosophy are two separate and rather unrelated fields of inquiry.[7] His political philosophy is based on an understanding of right which is developed directly from reflections on the nature of self-consciousness and freedom without any prior detour through the moral law. This leads him close to some form of political realism. This peculiarly non-moral political philosophy has found fuller expression in the work of sociologists like Max Weber, who tried to get to grips with authority without relying on any moral presuppositions.[8] Weber contented himself with simply describing the different, ideal-typical models according to which people tend to hold domination to be legitimate. He remained uncommitted about whether these beliefs are normatively grounded.

2 Conceptual Clarifications

What, then, are the concepts of authority and legitimacy that play such a prominent role in contemporary debate? There are several. Let us start by first considering a state that does not even attempt to justify its power, but rather controls its subjects by resorting to brute force and brute force alone. Suppose that this state neither claims to possess authority nor is recognised to have authority by those subject to it. While such a state can be said to exercise political power, it does not possess even the semblance of legitimacy.

It is important to recognise how rare states of this kind are. Even the most brutal tyrants are typically unable to retain control over large

[6] N. Machiavelli, *The Prince* (Cambridge University Press, 1988).
[7] J.G. Fichte, *Foundations of Natural Right* (Cambridge University Press, 2008).
[8] M. Weber, *Economy and Society* (University of California Press, 1979), 212ff.

territories unless they are believed to possess authority, at least by some (their henchmen, their most loyal officials). This is what explains how they can stay in power despite the fact that they could easily be overthrown by those around them if their power relied exclusively on their capacity to employ brute force. Thus, what starts as the mere exercise of brute force typically turns into something more substantive: the exercise of de facto *political authority*. Someone holds de facto political authority if in addition to holding political power, he claims the right to do so, or is at least perceived to possess this right by most of his subjects. The motives or reasons for this acceptance do not matter for the existence of de facto authority. Whether the ruler is obeyed because his subjects (rightly or wrongly) believe that he has superior powers, because they believe that he tends to do the morally right thing, or because they believe that they have a moral duty to obey him, does not matter for the question of whether the ruler possesses de facto authority. However, Joseph Raz, for instance, claims that a regime only possesses de facto authority if it both has effective control over a population and also *claims* legitimate authority for itself. Since such a claim to legitimate authority is necessary for the authoritative nature of law, Raz further argues, only such de facto authorities can issue law and have a legal system.

A regime has de jure political authority if in addition to exercising political power, it possesses the actual right to do so (as opposed to a claimed or perceived one), because it satisfies whichever normative requirements trigger the existence of this right.[9]

So far we have invoked the notion of authority in its de facto and de jure variants. But what does it mean to have authority? How can we analytically unpack this notion? In the literature, three understandings are predominant. Authority is usually understood either as

(a) the permission (or liberty) to coerce those subject to the authority, or
(b) the claim of right to command those subject to the authority, or
(c) the moral power to change the normative status of those subject to the authority.

The thinnest notion is the one according to which all a holder of authority possesses is the liberty to coerce. This simply means that he is not under a

[9] J. Raz, *The Morality of Freedom* (Clarendon Press, 1986), 26; L. Green, *The Authority of the State* (Clarendon Press, 1988), 60.

duty to abstain from coercing those subject to his authority. It is the thinnest notion of authority, as it does not even purport to produce any normative consequences in the subjects of authority or anybody else. According to this notion, the fact that someone possesses authority by itself tells you nothing about the normative status of people other than the holder of authority, for example, its subjects or other states. By itself, it does not involve any duties or obligations.[10] Many reject such a thin conception of authority, since it seems to imply that, for instance, other states have no duty to abstain from interfering with whoever has authority in the territory in question.[11]

Thickening our concept of authority one notch, we get a notion that involves not merely a liberty to coerce but a claim right to command. Claim rights come with corresponding duties, which apply both to those subject to the authority and to potential third parties. So, if a state has de jure authority, understood as the claim right to command, this means both that other states (or international institutions) have a duty not to interfere with its legitimate exercise of political power and that its citizens have special duties toward it. These duties are typically understood as general moral requirements to obey the laws and support the political institutions of the state in question, but they could be understood more modestly as duties not to interfere with its exercise of political power.

Some theorists argue that any thin notion of authority already involves a thicker one: if authority is understood to contain the permission to coerce, this permission, to be meaningful, also has to include the duty on the side of the subject at least not to interfere with the act of coercion.

A final concept of authority goes even further and conceives de jure authority as consisting not only in the power to impose moral obligations, but more generally as the power to shape the normative status of subjects by unilaterally changing their duties, liberties and claim rights.[12] Note that

[10] R. Ladenson, 'In defense of a Hobbesian conception of law', *Philosophy and Public Affairs* 9 (1980), 134–59; A. Ripstein, 'Authority and coercion', *Philosophy and Public Affairs* 32 (2004), 2–35;

[11] J. Simmons, 'Political obligation and authority' in R. Simon (ed.), *Blackwell Guide to Social and Political Philosophy* (Wiley, 2009), 19.

[12] D. Copp, 'The idea of a legitimate state', *Philosophy & Public Affairs* 28:1 (1999), 3–45; S. Perry, 'Political authority and political obligation' in L. Green and B. Leiter (eds.), *Oxford Studies in Philosophy of Law*, Vol. II (Oxford University Press, 2013), 1–74.

this concept of authority can be seen as supplementing the second concept of authority discussed above and is not necessarily at odds with it.[13]

With the notion of de jure authority we have already entered the territory of justification of authority. Now, the concept of legitimacy adds a further level of complexity to this debate and there is little agreement about what exactly legitimacy denotes and how it relates to authority. On one reading, legitimacy is simply what turns a de facto authority into de jure authority. According to this view, an authority is legitimate when it has the right to exercise de facto authority. Thus, in addition to being perceived as having the right to coerce and/or impose obligations on its own citizens, the authority in question has in fact the right to do so. Others, however, have stressed the independence of the idea of legitimacy from authority and taken the former to be the more fundamental idea. They take legitimacy to simply denote the moral justification of the right to wield political power, 'where to wield political power is to attempt to exercise a monopoly, within a jurisdiction, in the making, application, and enforcement of laws', whereas authority involves, in addition to wielding such power, 'the right to be obeyed by those subject to it'.[14] Insofar as we clearly indicate how these labels are used, not much hinges on this choice. We can now move to discussing the justification of political authority.

3 The Justification of Political Authority

A natural way to think about the justification of the political authority of states is by appealing to the benefits that they normally provide to their subjects. By performing their legislative, executive and judicial functions, states provide their citizens with the level of order and security we generally regard as necessary for acceptable lives. It is hard to imagine how we could pursue our plans of life if these benefits were not secured, so appealing to them seems a promising strategy. But simply pointing at these benefits is not enough. We need to explain *why* the fact that states provide these benefits gives them the right to rule by coercing or imposing obligations on their subjects.

[13] Ibid.
[14] A. Buchanan, 'Political legitimacy and democracy', *Ethics* 112 (2002), 689–90.

The most straightforward way to do that is by appealing to the thought that citizens consent to being subject to the authority of the state in exchange for the benefits in question. This idea goes back at least to Plato's *Crito*, though the canonical formulation of the view is the one offered in the seventeenth century by John Locke, and it is easy to see its appeal.[15] It is morally permissible (within limits) for others to treat us in ways that would otherwise be morally unacceptable, if we consent to them doing so. This provides a straightforward explanation of why states do no wrong in requiring that we act in certain ways, and backing their requests with a threat of sanction, if we consent to them doing so. Moreover, we normally accept that we give others the moral power to create moral obligations for us when we consent to being subject to their authority. This explains why states may pass laws that impose moral obligations on their citizens, if the latter consent to being subject to their authority. To be sure, consent is binding only if it is not the product of coercion or mistake, but to the extent that it is not, its capacity to trigger the sort of duties or liabilities we are discussing seems clear enough. What is controversial, however, is the idea that the citizens of modern states can be plausibly described as having consented to the state.

If we think about *actual* consent, which involves forming and communicating (explicitly or tacitly) the intention to accept the authority of the state, it looks as if too few people can be said to have consented. When did we consent and how? And to what exactly? It is sometimes suggested that simply by living in the territory of the state, we thereby consent to its authority, but this seems implausible for at least three reasons: First, doing x can be taken to be a way of consenting to y only if we can be reasonably expected to know that by doing x we consent to y. But it is not clear that we can be reasonably expected to know that by failing to leave a certain territory we thereby consent to being subject to the authority of the state. Second, even if we could be expected to know that, our failure to leave could be meaningfully taken to be a way of consenting only if leaving was not too costly. (Compare: your failure to leave the room might be reasonably taken to be an expression of your consenting to be in my company only if the option of leaving is available to you at a reasonable cost. If the room is locked, if there's a fire in the corridor, or if your sick mother is

[15] Plato, 'Crito' in *Five Dialogues* (Cambridge University Press, 2002); J. Locke, *Second Treatise of Government* (Hackett, 1980).

immobilised in the room, your remaining in the room could not be taken to be a genuine instance of consenting to be in my company). But the option of leaving the territory of the state where we live is indeed significantly costly, both financially and in terms of the relationships and personal projects that we would have to sacrifice to do so. Third, even if we were willing to bear these costs, it is not clear where we could go, since there are virtually no parts of the globe over which no states claim authority.

A second way in which we are sometimes said to consent to the authority of the state is by voting, but this suggestion is also problematic. Voting is best understood as a way of choosing who should rule, given that a ruler will have to be chosen, rather than as a way of authorising someone to rule. Since there is a state that passes and enforces laws on the territory where I live, I have reasons to do what I can to choose the better – or the least bad – ruler, but doing so cannot be taken to be a way to consent to being ruled over. (Compare: if a group of knife throwers is going to use you as a target and you can choose which of them should practice on you, you have reasons to choose the most skilful. But this choice can in no way be interpreted as a way for you to consent to being used as a target by him.)

Faced with these problems, we might decide that consent is not necessary after all. Even if we have not consented to obeying the law and supporting the state in exchange for the benefits it provides, failing to do so would be unfair. Since the state provides us with these benefits, and these benefits can be provided only if enough people obey the law and support the state, failing to obey the law and support the state would be morally wrong in the same way in which it is wrong to take the bus without paying the fare. In both cases we free ride on the contributions made by others to maintain a scheme that benefits us. We take advantage of their efforts to maintain the scheme without bearing our share of the costs associated with its maintenance.[16]

This view seems appealing in that it preserves the idea that our duty to obey the law and maintain the state is grounded in certain important goods provided by it, without having to identify an act whereby we can be said to have consented to the state. However, we might worry that the view moves too quickly from the premise that the state provides us with

[16] H.L.A. Hart, 'Are there any natural rights?', *Philosophical Review* 64 (1955), 175–91; J. Rawls, 'Legal obligation and the duty of fair play' in *Collected Papers* (Harvard University Press, 1999), 117–29.

important benefits to the conclusion that we have a duty to contribute to their production. The problem is that members of modern states are not given the opportunity to opt out from receiving these benefits. It is morally permissible, of course, to provide someone with some benefits, if nothing is asked in exchange for them. But if they come with costs attached, we normally think that it should be up to the recipient to decide whether to receive them and incur the relevant costs or not.[17] This is not how modern states operate, though. Modern states provide all those living on their territory with benefits such as security or the rule of law, and require everybody to contribute to their production.

In response, some have suggested that there is something special about the benefits provided by the state: since goods such as security or the rule of law are necessary for a minimally acceptable life, we can presume that everyone wants them, regardless of whatever else they want, and thus expect that everyone has the relevant obligations to the state.[18] This move is controversial though. For even if you are justified in presuming that I would want to receive a benefit because of its importance, I might nonetheless (unreasonably) fail to do so. And if I do, it looks as if I should not incur the obligations that would normally attach to it. This has led others to conclude that only those who accept the benefits can be said to be subject to the authority of the state, where acceptance requires that we fulfil certain psychological conditions (or that we would do so under some idealised conditions): we must understand the source and the cost of these benefits, and want to receive them at the relevant cost.[19] This view seems plausible, but cannot deliver the conclusion that all those living in the territory of the state are subject to its authority. Only those who have accepted the benefits provided by it are. Should we conclude that everybody else is off the hook?

Perhaps not. There is another way in which we can think about the relationship between the benefits provided by the state and our duty to support it and obey the law. Think about a world in which states do not exist and these benefits are not provided. This is a world in which general

[17] R. Nozick, *Anarchy, State and Utopia* (Blackwell, 1974), 90–5.

[18] G. Klosko, *Political Obligations* (Oxford University Press, 2005); R. Dagger, *Civic Virtues* (Oxford University Press, 1997).

[19] J. Simmons, *Justification and Legitimacy* (Cambridge University Press, 2001), chs. 1–2; M. Renzo, 'Fairness, self-deception and political obligation', *Philosophical Studies* 169 (2014), 471.

compliance with an authoritative set of rules, which is necessary to guarantee peace and respect for human rights, could not be secured. Indeed, we might think that in this world – call it, 'the state of nature'– the very possibility of respecting other people's rights and acting justly is absent, since the content of rights and duties is underdetermined and, similarly, we might reasonably disagree over what justice requires.[20] If so, it is plausible that we have a duty to prevent these dangers by creating states and complying with their directives.[21]

Notice how this approach avoids the main problem encountered by consent and fair-play theories. The problem for those theories was being under-inclusive with respect to the class of individuals that intuitively are subject to the authority of the state: since only few of those living on the territory of the state accept the benefits provided by it, let alone explicitly consent to it, only a limited number of subjects over whom states claim authority can be said to have a duty to support their state and obey its laws. Natural duty theories do not have the same problem, since everybody has a duty to create and support just institutions to prevent the dangers of the state of nature.

However, these theories seem to have the opposite problem – that of being over-inclusive. They seem unable to vindicate the idea that states normally have authority over a particular group of individuals (their citizens), and that this authority correlates to a special duty that these individuals have to obey and support their state in particular.[22] For if what grounds the duty to obey is the fact that our state successfully performs the functions required to ensure justice and respect for human rights, shouldn't we conclude that everyone has the same duty? And shouldn't we have the same duty toward any other state that performs the same functions?

A theory that promises to avoid both problems is one that instead of focusing on the benefits produced by the state, focuses on the special responsibilities that we have *qua* members of a political community.

[20] A. Stilz, *Liberal Loyalty* (Princeton University Press, 2009).

[21] J. Rawls, *A Theory of Justice* (Harvard University Press, 1999); Buchanan, 'Political legitimacy and democracy'; C. Wellman, 'Samaritanism and the duty to obey the law' in C. Wellman and J. Simmons (eds.), *Is There a Duty to Obey the Law?* (Cambridge University Press, 2005), 3–89; M. Renzo, 'State legitimacy and self-defence', *Law and Philosophy* 30 (2011), 575–601.

[22] Simmons, *Justification and Legitimacy*, ch. 7; M. Renzo, 'Duties of Samaritanism and political obligation', *Legal Theory* 14 (2008), 193–217.

According to this view, even when non-voluntarily incurred, membership in a political community can generate special obligations to support it, just like membership in other forms of association that are intrinsically valuable, such as family or friendships, does. Ronald Dworkin, the first to formulate this view in the contemporary debate, calls these 'associative obligations'.[23]

Appealing to associative obligations constitutes a significant departure from the accounts we have considered so far, in that it rejects the assumption that there should be an independent moral principle (such as consent, fairness or a natural duty of justice) capable of justifying political authority. What is required, instead, is some kind of interpretative effort to uncover how the obligations we have to our political community are constitutive of our very identity *qua* members of the community. Once we realise that we have 'a duty to honour our responsibilities under social practices that define groups and attach special responsibilities to membership', we can see that associative political obligations, far from needing justification, are themselves justificatory.[24]

If successful, this view would avoid both the problem of over-inclusiveness and the problem of under-inclusiveness, in that it would justify the intuitively correct claim that, say, France has political authority over all and only the members of the French political community. But is it true that our relationship with the members of our political community is intrinsically valuable in the same way in which family relationships and relationships of friendship are? If it is not, we should not expect it to generate obligations in the same way in which these other relationships do.[25] And even if it is intrinsically valuable, is it true that the problem of under-inclusiveness is avoided by associativist accounts?

After all, while Dworkin is right that I do not choose to become your friend (our friendship develops spontaneously) or a member of my family,[26] there is a sense in which I voluntarily occupy these roles. If we stop having the relevant attitude toward each other, our friendship is no longer in place, and we do not owe to each other the duties normally

[23] R. Dworkin, *Law's Empire* (Harvard University Press, 1988), 196.

[24] Dworkin, *Law's Empire*, 197–8; J. Horton, *Political Obligation* (Macmillan, 2010).

[25] S. Perry, 'Associative obligations and the obligation to obey the law' in S. Hershowitz (ed.), *Exploring Law's Empire* (Oxford University Press, 2008), 183–206.

[26] Dworkin, *Law's Empire*, 197–8.

attached to it. Similarly (though perhaps more controversially), if I reject my relationship with my parents and 'deny' them, the obligations attached to that role would be significantly reduced, if not altogether cancelled. The same must be true in the case of my relationship to the political community. Although we do not choose to be members of the political community where we are born, this role is voluntary in the sense that we could step out of it if we do not endorse it; and when this is the case, we stop having the obligations attached to it. If so, associativism also struggles with under-inclusiveness, since some of us might not have the relevant attitudes toward the rest of the political community.[27]

Of course, under-inclusiveness is a problem only if we believe that states should have political authority over all and only the individuals they identify as their citizens – typically, those living on their territory. But why think that? Suppose we take seriously the idea that political authority is grounded in certain important benefits that states provide to their subjects. The most important benefit, we might think, consists in enabling their subject to do what they have reason to do. Thus, following Joseph Raz's influential 'service conception' of authority, we might argue that the 'primary way to establish that a person should be acknowledged to have authority over another person involves showing that the alleged subject is likely better to comply with reasons which apply to him ... if he accepts the directives of the alleged authority as authoritatively binding, and tries to follow them, than if he tries to follow the reasons which apply to him directly'.[28] But if so, we should not expect states to have the same authority over all those living on their territory, as no doubt different subjects will be in more or less need of following the directives of their state in relation to different areas of conduct.

You might be an expert chemist and require no guidance from the state as to which substance you should refrain from taking, whereas I might be a skilled driver and require no guidance as to which speed I should maintain when I drive. Then perhaps you and I are subject to the authority of the state with respect to different matters. And if it is the case that in every

[27] M. Renzo, 'Associative responsibilities and political obligation', *Philosophical Quarterly* 62 (2012), 120.

[28] J. Raz, *Ethics in the Public Domain* (Clarendon Press, 1994), 214. See also Raz, *The Morality of Freedom*, chs. 2–4; J. Raz, 'The problem of authority: revisiting the service conception' in *Between Authority and Interpretation* (Oxford University Press, 2010), 126–65.

area of conduct you will do better in complying with reasons that apply to you by deliberating without following the directives of the state, then perhaps I am subject to the state's authority and you are not. This is how it should be, if we adopt the service conception. Over-inclusiveness is no longer a problem, because Raz's view 'invites a piecemeal approach to the question of the authority of governments, which yields the conclusion that the extent of governmental authority varies from individual to individual, and is more limited than the authority most governments claim for themselves in the case of most people'.[29]

This implication might sound odd at first (this is not how most people seem to think about the authority of the state), but Raz's account is worth careful consideration, as it arguably captures an important aspect of the justification of authority: authorities are primarily justified by virtue of the service they provide to those subject to them. It is no surprise then, that Raz's view has proven extremely popular. Equally unsurprisingly, however, the view has also attracted a number of criticisms.

A prominent objection is that while the service conception explains why states might have the moral power to determine what we should do (within given domains), it is not clear that it can explain why they also have the power to demand that we comply with their directives.[30] Indeed, some have argued that Raz's account blurs the distinction between being subject to someone's authority and merely receiving advice from an expert. When you tell me that I ought not to drive faster than 40 mph on a certain road, it seems to make no difference, as far as the service conception is concerned, whether you are a government official or an expert driver giving me a friendly tip. Either way, I should do as you say if following your directives in driving-related activities will enable me to better comply with the reasons that apply to me than deliberating about what to do in some other way. But this is not how we normally think about the directives issued by political authorities. We normally think that it makes a difference whether the directive comes from a legitimate authority trying to impose an obligation on us or an expert giving us a tip. Genuine authorities are normally thought to have the moral power to impose obligations over us, which includes the power to demand that their directives are followed and the power to call us to account when we fail to do so. Experts who share their

[29] Raz, *The Morality of Freedom*, 80.

[30] S. Perry, 'Law and obligation', *American Journal of Jurisprudence* 50 (2005), 263–95.

knowledge with us, lack such standing. While it might be foolish not follow their directives, they cannot demand that we do so or sanction us if we refuse.[31]

Some have concluded from these arguments that Raz's view is unable to justify political authority. While capable of justifying the existence of special reasons – perhaps even duties– for us to act as the state requires, the view is criticised as unable to justify the right of the state to demand that we act as its laws require or to sanction our failure to do so. Notice however, that some of the assumptions these arguments rest upon are themselves controversial. For example, should we simply assume that political authority is best understood as combining both the power to impose obligations and the power to sanction failure to comply with them? Arguably, a separate argument is required for this view. In line with his broader account, Raz has suggested that whether states are indeed entitled to exercise both powers will ultimately depend on whether being subject to an authority that has this feature (as opposed to one that can impose obligations, but not sanctions) enables us to better comply with reasons that apply to us.[32]

Suppose now that we remain unpersuaded by the arguments discussed so far. If so, we should conclude that states lack a right to exercise their authority, and that those over whom this alleged authority is routinely exercised lack a duty to obey them. Adopting this view is tantamount to adopting a form of anarchism. However, we should be clear about what this entails exactly. The term 'anarchism' is normally associated with the view that states are oppressive institutions to be overthrown.[33] But none of this follows from the simple rejection of the arguments considered so far. After all, states might perform valuable functions, even if they lack the right to subject us to their authority. When this is the case, we might well have good reasons to support them and to act as they require. This is not because states have the moral power to create duties for us in virtue of their legitimate authority, but rather because their doing as they say is the best way for us to discharge moral duties that we have independently. (Compare: while I am not under your authority, I might have a duty to

[31] Ibid.; S. Darwall, *Morality, Authority, and Law I* (Oxford University Press, 2013), chs. 8–9.

[32] J. Raz, 'On respect, authority, and neutrality: a response', *Ethics* 120 (2010), 300.

[33] Call this view 'political anarchism'. The view is normally contrasted with 'philosophical anarchism', the view described in the rest of this section.

follow your directives, if doing so is the best way to discharge some independent moral duty I have – say, rescuing someone's life, or evacuating a sinking ship without endangering others.[34]) Indeed, we can imagine cases in which states might be permitted to use coercion to enforce such duty, in the same way in which you might be permitted to enforce some of the duties I have (for example, the duty to perform an easy rescue that I am unwilling to perform for futile reasons).

As John Simmons puts it, 'states may be bullies, restricting our autonomy without warrant, but they may be useful bullies, and in resisting them we may both act imprudently and harm others who rely on their states'.[35] With this in mind, we can see that the question of legitimacy, while important, is certainly not the only question we need to address in deciding how to relate to political authorities.

[34] R.P. Wolff, *In Defense of Anarchism* (University of California Press, 1998), 15–16. But see D. Estlund, *Democratic Authority* (Princeton University Press, 2008), ch. 7. for the suggestion that in this case I am under your authority in virtue of the fact that I *should have consented* to being under your authority (even if I didn't consent).

[35] J. Simmons, *Political Philosophy* (Oxford University Press, 2007), 63.

11 The Ends and Limits of Law

John Stanton-Ife

Historically the end of law has often been taken to be something like this: to secure the realisation of moral goals or to promote the well-being of persons. The law is (or should be) based on what a well-known opponent of such a view, John Rawls, would describe as a 'comprehensive moral doctrine'. As Rawls puts it, a comprehensive moral conception 'includes conceptions of what is of value in human life, and ideals of personal character, as well as ideals of friendship and of familial and associational relationships, and much else that is to inform our conduct and in the limit to our life as a whole'.[1] He has in mind many ethical and philosophical doctrines that prescribe how one ought to act and live.

Of course the assumption is that it is the *right* moral goals or the *genuine* well-being of persons that are to be secured by the law. I will label that view, somewhat loosely, 'legal moralism'. Aristotle, for example, believed that political communities should aim at the good of their members when making laws – 'more specifically at the realisation of their powers as thinking, feeling and social beings'.[2] And today's academy is not short of (broadly) like-minded writers who, unlike Rawls, hold that the law should promote moral ends or human well-being or both, such as Michael Moore,[3] Joseph Raz[4] and Antony Duff.[5]

For example according to Raz: 'The law's task, put abstractly, is to secure a situation whereby moral goals . . . are realised' where – 'given

[1] J. Rawls, *Political Liberalism* (Columbia University Press, 2011), 13.

[2] There is a debate about how far terms like 'moral' are appropriate to Aristotle's world view, but I sidestep such niceties. I have in mind an Aristotelian view along the lines of that outlined and defended in R. Kraut, *Aristotle* (Oxford University Press, 2002) viii, 478 and throughout.

[3] M.S. Moore, *Placing Blame* (Oxford University Press, 1997), 662.

[4] J. Raz, *Morality of Freedom* (Oxford University Press, 1986).

[5] R.A. Duff, 'Towards a modest legal moralism', *Criminal Law and Philosophy* (2014), 217.

the current social situation in the country whose law it is' – the moral goal in question 'would be unlikely to be achieved without it', and 'whose achievement by the law is not counter-productive'.[6]

More specifically:

> The main purpose of government is to assist people, primarily its subjects, to lead successful and fulfilling lives, or, to put the same point in other terms, to protect and promote the well-being of people.[7]

Given that law, like people and institutions in general, are morally appraisable, the ends of law are to be fixed by the applicable moral norms, not in principle excluding recourse to what Rawls calls comprehensive doctrines. Against this, as we will see in more detail below, is another tradition of thought, which we can label 'liberal' (again loosely). Liberal views do not typically reject the proposition that the law ought to achieve any moral goals. They do, however, seek to *truncate* the range of moral reasons on which the law can legitimately rely or to limit the means available to the law where it does pursue moral goals. Thus Rawls seeks to rule out comprehensive moral conceptions and John Stuart Mill's 'harm principle' limits the use of legal coercion in certain contexts and in certain ways.

Aristotle's own views on the subject have often been accused of objectionable paternalism, even totalitarianism.[8] For particularly if the concern is with liberty or the autonomy of persons under the law, a commonly held view has been that laws cannot be legitimately allowed such moral powers; the cost to human freedom is too great. John Stuart Mill discussed among much else in *On Liberty* 'the legitimate sphere of legal control', arguing that the law should not seek to compel a person 'to do or forbear because it will be better for him to do so, because it will make him happier, because, in the opinion of others, to do so would be wise, or even right'.[9] Law, thought Mill, must be limited in its use of coercion and the key limiting idea is harm prevention. The 'harm principle', restricting legitimate

[6] J. Raz, 'About morality and the nature of law', ch. 6 in *Between Authority and Interpretation* (Oxford University Press, 2009), 178.

[7] J. Raz, 'Liberty and trust' in R.P. George (ed.), *Natural Law, Liberalism and Morality* (Oxford University Press, 1996), 113.

[8] For example J. Barnes, 'Aristotle and political liberty' in R. Kraut and S. Skultety (eds.), *Aristotle's Politics: Critical Essays* (Rowman & Littlefield, 2005), ch. 8. 185–202.

[9] J.S. Mill, *On Liberty and Other Essays* in J. Gray (ed.), World's Classics Edition (Oxford University Press, 1991), I.9.

coercion to the prevention of harm to others, is the tradition that remains the most developed response to the question of the ends and limits of the law.[10] Quite what it amounts to however is, as we will see, a matter of some controversy.[11]

One alternative to Mill's harm principle is the 'sovereignty principle', an attempt by Arthur Ripstein to formulate a principle similar in form to Mill's principle only claimed to be superior. Ripstein, in part drawing on an idea Mill took to be complementary to his own harm principle, argues that conduct should not be legally coerced if it does not wrongfully interfere with the sovereignty of others. In Ripstein's view the idea of sovereignty, of 'the mutual independence of persons from each other'[12] is powerful enough to replace Mill's harm principle, not merely to complement it. As we will see the relevance of independence to the debate stands in an often-uneasy relationship to the idea of harm prevention. In much of what follows we examine the harm principle and seek to separate out two of its strands discernible initially in Mill's version. We also consider an interesting attempt to reconcile what we are calling the legal moralist and the Millian aspects of debate on the ends and limits of the law.

As briefly alluded to above, another way of rejecting legal moralism has, in recent years, been gaining currency. This is the idea of public reason, originating in the writings of John Rawls. Rawls urges his readers to eschew

[10] This is especially true in relation to Joel Feinberg's four-volume study of criminalisation: J. Feinberg, *The Moral Limits of the Criminal Law* (4 volumes: *Harm to Others*, 1984; *Offense to Others*, 1985; *Harm to Self*, 1986; *Harmless Wrongdoing*, 1988) (Oxford University Press, 1984 and subsequent years). On criminalisation see also A. Simester and A. von Hirsch, *Crimes, Harms and Wrongs* (Hart, 2011). Also pertinent, albeit not restricted to a defence of the harm principle cf. the ambitious criminalisation project directed by the quintet of Antony Duff, Lindsay Farmer, Sandra Marshall, Massimo Renzo and Victor Tadros; for the launch volume, see R.A. Duff, L. Farmer, S.E. Marshall, M. Renzo and V. Tadros, *The Boundaries of the Criminal Law* (Oxford University Press, 2010). Among studies of other areas of the law where the harm principle looms large, see e.g. on contract: S.A. Smith, *Contract Theory* (Oxford University Press, 2004) and D. Kimel, *From Promise to Contract: Towards a Liberal Theory of Contract* (Hart Publishing, 2003); on taxation J.K. Lieberman, *Liberalism Undressed* (Oxford University Press, 2012), J. Stanton-Ife, '"Must we pay for the British Museum?", taxation and the harm principle' in M. Bhandari (ed.), *Philosophical Foundations of Tax Law* (Oxford University Press, 2017).

[11] J. Edwards, 'Harm principles', *Legal Theory* 20 (2014), 253, Simester and von Hirsch, *Crimes, Harms and Wrongs*.

[12] A. Ripstein, 'Beyond the harm principle', *Philosophy and Public Affairs* 34:3 (2006), 215–45, 231. On Ripstein's sovereignty principle see V. Tadros, 'Harm, sovereignty and prohibition', *Legal Theory* 17:1 (2011), 35–65.

'the zeal to embody the whole truth in politics'.[13] Contemporary legal systems of the sort Rawls has in mind – Western democracies of Europe and the USA, as well as democracies in India, Israel and elsewhere all must concern themselves with developing a suitable idea of *public reason,* a specialised form of reasoning for the constitutional essentials of modern democracies. We come to views of the sort at the end of the chapter.

It should be noted that most writing on the ends and limits of the law has assumed the debate to be centrally about the legitimate use of *coercion* on the part of the legal system. Thus Mill's harm principle limits the use of coercion, but not the use of non-coercive means. And for Rawls, a constituent element of the 'definite structure' of public reason is its application 'in discussions of coercive norms to be enacted in the form of legitimate law for a democratic people'.[14] Important as it is to interrogate the legitimate use of state coercion, it is also regrettable that the question of coercion has had such prominence in debates about the nature and limits of law. One of the major events of twentieth-century legal philosophy was of course the publication of H.L.A. Hart's *Concept of Law*. It is remembered, among other reasons, for its robust denial that law should be understood reductively, essentially in terms of coercion.[15] It is to be hoped that coming years will see more emphasis on questions of law's ends and limits that go beyond the question of the law's use of coercion. Below I shall largely (if not exclusively) similarly assume that it is the law's use of coercion that is in question.

1 The Harm Principle: Two Kinds of Meiosis

a A Harm-Prevention or an Anti-Harming Principle?

The harm principle was first devised in 1859 by John Stuart Mill, and its much-quoted canonical formulation reads: 'the only purpose for which power can rightfully be exercised over any member of a civilised community against his will is to prevent harm to others'. It was, Mill claimed, 'one very simple principle'.[16] A little over a hundred years later, Lord Devlin,

[13] J. Rawls, *The Law of Peoples (with 'The Idea of Public Reason Revisited')* (Harvard University Press, 1999), 132–3.

[14] Rawls, *The Law of Peoples*, 133.

[15] H.L.A. Hart, *The Concept of Law* (Oxford University Press, 1961).

[16] Mill, *On Liberty and Other Essays*, I.9; cf. D.E. Miller, *J.S. Mill* (Polity, 2010), 114: 'Mill may never be so far wrong as when he describes the liberty principle as "very simple".'

adopting a biological analogy, suggested that Mill's principle had undergone meiosis, a cell-division. If there ever truly was just one harm principle as Mill asserted, it had, Devlin thought, subdivided by the 1960s.[17] Changing his metaphor Devlin suggested that at a certain point 'some of the crew who sail under Mill's flag of liberty' mutinied and ran 'paternalism up the mast'.[18]

Before returning in the next section to the pro-paternalist mutiny against Mill, if that is what it was, we should observe another way not noted by Lord Devlin in which the Millian harm principle subdivided into separate, often rival, views. Here the division is visible in Mill's own writings. Mill's canonical formulation of the harm principle cited at the start of this section is what can be described as a harm-prevention principle.[19] Legal coercion against certain conduct is only permissible if such coercion has certain effects, here that it prevents harm to others. One might for example not be the one who is harming another but still be coerced consistently with Mill's canonical formulation to rescue that other by virtue of the fact that the other would be harmed (by someone or something else).

By contrast, a principle can be an 'anti-harming' principle so that only conduct of a certain kind – here harmful conduct – is permissibly coerced. At times in *On Liberty* Mill speaks as if he means his harm principle to be this sort of principle. Thus: 'to justify that [compulsion and sanctions], the conduct from which it is desired to deter him, must be calculated to produce evil to someone else'.[20] If the harm principle is truly an anti-harming principle, it is to be deployed to prevent the harming of others, to proscribe beating or thieving and so on, actions which will themselves harm or risk harming others.

If by contrast it is a harm-prevention principle, it is not in this way specific as to means. As David Lyons plausibly argues, the requirement that one give testimony in court – cited by Mill himself as a legitimate deployment of his harm principle – is not well explained on the basis that

[17] P. Devlin *The Enforcement of Morals* (Oxford University Press, 1965), 132.

[18] Ibid., 132.

[19] D.O. Brink, *Mill's Progressive Principles* (Oxford University Press, 2013), 184. See also V. Tadros, *Wrongs and Crimes* (Oxford University Press, 2016), 91–107, especially at 92, who draws a similar distinction between an 'effect-focused' principle and a 'conduct-focused' principle.

[20] Mill, *On Liberty and Other Essays*, I.9.

failing to do so itself harms or endangers others: 'For the point of such a rule is not to interfere with conduct that would independently be characterised as harmful or dangerous to others, but is rather to channel behaviour so as to help create or maintain a social practice that will help prevent harm.'[21] Again there is no requirement that any activity one is prevented from engaging in due to the need to pay compulsory taxation has itself to be harmful conduct. Because I am legally compelled to pay tax in order to do my bit to fund schools and hospitals etc., the more expensive holiday I fancy is not affordable to me. But the holiday I forgo is not harmful or dangerous to anyone else.

Plainly, then, if the harm principle is to be conceived of as an anti-harming principle,[22] its scope will likely be more limited, possibly limited only to serious conduct. If on the other hand, it is to be conceived of as a harm-prevention principle,[23] it may seem like a rather undemanding limitation on government and law. Provided *some* significant harm can be pointed to, a major hurdle is jumped which may license very significant legal coercion.

b Paternalism: A Harm Principle or a Harm-to-Others Principle?

Whether an anti-harming principle or a harm-prevention principle, Mill's harm principle was clearly intended to rule out the use of coercion against immoral or wrongful behaviour as such and also such coercion used paternalistically. Mill's is a harm-*to-others* principle not a harm principle simpliciter. A form of what is sometimes called 'soft paternalism' would

[21] D. Lyons, *Rights, Welfare and Mill's Moral Theory* (Oxford University Press, 1994), 94–5. Lyons anticipated the current debate on this ambiguity in Mill in his work in the 1970s reprinted in his 1994 collection of essays.

[22] L.W. Sumner, 'Criminalizing expression: hate speech and obscenity' in J. Deigh and D. Dolinko (eds.) *The Oxford Handbook of the Philosophy of Criminal Law* (Oxford University Press, 2011), 17, understands the harm principle as requiring 'conduct' that 'causes or threatens harm to others'. Simester and von Hirsch, *Crimes, Harms and Wrongs*, 35, formulate it thus: 'the state is justified in intervening coercively to regulate conduct only when that conduct causes or risks harm to others'. For critique see R.A. Duff and S.E. Marshall, 'Remote harms' and 'Two harm principles' in A. Simester, U. Neumann and A. Du-Bois Pedain (eds.) *Liberal Criminal Theory: Essays for Andreas Von Hirsch* (Hart Publishing, 2014), 205–23.

[23] Gardner and Shute champion the harm principle as an effect-focused principle in 'The wrongness of rape', reprinted in J. Gardner, *Offences and Defences* (Oxford University Press, 2008).

seem compatible with Mill's views for all that. Joel Feinberg understands soft paternalism as permitting the state through its law 'the right to prevent self-regarding harmful conduct ... when but only when that conduct is substantially non-voluntary or when temporary intervention is necessary to establish whether it is voluntary or not'.[24] Mill's principle rules out coercion *against the will* of the person coerced save on the basis of preventing harm to others and Feinberg's two riders – to do with self-regarding non-voluntary conduct and certain circumstances in which the true will of the person coerced is not known – appear not to run counter to the will of the coerced person.

Beyond such soft paternalism, can it be legitimate for the law to seek to prevent harm in the interests of the person coerced? It is on this question that Lord Devlin claimed some of Mill's leading followers mutinied against him. Devlin in particular had H.L.A. Hart in mind. Hart, in the course of defending Mill's harm principle, gives an account entirely in line with the canonical Mill in a number of ways, in particular his rejection of legal moralism as a legitimate basis for legal coercion. However, he pointedly declines to reject legal paternalism. Hart takes it that a plausible rationale for criminalising, say, the supply of heroin is the 'protection of would-be purchasers from themselves';[25] and declared Mill's protests at the interference with the liberty of such would-be purchasers 'extreme'[26] and 'fantastic'.[27]

Furthermore, he took Devlin to task over the place of consent in the criminal law. While consent is of course recognised as central to certain offences such as rape, it is not – especially in many common law jurisdictions – accepted as a defence to murder or to assault above a certain threshold of seriousness.[28] Consider the following hypothetical. A person (D) enjoys inflicting violence on others and enters into an agreement with another (V) that he will severely beat V with a baseball bat. V agrees to the beating in exchange for a significant sum of money as well as payment of

[24] Feinberg, *Harm to Self*, 12.

[25] Hart, *Law, Liberty and Morality*, 32.

[26] Ibid., 33.

[27] Ibid., 32.

[28] For example in England and Wales, the law will not take as valid consent to assault at the level of 'actual bodily harm', still less 'grievous bodily harm', unless the conduct falls in a short list of exceptional categories, sporting, surgical, etc.: *R* v. *Brown* [1992] UKHL 7; Hart, *Law, Liberty and Morality*, 30.

all resulting private hospital bills. Many legal systems would convict and punish D irrespective of V's consent. And both Devlin and Hart apparently agree the law would be right to do so. Their disagreement is over the justification for that agreed conclusion. In short Devlin says such justification is moralistic, Hart that it is paternalistic. For Devlin the law would take such a stance because it is 'enforcing a moral principle ... and nothing else'.[29] Hart, by contrast, accepts that a 'modification in Mill's principles is required' if, as he appeared to believe, this kind of case should be accounted for on the basis of 'protecting individuals against themselves'.[30] A serious difficulty here is that it is far from clear how one can keep moralism and paternalism separate.

To consider this further one might ask if V, the sufferer of the baseball bat attack, needs saving from himself given his consent to the beating. Answering requires an account of V's well-being, of where his best interests lie. Adopting Derek Parfit's three-way division of theories of self-interest,[31] a desire-fulfilment theory would likely suggest V's policy of 'take the money and recover' is in his best interest. It is true that such theories are concerned with desire fulfilment across a whole life, or significant part, and it does not follow from the fact that V wants the beating now that he would not come to regret the decision later on in life. For all that, he may well have very firm and stable desires for the money and what it will pay for, desires that are strong enough to override his lack of desire for the beating. Similarly, while a hedonist theory would count the pain of the beating as a negative, this could well be more than compensated for by the pleasure of receiving the money and the long-term consequences thereof. Matters would likely be different on Parfit's third kind of theory, an objective list theory, which holds 'certain things are good or bad for people, whether or not the people would want to have the good things, or to avoid the bad things'. The good things, says Parfit, 'might include moral goodness, rational activity, the development of one's abilities' and so on, 'while the bad things [might include] ... being deprived of dignity'. On such a theory we might conclude that the beating is *not* in V's interest, since it is morally bad and undignified and therefore – according to the theory – bad for V.

[29] Devlin, *The Enforcement of Morals*, 7.
[30] Hart, *Law, Liberty and Morality*, 31.
[31] D. Parfit, *Reasons and Persons* (Oxford University Press, 1986), 499.

It looks, then, as if both Hart and Devlin are right, albeit in a way that looks somewhat more damaging to Hart's argument. On the first two types of theory, desire fulfilment and hedonist, V does not need saving from himself, since he has probably not mistaken his self-interest in the first place. Of course, one might say he should have different desires but that looks suspiciously like making a moral judgement and thus stepping beyond the desire-fulfilment and hedonist theories. By contrast on the third, objective list, variety, the beating is plausibly thought not to be in V's interest, so the question of saving V from himself at least arises. However, the reason for this is most likely that it reveals moral badness and indignity in his life, which is bad for him. But the moralistic and paternalistic analyses look at best inextricably intertwined here. And if that is true it seems we do have a case in which the law is being used to enforce morality, one that surely generalises too many other cases, albeit because paternalism and moralism simply get too close to one another for any convincing separation to be possible.

c Raz on the Harm Principle and Paternalism

Hart's departure from Mill on paternalism is followed by other important thinkers advocating the harm principle. Raz was cited at the start of the chapter as a proponent of a broadly Aristotelian view that law's ends include the realisation of moral goals and human well-being. Unlike the other thinkers cited with him, however, he believes that view can be reconciled with the harm principle, which he endorses.[32] Below we will return to the question of how far the views can be reconciled. 'To harm a person', on Raz's account 'is to diminish his prospects, to affect adversely his possibilities.'[33] Moreover, he apparently follows Hart's rejection of Mill's anti-paternalism in what he describes as his 'ready embrace of various paternalistic measures', also suggesting it is 'senseless to formulate either a general pro- or a general anti-paternalistic conclusion'.[34] As he

[32] Raz, *Morality of Freedom*, 400–29.

[33] Ibid., 414. On various senses of harm J. Stanton-Ife, 'Horrific crime' in R.A. Duff, L. Farmer, S.E. Marshall, M. Renzo and V. Tadros (eds.), *The Boundaries of the Criminal Law* (Oxford University Press, 2010), 138–62, 159ff.; Stanton-Ife, 'Taxation and the harm principle'; Tadros, *Wrongs and Crimes*, 175–200.

[34] Raz, *Morality of Freedom*, 422. To the same effect: Simester and von Hirsch, *Crimes, Harms and Wrongs*, Part IV.

understands the harm principle, it 'regards the prevention of harm to anyone [including the person to be coerced] as the only justifiable ground for coercive interference with a person'.[35]

Raz's account of paternalism is somewhat complex, developed in his classic work of perfectionist liberalism *The Morality of Freedom* and also in a subsequent paper entitled 'Liberty and trust'.[36] His views in the former work turn initially on an interesting distinction between paternalism as ends and paternalism as means. At least in the conditions of modern Western states, governments should attempt to supply for all an adequate range of valuable options. Persons will have various valuable ends, for example to be a successful nurse or farmer or parent. We should then distinguish between conduct and decisions as to such *ends*, on the one hand, and conduct and decisions as to the *means* to those ends, on the other. The essential initial thought is that paternalistically restricting choice as to the former (means) is more easily justifiable than restricting choice as to the latter (ends).

> In particular, paternalism affecting matters which are regarded by all as of merely instrumental value does not interfere with autonomy if its effect is to improve safety, thus making the activities affected more likely to realise their aim. There is a difference between risky sports e.g. where the risk is part of the point of the activity or an inevitable by-product of its point and purpose, and the use of unsafe common consumer goods. Participation in sporting activities is intrinsically valuable. Consumer goods are normally used for instrumental reasons.[37]

Hence laws mandating the use of seatbelts in motor vehicles are paternalist in nature, but surely in a means-related sense only. If one considers why people standardly drive cars – to get to work, to see family, to go on holiday – it is hard to see what intrinsic value is at stake if seatbelts must be worn; and the enhanced safety is moreover a potential help to the intrinsic value that is at stake, family relations etc. Matters would be different, on Raz's account, if the risk the government seeks paternalistically to eliminate or reduce is part of the point of the activity. Mountaineering, presumably, would change in nature – cease to be the same valuable option for choice – if excessively shrouded in health and safety

[35] Raz, *Morality of Freedom*, 412–13.
[36] Raz, *Morality of Freedom*, 'Liberty and trust'.
[37] Raz, *Morality of Freedom*, 422–3.

requirements. While mountaineers observe firm standards of prudence, part of the point and value of the activity lies in skilfully responding to dangers one does not encounter in the city and elsewhere in ordinary life. Hence paternalistically banning or severely restricting mountaineering looks like end-related paternalism and hence illegitimate on the account under consideration, while the mandating of seatbelts is means-related paternalism and thus legitimate, other things being equal.

The distinction will not always be easy to apply. Laws requiring, say, food hygiene at first sight appear straightforwardly means-related. Consumers must buy food that has undergone various tests and met certain standards of food safety. The cost of the mandatory testing is typically passed on to consumers, who generally lack a choice between paying less for food that has not been tested and paying more for food that has, but in general safer food does not compromise intrinsically valuable ends. However, epicures and others with elevated tastes may find that the very best cuisine, involving say fish, requires produce sourced directly from a fishing vessel, which is fresher than tested fish but also less safe. Legally precluding such possibilities with compulsory food hygiene laws may therefore interfere with the intrinsic values of haute cuisine. However, the fact that the distinction between means-related and ends-related paternalism will on occasion be difficult to apply does not show that the distinction is not a valuable one. Indeed it anticipates and continues to be developed in the current literature on 'nudging'.[38]

One might hesitate to accept the distinction because it appears to focus only on one important aspect of autonomy. Paternalism is acceptable, it effectively says, if the valuable options (ends) of persons are left uninterfered with, while matters of mere instrumental value (means), although interfered with, leave the actor better off in terms of her pursuit of her valuable options or at least no worse off. But while addressing the adequacy of persons' valuable options, it seems to say nothing about our independence to choose. Independence, as briefly mentioned above, was one of Mill's animating ideas. Forcing people to wear seatbelts may not affect any of their valuable options; it may even help them live to see

[38] See the development of the idea of means-related paternalism in J. Le Grand and B. New, *Government Paternalism: Nanny State or Helpful Friend?* (Princeton University Press, 2015), 27–30 and generally. Cf. C.R. Sunstein, *Why Nudge? The Politics of Libertarian Paternalism* (Yale University Press, 2014).

another day so as to succeed in their valuable goals. But such motorists were not able to choose independently and is that not another important aspect of autonomy? Raz – who also elsewhere stresses the importance to autonomy of independent decision-making – stresses that independence is not all or nothing,[39] and that while 'significant loss of independence may be hard to justify, trivial loss of independence hardly calls for justification'.[40] Standing in between of course are partial losses of independence.

What, then, of paternalism, on Raz's account, which is not means-related, but end-related? Any such law or policy, he says, must be compatible with respect for autonomy and 'confined to the creation of the conditions of autonomy'.[41] And as anti-paternalism is not itself built into his harm principle such ends-related paternalism 'must respect the limitation on the use of coercion that is imposed by the harm principle, as well as the analogous restriction on manipulation'.[42] In other words in seeking to coerce persons to avoid them harming themselves, the law's justification should not moralistically seek to ensure that such persons act morally or not immorally. I have already expressed doubts about the possibility of keeping such paternalistic and moralistic reasons separate from one another. In Raz's later article he adds a further condition, viz. that 'barring emergencies', the paternalist coercion 'comes from the hands of someone reasonably trusted by the coerced'. Such a condition of trust, he adds, 'explains the way consent can be relevant to the justification of coercion. It can express or establish a relationship of trust.'[43] This is certainly plausible in relation to certain kinds of relationship between persons, when successful, such as carer and cared-for. The condition of trust is then connected by Raz to an account of citizenship. Citizenship is here conceived as a status making it rationally possible for people to regard themselves as fully belonging to the political community.[44] While someone enjoying full citizenship may legitimately be subjected to coercive paternalism where the coercion is also justified by right reason, the status of full citizenship is a demanding one on the account.

[39] Raz, 'Liberty and trust', 121.
[40] Ibid., 122.
[41] Raz, *Morality of Freedom*, 423.
[42] Ibid., 423.
[43] Raz, 'Liberty and trust', 122.
[44] Ibid., 124.

The account in all its complexity cannot be further explored here. And it is far from clear what the implications would be for the two kinds of case discussed in relation to Hart's endorsement of paternalism, the criminalisation of heroin supply to save persons from themselves and the refusal to recognise consent as a defence to serious violence or murder. Suffice it to note two points. First, leaving aside Raz's plausible account of means-related paternalism and the also plausible restrictions connected to soft paternalism noted above, Raz's views on ends-related paternalism seem closer to Mill's (and less mutinous than Hart's!). Secondly, for all that, he joins Hart in dropping the anti-paternalist element from the harm principle he endorses. Since his account of paternalism is presented outside the scope of his harm principle, this does rather raise the question of quite what work the harm principle is doing. The obvious answer is that the harm principle is there to exclude moralism. Let us turn to that concern now.

d Legal Moralism

According to one strand of Raz's thinking we noted above, government through its law encounters 'no fundamental principled inhibition on ... acting for *any* valid moral reason'.[45] Again: 'it makes no sense to say of a state of affairs that it is good but that fact is no reason to do anything about it';[46] presumably, by the same token, if a state of affairs is *bad*, there is a reason to do something about that also – for the law, for governments, as for anyone else. Moving down a level, then, according to the Millian strand of Raz's thought – his endorsement of the (modified) harm principle – coercion on the part of the law must *not* be used to push people into acting morally or not immorally. This is the main job for the harm principle to do. But how do the moral reasons that are valid at the initial stage mentioned above come to be silenced at the Millian stage? How does the argument work?

Of course, Raz is not endorsing just anything that could be described as a morality at the higher level: he is specifically endorsing a 'morality of freedom' tailored to the contemporary conditions present in modern nations and centred on the value of autonomy for all. The argument

[45] J. Raz, 'Facing up', *Southern California Law Review* 62 (1989) 1153, 1230. Emphasis added.
[46] Ibid.

deriving the harm principle is based on the nature of coercion and the special threat it poses to autonomy. Two features of coercion, Raz believes, allow a derivation of the harm principle from considerations related to autonomy. The first has to do with the *effect* coercion has or threatens to have on options; the second on *the way* in which coercion restricts choice. First, 'coercion by criminal penalties is a global and indiscriminate invasion of autonomy'.[47] Secondly, coercion 'violates the condition of independence', and 'expresses a relation of domination and an attitude of disrespect for the coerced individual'. For these reasons, coercion is ruled out if purportedly imposed on the basis of moral reasons, even those that are independently valid prior to the prospect of using coercion in order to enforce them. Hence the initial and Millian strands on the account are said to be reconciled.

Taking these arguments in turn, the first appears to have two difficulties. It is certainly plausible to say that imprisonment is often a global and indiscriminate invasion of autonomy. And the argument could be usefully extended in many cases to the compulsory detention of mentally disordered persons under the civil law. But many other criminal penalties are not this devastating to a person's ability to choose between an adequate range of valuable options. Fines, electronic tags and community service orders may be unpleasant and costly in various ways, but hardly 'global and indiscriminate'.[48] They may leave intact the adequacy of someone's range of valuable options. The argument, then, appears not to rule out moralism in general even in relation to criminalisation, provided the penalties are not global and indiscriminate invasions of autonomy. Secondly, it remains unclear why moralism is ruled out by such an autonomy-based consideration more generally, as the harm principle demands. It must be remembered that on Raz's account it is the adequacy of the range of *valuable* options that matters. In his own words:

> ... not all the constraints imposed by coercion are a restriction of the autonomy of the coerced. An autonomous life is valuable only to the extent that it is engaged in *valuable* activities and relationships. The loss of an opportunity to murder does nothing to reduce one's chances of having the sort of autonomous life which is of

[47] Raz, *Morality of Freedom*, 418.

[48] J. Stanton-Ife, 'The limits of law' in E.N. Zalta (ed.), *The Stanford Encyclopedia of Philosophy* (Winter 2016 ed.), https://plato.stanford.edu/archives/win2016/entries/law-limits/.

value, hence there is nothing lost in not having the opportunity to murder, and one's autonomy, in the sense of a capacity for valuable autonomous life, is not constrained by the absence of that option.[49]

It appears to follow that provided the law's coercion is genuinely directed at something immoral, its damage to opportunity is only the irrelevant damage to an activity *without* value and hence not ruled out by the value of autonomy or, in turn, by legal moralism. If one takes it that gambling for very high stakes is immoral (let us assume this here for the sake of argument), criminalising on such a moral ground appears not to violate Razian autonomy. Realistically one might find it very difficult to criminalise gambling. The activity might be driven underground; other valuable options might come under attack simultaneously. These considerations may make it unjustified to criminalise such gambling. This, however, will be for reasons independent of the harm principle as currently conceived.

That leaves most of the heavy lifting in establishing the derivation of the harm principle to Raz's other argument mentioned above based on coercion's threat to independence. This, however, takes us back to the issue of paternalism, opposition to which (as we have seen) Raz followed Hart in excluding from the harm principle. It turns out that soft paternalism and means-related paternalism aside, Raz's anti-paternalism is in reality more significant than his anti-moralism, which appears not to have been successfully derived, via the coercion argument, from the initial Aristotelianism or perfectionism of the position. If a moral reason is valid at the higher level, it has not been shown how it loses validity at the lower level. As far as the harm principle is concerned we are left with an important reminder about the damage long-term imprisonment and compulsory civil detention can do to the autonomy of persons. That point, however, highly significant as it is in practice, does not seem to need the harm principle for support. And the independence/anti-paternalist argument appears to float free of the Razian harm principle.

Ultimately, one might wonder if anything is gained by the invocation of the harm principle on the Razian account? We began the chapter quoting Raz's words on the end of the law and it is worth quoting them again: 'The law's task, put abstractly, is to secure a situation whereby moral goals ... are realised' where – 'given the current social situation in the country

[49] Raz, 'Liberty and trust', 120. Emphasis in the original.

whose law it is' – the moral goal in question 'would be unlikely to be achieved without it', and 'whose achievement by the law is not counterproductive'.[50]

The statement here makes no reference to the harm principle, but it does flag up a different sort of consideration, the possibility that the achievement of a moral goal might turn out to be counterproductive. If so, however good the moral reason, there may be a stronger reason for the law to stay its hand. There are a large variety of defeating conditions that will surely be accepted ecumenically, whatever principled view one takes on the ends and limits of the law. One may not be able to legislate against certain wrongful conduct without also coercing valuable or neutral conduct. One might not have the resources to enforce laws against other wrongful conduct, and legislating in such cases may risk making a 'scarecrow of the law', which if unenforced becomes a 'perch', not a 'terror'.[51]

One sort of case, according to Michael Moore, is conduct which, as experience teaches us, will be engaged in inevitably whether or not the law intervenes:

> for behaviour that will be engaged in anyway even if legislated against, there will be a peculiar effect of prohibition, namely the raising of the prices of the products or services necessary for such behaviour; this, in turn, may increase the profits of supplying such services or products, which in turn sustains organised criminal activities. This is typically known as the 'crime tariff'. Prostitution, for example, does not go away by being legislated against, as the experience of all societies has shown. By making it criminal, however, the supply is artificially restricted to those willing to engage in criminal behaviour, so that prices and profits are such as to draw in organised criminal activity.[52]

And so on. One sort of legal moralist view, therefore, will affirm as the end of law that it should seek to secure the realisation of moral goals or to promote the well-being of persons, but work with a developed understanding of defeating conditions of this sort. It will seek a sophisticated and realistic sense of what can be achieved by law and what cannot. When one thinks of what it is Rawls wishes to see ruled out under the heading of 'comprehensive doctrines' – 'conceptions of what is of value in human life, ideals of personal character, as well as ideals of friendship and of familial

[50] Raz, *Between Authority and Interpretation*, 178.
[51] Shakespeare, *Measure for Measure*, Act II, Scene 1.
[52] Moore, *Placing Blame*, 664.

and associational relationships', and so on – the legal moralist can argue that there is an alternative to dispensing with these important and attractive ideas altogether, namely working with a psychologically well-informed and realistic notion of how far the law is genuinely likely to help secure such ideas and when not. Promotion of well-being is likely to succeed where the conditions and environment for willing adoption of life plans are established, rather than any attempt to coerce persons into 'willing' or 'wholehearted' flourishing. Above we briefly alluded to Ripstein's sovereignty principle, his proposed alternative to Mill's harm principle. In proposing it, Ripstein suggested that 'the only way to unseat a time-honoured principle is to provide a superior alternative'.[53] Perhaps the lesson of the formidable difficulties into which the harm principle has been led is not that the superior alternative is a superior alternative *principle*. It is rather a form of legal moralism without any overarching master principle, but one that is sensitive in the way just described to the variety of potential defeating conditions to which any plausible legal moralism is subject.

That said, most proponents of legal moralism in fact take the view that one must truncate in some way the relevant moral reasons that the law may legitimately rely upon. For most legal moralists, not all wrongdoing is a reason (even one subject to defeat) for legal coercion; for example, trivial wrongdoing[54] or private wrongdoing[55] might be excluded. These are thought to be areas of law's morality that are simply not the law's business. Views of the sort are currently under development.[56]

2 Public Reason

In the introduction we briefly sketched another line of thought of significance for the question of the ends and limits of the law. This is the

[53] Ripstein, 'Beyond the harm principle', 215. Tadros, 'Harm, sovereignty and prohibition', plausibly argues that while Ripstein's sovereignty principle successfully accounts for certain cases better than does the harm principle, the opposite is also true: the harm principle does better accounting for other cases.

[54] Tadros, *Wrongs and Crimes*.

[55] R.A. Duff, 'Legal moralism and public wrongs' in K.K. Ferzan and S. Morse (eds.) *Legal, Moral, and Metaphysical Truths: The Philosophy of Michael S. Moore* (Oxford University Press, 2016).

[56] Ibid.

Rawlsian idea that, at least as far as constitutional essentials and matters of basic justice are concerned, a specialised 'public reason' is required. No recourse should be permissible to moral truth as conceived as part and parcel of a comprehensive moral doctrine, that is – as we saw above – a moral or ethical or religious understanding of what makes lives good or virtuous or worthwhile. Public reason thus involves a rejection of the legal moralist idea that law's end is to realise independently identified moral goals. The basic idea behind it is that 'our laws and political institutions must be justifiable to each of us by reference to some common point of view, despite our deep differences and disagreements'.[57] Rather than ask what the truth is, we ask how the law is to be justified *to* those who are to be subject to it. In Rawls' own somewhat convoluted wording a legal system must give 'reasons we might reasonably expect . . . free and equal citizens might reasonably also accept'.[58]

Moreover:

> What we cannot do in public reason is to proceed directly from our comprehensive doctrine, or a part thereof, to one or several political principles and values, and the particular institutions they support. Instead, we are required first to work to the basic ideas of a complete political conception and from there to elaborate its principles and ideals, and to use the arguments they provide.[59]

Public reason is to be derived from a set of reasonable political conceptions of justice. One such reasonable political conception – Rawls stresses it is only one – is the conception he himself famously argues would be chosen in the 'original position'.[60] While the doctrines of Roman Catholicism would be a paradigmatic example of what public reason seeks to *rule out*, Rawls states that 'Catholic views of the common good and solidarity when they are expressed in terms of political values' *can* be one grounding for the political conception that gives the content of public reason, as could Habermas' 'discourse conception of legitimacy (sometimes said to be radically democratic rather than liberal)'. Rawls emphasises that 'new variations' of reasonable political conceptions 'may be proposed from time

[57] J. Quong, 'On the idea of public reason', in J. Mandle, and D.A. Reidy (eds.), *A Companion to Rawls* (Wiley, Blackwell, 2014), 265. For critique see D. Enoch, *Against Public Reason* (Oxford University Press, 2015).

[58] Rawls, *The Law of Peoples* 138.

[59] Ibid., 145–6.

[60] Rawls, *Political Liberalism*, lecture I, sec. 4, 22–8.

to time and older ones may cease to be represented'. Thus the political conceptions from which he envisages principles of public reason should be drawn are not fixed in time and will maintain some fluidity, allowing scope for the claims of groups and interests arising from social change.[61]

In insisting we must not proceed directly from comprehensive moral doctrines, Rawls stresses the plurality and the irreconcilability of contemporary moral doctrines and conceptions of the good life. Such plurality and irreconcilability implies, he argues, that these conceptions cannot practically be the basis of agreement 'or even approach mutual understanding'.[62] He does not just mean that reasonable conceptions of the good life will conflict with unreasonable ones. He means that the reasonable doctrines will themselves be numerous and irreconcilable. We must therefore eschew them and insulate central aspects of the law from more general issues of ethics, morality and theology by means of a sensitive development of public reason derived in the way briefly sketched above. Public reason is something that all people subject to law can understand, appreciate and endorse. This, Rawls holds, is unlike any partisan comprehensive moral doctrine.

It is impossible in a work of this length to get anywhere close to a fair representation of Rawls' detailed and subtle account and its relationship with his vast body of work on justice and political liberalism. He himself summarises the 'definite structure' of public reason as having five different aspects:

> (1) the fundamental political questions to which it applies; (2) the persons to whom it applies (government officials and candidates for public office); (3) its content as given by a family of reasonable political conceptions of justice; (4) the application of these in discussions of coercive norms to be enacted in the form of legitimate law for a democratic people; and (5) citizens' checking that the principles derived from their conceptions of justice satisfy the criterion of reciprocity.[63]

Here we can comment only very selectively. One area of controversy (including from within the group of authors sympathetic to Rawlsian public reason) is the restriction of the scope of the idea of public reason. Rawls states that public reason is the reason of the public *qua* free and

[61] Rawls, *The Law of Peoples*, 142.
[62] Rawls, *The Law of Peoples*, 132.
[63] Ibid., 133.

equal citizens and that its subject is 'the public good' compounded of the two kinds: 'constitutional essentials and matters of basic justice'.[64] Constitutional essentials are said by him to 'concern questions about what political rights and liberties ... may reasonably be included in a written constitution, when assuming the constitution may be interpreted by a supreme court, or some similar body'. Matters of basic justice in turn 'relate to the basic structure of society and so would concern questions of basic economic and social justice and other things not covered by a constitution'.[65] Naturally Rawls emphasises that public reason is not to be applied to the media – newspapers, reviews, the Internet – for that would be inimical to liberties of thought and speech.[66] He also states it is not to be applied to what he calls 'the background culture', institutions of learning, scientific and other societies, churches and associations of all kinds.[67]

Jonathan Quong, while sympathetic to the idea of public reason, objects that there seems to be plenty of space in which political power may be exercised in between the twin matters of constitutional essentials and matters of basic justice – on the one hand – and the workings of the media, churches, universities, etc. – on the other.[68] Space where, in his view, Rawls is too permissive of comprehensive doctrines of the good life or 'perfectionist' values. For example Rawls states:

> It does not follow that perfectionist values can never be appealed to in any form, say in suitably circumscribed questions legislators must consider, or on certain matters of policy. The main point is that there should be a good-faith commitment not to appeal to them to settle constitutional essentials and basic matters of justice. Fundamental justice must be achieved first. After that a democratic electorate may devote large resources to grand projects in the arts and science if it so chooses.[69]

To develop his objection Quong imagines a case in which a group of citizens would like an art gallery to be built with public money in order to honour the beauty of fine art, that is, in support of a comprehensive doctrine regarding what makes life worthwhile. The city already has one art gallery but no football stadium. The football stadium supporters offer,

[64] Ibid., 133.
[65] Ibid., 133, n. 7.
[66] Ibid., 134.
[67] Ibid., 134.
[68] J. Quong, *Liberalism without Perfectionism* (Oxford University Press, 2011).
[69] Rawls, 'Justice as fairness', 152. Quoted in Quong, *Liberalism without Perfectionism*, 281.

by contrast, what look like a set of public reasons in favour of building the stadium instead. They cite the issue of fairness in the light of the fact that there already is an art gallery and evidence that the stadium will stimulate the broader economy unlike the extra art gallery and so on. However, on Rawls' account we would apparently have 'no cause for concern if the art gallery proposal wins out in a fair procedural vote'.[70] As these are not constitutional essentials or basic matters of justice, the comprehensive view of the good life is apparently acceptably allowed significant sway. So much the worse for Rawls' account of public reason in Quong's view; he believes examples such as this should propel us away from Rawls' view toward the endorsement of 'The Broad View', according to which 'the idea of public reason ought to apply, whenever possible, to *all* decisions where citizens exercise political power over one another'.[71] What animates public reason in relation to constitutional essentials and matters of basic justice should animate it in the domain of political power generally.

Moving away from what some would see as marginal cases of legitimate legal regulation, others less sympathetic to Rawlsian public reason have questioned the ability of Rawlsian public reasoning to account fully or satisfactorily for certain central domains in which the law's coercive presence is plainly legitimate. For example beyond the uncontroversial judgement that a legal system should criminalise rape or serious sexual assault, many questions emerge about what should be the appropriate content of sexual offence laws. On some views and in some legal systems rape is seen as an attack on sexual autonomy – intercourse without consent is rape, irrespective of whether violence was present. On other views and in other legal systems force or violence is necessary for a rape conviction, perhaps due to the effect such traumatic experience will typically have on a life. Victor Tadros argues that issues of the sort turn on 'controversial views of which features of a person ground his or her moral significance'.[72] And there seems to be no more prospect of these deep

[70] J. Quong, *Liberalism without Perfectionism* (Oxford University Press, 2011), 280. Cf. J. Stanton-Ife, 'Must we pay for the British Museum?', taxation and the harm principle' in M. Bhandari (ed.), *Philosophical Foundations of Tax Law* (Oxford University Press, 2017).

[71] Quong, *Liberalism without Perfectionism*, 274. Emphasis added.

[72] V. Tadros, 'Fair labelling and social solidarity' in L. Zedner and J.V. Roberts (eds.) *Principles and Values in Criminal Law and Criminal Justice* (Oxford University Press, 2012), 67–80, 77. Cf. J. Rubenfeld, 'The riddle of rape-by-deception and the myth of sexual autonomy', *Yale Law Journal* 122 (2013), 1372.

differences being resolved any sooner than the other inveterate differences in comprehensive doctrines and moral understandings that we have seen Rawls emphasise. Legal systems choose as they must between these different underlying moral understandings. In doing so they apparently break the bounds of public reason, putting in question the ability of the view to account adequately for cases of the sort that no one doubts are proper objects of legal proscription.

More recently, Tadros has taken further this form of critique of public reason – based on its inability to handle adequately some of the most serious wrongs with which the law deals. Tadros believes that an important advantage of the public reason view is that it takes seriously the independence of persons.[73] He argues, however, that the value of independence is not engaged in relation to seriously harmful wrongs, in particular those with which the criminal law is concerned. The content and scope of serious wrongs is 'not determined by the ambition to ensure that the law is acceptable to those with different basic moral views'. Tadros continues:

> Those who reject the scope of the law because of their mistaken views, in such cases, have no objection to state interference to prevent them from acting wrongly. They may feel alienated from their state, but any disvalue in their alienation is outweighed or negated by the importance of ensuring that serious wrongdoing does not occur.[74]

At least as far as core cases of criminalisation are concerned, Tadros concludes, the fact that people reasonably disagree about what is wrong is not a matter of great importance and is certainly not a decisive consideration.[75]

Perhaps the most common form of objection to public reason accounts, however, has focused on the division between public reasons and non-public reasons. Ronald Dworkin for one alleged that Rawls himself describes the weakness of his own proposal. For Rawls asks of his own account of public reason 'How is it possible – or is it – for those of faith, as well as the non-religious (secular), to endorse a constitutional regime even when their comprehensive doctrines may not prosper under it, and indeed

[73] Tadros, *Wrongs and Crimes*, ch. 8.
[74] Ibid., 156.
[75] Ibid., 157; cf. J. Stanton-Ife, 'Horrific crime' in R.A. Duff, L. Farmer, S.E. Marshall, M. Renzo and V. Tadros, (eds.), *The Boundaries of the Criminal Law* (Oxford University Press, 2010), 138–62.

may decline?'[76] Consider what Dworkin calls 'the schism over religion in America'. For here, Dworkin suggests, we see that the religious convictions of many Americans *are* political principles, not something ultimately distinguishable from political principles. Dworkin quotes the religious conservative Newt Gingrich as saying, 'We must re-establish that our rights come from our Creator, and that an America that has driven God out of the public arena is an America on the way to decay and defeat.'[77] Dworkin's religious conservatives 'do not accept private observance as a substitute for public religious endorsement; they want to celebrate their god not just as private worshipers but as citizens'. Further they do not believe that religion is inaccessible to atheists, but rather that such people stubbornly and wilfully close their hearts to the truth. As well as denying the psychological possibility of demanding from the citizens in question that they separate their ethical or religious convictions from their political ones in the way that the idea of public reason demands, Dworkin also questions the *desirability* of so doing. After all, did not Martin Luther King Jr – a man of faith – not invoke his religion to condemn prejudice with great effect?

In part at least Dworkin's criticism of Rawls overlooks what the latter calls the 'proviso' to his idea of public reason. Rawls' proviso holds that

> reasonable comprehensive doctrines, religious or non-religious, *may* be introduced in public political discussion at any time, provided that in due course proper political reasons – and not reasons given solely by comprehensive doctrines – are presented that are sufficient to support whatever the comprehensive doctrines introduced are said to support.[78]

There are no restrictions, Rawls emphasises, on how religious or secular doctrines are to be expressed; they need not for example be 'by some standards logically correct, or open to rational appraisal, or evidentially supportable'.[79] Rawls also declares that the religiously based arguments of the Civil Rights Movement – for which Martin Luther King Jr was of course a leading light – can be seen as entirely consistent with his idea of public

[76] Rawls, *Law of Peoples (with 'The Idea of Public Reason Revisited')*, 149.

[77] Dworkin, *Is Democracy Possible*, 64. Cf. the discussion in C. Taylor, *A Secular Age* (Belknap Press, 2007), 42.

[78] Rawls, *The Law of Peoples*, 152. Emphasis added.

[79] Ibid., 153.

reason. Notwithstanding the religious roots of many civil rights arguments 'these doctrines supported basic constitutional values – as they themselves asserted – and so supported reasonable conceptions of political justice'.[80] Dworkin is surely right to say that it would be unrealistic to demand of the religious citizens he has in mind that they refrain altogether from praying in aid their deepest religious convictions when engaged in political reasoning. But Rawls denies that his notion of public reason requires that. Citizens of faith, in Rawls' own example, *may* cite the Gospel parable of the Good Samaritan, provided they 'do not stop there, but go on to give a public justification for that parable's conclusions in terms of political values'.[81]

One might wonder about how well public reason could operate in practice on this understanding. Quite how, in such a climate permissibly replete with religious and non-religious comprehensive doctrines, one is to police how far 'sufficient' public reasons have also been given and to discern the relative persuasive force of those public reasons (that must be eventually decisive) as against the comprehensive doctrines (that must eventually be ruled out). Perhaps it is enough to say with Rawls that 'the details about how to satisfy this proviso must be worked out in practice and cannot feasibly be governed by a clear family of rules given in advance'.[82]

Alternatively one might want to press harder on the feasibility and/or desirability of detaching public reasons from the reasons of reasonable comprehensive doctrines. Certain kinds of theory may work better with the idea of public reason than others. Jeremy Waldron characterises the idea of a public reason as a 'search for common ground involv[ing] the identification and isolation of particular items in the set of reasons that one person brings to a public issue and their detachment and the matching of them with items in the set of reasons that another person brings to the same public issue'.[83] This might, Waldron allows, work fine for some consequentialist views, where the set of reasons that a given person brings to the public issue is a simple aggregation of distinct items: 'that a given proposal would advance *this* interest is one thing, that it would advance *that* other interest is another

[80] Ibid., 155.
[81] Ibid., 155.
[82] Ibid., 153.
[83] J. Waldron, 'Isolating public reasons' in T. Brooks and M.C. Nussbaum, *Rawls's Political Liberalism* (Columbia University Press, 2015), 113–37, 135.

thing, and so on'. But, he argues, this model works badly in the case of rights-based and deontological theories in which 'reasons often work as a system and take their shape and importance from their context, from other reasons in their vicinity in a given person's package of reasons'.

Still more fundamentally, a number of critics of public reason have fastened on to the idealisation the approach involves.[84] When we ask what is 'reasonably acceptable to free and equal citizens' this does not mean exactly whatever the actual citizens will in fact accept, for they may not accept reasonably. The citizens need to be idealised to an extent; constraints of reasonableness must be placed on what it is that they can accept. But then there seems a danger that 'reasonable' acceptance may collapse into simply accepting that which is true. If so, there may be no genuine alternative to 'the zeal to embody the whole truth in politics'.[85] Worse, those who purport to argue from the standpoint of public reason will have illegitimately used a purportedly neutral procedure which is in reality nothing of the kind. As Raz puts the concern: 'There may be no middle way between actual (including implied) agreement and rational justification.'[86] Whether the public reason approach can overcome such objections will surely in part depend on how successfully it can be developed through the careful development of case studies and real-world applications of the view. The aspiration to find common ground in law and politics is a worthy one.

Conclusion

While some authors write as if there is only one version of the harm principle,[87] I have stressed the variety of such approaches; in particular attention has been drawn to the tension in Mill's original version between harm prevention and independence. I have acknowledged as a central bone of contention the place of moral goals and the well-being of persons in our

[84] J. Raz, 'Facing diversity: the case of epistemic abstinence', *Philosophy & Public Affairs* 19:1 (1990), 3–46, Enoch, *Against Public Reason*.
[85] Rawls, *The Law of Peoples*, 132–3.
[86] Raz, 'Facing diversity: the case of epistemic abstinence', 46.
[87] J. Wolff, *Ethics and Public Policy: A Philosophical Inquiry* (Routledge, 2011) 37–60 in a fine study of the legal regulation of gambling and other areas of conduct, however, might appear to dismiss 'the harm principle' on grounds that might be accommodated on other versions of the principle.

understanding of the ends of laws. To many, such moral goals must be subjected to limiting principles, most famously the harm principle itself. I examined in some detail Raz's attempt to reconcile legal moralist and Millian themes. To others the very invocation of 'true morality' is anathema and must be replaced by a specialised public reason for legal matters of central importance. I have also emphasised that even the staunchest of legal moralists must recognise a large range of limitations on securing moral ends through the law. It will be interesting to see the development of legal moralist approaches that avoid any master principle, be that a harm or sovereignty principle or whatever, and which develop sophisticated understandings of what can and cannot be achieved by legal implementing techniques.

To this end it will be important to focus more than has been the case in the past on law's implementing techniques beyond coercion. It would of course be folly to deny the importance of the coercive mechanisms to the law, most obviously imprisoning and fining. But there are a number of others. Hart famously identified nullity as a further device of legal implementation of law's ends, stressing *pace* Kelsen that it could not sensibly be reduced to coercion.[88] Among other implementing devices available to law, Robert Summers adds 'educational effort, rewards and other incentives, symbolic deployment of legal forms, publicity (favourable or adverse), continuous supervision, public signs and signals, recognised statuses and entities' and 'grants with strings attached'.[89] Examination of the ends and limits of the law will benefit from close attention to all of these implementing techniques. These debates have long been central to our understanding of law and will continue to be so. It is to be hoped that more work is to come on the ends and limits of law conceived widely and without overemphasis on the justification of legal coercion.

[88] Hart, *Concept of Law*, 33ff.

[89] R.S. Summers, 'Naïve instrumentalism and the law', in P.M.S. Hacker and J. Raz, *Law, Morality and Society* (Oxford University Press, 1977), 119, 126. For a recent study see R.H. McAdams, *The Expressive Powers of Law: Theories and Limits* (Harvard University Press, 2015).

Part III

Special Theory

Causation and Responsibility 12

Richard Holton

The notions of causation and responsibility are deeply entwined in the law. Two questions about responsibility are central to any legal system: (i) for which consequences of your actions are you responsible? And (ii) for which of your actions themselves are you responsible? Our main focus will be on the former, but causation plays a fundamental role in both.

What is the responsibility in question? It is not moral responsibility but legal. Just as legal obligation is distinct from moral obligation, so legal responsibility is distinct from moral responsibility: one can have moral responsibilities that are not legal, and, barring a general moral responsibility to obey the law, legal responsibilities that are not moral. Equally though, legal responsibility should not be equated with legal culpability; I may have a legal responsibility in an area in which I have no culpability: perhaps I have done nothing even *prima facie* illegal, or I have but I have a justification or an excuse. We can think of legal responsibility as something like answerability: I am legally responsible for those things I must legally answer for.[1]

Understood this way, the importance of causation in determining which consequences of my actions I am legally responsible for is obvious. The very notion of consequence is itself a causal one: by and large, the things for which one is responsible, whether in criminal law or in torts, are those that causally issue from one's actions. Sometimes the causal element is explicitly noted in the law; sometimes it is implicit in the causal terms that the law uses. Notions such as 'murder', 'battery' or 'negligence' all involve

[1] For different ways of developing this approach, see A. Duff, *Answering for Crime: Responsibility and Liability in the Criminal Law* (Hart Publishing, 2007); J. Gardner, *Offences and Defences* (Oxford University Press, 2007); J. Gardner, 'Relations of responsibility' in R. Cruft, M. Kramer and M. Reiff (eds.), *Crime, Punishment and Responsibility* (Oxford University Press, 2011) 87–102.

causal relations: a necessary condition for murder is that the defendant *caused* the victim to die.

So should we understand causation as a *necessary* condition on responsibility for outcome? That rather depends on how we understand causation. Take, for instance, a case of overdetermination: you and I each do something that would have been enough on its own to bring about the effect. It might seem that each of us should be responsible for it, but on some prevalent accounts of causation – most notably those which say that a cause is something without which the effect would not have occurred – neither of us looks to count as a cause. So either we have to give up on the idea that causation is necessary for responsibility, or we have to give an alternative account of causation. A great deal of the discussion here has been devoted to trying to formulate an alternative account that will do the work.

A second issue concerns whether having caused an outcome is *sufficient* to be legally responsible for it. In an unqualified form that claim is surely too strong. Other people, or rogue happenings, might intervene in the chain of events, and that might affect responsibility. Moreover, if causation is, as many think, a transitive notion – so that if A causes B, and B causes C, it follows that A causes C – then the consequences of one's actions extend indefinitely into the future. Are we responsible for all of them? Or only some, those that are sufficiently close to the action, those that have the requisite proximity? And if we take the latter course, how do we characterise 'sufficiently close'? Is that itself to be characterised in terms of the metaphysics of causation – in terms of 'cause in fact' as it is often called? Or is it rather a normative question, to be settled by reference to other factors about what we ought to be held responsible for? Much of the debate around the legal notion of causation has focused on how to draw the boundary here.

Turning to the role of causation in determining which actions we are responsible for, we find that parallel issues arise. Most jurisdictions recognise some kind of insanity defence. If someone kills while suffering from paranoid schizophrenia, they may not be legally responsible for what they have done. But in most jurisdictions, it is not enough that they kill and that they suffer from the illness: it needs to be shown that the illness was relevantly implicated in the killing. The natural way to understand this is again in terms of causation: there has to be a causal influence of the illness on the killing. If so, many of the issues that arose in determining responsibility for outcome – issues around pre-emption, overdetermination and proximity – will have parallels here.

We will look at these two issues in turn, with our focus on responsibility for outcome, but first it will be helpful to examine ways of understanding the metaphysical framework surrounding the notion of causation.

1 The Metaphysical Framework

The philosophical literature on causation is enormous and increasingly complicated; there is no chance of summarising it. Still, two debates can be identified which will be enough to structure the discussion.

The first debate is over which kind of relation captures the essence of causation. There are two distinct ideas that underpin much of our everyday thinking. One is that a cause is *sufficient* for its effect: the cause is whatever it takes to bring the effect about. The other is that a cause is *necessary* for its effect: that in the absence of the cause, the effect would not have happened. Philosophical *analyses* of causation – that is, accounts that seek to define causation in terms that do not mention causation themselves – typically take one or the other as fundamental. For many years, particularly under the influence of David Hume, philosophical theories focused on the sufficiency side. But since the 1970s the philosophical orthodoxy has shifted radically, so that now most accounts focus on necessity: causes are those things without which the effect would not have happened.

Part of the explanation for that shift is tied up with the second major philosophical debate around causation, which concerns the metaphysical machinery to be used in the account. In characterising causation, should we make use of modal notions, most centrally of counterfactuals, statements that make reference to how things *would have* turned out under other circumstances? Or is such talk philosophically illegitimate? Here again Hume's work casts a long shadow. Hume was suspicious of talk that did not concern how things can be observed to be; modal notions tended to fall prey to this suspicion. So his version of the sufficiency claim was formulated in terms of regularity: very roughly, C causes E if and only if things of the same type as C are always followed by things of the same type as E. Such an account makes no mention of how things would have been (although oddly Hume does at one point say that it is equivalent to a counterfactual formulation). After Hume, many have realised that such an account is vulnerable to various kinds of counterexample (what if C is the only one of its type? What if C and E are both effects of some common cause? What if C has been invariably followed by E as a result of some great coincidence?) and so later empiricist accounts, from Mill to Mackie, typically made use of the idea of a natural law – C causes E if there is some *law-like regularity* linking C and E – where the idea of a law is not itself defined in counterfactual terms.

In contrast to all this, accounts that focus on the necessity of the cause for the effect have typically been formulated using explicitly counterfactual machinery. The most influential are from David Lewis, whose accounts of causation are couched in terms of the semantics of counterfactuals that he developed: again roughly, a counterfactual of the form 'If it were the case that P it would be the case that Q' is true just in case the closest possible world (i.e. closest to the actual world) in which P obtains is a world in which Q obtains. (Closeness is to be understood in terms of similarity.) Using this account, Lewis defined a notion of *causal dependence*: E is causally dependent on C if and only if (i) if C were to occur, then E would occur, and (ii) if C were to fail to occur, then E would also fail to occur. Causation itself was then analysed by Lewis in terms of a chain of causal dependencies.[2] C causes E just in case either E causally depends directly on C, or there is a chain of dependencies between events more or less long stretching back from E to C. This guarantees that causation will be a transitive notion.[3]

However, this association of sufficiency with regularity accounts, and of necessity with counterfactual accounts, is largely a historical accident. Lewis, as we have just seen, defines causal dependence in terms of two clauses: while the second (if C were to fail to occur, E would fail to occur) is clearly a necessity condition, the first (if C were to occur, E would occur) looks like a sufficiency condition. In fact, on Lewis' account of counterfactuals, that condition is trivially satisfied when C and E have both happened (the closest world to the actual world in which C obtains is the actual world itself, and that is a world in which E obtains), but on other accounts of counterfactuals – those that reject 'strong centring' – it will not be. On such accounts C is sufficient for E just in case in *every close world* to the actual world in which C happens, E happens – here Hume's quantification across different actual events is replaced by quantification

[2] D. Lewis, 'Causation', *Journal of Philosophy* 70 (1973), 556–67.

[3] Lewis came to refine his account in significant ways, but this will not concern us here. D. Lewis, 'Causation as influence', *Journal of Philosophy* 97 (2000), 182–97.

across different occurrences of the same event in different possible circumstances. Or, more plausibly, since most causes will require other factors to be present if they are to be sufficient we might say that something is a cause just in case it is a non-redundant member of a set of conditions that suffice for the effect; we will return to such an account – propounded by Mackie, and in the legal literature by Wright[4] – shortly.

We will not be further concerned with regularity accounts here, or with the empiricist scruples that motivate them. Attempts to dispense with all modal talk and to replace it with notions of law-like regularity or of entailment, where these are not in turn cashed out in modal talk, have not been very successful.[5] Moreover empiricist scruples themselves are far from natural. Ordinary speech is full of counterfactual constructions, as is most legal practice and legal theorising. So the focus here will rather be on whether necessity or sufficiency conditions should be central – or whether we need some mixture of the two – where both of these are to be understood in explicitly modal counterfactual terms. Before examining how this has played out in the law, let us first examine the problems that the two approaches face.

2 Problems for the Accounts

a Problems for Necessity Accounts

The first problem facing necessity accounts is that they under-count causes, because of how they handle cases of redundancy: cases in which there are other causes that would bring the effect about if the cause in question did not do so. Such cases are typically divided into two types:

(i) Cases of *pre-emption*, where it is intuitively clear that there is one factor that is the cause – the pre-empting cause – but where something else would have caused the same (or a very similar) effect if the pre-empting cause had not already done so: assassin A shoots V before

[4] J.L. Mackie, 'Causes and conditions', *American Philosophical Quarterly* 2 (1965), 245–64. R. Wright, 'Once more into the bramble bush: duty, causal contribution, and the extent of legal responsibility', *Vanderbilt Law Review* 54 (2001), 1071–132; R. Wright, 'The nightmare and the noble dream' in M. Kramer, C. Grant, B. Colburn and A. Hatzistavrou (eds.) *The Legacy of H.L.A. Hart: Legal, Political, and Moral Philosophy* (Oxford University Press, 2007), 165–77.

[5] L.A. Paul and N. Hall, *Causation, A User's Guide* (Oxford University Press, 2013), 42–3.

assassin B can do so. These are further divided into cases of *early* pre-emption, where the pre-empting cause stops or interrupts the alternative cause – hearing A's shot, B does not fire; and cases of *late* pre-emption, where the alternative cause is not interrupted but simply happens too late – A's shot kills V before B's shot hits.

(ii) Cases of *overdetermination*, where there is redundancy and yet there is a symmetry, so that each putative cause does intuitively seem to contribute to the effect. These are further divided into cases of *sufficient overdetermination* where each of the causes would have been sufficient on its own, and so each of which is redundant (assassins A and B both shoot V simultaneously; each is enough to kill), or cases of *insufficient overdetermination* where the causes, while being individually redundant, are not individually sufficient, since several but not all of them are required for the effect (assassins A, B and C all shoot V simultaneously; two shots are needed to kill).

Necessity accounts clearly do badly on all of these redundancy cases: in their simplest form they will conclude that there is no cause, because in each case no single factor is necessary.

A second problem with necessity accounts concerns the *over-counting* of causes. Everything that is necessary for an effect counts as one of its causes: not just the action of the arsonist in striking the match, but also the presence of oxygen, the action of her parents in conceiving her, and the origins of the universe. Perhaps more counterintuitive still, *absences* seem to count as causes, and, again, these may be very distant: so not just the failure of the police officer to check what the arsonist was doing, and the absence of a sprinkler system, but also the failure of a thief to steal her car thereby stopping her getting to the site, and, more distant still, the failure of other suitors to have stopped her parents ever conceiving her. Philosophers tend to be rather dismissive of such worries, happy to say that, once we stop talking about *the cause* of an event and start talking about *causes*, all can be welcomed in. But in the legal world, where cause brings responsibility, such liberality is a problem.

b Problems for Sufficiency Accounts

Sufficiency accounts also face substantial problems, some of their own, and some that they share with necessity accounts. The first concerns how to understand the relevant notion of sufficiency. Obviously what we think of as a cause is not sufficient on its own: pulling the trigger would not have caused the gun to fire if there had not been oxygen present to react with the explosives in the cartridge. So a first move, as with necessity accounts, is to think in terms, not of the single cause, but of a set of causes. We might try to formulate a sufficiency account by saying that something is a cause if it is one of a set of factors that are sufficient for the effect. But that is too liberal: each of the factors in the set had better do some work. If we add this requirement that they do some work, saying that something is a cause if it is a *necessary* member of a set of factors that are jointly sufficient for the cause, we arrive at the kind of account that was introduced into legal theory by Hart and Honoré[6] and has been most influentially defended in the philosophical literature by Mackie[7] (under the heading INUS: Insufficient but Necessary part of a condition which is itself Unnecessary but Sufficient). This of course builds in elements of necessity as well as sufficiency. Moved by empiricist scruples, Mackie tried to account for both in terms of laws; but both can more naturally be analysed in terms of counterfactuals.

How does a mixed sufficient account along these lines fare with the redundancy problems that beset the necessity account? In cases of pre-emption, where A shoots and kills V before B has the chance to do so, it has the mirror image problem. The sufficiency account has no difficulty classing A's shooting as a cause of V's death: A is a member of a set of factors that are sufficient for it. Its problem comes with the pre-empted event: since B's shooting is also a member of a set of factors that are sufficient for V's death, it will wrongly identify it as a cause. (There is some debate about this – some[8] have argued that it will not count, since V will not be alive to be killed; but for an effective response see Maslen.[9]) When it comes to overdetermination, sufficiency accounts do better. In cases of sufficient overdetermination (A and B each shoot V simultaneously; each shot would be enough for V's death), both A's shooting and B's count as causes, since

[6] H.L.A. Hart and T. Honoré, *Causation in the Law*, 2nd ed. (Clarendon Press, 1985).
[7] Mackie, 'Causes and conditions'.
[8] M. Strevens, 'Mackie remixed' in J. Campbell, M. O'Rourke and H. Silverstein (eds.), *Causation and Explanation* (MIT Press, 2007); M. Moore, *Causation and Responsibility* (Oxford University Press, 2009).
[9] C. Maslen, 'Regularity accounts of causation and the problem of pre-emption: dark prospects indeed', *Erkenntnis* 77 (2012), 419–34.

each is a necessary part of a sufficient set: A's of a set that does not include B's, and B's of a set that does not include A's. They likewise do well with cases of insufficient overdetermination (A, B and C all shoot; any two shots would be enough for V's death): each counts as a cause since, for instance, A's shooting is a necessary member of a sufficient set that contains just A's shooting and B's shooting, and so on for the others.

With respect to the issue of counting everything in the causal history of an event as a cause, INUS-style sufficiency accounts are in much the same boat as necessity accounts: since any set that contains the sufficient causes must contain all of the conditions needed for the outcome, very distant conditions will count. Indeed, given that necessity accounts typically deny causation in cases of overdetermination, sufficiency accounts will tend to include more things under their tally. (Whether it will contain all of the relevant omissions and absences depends on quite how sufficiency is understood: if it is phrased in terms of counterfactuals, they will be included; but if it is phrased in terms of natural laws, the question will hinge on whether the relevant laws will need to mention them.)

The philosophical literature looking at ways of avoiding these problems for the two accounts is enormous. It is safe to say that there is no agreed solution.[10] As with so many philosophical issues, the thought arises that there may not be an analysis of the notion of causation. Perhaps the notion is primitive; after all, on pain of regress, some notions have to be. If so, the two accounts might be better viewed as heuristics rather than analyses; we can look to that in the context of the legal practice.

3 Accounts of Causation in the Law

Far and away the most prevalent account of causation in the law, regularly invoked both in courtroom practice and in legal writings, is a necessity approach: the 'but for' or *sine qua non* test. But in the light of the problems already mentioned, its inadequacy given a simple formulation has been widely recognised: 'It is now, I think, generally accepted that the "but for" test does not provide a comprehensive or exclusive test of causation in the

[10] For a recent review of options see Paul and Hall, *Causation, A User's Guide*.

law of tort' said Lord Bingham in *Chester* v. *Afshar* [2005], going on to cite both issues of under-counting and over-counting.

So what should stand in its place? Much academic writing, though less courtroom practice, has focused on sufficiency accounts, especially as given by Richard Wright in his NESS (Necessary Element of a Sufficient Set) formulation, which follows Mackie's INUS account fairly closely.[11] Again though, as we have seen, sufficiency accounts have problems with redundancy, so, despite the amount of work devoted to their development, it is far from clear that they can work on their own.

One response is to produce a new account by disjoining the two rivals: something counts as a cause if it passes either the 'but for' test, or the NESS test.[12] This helps where one test is accurate but the other under-counts, as with overdetermination. But it does not help if one of them over-counts, as happens with pre-emption: since the necessity test is positive for both the pre-empting cause and the pre-empted potential cause, the disjunctive account will classify both of them as causes.

A more nuanced approach makes use of the tests selectively: using one or the other, suitably modified if need be, in the cases where we have reason to believe that they will work well. Compare our use of common-sense tests in other domains. We may test for the presence of water on the path by checking if it feels wet. But if the temperature is below freezing that test will not work; now we check if it feels slippery. Indeed, if it feels wet at such a temperature, then that is good grounds for thinking that any liquid present is not water. Conversely, if we are not sure what the temperature is, but are confident that the liquid on the ground is water, we might use its feel to estimate the temperature. And if we know that there are interfering factors – perhaps someone has spread salt on the path – things change again. We employ tests defeasibly and flexibly, amending our beliefs on the outcome of the tests we deploy, but also amending the tests we deploy on the basis of our beliefs.

Likewise, it is plausible that the necessity and sufficiency criteria should be seen as *defeasible* tests for causation. In a case of overdetermination, the

[11] For discussion of the differences, and responses to criticisms, see R. Wright, 'The NESS account of natural causation: a response to criticisms' in R. Goldberg (ed.), *Perspectives on Causation* (Hart Publishing, 2011), 285–322.

[12] See Steel for a proposal along these lines. S. Steel, *Proof of Causation in Tort Law* (Cambridge University Press, 2015).

sufficiency test will work better than the necessity test. In a case of pre-emption, neither test will work well, so we will need to look to other tests; but the fact that the necessity and sufficiency tests give such divergent results is itself an indication that pre-emption is involved.[13] On such an approach we cannot define cause in terms of one of these tests: they could not be used to introduce the notion of causation to someone who had no understanding of it. It is our prior grip on the notion of causation that enables us to see where the tests can be usefully employed. But it does not follow that the tests have no function. They may work, as we have seen, as heuristics, enabling us to identify cases of causation in many concrete cases: this is plausibly how a jury might deploy them. Moreover, they might help us articulate the reasons for coming to conclusions in particular cases, and then to build up a body of precedent to deal with future cases.[14]

What though of the problem of counting everything in the causal history of an event as a cause in equal standing, no matter how distant from the event, or how insignificant its contribution appears to be? We focus first on the latter of these two issues: the need to estimate the degree of contribution that a given factor makes to an outcome.

The legal need for such a test has been somewhat obscured by two features of legal practice. First, in many jurisdictions, the degree of causal contribution is irrelevant to criminal responsibility: even someone who merely aids or abets the commission of a crime is as responsible as the principal offender. Second, within torts, the widely applied doctrine of joint and several liability means that each of the defendants will be liable up to the full amount of the obligation: the plaintiff may recover damages from any one of the defendants, leaving it up to that defendant to recover the due share from the others. These doctrines have had the consequence that it has been somewhat less important to determine the degree of causal contribution than might be expected. But causal contribution is not legally

[13] To get an idea of the kinds of further tests that may help here, see Paul and Hall, *Causation, A User's Guide*, though there they are *formulated* as candidate analyses.

[14] For an approach along these lines, see J.J. Thomson, 'Some reflections on Hart and Honoré, causation in the law' in M. Kramer, C. Grant, B. Colburn and A. Hatzistavrou (eds.) *The Legacy of H.L.A. Hart: Legal, Political, and Moral Philosophy* (Oxford University Press, 2007) 143–64. For the general issue of whether rules in law work as decision procedures that could be used by someone who had no prior grip on the issues, or whether they serve to articulate our implicit reasoning and make them useful for future application, see J. Dewey, 'Logical method and law', *The Philosophical Review* 33 (1924), 560–72.

irrelevant. For a start, not all jurisdictions embrace joint and several liability; and even those that do need some way of addressing the apportionment of liability among the defendants if one of them goes on to sue the others.

We concentrate on cases of insufficient overdetermination. Such cases are real in tort and criminal law: pollution by many manufacturers causes illness or damage, but no one polluter's contribution was necessary; the members of a company board vote unanimously not to recall a dangerous product, where a simple majority would have been sufficient to carry the policy.[15] Here courts tend to talk of 'contribution' rather than cause, a graded notion rather than all or nothing; but how is this to be understood?

In cases where direct physical forces are involved, we can measure the contribution in terms of those forces. If A, B and C push a car off a cliff, or hold another person down, we can measure their physical contributions, even if the total force is greater than is needed.[16] Perhaps the same reasoning can be applied to polluters: we can measure the amount of pollutant introduced by each of the defendants. But it is hard to see how to do this for the votes of the board: there are no physical forces involved there. If the board members all have the same voting power it is natural to think of their contributions as equal, but this does not have to be the case: some could be assigned more votes than others. Other cases will be even harder to assess: a suicide may be overdetermined by the bullying and harassment that led to it, yet the contributions of those involved may differ.

Two approaches have been suggested. One involves counterfactuals: an attempt to measure how big a contribution is made by each factor to the change from the world in which the effect does not take place, to the world in which it does.[17] The other involves probabilities: how great an impact does each factor have on the likelihood that the effect will take place.[18] Again though the chances of providing a reductive analysis of the notion

[15] See J. Stapleton, 'Unnecessary causes', *Law Quarterly Review* 129 (2013), 39–65 and Steel, *Proof of Causation in Tort Law*, for a discussion of such cases.

[16] Stapleton, 'Unnecessary causes'.

[17] For different approaches, see H. Chockler and J. Halpern, 'Responsibility and blame: a structural-model approach', *Journal of Artificial Intelligence Research* 22 (2004), 93–115; M. Braham and M. van Hees, 'Degrees of causation', *Erkenntnis* 71 (2009), 323–44.

[18] A. Kaiserman, 'Partial liability', *Legal Theory* 23 (2017), 1–26.

look bleak. Counterfactual accounts require a prior individuation of the relevant events if they are to get a grip: they are better suited to measuring contributions in the case of the voters than of the suicide. Probabilistic accounts avoid this problem, but face others. In general a factor can fortuitously cause an outcome even though it lowered the chance that that outcome would happen;[19] likewise there will be cases where a factor can be non-redundantly involved in causing an outcome even though it lowered the chance of that outcome. Again though, this does not show that these accounts have no place. It suggests rather than they should be used as defeasible tests for contribution to causation, rather than as reductive analyses of it.

Such accounts might also help shed some light on the other problem that faces both the necessity and the sufficiency accounts: where to draw the line between causes that are sufficiently close to the effect that the author of the cause bears responsibility for it, and those that are not. This issue, that of proximity or remoteness, the idea that in some sense remoteness decreases liability, remains the subject of intense legal controversy.

Clearly we should not take the idea of spatial or temporal proximity too literally. A defendant who acts, using the appropriate technology, at great distance, does not thereby avoid liability – a defendant who places a bomb on a plane so that it explodes on the other side of the globe, or fits it with a slow fuse so that it explodes after many months, is just as liable as one who detonates it here and now. Nor does the complexity of the causal process in itself make a difference: using a sophisticated detonator that involves many causal stages is no different to directly lighting a simple fuse. The distance should rather be causal distance.

One approach applies the idea of degree of causation directly here: if causes come in degrees, then we might think that responsibility attaches only if an agent's causal contribution is sufficiently large. We might think of cause as diminishing to zero over enough steps; this would be to deny its transitivity.[20] Or we could maintain the idea that cause is a transitive notion, while saying that having a large causal influence is not; what we need to do is quantify the size needed for responsibility.

[19] C. Hitchcock, 'The mishap at Reichenbach Fall: singular vs. general causation', *Philosophical Studies* 78 (1995), 257–91.

[20] Moore, *Causation and Responsibility*.

The alternative (probably more widespread) approach takes the view that proximate causation is concerned with other issues, to be contrasted with the kinds of metaphysical issues that we have looked at so far. That is, it is not a species of 'cause in fact', but a specifically legal notion.[21] We need to distinguish two different ways of spelling this out. The first is that proximate causation is badly named: it has nothing specially to do with causation, as ordinarily understood, at all. Rather it is to do with some other issue, most plausibly something to do with the intention or foresight of the defendant. The second view is that proximate causation is indeed centrally concerned with causation, but that it involves a normative constraint on which causal chains bring responsibility. These constraints might themselves need to make use of causal distinctions; but they are not distinctions that would naturally stem from metaphysical considerations independently of their normative significance.

On the first approach, responsibility runs out if the agent did not intend, or could not have reasonably foreseen, the consequences of their act (the details here would depend on the *mens rea* attaching to the particular offence). Or, if the outcome was foreseen, whether the way it came about was foreseen: whether there was the appropriate 'harm within the risk'. An attempted murder would not be a successful murder if the death of the victim resulted, quite unexpectedly, from their suicide in response to the attempt.[22] However, once proximity is understood in this way, the question arises whether it is needed as a separate category: why not let the *mens rea* requirement do all of the work?

On the second approach proximity is understood in terms of the specific kinds of causal chain that are needed for legal responsibility. A central consideration here is the one that Hart and Honoré drew from their discussion of a large body of case law: that responsibility is blocked if other agents, or some freak events, supersede the initial cause. Take one of their examples: suppose D, aiming to kill V, knocks him to the ground, where he is killed by the freak falling of a tree, or by the actions of some third-party, who, seeing V helpless on the ground, maliciously fells the tree onto him. D would not be responsible for V's death.

[21] J. Stapleton, 'Choosing what we mean by "causation" in the law', *Missouri Law Review* 73 (2008), 433–80.

[22] Moore, *Causation and Responsibility*.

Hart and Honoré take this to show that in such circumstances D would not have caused V's death, but this is implausible. To see this, note that in both cases, lack of intention on D's part is still required if D is to avoid responsibility. If D's plan had involved the falling tree, or the expectation that the third-party would become involved, it would still be a case of murder. But how can the issue of whether or not D was the cause of V's death turn on issues of D's beliefs?[23] Much more plausible is the thought that causation is present in all cases, but that only certain types of causation are sufficient for responsibility.

Similar ideas can be applied to the issue of complicity. In cases where being an accomplice rather than a principal is important, the difference is not to be understood in terms of the principal being the cause of the offence whereas the accomplice is not. If a would-be accomplice has no causal impact they are not an accomplice (although the impact might be overdetermined, and so badly assessed using necessity tests). It is rather that the accomplice causes the principal to cause the offence, and not vice versa.[24]

The point is equally plausible in the case of omissions. As we saw, both necessity and sufficiency accounts find it hard to distinguish between the causal strength of acts and that of omissions; both tend to count equally as causes, and it is hard to see how that could be avoided (though see Moore[25] for a valiant attempt). Nevertheless, in general Anglo-American law is reluctant to prosecute for omissions except those that contravene an established duty to act (for general discussion here, see Alexander[26]). While the philosophical attempt to delineate general principles that distinguish acts from omissions (or distinguish doing from allowing, which is clearly not the same thing) has certainly not reached consensus,[27] most approaches look to establish different sorts of causal chains, rather than to class omissions as fundamentally not causal. Recent

[23] Thomson, 'Some reflections on Hart and Honoré, causation in the law'. For a broader criticism to the same conclusion see Wright, 'The nightmare and the noble dream'.

[24] See J. Gardner, *Offences and Defences* (Oxford University Press, 2007), ch. 3.

[25] Moore, *Causation and Responsibility*.

[26] L. Alexander, 'Criminal liability for omissions: an inventory of issues' in S. Shute and A. Simester (eds.) *Criminal Law Theory: Doctrines of the General Part* (Oxford University Press, 2002), 121–42.

[27] See Steinbock and Norcross for a sense of the difficulties. B. Steinbock and A. Norcross (eds.) *Killing and Letting Die*, 2nd ed. (Fordham University Press, 1994).

attempts to distinguish those omissions that are relevant from those that are not have made use of contrastive accounts: accounts that make reference to salient alternatives among those that could have happened if the cause and effect had not taken place (Schaffer[28]).

4 Which Actions Are We Responsible for?

So far we have examined the role of causation in the attribution of responsibility *downstream* of the agent's action; in closing we briefly examine its role *upstream* of it.

To fix ideas, consider the case of the right-wing terrorist Anders Breivik. In 2011 he detonated a bomb in Oslo that killed eight, and then shot dead 69 young supporters of the Workers' Youth League at an island summer camp. An initial psychiatric assessment found him insane on the grounds of paranoid schizophrenia. Under Norwegian law that would have been enough to provide a defence, even though no evidence was given that the insanity was the cause of his actions – it was not argued, for instance, that he thought the children were trying to kill him. (A second psychiatric assessment came to a different conclusion, judging him as suffering from personality disorders, hence not psychotic, and so not insane under Norwegian law; the court agreed.) On the Norwegian approach, insanity defences are a form of *status* excuse, like that conferred in Anglo-American law on children under the age of seven, who are held incapable of being criminally responsible. On such an approach, the insane are simply not taken to be moral agents in the first place; issues of causation do not enter in.

Such an approach is very foreign to most Anglo-American accounts of insanity.[29] Instead the standard approach is to think that the illness must be causally involved in the act if it is to remove responsibility. (The same is typically true for justifications and excuses: thus it is not enough for a partial defence of provocation that the accused kills having been provoked; it must be that the provocation causes them to lose self-control

[28] J. Schaffer, 'Contrastive causation in the law', *Legal Theory* 16 (2010), 259–97.

[29] Though see Moore for a contrary view. M. Moore, 'The quest for a responsible responsibility test: Norwegian insanity law after Breivik', *Criminal Law and Philosophy* 9 (2015), 64–93.

which in turn causes the killing.[30] Given this, we might expect to see many of the issues discussed so far arising here. What if an act is overdetermined by the illness and something else? What if the causal effects of the illness lack proximity? That such issues have not been to the fore in legal contexts probably shows the difficulty of establishing the causal effects of mental happenings. As neuroimaging becomes more sophisticated, we may start to see it more.

[30] R. Holton and S. Shute: 'Self-control in the modern provocation defence', *Oxford Journal of Legal Studies* 27 (2007), 49–73.

Punishment 13

Christopher Bennett and Kimberley Brownlee*

Introduction

Punishment is a burden that some agent with relevant powers deliberately imposes on someone else as a purportedly justified response to conduct that she, the punishing agent, views as wrong.[1] The agent might view the conduct as wrong *in itself* or as wrong simply because it breaches an authoritative rule. But the burden imposed on the supposed wrongdoer is normally intended to communicate the punisher's justified condemnation of the wrong in question. The punishing agent not only has the *power* to inflict hard treatment in response to the conduct, but also, usually, claims to have the *authority* – the right – to do so. The punishee is *allegedly* responsible for the (putative) wrong, in the sense of meeting the conditions that would make it fair or fitting or otherwise appropriate to impose the punishment – though of course he in fact might not be responsible for it. These features – that punishment is justified, that the punishing agent has the relevant authority, and that those punished are responsible – are the sources of most of the philosophical issues that arise in regard to punishment, and we examine them in more detail in this chapter.

People impose punishments on each other in various contexts and forms for various reasons. For instance, parents may use punishments as a technique in rearing their children to discipline them, and to teach them what behaviour is acceptable. Creedal associations such as the Christian Church have sometimes used harsh punishments like excommunication or public shaming to condemn members whose behaviour they could not tolerate. Employers often use punishments – such as the denial of

* We are very grateful to Jules Holroyd and John Tasioulas for helpful comments on a draft of this paper.

1 See N. Lacey, *State Punishment: Political Principles and Community Values* (Routledge, 1988), ch. 1, for a discussion of the assumptions built into this kind of conception. See also D. Boonin, *The Problem of Punishment* (Cambridge University Press, 2008), ch. 1.

promotions or benefits, or the assignment of unpopular tasks – to control or express disapproval of uncooperative employees. And in intimate relationships with friends, family members, partners and spouses, people often respond to the conduct they disapprove of with treatment such as blame, resentment, indignation, anger, shaming and shunning.

The arena of punishment that is the focus of this chapter, however, is legal punishment. The specific forms that our legal punishments tend to take can be viewed against the backdrop of the various, broadly punitive, responses that we give to each other's wrongdoing in the non-legal contexts noted above. Those non-legal uses of punishment by employers, friends, associations and families – flawed and debatable as they may be – provide us with a rough set of reference points by which to judge the credibility, defensibility and harshness of our legal punishment institutions. Those reference points pertain to our motivations and aims in punishing each other; the chance that punishing each other in the ways we do will achieve our desired aims; and the merits or demerits of alternative responses to wrongdoing.

Punishment practices vary widely across jurisdictions in how harsh or mild they are. For instance, punishment regimes vary in the severity of the punishments provided by the criminal law of that jurisdiction (e.g. community service, fines, imprisonment, exile, solitary confinement, torture, or even execution); the harshness with which those punishments are administered by officials in that jurisdiction; and the flexibility or inflexibility of sentencing practices to attend or not to the particular features of a case.[2] Anglo-American systems are often said to be harsher along most measures than more progressive continental-European systems.[3] Some less harsh criminal justice systems allow people to opt for mediation, arbitration, victim restitution and non-punitive restorative justice. Harsher systems which impose punishments such as long-term imprisonment or, worse, solitary confinement tend also to generate distinctive moral problems related to slopping out, caging, sexual violence, disease, psychological trauma and the cultivation of survival mechanisms.[4]

[2] J.Q. Whitman, *Harsh Justice: Criminal Punishment and the Widening Divide between America and Europe* (Oxford University Press, 2005).

[3] N. Lacey, *The Prisoner's Dilemma: Political Economy and Punishment in Contemporary Democracies* (Cambridge University Press, 2008).

[4] R.A. Duff, 'Punishment, dignity, and degradation', *Oxford Journal of Legal Studies* 25:1 (2005), 141–55.

Of course, the credibility of our legal punishment institutions depends also on other factors, such as the level of collateral damage that these institutions can do to the dependents of people who have offended as well as the gravity of any pre-existing social injustices whereby some people and communities who are already disadvantaged are disproportionately affected by the punishment regime.

Given the problems of punishment regimes, we must confront some basic questions about whether we need to punish, and whether our forms of punishment are fit for purpose or should be replaced by alternatives. We will shape this chapter around these issues, which can be captured by three questions about the general justification of legal punishment: (a) why punish? (b) Who may legitimately punish? And (c) who may legitimately be punished, for what, and how much? We will see that the answers to these questions depend on the philosophical approach one takes to the overall justifiability of punishment.

1 Why Punish?

In this section, we look at the main routes by which theorists attempt to justify the practice of legal punishment. These are only *potential* justifications: that is to say, the conditions theorists have put forward under which a society's intentional and authoritative infliction of hard treatment on human beings could be justified. We should be wary of accepting these conditions for two reasons. First, we should be aware of our tendency to be biased toward the *status quo*. Since we are familiar with the practice of punishment we may be inclined to conclude too quickly that it is necessary and defensible. Second, because the consequences of punishment are so drastic, we should pay particular attention to the validity of theorists' claims to have shown that the practice is morally acceptable.

We can begin by categorising accounts of the justification of punishment as *forward-looking*, *backward-looking* or some combination of the two. Theories of punishment are either *pure*, and hence purely forward-looking or purely backward-looking, or else *hybrid*, in which case they contain some mixture of forward- and backward-looking justifications.

The forward-looking justifications comprise attempts to justify punishment by claiming that some future good is best realised (or made more likely) by punishing. The backward-looking accounts, by contrast, claim that there is something about the criminal or wrongful action itself, as we look back at it, that requires punishment as an appropriate response, regardless of whether punishment is the best available means to realise some future good. The crucial difference between the two types of accounts is that forward-looking justifications require evidence that punishment is the best available means to realise some desired end, whatever that end is, and backward-looking justifications require instead some argument that punishment is somehow inherently fitting as a response to crime or wrongdoing.

For instance, the claim that punishment is justified because it deters crime, and thereby reduces harm and makes people safer, is a forward-looking justification. To show that punishment would be justified in these terms, we would need to look at whether there are more effective and less harmful ways to increase people's safety than by punishment (such as pre-emptive measures like increasing policing, improving education, reducing social inequality, or becoming a less acquisitive society).

By contrast, the view that punishment is justified because wrongs done to one person need to be avenged on the perpetrator in like manner and extent (something like 'an eye for an eye') is a backward-looking justification since it relies on normative claims about the necessity and proper mode of avenging wrongdoing, rather than on empirical evidence about how likely it is that punishment will lead to some desired future state.

Backward-looking justifications might seem to have their own *end* in view, that is, their own forward-looking aim, which is to avenge the victim or to take revenge against the wrongdoer. The reason that such views are nonetheless well-characterised as *backward-looking* is that the wrong done is the essential reference point by which to determine what kind of punitive response is justified.

If we look more closely at forward-looking justifications, we can ask what kinds of important ends punishment could be thought to serve. We have already seen that one answer is deterrence and the contribution deterrence makes to security. This is in fact the overwhelmingly most popular answer – that punishment is necessary because of the contribution it makes to peace, security and people's ability to plan their lives into the future without threat from those more powerful than themselves. Other related ends that are often identified are rehabilitation, education, reconciliation and forgiveness.

We can note a number of common criticisms of forward-looking theories. First of all, it is not normally thought to be legitimate to inflict suffering on people in order to further important social ends. Rather, people are thought to have stringent rights to non-interference and self-determination. If that is correct, then we would need to show that, in order to be permissibly punished, someone would have to have lost or forfeited the right to non-interference or non-punishment. But, this means that forward-looking views would have to incorporate something backward-looking, showing why it is that those people who have committed certain wrongs thereby lose or forfeit their rights. This suggests that theories with a forward-looking element might have to be hybrid theories. Examples of such hybrid theories might be those that aim to model justified punishment on self- and other-defence, where there is likewise a claim that, in launching an unjustified attack on another person, one alters one's own moral immunity to an aggressive response.

Second, and leading on from this, it might be argued that, without a backward-looking element, forward-looking theories will be unable to explain why it is important to punish only the guilty. If, in some circumstance, the relevant valuable social end can be furthered most effectively by punishing an innocent person, and if it is the effective pursuit of that valuable social end that is sufficient to justify punishment, as the forward-looking views suggest, then the punishment of an innocent person would be justified. However, given that we should reject this conclusion – surely the punishment of the innocent is unacceptable – the premises must be mistaken.

Third, because, in the end, forward-looking justifications are hostage to empirical evidence about the effectiveness of punishment to achieve certain goals, as compared to alternative ways of bringing about those goals, there is always scope for criticism that the evidence shows otherwise. Although at some level it seems commonsensical to say that, if we threaten rational agents with a bad consequence if they decide to opt for some proscribed action, then that will reduce the likelihood of their doing that action, the evidence that punishment deters is actually very unclear.[5] Furthermore, as proponents of informal justice point out, a large number of criminalisable actions are never reported – perhaps far more than *are* reported – and are hence dealt with within communities and families without ever formally being labelled as crimes. If this is true, it gives the lie to the view that the threat of punishment is necessary to maintain social order.

[5] D. Nagin, 'Deterrence in the twenty-first century: a review of the evidence', *Crime and Justice* 42:1 (2013), 199–263.

Turning now to criticisms of backward-looking justifications, as the label suggests, *backward*-looking justifications do not claim to bring about any future good, and for many people this is precisely their weakness.[6] These justifications seem to be suggesting that we make someone suffer – indeed, that we pour huge amounts of public money into maintaining expensive social institutions to make large numbers of often already disadvantaged people suffer – for no good end. For this reason, the backward-looking views are often portrayed as barbaric, as giving vent to a cruel or vindictive aspect of human nature that we should be looking to overcome, or as rooted in an outdated cosmology of good and evil, heaven and hell. To compound the problem, many think that these backward-looking justifications would make sense only if human beings had free will. After all, if human beings are not free to comply with moral standards for the reason that they are causally determined to act as they do, how can they be fairly punished for failing to comply?[7]

Nevertheless there are many theorists who continue to see backward-looking justifications for punishment as having some resonance. The ways in which these theorists have tried to articulate the backward-looking justification that punishment is an inherently fitting response to wrong-doing fall into three categories.

First of all, there are those who claim that there is an abstract moral principle according to which justice should be done against wrongdoers, in the name of those wronged – and specifically that doing justice requires punishment directed at the evil will of the wrongdoer in order to vindicate the victim.[8] While this route has the virtue of tying punishment to moral seriousness – upholding moral standards and showing concern for the rights and status of the victim as one to whom this should not have been done – the crucial thing is whether these views can really show that such moral seriousness requires punishment, and that an unwillingness to

[6] V. Tadros, *The Ends of Harm: The Moral Foundations of Criminal Law* (Oxford University Press, 2011), ch. 1.

[7] N. Levy and M. McKenna, 'Recent work on free will and moral responsibility', *Philosophy Compass* 4 (2009), 96–133; B. Vilhauer, 'Persons, punishment, and free will skepticism', *Philosophical Studies* 162 (2013), 143–63.

[8] I. Kant, *The Metaphysics of Morals*, M. Gregor (trans.) (Cambridge University Press, 1991, orig. published 1797). Cf. R. Shafer-Landau, 'The failure of retributivism', *Philosophical Studies* 82 (1996), 289–316; and 'Retributivism and desert', *Pacific Philosophical Quarterly* 81 (2000), 189–214.

punish involves in some way condoning or acquiescing in the initial wrongdoing by failing to stand up for the victim.

Second, there are those who claim that punishment, or close analogues to punishment, are found in everyday interpersonal relations when we criticise, blame and get angry with one another, and generally hold one another to account for what we take to be important moral standards of behaviour and concern.[9] Thus, it might be argued, we have firmly embedded intuitions that moral criticism, remorse and apologies are fitting responses to wrongs, not just when they are the most effective way to realise some future good, but, for backward-looking reasons, in order to acknowledge properly the seriousness of the wrong.[10] Yet these practices of accountability are rarely targeted as being cruel or barbaric. The critic might nevertheless argue that our practices of accountability *are* in fact unacceptable, or that formal types of punishment are too far removed from those practices to be justified by analogy with them.

Third, there are those who take a specifically political route in attempting to make a backward-looking justification plausible. They claim that punishment is necessary as part of political society: for instance, as part of the authority of the state to make law and to set boundaries to permissible actions. If there were no such thing as punishment to mark a violation of these boundaries, it might be said, the authority of the state would amount to nothing.[11] Therefore, the state needs a right to punish, on this type of view, not to vindicate the rights of the victim, but to vindicate its own rights as the agent that has the final say in how citizens are permitted to act.

2 Who Has the Right to Punish?

Some theorists argue that, in order to justify punishment, it is not enough to show either that punishment brings about some good, such as crime control,

[9] See P.F. Strawson, 'Freedom and resentment', *Proceedings of the British Academy* 48 (1962), 187–211; T.M. Scanlon, *Moral Dimensions: Permissibility, Meaning, Blame* (Harvard University Press, 2008).

[10] C. Bennett, *The Apology Ritual: A Philosophical Theory of Punishment* (Cambridge University Press, 2008).

[11] G.W.F. Hegel, *Philosophy of Right* (various editions), §101. See also H. Fingarette, 'Punishment and suffering', *Proceedings and Addresses of the American Philosophical Association* 50:6 (1977), 499–525.

or responds appropriately to a wrong by imposing deserved censure. It is also necessary to show that the party who punishes has a right to punish the person she punishes. There are two aspects to such a right. First, something must be true of the party who is doing the punishing; it is not the case that just anyone can punish just any wrongdoer if they have the opportunity to do so. Second, something must be true of the person to be punished; as just noted, in general, people have a right against being used without their consent even if using them would bring about some good, because people have strong rights to self-determination/non-interference, and therefore the person to be punished must have lost or forfeited certain rights by their wrongdoing. We will focus on the necessary features of the punisher in the current section and on the necessary features of the punishee in Section 3.

Theorists who argue that the state and its relevantly placed officials have a right, indeed an *exclusive* right, to punish must respond to several objections. One such objection is that states are usually engaged in worse conduct than that for which they would seek to hold their citizens to account. If *tu quoque* arguments are credible, then the state and its officers are not in a position to condemn people for doing some of what the state itself is doing.

A second objection is that the state and its officials lack the *standing* to punish.[12] The strongest version of this objection says that no human being or institution has the standing to punish another human being. In Herman Bianchi's words:

> The very thought that one grown up human being should ever have a right, or duty, to punish another grown up human being is a gross moral indecency, and the phenomenon cannot stand up to any ethical test.[13]

In this kind of view, vengeance, retribution and punitive threats, if they belong to anyone, properly belong to God alone, and therefore only God has the standing to condemn and punish people for their conduct. A less radical version of the objection states that vengeance can properly belong to human beings, but it belongs to victims and their affiliates, not to the

[12] Cf. R.A. Duff, *Answering for Crime* (Hart, 2006); and J. Gardner, 'The mark of responsibility', *Oxford Journal of Legal Studies* 23 (2003), 157–71.

[13] H. Bianchi, 'Abolition: assensus and sanctuary' in R.A. Duff and D. Garland (eds.), *A Reader on Punishment* (Oxford University Press, 1994), ch. 15. See also H. Bianchi, *Justice as Sanctuary: Toward a New System of Crime Control* (Indiana University Press, 1994).

state, and therefore only victims have a right to punish the people who wrong them. Victims could delegate that right to a third-party such as the state, but they need not do so. A third version of the objection challenges the victim's exclusive right to punish while still denying that the state has the exclusive right. This view holds that *everyone* has a natural executive right to punish people for wrongdoing. Here, 'everyone' includes the state, but the state is not the only party with the right to call people to account for criminal wrongdoing within its jurisdiction.[14]

Some responses to these objections are voluntaristic, and some are non-voluntaristic. The theorists who give a voluntaristic argument for the state's exclusive right to punish either root that right in people's explicit or implicit contractual arrangements with the state, which transfer to it the rights they would naturally have to punish each other for wrongdoing, or, less contentiously, root that right in citizens' ongoing democratic endorsement of the state's punishment practices.[15]

Theorists who give a non-voluntaristic explanation root the state's exclusive right to punish in the public goods that are derived from the state having an exclusive right. Some argue that the state must have an exclusive right to punish because only that arrangement maintains the link between the state's judgement that some action is wrong and the appropriateness of the state inflicting a certain sanction and mode of suffering on the person who did the wrong.[16] Others focus on the state's relative effectiveness and truth-seeking ability in criminal justice matters. They claim that formal, institutional processes and procedures are, under certain conditions, more reliable than private exercises of judgement, and, for that reason, both criminal justice officials and ordinary citizens should follow the rules of legal punishment even when, on occasion, the institutional criminal justice process arrives at the wrong conclusion.[17]

A more general account of the state's exclusive right to punish is rooted in the distinctive aims of legal punishment, which include, as discussed

[14] For a defence of this Lockean view, see C.H. Wellman, *Rights Forfeiture and Punishment* (Oxford University Press, 2017), ch. 3.

[15] Cf. R. Dagger, 'Social contracts, fair play, and the justifications of punishment', *Ohio State Journal of Criminal Law* 8 (2010–11), 341–68.

[16] A. Harel, 'Why only the state may inflict criminal sanctions: the case against privately inflicted sanctions', *Legal Theory* 14 (2008), 113–33.

[17] D. Estlund, 'On following orders in an unjust war', *Journal of Political Philosophy* 15 (2007), 213–34.

above: (1) retributive justice, (2) general deterrence, (3) moral education, (4) the expression of certain societal values, (5) the restoration of victims, and (6) the release of socially disruptive tensions. The most notable aim, some argue, is deterrence: circumstances would deteriorate rapidly if the state did not concern itself with these six aims and, particularly, the aim of deterring.[18]

Of course, even if the state were to achieve these aims *best*, that would not necessarily give it an exclusive right to punish. What gives it that right, some argue, is the *importance* of the aims in question. That is, given the grave risks and high stakes for both people and society, criminal justice and punishment are distinct from other political issues and this explains why the state's right to respond must prevail over individuals' rights to answer certain wrongs done to them.[19]

That said, we could make a similar claim about childrearing, namely that it is fundamentally important to get it right since the stakes are high and the risks are grave. Would this justify allocating childrearing rights exclusively to those people who are best placed to rear children well, who often may not be the biological parents? Surely not. A redistributive childrearing scheme is highly counterintuitive. Therefore, by analogy, we may question whether *importance* is sufficient to give the (legitimate) state an exclusive right to punish.

Moreover, even if states are best placed, in principle, to achieve the important aims of punishment, they do not necessarily achieve those aims best or well through the kinds of punishment practices that they currently use, especially in Anglo-American systems where punishment is practised in harsh ways that include, in addition to fines and community service, public shaming, incarceration, mandatory minimum sentences, life sentences, life sentences without parole, and, in some jurisdictions, solitary confinement, severe physical strain and execution. These are the practices that are openly acknowledged to be part of the legal punishment regime. With them comes a host of incidental, accidental, careless and unacknowledged burdens that seem to be part of doing punitive business. First, punitive practices often deny people the freedom to pursue and maintain an ordinary family life as well as rights to care for others, to have privacy, and to exercise a meaningful degree of associative control. Second, in consequence, punitive practices harm the dependents and associates of people who have offended by

[18] Wellman, *Rights-Forfeiture*, ch. 3.
[19] Wellman, *Rights-Forfeiture*, ch. 3.

severing their social bonds. Third, punitive practices often stigmatise, blame, shame and dehumanise people who have offended; label them for life as *crooks*, *jailbirds* and *criminals*; expose them to the risks of disease, injury, violence and sexual abuse; use them as a means of cheap or free labour; and deny them personal control, respect and self-respect.

Although some theorists, and politicians, view burdens such as stigmatisation and comprehensive rights-forfeiture as core aspects of legitimate punishment,[20] many theorists wish to see punishment practised in humane ways. The benefits that harsh measures purport to achieve could possibly be approximated, achieved or optimised through more humane measures.[21] More modest punishment practices or non-punitive institutions, such as mediation, arbitration, education, health, housing and work, might secure these aims better than our present punishment practices do. Most thinkers also recognise that, possibly, the purported benefits of any form of punitive hard treatment could be less important than other benefits that we could secure by prioritising other objectives.

Additional, more general, questions about the state's standing to punish include the following: could *any* state assert an exclusive right to punish or must it satisfy certain criteria of democratic, liberal, legitimate authority and normative power to enact criminal law? Must its criminal law coincide to a reasonable degree with objectively correct moral standards? Must it serve all of its citizens equally well, giving them a genuinely good chance, at least, of avoiding breaching the law? Must it punish fairly and equitably? Theorists who wish to defend the use of punishment as it is practised in societies like ours must explain why a state need not meet all of these criteria, since few if any real states do.

3 Who May Legitimately Be Punished, For What, and How Much?

The second condition on the state's right to punish pertains to features of the person to be punished. Even if the state has an exclusive right to

[20] C.W. Morris, 'Punishment and loss of moral standing', *Canadian Journal of Philosophy* 21 (1991), 53–79. See also D. Kahan, 'What do alternative sanctions mean?', *University of Chicago Law Review* 63 (1996), 591–653.

[21] For the view that societies that have more modest punishment systems also tend to have lower levels of crime and recidivism, see Whitman, *Harsh Justice*.

punish, that does not entail a right to punish all people who do criminal wrong and can be punished for it. Theorists of punishment must answer several questions, such as: who is liable to punishment? What should the conditions of culpability be? Can we be punished for an act only, or also for emotions and thought? Can we be punished for acts (*actus reus*) alone, or only with an accompanying mental states (*mens rea*)?[22]

The answers to these questions will be different depending on what we think are the ends at which punishment properly aims. On a purely forward-looking crime control model such as the deterrence view, a punishment being an efficient way of reducing crime is a sufficient condition of justification. But this seems to mean that there is no requirement of individual culpability. Little or even no degree of culpability might be compatible with liability to punishment: it depends on what is most efficient. That is why the forward-looking view is compatible with strict liability (*actus reus* only), or even, as we saw above, with the punishment of the innocent (i.e. not even the *actus reus*). The reasons for thinking that individual culpability, with the familiar pattern of excuses, is necessary would be empirical reasons, namely, that restricting punishment to a certain construction of individual culpability best serves crime reduction aims. This might be the case, for instance, if, following Jeremy Bentham, we take it that people who commit crimes unintentionally are less likely to be dangerous, and therefore less in need of deterrence, than those who commit them intentionally.

By contrast, on a backward-looking view that sees individual wrongdoing as *ceteris paribus* sufficient to justify punishment, it is also a necessary condition of punishment being justified that the individual has done (moral) wrong. So fault of some kind is necessary and the liability cannot be strict. On this view, the action has to manifest some form of ill will or moral failing in the agent – disrespect for the law or for moral standards or for the interests of the victims of the action – in order for it to be the case that justice requires punishment. This in turn requires some type of freedom of will – for the action must really represent the person's will and not simply be the effect of an accident, a mental illness or justifiable ignorance, all of which are compatible with the agent's orientation to the relevant moral standards being impeccable. There is room for a

[22] For a discussion of related issues, see Holton, 'Causation and responsibility', in this volume.

range of views here regarding what it means for the agent's action to represent their attitudes, and what kinds of impairments we should accept in overlooking some of an agent's attitudes as being products more of circumstance than their own 'deep self'.[23] In short, the justification of backward-looking punishment requires a conception of moral responsibility that explains which conditions of agency have to be met for punishment to be an inherently fitting response.

There are two types of hybrid theories that we can quickly note. The first is principally a forward-looking view, but one that acknowledges moral values other than the imperative to maximise overall social good. For instance, if there were deontological constraints of some sort that rule out treating individuals as a mere means to an end, then it might be that people who have offended would have to be morally culpable before it can become permissible to use their punishment to deter others. This combination of moral responsibility with forward-looking aims is characteristic of 'negative retributivism' – the view that individual wrongdoing makes a person liable to punishment, but denies that such punishment is inherently fitting; if there is to be punishment, it must be only because it serves forward-looking ends to punish. The second view is based on H.L.A. Hart's position in his classic paper, 'Legal responsibility and excuses'.[24] Here the idea is that individual culpability is important, not because retributive desert is important, but rather because it allows a basically forward-looking crime control institution to make room for individual freedom by ensuring that the individual has some control over whether they are liable to punishment. Hart argues that the significance of non-strict liability conditions – which effectively require some voluntary action in order to incur liability – is that one must act voluntarily to incur liability, and hence retain freedom to avoid punishment. If liability is strict, one cannot determine what might happen that will incur a risk of punishment, and Hart saw such a prospect as an unjustifiable restriction on individual freedom. Hart's model therefore supports non-strict liability without agreeing with the retributivist claim that through wrongdoing a person inherently changes their moral liability to be harmed.

[23] S. Wolf, *Freedom within Reason* (Oxford University Press, 1993).

[24] H.L.A. Hart, *Punishment and Responsibility* (Oxford University Press (2008, orig. published 1958).

To be plausible, the above models must be reconciled with various intuitions about liability to punishment. For instance, there is a common-sense intuition that young children, people with severe cognitive impairments, and people who have committed no crime are not liable to punishment. There is also a settled range of justifications and excuses such as self-defence, provocation/loss of control, duress and so on which take punishment off the table.

There is another common-sense intuition that people who repent, apologise, and seek to make amends for their wrongdoing prior to being punished should not be viewed in the same light as people who are unrepentant about their wrongdoing. If severity of a wrong can be lessened through repentance and repair, and if punishments are meant to track the general aims that purport to justify them, then oftentimes we should punish repentant people less than otherwise, if at all, since most of the declared aims of punishment will have been achieved prior to punishing them.

Another intuition that many have is that people who live in criminogenic conditions – such as persecution or poverty or environments where violence among young males is the norm – due to distributive or structural injustice and who are more likely to commit crimes as a result of that, are less culpable than people who have committed the same crimes but who did not inhabit the same conditions and, hence, the former should be deemed less liable to punishment.[25]

As we said at the outset of this section, views of liability dovetail with views of the overall purpose of punishment. One way to adjudicate among the various forward- and backward-looking views of punishment is to ask which gives the most plausible answer to the question of what would justify punishment. But also relevant is its corollary view on the conditions of liability. For instance, if we have the intuition that remorse or criminogenic upbringing is relevant to reducing liability, could this be because, as it happens, punishing such people is less likely to reduce crime? Or is it simply a firm intuition that such people deserve less punishment because their actions do not show such flagrant disregard of law and morality as they would have shown if they had been performed in the absence of remorse or criminogenic upbringing?

[25] V. Tadros, 'Poverty and criminal responsibility', *Journal of Value Inquiry* 43 (2009), 391–413.

4 Alternatives to Punishment

We end this chapter by looking at alternatives to punishment. Although we have followed the contours of traditional ethical debates about punishment by looking at *how* rather than *whether* punishment can be justified, we would like to make it clear that it is very much a live question whether punishment can be justified. This is a possibility that tends to be overlooked. Even though philosophers will often say that their attempts to justify punishment build it in as a structural presupposition that such attempts may fail, far more intellectual effort is spent on justifying punishment than on coming up with realistic alternatives.

For this reason, there is nothing like the same well-versed literature on alternatives to punishment. However, we would like to set out the argumentative strategies that are open to abolitionists, and what they would need to show to make a success of their case. Some who reject punishment and its alternatives do so because they think that punishment could never be justified, at least not for beings like us. Others take the view that punishment is unjustified because of the way that society and its particular forms of punishment are presently structured – and this might change. This latter, less radical, view might be compared to what is called 'contingent pacifism' – the view that pacifism is required, not because the use of lethal force in self-defence is always unjustified, but rather because the realities of modern warfare mean that there is no way of realistically discriminating between innocent and non-innocent, or simply repelling an unjustified attack. Related to punishment, this 'contingent abolitionism' might be the view that, given the prison–industrial complex and the nexus between democratic politics and law and order, there is no realistic way in which punishment could be carried out in a justifiable manner in our societies.

How would one go about arguing for the stronger conclusion that punishment is in principle unjustified? The arguments for alternatives to punishment tend to mirror the attempted justifications that we have looked at in previous sections. As we have seen, in order for a particular act of state punishment to be justified, it would have to be the case that punishment serves an important aim, and that there are no better, less harmful ways to serve that aim; that the agency carrying out the punishment has the right to do so; and that the capacities of the agent to be punished are such as to make the punishment fair or deserved or otherwise justified. These conditions are each necessary and jointly sufficient. This means that a proponent of alternatives to punishment need show only that the case for punishment is vulnerable on any one of these grounds in order to show that some alternative is called for.

Are the vivid measures of punishment really necessary for societies like ours to convey effectively that certain behaviours are prohibited and that the people who engage in them must undertake to repent, apologise and restore relations? Or, are there other equally credible or more credible mechanisms for restoring and repairing wrongs, such as victim restitution? Additionally, are there less costly mechanisms by which to influence and guide people's behaviour than through the threat of punishment?

Some possibilities that theorists are currently exploring include nudging, social pressure, status and cultural norms.[26] Such social influences can affect how we view the demands of the law because the demandingness of a norm, rule or law is not a fixed quantity. It is elastic and depends greatly on our circumstances, or what psychologists call *situationism.*[27] We tend to want what the people around us want and have. Hence, the demandingness of following the law, or of apologising and remedying a wrong when we breach the law, can diminish for us when our surrounding infrastructure, habituation and concerns about status all support law-abidance. In short, if we can change relevant social norms and attitudes about the law, we can make it less demanding to follow the law.

Attending to our situated position generates a response to theorists who argue that blame and resentment are natural and appropriate responses to wrongful behaviour. If these responses are natural (that is to say, typical) and appropriate, they are not the only responses that are natural and appropriate. Compassion, forgiveness, kindness and mercy are also natural and appropriate responses to wrongdoing, especially when we remember that we are all fallible, predictably irrational human beings who are likely to respond in aggressive, acquisitive or self-protective ways when confronted with certain kinds of stresses. To appreciate the appropriateness of compassionate responses, we would need to adjust our social norms surrounding crime and punishment.

In our present society, such an adjustment would amount to something of a moral revolution. But, moral revolutions can happen, and sometimes

[26] See, for example, R.T. Thaler and C.R. Sunstein, *Nudge: Important Decisions about Health, Wealth and Happiness* (Yale University Press, 2008).

[27] J. Lichtenberg, *Distant Strangers: Ethics, Psychology, and Global Poverty* (Cambridge University Press, 2014), 122ff.

can happen quickly. As Kwame Anthony Appiah observes, within a generation, China abandoned the practice of foot-binding and English gentlemen gave up duelling as a way to defend their honour. In both cases, the societies in question came to care about how the practices made them look. Foot-binding came to be viewed as a stain on the national honour of China. Duelling came to seem ridiculous to aristocrats as a way to defend their honour.[28] A similar moral revolution might be possible in our responses to criminal wrongdoing if we came to view our contemporary practices as dishonourable. Such a revolution could take various forms. One option is that we do away with everything associated with punishment. As previously noted, some communities, including some legal jurisdictions, have adopted non-punitive, restorative responses such as healing rituals, mediation, restorative probation, and family group conferences.[29]

Another option is to try to find institutional forms of punishment that better do justice to the spirit of those responses to wrongdoing that we find important in ordinary interpersonal relationships, such as educating, airing legitimate grievances, restoring relations, and improving cooperation and cohesion. Measures that might support these aims best are formal condemnation without punitive hard treatment, compulsory victim restitution, sanctuary and community service. In moving toward such approaches, we might nonetheless have to retain a set of harsher measures with which to respond to 'dangerous' people for whom preventive detention will be necessary; whether such detention would be a punishment or not depends, in part, on our intentions. A related alternative is to do away with criminal justice altogether and replace it with a combination of private law measures and mediation, retaining a small preventive detention resource for deployment against the relatively small number of people who persistently offend and cannot be expected to 'go straight' once they leave their early twenties.

Conclusion

In this chapter, we have surveyed the main considerations that are identified as legitimate aims pursued through the criminal justice system. These

[28] K.A. Appiah, *Honor Code: How Moral Revolutions Happen* (Norton, 2011).

[29] J. Braithwaite, 'Repentance rituals and restorative justice', *Journal of Political Philosophy* 8 (2002), 115–31.

include deterrence, incapacitation, reform, retribution, victim-restoration, security, moral education, the expression of certain societal values, and the release of disruptive tensions. We have noted some of the key objections against forward-looking and backward-looking accounts of the justification of punishment. We have also identified specific conditions that both the punisher and the punishee must satisfy in order for punishment to be legitimate.

14 Constitutional Law

Mitchell N. Berman

Constitutional law is a sprawling subject, encompassing many topics of legal–philosophical interest. This chapter addresses several of the most fundamental and widely discussed issues, organised into three clusters. First, what is constitutional law and what are its necessary or central features or functions? Second, what is the proper role for the judiciary in enforcing constitutional law? Third, how should constitutions be interpreted? Under these headings, the chapter examines, among other things: the puzzle of 'unwritten' constitutions, differences between constitutional 'conventions' and constitutional law, and the relationship between theories of constitutional interpretation and general jurisprudential accounts of the nature or contents of law. Most issues that especially concern constitutional rights lie beyond the scope of this chapter.

1 Concepts, Terminology, Features, and Functions

What is constitutional law? If that is a natural first question to ask, equally natural is this answer: constitutional law is the law of, or concerning, the constitution. This response, though plausibly true, is not terribly informative, for it provokes the further question: what is the 'constitution'? And to that question there are at least two answers.

The first meaning of 'constitution' traces to Aristotle, who defined it broadly as 'an organisation of offices in a state, by which the method of their distribution is fixed, the sovereign authority is determined, and the nature of the end to be pursued by the association and all its members is prescribed'.[1] In a loosely Aristotelian sense, a state's constitution is the set of fundamental rules, standards, principles and practices that govern the distribution and exercise of political power.

[1] Aristotle, *Politics*, Book III.

More often, however, when people speak of a state's constitution, they are referring not to the central ways of arranging and exercising political power, but to a specific written instrument that purports to establish those fundamental arrangements. The historical models are the Constitution of the United States, ratified in 1789 and still in force, and the short-lived French Constitution of 1791. Despite a flurry of constitution-writing in the nineteenth century, the true age of written constitutions dates to the second half of the twentieth century, the product of successive bursts of constitution-making after the Second World War, decolonisation, democratisation in Latin America, and the fall of the Soviet Union. Today, by one recent count, 203 nations boast constitutional charters, as do an equal or greater number of sub-national political entities such as American states and German Länder.[2] Most such instruments are formally denominated 'the constitution' – as in 'The Constitution of the Republic of South Africa' – but a constitution, as a foundational instrument, need not be labelled 'the Constitution' to qualify. The German 'Basic Law' is plainly a constitution.

To keep these two meanings of 'constitution' clear, scholars sometimes distinguish between 'ancient' and 'modern' constitutions, or between 'small-c' and 'big-C' constitutions. The 'ancient' or 'small-c' constitution refers to the fundamental structure or organisation of a state, and the 'modern' or 'big-C' constitution refers to the 'constitutional instrument' or 'constitutional charter'.

Although constitutional instruments vary in innumerable particulars, several features are nearly ubiquitous. Here are four. First, constitutional instruments almost universally provide that the law to which they give rise is legally superior to 'ordinary' law in that a conflict between legal norms of constitutional and non-constitutional status is resolved in favour of the former and not, say, by last enactment. Second, constitutional instruments are generally hard to change. Third, such instruments routinely confer or recognise constitutional rights, such as rights of free expression and of conscience, rights to equality of treatment or non-discrimination, and criminal-procedural protections. Fourth, many written constitutions

[2] There is no generally recognised supranational written constitution. A 'Treaty establishing a Constitution for Europe' was drafted in 2004 but fell short of ratification. Supranational and international constitutionalism are topics of growing scholarly interest that lie beyond the scope of this chapter.

contain language, especially concerning rights, that is more vague or general than is characteristic of legally authoritative texts in that legal system. All four features raise issues of philosophic interest. The fourth bears on the who and the how of constitutional interpretation, as will be noted in the subsequent sections. The other features deserve brief comment here.

The first two factors – superiority and entrenchment – are closely intertwined. Constitutional instruments are almost always adopted by unusually stringent means, including by plebiscite or by temporary single-purpose representative bodies. The rationale is often encapsulated this way: ordinary law is enacted by the government to regulate the people, whereas constitutions are adopted by the people to regulate the government. It follows both that legislative enactments should be legally subordinate to the constitution and that the constitution cannot be revised by ordinary legislation. Were it otherwise, legislatures could easily escape whatever strictures the constitution aims to impose.

As for rights, it is sometimes said that constitutional protection for rights is not merely standard or advisable, but somehow essential. This seems unduly stipulative if read as a claim about the conceptually necessary features of a constitution, or about the concept of *having a constitution*. Possibly, such claims confuse constitutions (and constitutional law) with *constitutionalism*.

According to one influential definition, 'constitutionalism has one essential quality; it is a legal limitation on government; it is the antithesis of arbitrary rule; its opposite is despotic government, the government of will instead of law'.[3] Constitutionalism, in other words, is an ideal of political morality with close affinities to 'the rule of law': it is the practice and means of establishing, maintaining and enforcing limits on governmental power. And like the rule of law, constitutionalism is a scalar, not a binary, quality: a state can instantiate the value of constitutionalism to a greater or lesser degree. Still, it is plausible that a state does not warrant the honorific label 'constitutional' unless it respects constitutionalism to some hard-to-specify minimum degree, and it is additionally plausible, if controversial, that that minimum degree requires that the regime have a written constitution that protects some specified rights.

[3] C.H. McIlwain, *Constitutionalism: Ancient and Modern* (Cornell University Press, 1940), 21.

Even if that is true, we should guard against a common equivocation. The phrase 'constitutional state' or 'constitutional regime' can describe a state or regime that either (a) respects the minimum requirements of constitutionalism, or (b) possesses a written constitution. (There are other possibilities too.) One not attuned to this ambiguity might infer, from the claimed fact that a state does not satisfactorily embody the values of constitutionalism, hence is not 'constitutional' in the first sense, that it is not 'constitutional', full stop. And that mistaken inference suggests that a putative constitution (in the big-C sense) is not a constitution rightly understood, or 'in the strict sense', if it does not guarantee certain rights or liberties. Such a claim generates more confusion than clarity: whether (or to what extent) a state lives up to the values of constitutionalism is one thing; whether it has a constitutional instrument is a second; and whether (or to what extent) the legal requirements derivable from that instrument are followed in practice is a third.

Whatever may be the central features and functions of constitutional instruments, failure to keep separate the ancient and modern, small-c and big-C, conceptions of constitution has occasionally fuelled doubts that Great Britain, which is said to have an 'unwritten constitution', has a constitution at all.

Now, the British 'unwritten' constitution of lore is far from unwritten in fact. It is grounded not only in longstanding practice and custom, but in vastly many written judicial opinions and a host of statutory texts. Exactly which portions of which texts have constitutional status is controversial – as is unavoidable in nations that lack a canonical constitutional instrument – but a 2003 Joint Committee of the House of Commons and the House of Lords identified over twenty statutes that contribute to 'the statutory patchwork of the British constitution'.[4] These range from old instruments such as Magna Carta 1297, the Bill of Rights and the Crown and Parliament Recognition Act that capped the Glorious Revolution of 1688, and the eighteenth-century Acts of Union, to recent enactments such as the Human Rights Act 1998 and the House of Lords Act 1999. Accordingly, commentators increasingly refer to the British constitution (or the UK constitution, which terms are generally used interchangeably) as 'uncodified' rather than 'unwritten'. Be that as it may, there is no doubt

[4] Joint Committee on Draft Civil Contingencies Bill - First Report (2003): https://publications.parliament.uk/pa/jt200203/jtselect/jtdcc/184/18402.htm

that the few nations that lack constitutional instruments (Israel and New Zealand, in addition to Britain) have small-c constitutions. It is conceptually necessary that every state has a constitution, in the Aristotelian sense. Of course, and to reiterate, the boundaries are bound to be unclear and contestable.

Today, the two distinct senses of 'constitution' are well appreciated. Not as well appreciated is that these two senses of constitution naturally suggest two senses of constitutional law: constitutional law as the law encoded in, or derivable from, the constitutional instrument; and constitutional law as the law that concerns the small-c constitution – that is, the law that governs the central or most fundamental arrangements regarding the exercise of state power.

That these are different conceptions of constitutional law emerges from the standard case: nations that have constitutional instruments. Recall that we earlier defined a big-C constitution as the instrument that purports to create the basic institutions of the state and to establish the most fundamental rules governing their operation. If such an instrument concerns *only* what might loosely be described as governing fundamentals, and if *all* legal rules that concern those fundamentals derive from the instrument, then these two definitions of constitutional law would coincide: constitutional law would be, equally, the law that derives from the constitutional instrument and the law that governs fundamental arrangements regarding the exercise of state power. But neither of those conditions obtains.

First, many constitutions are full of trivialities. Students of American constitutional law are likely to be misled on this score. The US Constitution is not only the oldest extant national constitution, it is also, at just 7500 words, the shortest. Few of its provisions concern matters of little importance. But things are different even in the American states. For instance, the constitution of the state of Alabama runs to a staggering 376,000 words (more than 100,000 words longer than *Ulysses*) and includes separate provisions to criminalise prostitution in part of Jefferson County (Amendment 688) and to authorise the legislature to promote the soybean industry (Amendment 315). The longest national constitution, India's, specifically provides (Article 268) for the imposition of duties on toiletries. Second, in most nations with constitutional instruments, at least some legal arrangements that, intuitively, are fundamental or belong to the small-c constitution, do not derive from the constitutional instrument. An example from the USA is the Administrative Procedure Act of 1946, which governs the basic operations of administrative agencies – the fourth branch of government.

For both these reasons, what the constitutional law is in nations with constitutional instruments depends on how the very idea of constitutional law is conceptualised. If constitutional law consists in the set of legal norms that concern the state's fundamental structure and commitments, then legal norms that are encoded in a constitutional instrument but marginal will not count as constitutional law and some legal norms that derive from an ordinary statutory enactment will. Alternatively, if constitutional law is the law traceable to the instrument, and if the instrument addresses some quotidian matters, then some constitutional law will not concern basic or fundamental issues and some fundamental legal arrangements will not be 'constitutional'. German constitutional theory navigates this modest quandary by distinguishing between 'formal' constitutional law (the law that traces to the Basic Law), and 'substantive' constitutional law (the law that concerns the small-c constitution). American constitutional theory, which does not recognise the German distinction, simply treats all law that derives from the instrument (and thus is entrenched and legally superior to other norms) as 'constitutional law' no matter how trivial.[5] That is a sensible choice, but it invites the question whether there are any respects in which statutory law that is in some sense fundamental or constitutive should be treated unlike ordinary statutory law and more like norms that derive from the constitutional instrument. Perhaps, for example, statutes that bear significantly on the small-c constitution should be interpreted more like constitutional charters and less like ordinary statutes – if the two types of instruments are generally interpreted differently in the first place.[6]

What is constitutional law in nations that lack constitutional instruments? Jurists in such nations cannot conceive of constitutional law as all the law encoded in, or derivable from, a canonical instrument. Instead, they might naturally think of constitutional law as the law that concerns what we could call 'constitutional arrangements'. Not all the basic and

[5] I mean to be as agnostic as possible regarding what the idea of 'deriving' from the instrument involves. We will examine some possibilities in Section 3. The important point for the present is to exclude legal norms that are grounded or encoded in a statutory text.

[6] W.N. Eskridge and J. Ferejohn, *A Republic of Statutes: The New American Constitution* (Yale University Press, 2013).

stable features that describe the distribution and exercise of state power are 'legal' or belong to constitutional 'law'. Some arrangements are merely 'practices' – habitual, not normative. And others that do involve obedience to norms may nonetheless not involve *law:* the norms could be ones of morality or etiquette, for example. What is needed, then, is a way to mark the *legal* part of a state's small-c constitution. The celebrated British constitutional theorist A.V. Dicey offered one proposal. Constitutional law in the strict sense, he contended, includes only those 'rules which (whether written or unwritten, whether enacted by statute or derived from the mass of custom, tradition, or judge-made maxims known as the Common Law) are enforced by the Courts'. These contrast with 'rules that consist of conventions, understandings, habits, or practices which, though they may regulate the conduct of the several members of the sovereign power, of the Ministry, or of other officials, are not in reality laws at all since they are not enforced by the Courts'.[7] Dicey dubbed the latter 'constitutional conventions' or 'constitutional morality'. A representative constitutional convention in Britain holds that 'A Cabinet, when outvoted on any vital question, may appeal once to the country by means of a dissolution';[8] an American constitutional convention is that members of the electoral college will cast their ballots for the candidate to whom they have committed, without discretion or deliberation.

Although many commentators still invoke Dicey's distinction, his way of carving the terrain is doubtful. One oft-voiced worry is that Dicey runs together too many disparate things as 'constitutional conventions' – 'conventions', 'understandings', 'habits', 'practices', 'customs', 'maxims', 'precepts'[9] – and their relationship to 'rules' is obscure. If a rule, for Dicey, can consist of just a habit or an 'understanding', it is unclear what sort of thing a rule is and what its normative force is. In sum, other than it being necessary that they are *not* judicially enforceable, precisely what 'constitutional conventions' *are* remains murky (e.g. Marshall[10]).

A more profound objection attaches to the law side of Dicey's convention/law distinction. Dicey conceives of constitutional law as a subset of

[7] A.V. Dicey, *Introductory to the Study of the Law of the Constitution*, 10th ed. (Oxford University Press, 1959), 24.

[8] Ibid., 420.

[9] Ibid., 417.

[10] G. Marshall, *Constitutional Conventions: The Rules and Forms of Political Accountability* (Oxford University Press, 1984).

the larger set consisting of what we are calling constitutional arrangements. But that subset can also be conceived as the intersection of two sets: the set of constitutional arrangements, and the set of legal norms. That is, constitutional law consists of those basic arrangements that are law and those laws that concern basic arrangements. So to separate conventions that are law from those that are not by the criterion of whether they are judicially enforceable is to maintain that judicial enforcement is a necessary condition of law. And this is a very ambitious jurisprudential claim. For even granting *arguendo* that there can be no legal system without a recognisably 'judicial' institution empowered to enforce legal norms, it is a separate matter whether any given norm must be judicially enforceable for it to qualify as a norm of that system. In the US legal system, courts will hold some disputes 'non-justiciable' – not meet for *judicial* resolution – on the ground that the legal provision invoked does not present a 'judicially manageable standard'. On the orthodox American understanding, however, state actors are still *legally* bound to comply with these non-justiciable constitutional norms.[11]

Even if Dicey's particular proposal is wrong, it is the wrong answer to the right question. The question is: if not all the norms and practices that make up a state's small-c constitution are part of its constitutional *law*, what determines which are and which are not? Put more generally, the question is what are the general facts or principles that validate or constitute legal norms? Answering this question is the central task of general jurisprudence.

2 Constitutional Law and the Judicial Role

We will return to the relevance of jurisprudence to constitutional law at the end of this chapter. For now, let us explore the idea of judicial enforcement of constitutional norms. The central question concerns the distribution of authority to decide constitutional matters between the judiciary and other branches of government, especially the legislature. It is generally agreed that courts should enforce constitutional law against executive action. More controversial is whether the judicial branch should have authority

[11] L.G. Sager, *Justice in Plainclothes: A Theory of American Constitutional Practice* (Yale University Press, 2006), ch. 6.

to strike down or deny effect to legislation on the ground that it violates constitutional norms – whether, that is, courts should enjoy 'the power of judicial review' – and, if so, whether such judicial authority should be 'strong' or 'weak'.[12,13]

The power of judicial review is conventionally traced to the US Supreme Court's 1803 decision in *Marbury* v. *Madison.* In that decision, the Court interpreted an Act of Congress to confer upon the Supreme Court jurisdiction over a class of suits that exceeded what, in the Court's determination, the Constitution allowed. Although the US Constitution did not (and still does not) explicitly authorise courts to invalidate legislation as contravening constitutional norms, the Court held that it could not give effect to the statute. Because '[i]t is emphatically the province and duty of the judicial department to say what the law is', Chief Justice John Marshall reasoned, '[i]f two laws conflict with each other, the courts must decide on the operation of each'. The precise scope and force of the power of judicial review contemplated in *Marbury* is unclear, for the statute at issue did particularly concern the judiciary, and Marshall conspicuously did not say that the coordinate branches were in all cases and respects bound by a judicial determination that some legislative enactment was unconstitutional, hence 'void'. Therefore, *Marbury* could have come to stand for some form of 'departmentalism' in which no branch has final interpretive authority or different branches have final authority over different types of issues. But whatever Marshall might have had in mind, the power that *Marbury* birthed has become more robust over the ensuing two centuries. The Supreme Court made this clear when, more than 150 years after *Marbury*, it confronted the southern states' 'massive resistance' to its holding, in *Brown* v. *Board of Education*, that racial segregation in public schools was unconstitutional. *Marbury*, said a unanimous court in *Cooper* v. *Aaron* (1958),

> declared the basic principle that the federal judiciary is supreme in the exposition of the law of the Constitution, and that principle has ever since been respected by this Court and the Country as a permanent and indispensable feature of our constitutional system. It follows that the interpretation of the [Constitution] enunciated by this Court in the *Brown* case is the supreme law of the land.

[12] M. Tushnet, 'Alternative forms of judicial review', *Michigan Law Review* 101 (2003), 2781.

[13] A system with any form of judicial review must decide whether to entrust that power to ordinary courts or only to a centralised 'constitutional court', a matter that this chapter does not address.

Cooper embodies the strong form of judicial review frequently labelled 'judicial supremacy'. Though broadly apt, the label is overstated in at least one respect and misleading in others. It is misleading because, given that federal courts in the US (like those in, say, Australia and unlike those in Canada) exercise judicial review only in 'concrete' disputes, not in the 'abstract', and given that the rules of 'justiciability' ensure that many actual concrete disputes will not gain a judicial hearing, the political branches do get the last word on many constitutional issues. The moniker is overstated because when courts do issue constitutional rulings, only holdings of *unconstitutionality* bind other state actors; a holding that some challenged legislation is *constitutional* will not preclude legislators who believe otherwise from seeking to repeal the legislation on precisely that ground. Subject to those qualifications, however, it is true that American-style judicial review gives courts ultimate authority to interpret and enforce constitutional norms.

There are many reasons to invest courts with a strong power of judicial review. Most notably, thanks to their long terms in office (up to life tenure, in some jurisdictions), judges are better insulated against political pressures than are electorally accountable actors such as legislators. Insofar as a central function of a constitutional instrument is to codify and entrench limitations on what political majorities are authorised to do, it seems likely that those limitations will be more faithfully enforced by agents whose continued employment does not depend (or depends less tightly) upon the preferences of those very majorities. It is additionally plausible that the sources of job satisfaction and professional status differ, in relevant ways, for legislators and judges: possibly, legislators gain satisfaction and prestige mostly from accumulating greater effective political power and influence, whereas a judge's satisfaction and prestige may depend more heavily on her believing of herself, and on others believing of her, that she subordinates her political commitments to her judgement regarding what the law requires. And even if legislators and judges are comparably motivated to sincerely enforce constitutional norms (as the first two considerations challenge), judges may be better equipped to get those norms right – especially to the extent that constitutional reasoning is similar to other forms of legal reasoning. Judges have task-relevant training and experience; they benefit from adversarial argumentation, and are disciplined by the demand that they articulate their reasons in written opinions; and, insofar as they review legislation as applied to concrete disputes, they may have access to constitutionally relevant facts (such as the character and magnitude of the statute's impact on constitutionally protected interests) that were unknown when the legislators voted. In short, judges may enjoy motivational, situational and cognitive advantages over legislators that are relevant to constitutional enforcement.

Considerations such as these have resonated with constitutional designers across the globe, and nearly every modern constitutional instrument (the Constitution of the Netherlands is one conspicuous exception) expressly provides for some form of judicial review. Indeed, just as many theorists maintain that constitutionalism requires the codification of rights, some also insist that such constitutional rights must be judicially enforceable. And in a development that reflects very substantial enthusiasm for judicial review, courts in some nations, following the Indian Supreme Court's lead, have even invalidated some constitutional amendments as contravening the 'basic structure' or 'basic features' of the constitution.

Despite the worldwide spread of judicial review, a longstanding tradition challenges the practice as presenting what Alexander Bickel dubbed a 'countermajoritarian difficulty'. When a court declares legislative or executive action unconstitutional, Bickel explained, 'it thwarts the will of representatives of the actual people of the here and now; it exercises control, not in behalf of the prevailing majority, but against it ... [I]t is the reason the charge can be made that judicial review is undemocratic'.[14] Bickel was an American constitutional theorist writing more than half a century ago, but his objection has been echoed by critics of judicial review in other nations and to the present day.

Many things can be said in response to the Bickelian objection. Perhaps the most obvious is that the majoritarian bona fides of legislative outputs cannot be taken for granted. Given the teachings of social choice theory that problematise the very idea of a popular or majoritarian will, as well as countless features of actual representative democracies that combine to allow the wealthy few vastly disproportionate political influence, we cannot blithely assume that any particular legislative enactment enjoys more popular support than does a judicial declaration that the legislation cannot stand. But even granting, as is uncertain, that judicial decisions

[14] A.M. Bickel, *The Least Dangerous Branch: The Supreme Court at the Bar of Politics* (Bobbs-Merrill, 1962), 16–17.

invalidating legislation are countermajoritarian more often than not, this fact does not clearly underwrite a sound objection to judicial review.

To see why not, we should distinguish between policy preferences (what some individual or group wants the state to do or pursue) and constitutional judgements (what some individual or group concludes is constitutionally permitted or required) and note that, in most recitations of the countermajoritarian difficulty, judicial review is objectionable because it frustrates majoritarian preferences; majoritarian judgements are offstage. In the passage quoted above, for example, Bickel speaks of the representatives' 'will' and elsewhere he describes judicial review as 'the power to apply and construe the Constitution, in matters of the greatest moment, against the *wishes* of a legislative majority'.[15]

With the (admittedly imprecise) distinction between preferences and judgements in mind, suppose that the judiciary in a jurisdiction lacks authority to invalidate legislation, but that the legislature takes seriously *its* responsibility to conform to constitutional requirements. As a thought experiment, imagine that the legislature follows a two-step procedure when considering any bill: first, the legislators vote on the bill on the assumption that it is constitutional; then, if the bill garners a majority at the first stage, the representatives scrutinise that assumption. If, at this second stage, a legislative majority determines that the legislation is not constitutional, the bill is not enacted. Plausibly, representatives would cater to constituent preferences at the first stage and exercise independent constitutional judgement at the second. There is no judicial review in this picture but there is countermajoritarianism: any bill that passes the first hurdle and fails the second is defeated despite the 'wishes of a legislative majority'. The lesson is that any sincere obedience to constitutional norms – especially norms that recognise rights as constraints on 'democratic' outcomes – is countermajoritarian in the sense of frustrating the preferences of a contemporary majority of voters or legislators or both. Rights-respecting constitutionalism is countermajoritarian no matter who does the enforcing, so long as that enforcement is genuine.

Even if 'countermajoritarianism' does not most accurately capture what is problematic about judicial review (countermajoritarianism, to restate things, is baked into a constitutional order that protects individual rights,

[15] Ibid., 20, emphasis added.

with or without judicial review), the enforcement of constitutional norms by an unelected judiciary is hardly worry-free. The most extreme fear is of 'judicial tyranny': under the guise of enforcing constitutional norms, judges may simply pursue their own parochial interests. But even to the extent that judges exercise judicial review in good faith, their possession of this power may breed apathy and irresponsibility on the part of the people and their elected representatives. James Bradley Thayer sounded this alarm over a century ago, warning that '[t]he tendency of a common and easy resort to this great function [of judicial review] . . . is to dwarf the political capacity of the people, and to deaden its sense of moral responsibility'.[16]

Furthermore, when it comes to the enforcement of constitutional rights (as contrasted with constitutional norms that govern, say, the distribution of power between national and state or local governments), the premise, flagged earlier, that constitutional interpretation is much like 'ordinary' legal interpretation, might be mistaken. Jeremy Waldron has argued that the enforcement of constitutional rights depends more upon moral reasoning than on any form of reasoning properly denominated 'legal', and that there are no good reasons to believe that judges are better than elected representatives at reasoning about these matters. To the contrary, Waldron says, a careful comparison of the ways that legislatures and courts have grappled with actual rights claims suggests that legislators often reason about moral rights in subtle and responsible fashion while courts too often engage in legalistic logic-chopping. And if courts do not have a substantive advantage over legislatures, legislatures plainly have a procedural advantage over courts: they are more legitimate, participatory and egalitarian.[17]

Although academic scepticism about judicial review is growing, many or most constitutional theorists remain unpersuaded. To start, fear that anything fairly describable as 'judicial tyranny' will materialise seems overwrought. Because courts lack powers of sword or purse, it is doubtful that they have the levers necessary to oppose robust popular will on many issues over an extended period of time. Revealingly, as recent scholarship has shown[18]), even the US Supreme Court of the 1960s and 1970s – thought by

[16] J.B. Thayer, *John Marshall* (Houghton Mifflin, 1901), 106–7.

[17] J. Waldron, *Law and Disagreement* (Oxford University Press, 1999).

[18] L.A. Powe, *The Supreme Court and the American Elite, 1789–2008* (Harvard University Press, 2009); B. Friedman, *The Will of the People* (Farrar, Straus and Giroux, 2009).

many critics, not only on the political right, to have been particularly adventurist – was never far out of step with the dominant coalition in Congress. Many commentators also deem Waldron and other sceptics of judicial review too sanguine about legislators' ability or motivation to engage with moral claims very seriously, given crushing limitations of time and the logic of electoral politics.

In any event, the common belief that investing courts with the power of judicial review over constitutional rights is defensible only if they will ascertain those rights more accurately than will legislatures is, for two different reasons, mistaken. First, as Richard Fallon has explained,[19] the justification of judicial review could be rooted in the far more modest assumption that constitutional rights are sufficiently important to warrant a double layer of protection. Recall an earlier observation: even in the US, with its 'judicial supremacy', only judicial determinations that some legislative or executive action is constitutionally *prohibited* binds other branches; if courts determine that some action is constitutionally *permissible*, legislators who conclude otherwise are wholly free to vote against the legislation in question.[20] Therefore, even if courts are not better than legislatures at correctly identifying constitutional rights – indeed, even if they are *worse* – investing courts with power to invalidate legislation that they conclude violates rights could maximise the system's overall protection of 'true' constitutional rights because a rights claim will be vindicated if accepted by *either* a legislative majority *or* a final reviewing court. In the former case, the supposedly rights-violative legislation will not be enacted; in the latter, it will be enacted but invalidated. Second, some scholars defend judicial review on grounds that do not depend upon the premise that the practice will have any instrumental value. In Alon Harel's view, for example, judicial review is justified simply because it respects an individual's right to a hearing. On this account, '[t]he justification for judicial review is grounded ... not in the superior quality of the decisions resulting from judicial review but in the willingness to hear individual grievances, consider their

[19] R.H. Fallon Jr, 'The core of an uneasy case for judicial review', *Harvard Law Review* 121 (2008), 1693.

[20] Similarly, an executive that concludes that enacted legislation that has survived judicial review is unconstitutional may decide not to enforce it, although the executive's latitude to do so might be more circumscribed.

soundness, address these grievances in good faith, and act in accordance with the outcomes of the deliberation'.[21]

Wherever the truth lies in this debate, plenty of room exists for compromise between strong, American-style judicial review and the British tradition of legislative supremacy. Canada has pioneered exploration of this broad middle ground in Section 33 of its Charter of Rights and Freedoms, which provides that 'Parliament or the legislature of a province may expressly declare in an Act of Parliament or of the legislature, as the case may be, that the Act or a provision thereof shall operate notwithstanding [the enumerated fundamental freedoms, legal rights and equality rights]'. Any such declaration expires after five years but may be re-enacted indefinitely. Stephen Gardbaum argues that, far from a lonely innovation, the Canadian 'notwithstanding' power exemplifies an approach to judicial review that is finding increasing acceptance throughout the British Commonwealth – in New Zealand, the Australian state of Victoria, and the UK itself – and that, when joined to a requirement that the elective branches formally review any proposed legislation for conformity with constitutional rights, offers the most promising way to protect rights while respecting democracy.[22]

3 Constitutional Interpretation

How, finally, should a nation's constitution be interpreted? Or: how should a judiciary interpret and enforce a constitutional instrument? In many countries, the literature concerning 'theories of constitutional interpretation' is voluminous and highly nuanced. Of necessity, our discussion must be general and abbreviated.

At the outset, we need be clear on what a theory of constitutional interpretation is a theory *about*. To simplify, distinguish two types (or aspects) of theories: a theory could provide an account of how a court (a) should ascertain what the law is or (b) should exercise its power of judicial

[21] A. Harel, *Why Law Matters* (Oxford University Press, 2014), 2; Sager, *Justice in Plainclothes*, ch. 10.

[22] S. Gardbaum, *The New Commonwealth Model of Constitutionalism: Theory and Practice* (Cambridge University Press, 2013).

review. Take a theory (e.g. Ely) that advises courts to enforce constitutional norms against the legislature only when necessary to rectify defects in the mechanisms of political accountability.[23] Because an account of this sort concerns when courts should intervene, and not how courts should figure out what the content of constitutional norms is, it is a theory of the second type, not of the first. Or consider theories that elaborate on whether and how courts should make, revise or refine legal doctrine either (i) when there is no law on point (because, say, relevant sources are contradictory or too gappy) or (ii) when the discoverable law on point is not well suited for judicial enforcement.[24] Again, directions regarding such matters concern what courts should and should not do when exercising their power of judicial review, but do not concern how to derive legal norms from the constitutional instrument. In short, a 'theory of judicial review' or a 'theory of constitutional adjudication', as type (b) theories could be called, can be less than, or more than, a theory of constitutional interpretation proper, as I will call type (a) theories. The remainder of this chapter discusses theories of constitutional interpretation proper.

It would be impossible here to examine in any depth more than a tiny handful of such theories. So let us focus not on distinct full-blown theories but on the ingredients that go into those theories. As one illuminating recent study (Goldsworthy) shows, courts and theorists across countries generally draw from the same types of considerations, even if the catalogue of possibilities differs from one telling to another.[25] Here is one list that contains more factors, sliced more thinly, than is the norm: the meaning that would be attributed to a textual provision by a contemporary reader (where 'meaning' is one or another linguistic, semantic or communicative concept); the meaning of a provision as it was understood at enactment; the meaning that authors or ratifiers intended to communicate; the specific consequences or legal changes that the authors or ratifiers of a

[23] J.H. Ely, *Democracy and Distrust: A Theory of Judicial Review* (Harvard University Press, 1980).

[24] A growing literature addresses topic (ii) – the propriety of courts refining or supplementing 'discovered' constitutional norms with judge-made doctrines that provide greater determinacy or greater ease of judicial enforcement. See R.H. Fallon Jr, *Implementing the Constitution* (Harvard University Press, 2001); M.N. Berman, 'Constitutional decision rules', *Virginia Law Review* 90 (2004), 1.

[25] J. Goldsworthy (ed.), *Interpreting Constitutions: A Comparative Study* (Oxford University Press, 2006).

provision intended to accomplish by means of the enactment, or their more general 'purposes'; judicial precedents; historical practices of the political branches; structural principles underlying the small-c constitution (e.g. federalism, democracy); moral principles to which the society is committed; purportedly true moral principles; and pragmatic or instrumental considerations. What distinguishes theories is which considerations they advocate, in what balance, and what they exclude.

Commentators often classify approaches into broad families, such as theories of 'strict' or 'loose' interpretation, or theories of 'fixed' or 'evolving' meaning, or 'monistic' or 'pluralistic' theories. Roughly, theories characterised as 'strict' (or 'legalistic') emphasise textual meanings and fairly specific intentions; loose (or 'creative') theories invoke structural and moral principles, along with 'pragmatic' judgements about what 'works'. Fixed theories (standardly called 'originalism') look only to facts that obtained at the moment of enactment, whereas evolving theories (sometimes called 'living constitutionalism') emphasise judicial precedents or other historical practices, and changing moral commitments of the community. Most originalists are monists: they believe there is one particular interpretive target (though they disagree about what that target is) and often struggle even to accommodate judicial precedents. Non-originalists are almost invariably pluralists.

Defenders of different theories tend to advance arguments more jurisdiction-specific than universal. Their arguments are too diverse and complex to permit easy summary. But they often draw upon assumptions regarding how continuous constitutional interpretation is with statutory interpretation, and also on supposed facts about that jurisdiction's constitutional instrument or about its legal culture. For example, in the US, originalists typically contend that all legal interpretation – whether of statutes or of constitutions (and sometimes even of contracts and wills) – properly proceeds according to the same rules, and also emphasise the nation's commitment to popular sovereignty and the supposed incompatibility of such a commitment with creative styles of interpretation by an unelected judiciary. Non-originalists argue that the unusual vagueness and generality of the US Constitution, along with its extraordinary obduracy to formal amendment, explain and justify judicial recourse to more creative and evolving factors.

I earlier described theories of constitutional interpretation proper as theories that concern how courts should ascertain the constitutional law.

Putting the matter this way suggests that the theory will sound in epistemic or practical advice. That is indeed how many accounts read. The iconic American originalist Robert Bork, for example, insists that '[t]he judge should stick close to the text and the [constitutional] history, and their fair implications'.[26] The pragmatist US Supreme Court Justice Stephen Breyer[27] urges that 'Judges should use traditional legal tools, such as text, history, tradition, precedent, and purposes and related consequences, to help find proper legal answers'.

But a theory of judicial interpretation that couches things in terms of what judges should do obscures what is most fundamentally at issue. It is true that the line between what Joseph Raz calls 'conserving' and 'innovative' interpretations is hazy. However, as Raz also emphasises,[28] a line often exists precisely because there is some constitutional law. That is, statements of the form 'the constitutional law forbids φ' are truth-apt and at least some of them are true before the court deliberates. Interpretation in such cases is the activity of trying to figure out what the law is. In consequence, a theory of interpretation understood as a theory regarding how judges should interpret the constitution is parasitic upon a theory of what determines or constitutes the law in that jurisdiction.

Ronald Dworkin recognised this. On his account,[29] judges should try to identify the moral principles that best fit and justify the institutional history of the legal system because it is those principles that determine what the law is. Similarly, a central theme among contemporary originalists likewise emphasises that we should focus less on what judges should do and more on what makes out the constitutional law. As two prominent American originalists explained: 'Originalists do not give priority to the plain dictionary meaning of the Constitution's text because they like grammar more than history. They give priority to it because they believe that it and it alone is law.'[30] This appears to be Justice Antonin Scalia's

[26] R.H. Bork, 'Neutral principles and some first amendment problems', *Indiana Law Journal* 47 (1971), 8.

[27] S. Breyer, *Making Our Democracy Work: A Judge's View* (Harvard University Press, 2010), 73–4.

[28] J. Raz, 'On the authority and interpretation of constitutions: some preliminaries', in L. Alexander (ed.), *Constitutionalism: Philosophical Foundations* (Cambridge University Press, 1998), 181–2.

[29] R. Dworkin, *Law's Empire* (Harvard University Press, 1986).

[30] S.G. Calabresi and S.B. Prakash, 'The President's power to execute the laws', *Yale Law Journal* 104 (1994), 541, 552.

view too, although he equivocates between claims about what judges should do and about what the law is.[31] Arguably, originalism's embrace of this simple and straightforward account of law partially explains its success in the political marketplace, for the claim that what the text means or says is the law is highly intuitive.

But if this formulation and defence of originalism – judges should follow the original meaning of the constitutional text precisely because the original meaning of the text makes out the law – earns that theory plausibility points on the street, it costs the theory plausibility points among philosophers of law. No general theory of law actively defended or debated by legal philosophers maintains that, where an authoritative legal text is in force, the law is necessarily the communicative content of that text. So if the meaning of a constitutional instrument 'and it alone' is the law, that will not be a general jurisprudential truth but will be true in virtue of other facts that are themselves made relevant by a general jurisprudential truth. To illustrate, consider H.L.A. Hart's celebrated theory.[32] As conventionally understood, Hart maintained that the law is the set of norms identified or validated by a convergent practice among officials that Hart termed a 'rule of recognition'. So if the convergent practice in a given jurisdiction holds that the dictionary meaning of constitutional provisions is the law, then originalism would be true of that jurisdiction even if not true elsewhere or necessarily. But most commentators (see the essays in Adler and Himma) think it plain that the recognitional practice in the US is pluralist, not originalist.[33] And the rejection of originalism among legal officials is even more total in many other jurisdictions, such as Canada.

To sum up: theories of constitutional interpretation proper (as distinct from theories of judicial review or of constitutional adjudication) are often better understood not as accounts of what interpreters should *do* but as accounts of what the (constitutional) law *is*; as such, they must be reconcilable with a theory of legal content. A constitutional theorist who appreciates this fact faces a choice: either to explain how her jurisdiction-specific account of the content of constitutional law meshes

[31] M.N. Berman, 'Judge Posner's simple law', *Michigan Law Review* 113 (2015), 777, 801–5.

[32] H.L.A. Hart, *The Concept of Law* (Oxford University Press, 1961).

[33] See the essays in M.D. Adler and K.E. Himma (eds.), *The Rule of Recognition and the US Constitution* (Oxford University Press, 2009).

with a credible general account of the determinants or constituents of legal content, or to avow that what we call 'constitutional interpretation' is lawmaking, not law discovery, through and through. Either way, constitutional theorists will find it profitable to pay greater attention to general jurisprudence. At the same time, general jurisprudes should find constitutional law an especially fertile ground for testing and refining their theories of law.

Civil Rights and Liberties 15

Sherif Girgis and Robert P. George

Any adequate normative theoretical account, or philosophy, of civil rights and liberties must accommodate, among other norms, those set out in the French Declaration of the Rights of Man and the Citizen (1789), the US Bill of Rights (1791), and the first twenty-one Articles of the Universal Declaration on Human Rights (1948). Paradigm cases include rights to life, physical integrity, security, privacy, property, and a fair trial; and freedoms of religion, expression, movement, contract, and association or assembly.

Our catalogue of these rights has expanded over time. In the nineteenth-century United States, civil rights included roughly those listed above, and they were enjoyed by aliens and (unmarried free) women as well as men. So-called *political* rights – to vote, hold office, and serve on juries – were limited to adult male citizens. An unmarried woman in Boston, a Frenchman on vacation in New York, could speak and worship freely, form contracts, acquire property and file lawsuits. But only adult male citizens could approach the ballot box or sit in the jury box, in Congress, or in the Oval Office.[1]

As this way of drawing the civil–political line was radically unjust, some theorists would erase it entirely, identifying civil rights with 'the general category of basic rights necessary for free and equal citizenship'.[2] But beyond such summary statements, what defines civil rights – as opposed to moral or human or legal rights – has received little philosophical attention.

And the summary just stated is questionable. It implies that it is simply confused to speak of a non-citizen's civil rights being violated. Yet US law, for example, guarantees due process of law for *persons*, citizens or not,

[1] A.R. Amar, *The Bill of Rights: Creation and Reconstruction* (Yale University Press, 1998) 48. Thus, even after the Fourteenth Amendment to the US Constitution guaranteed the 'privileges and immunities' of American citizens, the Fifteenth Amendment was still needed to guarantee blacks the right to vote.

[2] A. Altman, 'Civil rights' in E.N. Zalta (ed.), *The Stanford Encyclopedia of Philosophy* (Summer 2013 ed.), http://plato.stanford.edu/archives/sum2013/entries/civil-rights/.

which seems coherent as well as just.[3] On the other hand, it does deny non-citizens suffrage, and no one thinks this a *civil rights* violation.

Maybe, then, our category tracks what Ronald Dworkin called political rights: individuals' 'trumps' against their political communities' pursuit of collective interests.[4] Yet civil rights govern not just relations between government and private parties, but also (sometimes) *among* private ones. They are infringed not just when government curbs your right to contract on account of your race, but when a hotelier is free to deny you a room for the same reason – something banned by the *Civil Rights* Act of 1964.

Then again, it is equally arbitrary, but not obviously a *civil rights* violation, for the hotelier to turn you away because, say, he envies your good looks. So maybe the special link in some jurisdictions between civil rights and *racial* (and/or sex-based, or . . .) prejudice is based on their history of *state*-perpetrated racial (or other forms of) injustice. Maybe protections against invidious private discrimination count as civil rights protections when they are meant to reverse the social effects of the state's denial of more traditional civil rights.

In the end, we suspect, any convincing analysis of civil rights and liberties will deploy the Aristotelian idea of focal and more marginal cases.[5] Suppose rights in general are normative claims possessed by someone, against someone else, with respect to some subject matter: actions, resources, etc. Then at a first pass, we might identify the focal case of a *civil* right as one possessed (i) against government, (ii) by those in its jurisdiction,[6] (iii) whose main subject matter is governmental treatment (e.g. rights against censorship or summary execution) or its institutional resources (e.g. rights to contract or a fair trial).

And then there will be non-focal (one might say 'analogous') cases – rights that share just some of these features.[7] Some involve the same

[3] One could reply, of course, that due process (or due process just in the non-citizen's case) is a *human* right and not specifically *civil*, but this would seem to involve ahistorical gerrymandering.

[4] R.M. Dworkin, *Justice for Hedgehogs* (Harvard University Press, 2011), 329.

[5] On this sort of analysis, see J. Finnis, *Natural Law and Natural Rights*, 2nd ed. (Oxford University Press, 2011), 9–11.

[6] That everyone generally has a right doesn't make it absolute or unlimited. See Section 4.

[7] 'Non-focal' does not mean 'weaker' or 'less important'. It means that the right shares only some of the features of the paradigm civil rights; the contrasting features – e.g. the right's addressee, or its primary subject matter – needn't diminish its moral importance by an ounce.

subject matter (governmental) and addressee (government) but are not *automatically* owed to everyone in the jurisdiction. An example might be rights to participate in the government's legislative, executive and judicial functions by voting, holding office and sitting on juries. We have already seen another set of analogous cases: protections against certain forms of invidious private discrimination. Still another might be what some call 'second-generation' civil rights,[8] but some historical sources treat under the separate headings of economic, social or cultural rights: guarantees of a minimum share of essentially *non*-governmental resources.[9]

We will return to the conceptual analysis of civil rights and liberties after discussing their justifications, for methodological reasons that will emerge. For now, even this tentative grip allows us to address important issues: whatever might distinguish *civil* rights and liberties, what is their basic structure *as rights*? And what justifies or grounds them?

Reviewing important treatments of both questions,[10] we will see that they bleed into each other – that the boundary between the nature and grounds of civil rights is porous. Our own view of both will invite two other longstanding questions, about strength (or what is sometimes called 'stringency') and scope: are any civil rights absolute? And do our civil liberties include, within certain domains, a right to do a moral wrong?

1 Analysis: Hohfeldian Incidents

Whatever else is true, civil rights and liberties are of course *rights and liberties*. So they can be expected to share something with rights and liberties that are obviously *not* 'civil rights' – say, a spouse's moral right not to be cheated on, or a president's legal freedom to keep conversations with aides private. What then distinguishes *rights* as such? Alan Buchanan offers a critical review of several prominent proposals, including the idea that rights 'trump' appeals to general utility, that their infringement calls for compensation, and that they express what someone is *owed*.[11]

[8] Altman, 'Civil rights'.

[9] United Nations General Assembly, International Covenant on Economic, Social and Cultural Rights, 16 December 1966.

[10] Though sometimes by adapting philosophical treatments of rights *generally*.

[11] A. Buchanan, 'What's so special about rights?', *Social Philosophy & Policy* 2:1 (1984).

Surely the last proposal is part of the answer. Rights are norms with a *direction*: they are possessed by someone, and (usually at least) addressed to – or held against – someone. How many forms can this structure take? The most influential answer in Anglophone philosophy comes from Wesley Hohfeld.[12] Reviewing and applying his schema will give us precise tools for identifying possible civil rights and liberties by their component parts.

Hohfeld showed that legal rights could be broken down into four elements: claims, privileges (or liberties), powers and immunities. The first two are defined in terms of duties:

- Jones has a **claim** that Smith do *X* if and only if Smith has a **duty** to Jones to do *X*.
- Jones has a **liberty** (with respect to Smith) to do *X* if and only if Jones has **no duty** (to Smith) to do *X*.

In short, claims are duties *owed to* someone, and a liberty is the lack of any contrary duty. Parents have a duty to care for their children, so children have a claim on their parents to feed them. But parents have a liberty to deprive their children of visits to Disney World; they have no duty to take them there. Everyone is obligated not to torture, so you have a claim against anyone else that they not torture you, and no one has a liberty to do so.

The other two Hohfeldian 'incidents' are powers and immunities:

- Jones has a **power** (with respect to Smith) if and only if Jones **can alter** (Smith's) Hohfeldian incidents under the system of rules in question.
- Jones has an **immunity** against Smith if and only if Smith **cannot alter** Jones' Hohfeldian incidents under the system of rules in question.

Powers and immunities are thus 'second-order' incidents: they are defined in terms of others – claims or liberties, or even other powers or immunities. Freedom of contract involves Hohfeldian powers. By entering a contract with your plumber, you exercise a power to change your own (and the plumber's) duties and claims under law. But because others lack the legal ability to enslave you – to create in you legal claims to do whatever they wish, or deprive you of legal powers to lead your own life by marrying,

[12] W. Hohfeld, *Fundamental Legal Conceptions*, Ed. W. Cook (Yale University Press, 1919).

entering your own contractual agreements, etc. – you have legal immunity against enslavement by anyone.

Now most familiar civil rights and liberties correspond not to a single Hohfeldian incident, but to a cluster of them.[13] Take property rights. Your property right over an iPhone covers (i) a claim against others cracking its screen; (ii) the liberty to do so yourself, if you please; (iii) the power to give this claim and liberty to your friend (by sale or gift); and (iv) immunity against the government's depriving you of these incidents without due process.

Religious freedom might include (i) the liberties to inquire, assent, worship and give witness – or not – as you judge appropriate; (ii) claims against being penalised by government just for exercising those liberties; (iii) powers to devolve money or other property to your religious community; and (iv) immunities against being legally obligated (e.g. by legislatures or courts) to adhere to any religion.

But if civil rights and liberties are clusters of Hohfeldian incidents, it certainly is not true that all such clusters make up a right, much less a *civil* right. What else is needed?

2 Analysis: Will or Interest Theory?

We began exploring this question in the introduction by asking what made a right 'civil'. But it will be instructive here to ask of civil rights a more *general* question that has long vexed theorists of rights of *any* sort: Granted that rights are norms with a 'direction' – possessed by someone, and directed at someone – what do they do *for* the rights-holder? Are they for that person's benefit, as 'interest theorists' hold? Or do they simply function to protect his or her choices within certain domains, especially regarding others' actions?

H.L.A. Hart was a major proponent of the latter, 'choice' or 'will' theory. For Hart, the defining function of rights is to make the rights-bearer

[13] We should note that this is a controversial view. Some philosophers, like Jeremy Waldron and Joseph Raz, think that rights give rise only to duties – e.g. of non-interference. J. Waldron, 'A right to do wrong', *Ethics* 92 (1981), 21–39; J. Raz, 'Legal rights', *Oxford Journal of Legal Studies* 4 (1984). And some think of immunities not as parts of any right but as protections for some. We think the most natural view is that what we call rights and liberties are packages of several Hohfeldian incidents.

'a small-scale sovereign'.[14] To have a right is *either* to be free to do something or not, perhaps together with immunities protecting that liberty, *or* to have control over someone else's duty to you. Your property rights over your iPhone cover not just your liberty to destroy it and a claim against others doing so, but a power over that claim, to choose to enforce or annul it.

So rights are always about freedom: the right-holder's own liberties, and his or her power to make or drop claims against others. This is how rights constitute a distinct 'branch of morality'. They are 'specifically concerned to determine when one person's freedom may be limited by another's'.[15] And in rights logic, that determination has nothing to do with the alleged *benefit* to the rights-bearer of the action that he is empowered to enforce. Rather

> the possessor of [a moral right] is conceived as having a moral justification for limiting the freedom of another . . . not because the action he is entitled to require of another has some moral quality but simply because in the circumstances a certain distribution of human freedom will be maintained if he by his choice is allowed to determine how that other shall act.[16]

The contrary view, Hart thinks, just collapses the category of rights back into the rest of morality. If rights function just by serving their bearers' interests, he supposes, nothing could set them apart from other moral norms. There would be nothing special about them.

But this analysis is too narrow,[17] artificially limiting the range of possible rights *and* of possible rights-bearers. It suggests that unwaivable claims cannot be rights – that it is a *conceptual mistake* to think that you can have a right not to be tortured, for example (granted that you cannot waive the associated claims). And it implies that infants and the severely cognitively disabled cannot have rights since they cannot exercise discretion.

[14] H.L.A. Hart, 'Legal rights' in H.L.A. Hart (ed.), *Essays on Bentham* (Clarendon Press, 1982), 162–93, 182.

[15] H.L.A. Hart, 'Are there any natural rights?', reprinted in J. Waldron (ed.), *Theories of Rights* (Oxford University Press, 1984), 77–90, 79.

[16] Ibid., 80.

[17] See N. MacCormick, 'Rights in legislation' in P.M.S. Hacker and J. Raz (eds.) *Law, Morality and Society: Essays in Honour of H.L.A. Hart* (Oxford University Press, 1977), 189–209, 197. N. MacCormick, *Legal Right and Social Democracy* (Oxford University Press, 1982), 154–66.

These criticisms have been explored at length, and will theorists have offered their replies.[18] But Hart himself granted the first.[19] He allowed that his analysis applies only to rights talk within 'the working of the "ordinary" law'. In discussion of constitutional rights, he conceded, 'the core of the notion' is not 'individual choice' but 'basic or fundamental individual needs'.[20] This certainly seems true of civil rights and liberties, though the will theory is not entirely without appeal even here – on which, more later.[21]

The main rival theory of the function of rights – or an early iteration of it – is traced to Jeremy Bentham. For Bentham, a utilitarian, morality requires choosing whichever option yields the best balance of pleasure over pain. So rights[22] – like other principles or institutions – are to promote interests in the aggregate. But this makes rights hostage to the utilitarian calculus. On a consistent utilitarian view, your legal right against torture should depend on others having alternatives to torturing you that promise more utility; it will flicker in and out with the slightest change of circumstance. This makes rights fragile, even evanescent.

And sure enough, the interest theory's champions today – for example, Jeremy Waldron, Joseph Raz, Matthew Kramer – are not utilitarians. Indeed, Bentham's view is sometimes dubbed the 'benefit theory' precisely by way of contrast with its successor 'interest' theory. As Waldron writes, 'the essence of the so-called "interest theory" of rights' is to take 'single individuated aims as the basis for generating genuine and full-blooded moral constraints whereas utilitarian theories do not'.[23] In Joseph Raz's formulation, for example, a person x possesses a right if and only if 'other things being equal, an aspect of x's well-being (his interest) is a sufficient reason for holding some other person(s) to be under a duty'.[24]

[18] For a quick recent summary of the dialectic, see L. Wenar, 'The nature of rights', *Philosophy & Public Affairs* 33 (2005), 223–53.

[19] As for the second, he thought the will theory could accommodate children's rights by reference to the choice or discretion of their representatives. Hart, 'Legal rights', 184.

[20] Ibid., 185–6, 192–3.

[21] See Section 5.

[22] Bentham was deeply dismissive of the idea of *natural moral* rights (famously deriding it as not only nonsense but 'nonsense upon stilts'). What he offered a functional analysis of was legal rights – an analysis that we are considering now in connection with civil rights and liberties. See J. Bentham, *Of Laws in General*, Ed. H.L.A. Hart (Athlone Press, 1970).

[23] J. Waldron, *The Right to Private Property* (Oxford University Press, 1988), 79.

[24] J. Raz, 'On the nature of rights', *Mind* 93 (1984), 195.

Of course, the new-and-improved interest theory faces its own hard cases. There are rights that seem to benefit not their bearers, but third parties. The classic example: *A* makes a promise to *B* to help *C*. The benefit redounds to *C*, but it is *B* who has a claim on *A*. Rights attaching to certain social roles – like a judge's liberty to dismiss spurious lawsuits – seem to have diffuse benefits to society at large, not the rights-holder. And so on.

Interest theorists have responded with increasingly elaborate refinements. (Matthew Kramer's is a particularly sophisticated recent effort.[25]) But others have declared the contest a stalemate and explored ways to combine or go beyond the two approaches.[26]

As will emerge, our sympathies lie closer to the interest theory. But we agree that this debate about rights has stalled, for reasons that will inform our exploration of *civil* rights and liberties here. The mistake, in our view, has been to think that one can develop a conceptual analysis of rights (civil or otherwise) without reference to their *justifications*.

With Aristotle, we think that when it comes to social phenomena – phenomena constituted in part by human deliberation, judgement, choice and action – to ask *what* is to ask *why* and *what for*. In fact, it was Hart's great contribution to drive home this very point in the field of legal theory. Laws and legal systems, he showed, could be understood only by reference to their practical point. It is not enough to go around to different actual systems, observing and recording their statistically frequent features in a sheer list: rules, general in scope, backed up by threats, etc. Such a 'theory' will fail to account for *why* people develop legal systems in the first place, and in the process will miss some of their salient features.

No, Hart argued, legal theorists must assume the internal perspective of those who *use* law and see *reasons* to do so. They can capture – and explain in a unified way – law's characteristic features only if they attend to its nested *purposes*: a society's survival, which calls for resolving coordination problems, which calls for a system of regulations and orderly

[25] For his latest articulation, see M.H. Kramer, 'Refining the interest theory of rights', *American Journal of Jurisprudence* 55 (2010), 31–9. For a sophisticated debate among will and choice theorists, see M.H. Kramer, N.E. Simmonds and H. Steiner, *A Debate Over Rights: Philosophical Enquiries* (Oxford University Press, 1998).

[26] See e.g. R. Cruft, 'Rights: beyond interest theory and will theory?', *Law and Philosophy* 23 (2004), 347–97; E. Mack, 'In defense of the jurisdiction theory of rights', *Journal of Ethics* 4 (2000), 71–98; Wenar, 'Nature of rights'.

ways of amending them over time – which in turn calls for secondary rules, and so on.[27]

Of this methodological point, Hart's student John Finnis argued that it was sound but incomplete.[28] Yes, in doing legal theory, we should distinguish perspectives 'external' and 'internal' to law, and take on the latter. Doing so will help us develop a more complete theory of law – one that can better explain why communities should have law at all.

But by the same token, we should distinguish *among internal* perspectives. Over the viewpoint of people just out to satisfy their own desires, we should take the view of those concerned for the common good (and hence keener to maintain a system of social coordination in the first place). And within this latter class, we should prefer the perspective of those with the most reasonable vision of that common good; their explanations of law's point and existence will be still more robust.[29]

From this vantage point, Finnis concludes, *the* central case of law will involve *just* rules for coordination – rules that really serve the common good. Likewise, we think, a good theory of rights as social phenomena – and of civil rights and liberties in particular – cannot rest with an entirely value-free conceptual analysis. It will address not just their function in some amoral sense – as Hart's theory tries to do – but their ground or justification. Indeed, if Finnis' development of Hart's insight is right, any attempt to seal off conceptual analysis from justification must be not just mistaken but unstable.[30]

And that is just what a review of the literature on interest and choice theories shows. Time and again, these analyses of rights have shaded into accounts of their justification. Bentham's is a clear example. But so is Raz's; as we have seen, it defines rights in terms of interests that *in fact* ground moral duties – leading one commentator to think this just an obvious error to fix before seriously engaging Raz's view.[31] Indeed, Hart himself, while claiming to define the freedoms that constitute rights without appeal to the 'moral quality' of the associated actions, wavers on the point. He defines rights sometimes in purely procedural terms, as arising

[27] H.L.A. Hart, *Concept of Law* (Clarendon Press, 1961), 96.
[28] Finnis, *Natural Law*, 13–15.
[29] Ibid.
[30] This is not to deny the legitimacy of legal scholars' aspiration to *descriptive accuracy*, free of distortion by their normative judgments about the phenomena described.
[31] Cruft, 'Rights', 275.

from a 'transaction or antecedent situation'; and sometimes morally, in terms of a 'distribution of freedom' determined by 'principles of fairness'.[32]

Leif Wenar has noted a similar pattern. He faults both will and interest theorists for developing 'analyses framed to favour their commitments in normative theory', which has 'turned the debate between them into a proxy for' their first-order moral disagreements. Wenar chides them on the ground that their 'normative dispute[s] cannot be resolved through a conceptual analysis of rights'.[33] No, but we think something close to the reverse is true: disputes about the proper analysis of rights can be resolved, in part, by normative debate – debate over the political-moral *grounds* of our rights and liberties, civil or otherwise.

So we will put the conceptual question on hold as we consider more direct treatments of the justifications of basic rights and liberties.

3 Justifications

If the foregoing analysis is sound, there is no sharp, easy distinction between the function and ground (or justification) of civil rights. The functions on which legal theorists have focused may be candidates for *a* (perhaps intermediate) purpose of a right; its ground is its *ultimate* (or *fully* specified) purpose. The question is whether the latter is to be identified with the interest or the choice theorist's proposal for the former; this reframes the debate in light of Finnis' methodological insight. Is the protection of agents' choice the most basic ground of the norms we call civil rights? Is it promotion of their interests? Something else?

James Griffin's account plants the value of choice into the justificatory bedrock. He grounds rights in the value of personhood and its effective exercise. This three-part value involves freely choosing a vision of the good life, pursuing it free of coercive interference, and having the minimum resources to do so effectively. Exercising these personal capacities contributes to our well-being, on Griffin's view, and thereby grounds our rights.[34]

In this last respect, we should pause to note, Griffin's argument differs from so-called 'status-based' justifications of rights that also focus on our agency and autonomy but, following Kant, take these to ground others'

[32] For criticism along these lines, see Mack, 'Jurisdiction theory', 89.

[33] Wenar, 'Nature of rights', 224.

[34] J. Griffin, *On Human Rights* (Oxford University Press, 2008), 27–44.

duties toward us *directly*. On these views, rights are not grounded in what serves our well-being. Instead, they reflect the only attitudes that it is fitting to take toward rational beings; to violate them just is to fail to respect people. 'The right to speak', Frances Kamm writes, 'may simply be the only appropriate way to treat people with minds of their own and the capacity to use means to express it.'[35] But in rejecting appeal to substantive values, status-based views have trouble explaining, when pressed, *why* we should honour people's rights. It is also unclear how something as abstract as respect, even supplemented by an appeal to our capacity for speech, could explain why freedom of speech and press matters more in political discourse than in writing instruction manuals. Or how an appeal to our autonomy could explain why choice matters more in choosing friends or a spouse than in choosing which side of the road to drive on.

Unlike these theorists, Griffin takes the exercise of 'personhood values' like autonomy and liberty to be important as parts of a flourishing life. It is their value, and theirs alone, that he thinks grounds our rights, though he affirms that we have other interests – like knowledge – which can sometimes justify curbing rights.

But are personhood values enough? They imply (as Griffin concedes[36]) that humans unable to make choices lack rights. And by ruling out appeal to other interests – like knowledge or leisure – Griffin's view forces convoluted justifications of familiar rights in terms of their alleged effects on our capacities for autonomy and choice. Such a justification, as John Tasioulas points out, is too 'precarious' and 'roundabout'.[37] It is too narrow.

And too *broad*. Exercises of autonomy in Griffin's sense are not, we think, always valuable in themselves. Yes, free choice is integral to some basic human interests. Nothing deserves the name 'friendship', or has its basic value, unless freely formed and maintained. Even when it comes to goods (like knowledge) that have value whether we choose them or not, it is better to realise them by choice than by chance or force.

But autonomy by itself is not enough. If Jones freely judges that the good life consists in trotting the globe to burn ants from every continent under a magnifying glass, this does not become for him 'an end the

[35] F. Kamm, *Intricate Ethics* (Oxford University Press, 2007), 247.

[36] Griffin, *Human Rights*, ch. 4.

[37] J. Tasioulas, 'Human rights' in A. Marmor (ed.), *The Routledge Companion to Philosophy of Law* (Routledge, 2012), 256.

realisation of which enhances the value of [his] life'.[38] It is not just an *overridden* value; it is worthless. That is because exercises of freedom have value in themselves when what we are pursuing has its own value – but not otherwise. In focusing on autonomy to the exclusion of other interests, Griffin does not just eliminate the most natural grounds for some rights. He also misconstrues the one he considers.

So while Griffin's interest-based view has advantages over purer Kantian views, Raz's theory – which allows *any* important human interest to ground rights – is better still.

Yet it has been criticised as unstable. Eric Mack argues that any interest theory risks collapsing back into the (consequentialist) benefit theory it was meant to overtake. If Smith's interests bind any agent and not just Smith – as the interest theory of rights requires – must they not have *agent-neutral* value? But then, Mack thinks, different people's interests can be aggregated, compared and netted.[39] And if they can, shouldn't they be? Why *shouldn't* officials deny one person's freedom from arbitrary detention, for instance, if doing so really led to a surplus in the human interest(s) served by that freedom across society? Yet this is just the consequentialism that interest theories like Waldron's or Raz's are meant to avoid.

What Mack's argument shows is that interest theory requires the interests that ground one person's rights to be incommensurably valuable with those that ground another's. By this we mean that neither interest contains (much less contains *and surpasses*) all the basic value of the other. So neither offers more value, but they also are not *equal* in value: they are apples and oranges. The loss of one cannot be cancelled by gains in the other, for they cannot be compared along a single scale of total value in the first place.

In fact, Raz affirms some forms of incommensurability. He grants that careers in philosophy and medicine, for instance, are incommensurable in their value.[40] But if Mack is right, that is not enough.[41] For the interest

[38] Griffin, *Human Rights*, 58.

[39] '[I]t is hard to understand why, if I and I_I exemplify the *same agent-neutral value*, their comparative value is not simply a matter of their comparative magnitude'. Mack, 'Jurisdiction theory', 82.

[40] J. Raz, 'Incommensurability', ch. 13, *The Morality of Freedom* (Oxford University Press, 1986).

[41] He thinks what is needed is 'incommensurability among instances of the *same type* of valuable condition'. Mack, 'Jurisdiction theory', 79.

theory to work, philosophical knowledge in one person must be incommensurable even with the same sort of knowledge in another.

As it happens, Raz's colleague Finnis affirms (on independent grounds) this stronger incommensurability thesis; call it 'thoroughgoing pluralism'.[42] A perfectionist political theory based on thoroughgoing pluralism, then, might offer the richest and surest ground (and, hence, the most robust general theory) of civil rights and liberties. In reviewing how, we will rely on a version that Finnis and several collaborators (including one of us[43]) have developed over many years.

4 Plural and Incommensurable Interests

Applied to civil rights and liberties, thoroughgoing pluralist perfectionism provides an alternative to broadly Kantian *and* consequentialist justifications. Unlike the first, it is perfectionist: it holds that (political) morality is about having and acting on concern for the human good. Unlike the second, it holds that basic human goods are incommensurable in value (as are instances in different people of the same broad category of good). So moral and political norms *cannot* be simply about maximising value.

What this vision instead demands is responsiveness and openness to all the basic interests in everyone affected. It requires acting on right reason: on our rational appreciation of basic human goods or interests, undistorted by emotions like partiality or hostility that would have us discount some of

[42] J. Finnis, *Fundamentals of Ethics* (Georgetown University Press, 1983), 86–90. Against this sort of view, Mack asks how two instances of the same *type* of value could be incommensurable. On the other hand, if Smith's knowledge and Jones' knowledge *are* incommensurable, must we not be measuring them by two different scales: value-for-Smith, and value-for-Jones? But then the values are *agent-relative* – not binding on others, as they must be to ground rights.

What Mack denies, then, is the possibility that two instances of the *same type* of value, but *considered agent-neutrally*, should be incommensurable. But he ignores another possibility.

Smith's knowledge and Jones' knowledge could belong to the same *genus* of value (knowledge) without being instances of the same *fully determinate* type. There may be Smith-knowledge, and Jones-knowledge: actually two types of value, but both conceived agent-neutrally. Something like this analysis seems to fit best with Finnis' – and our own – vision of the plural and incommensurable components of the common good – and, as we will see, with the inviolability of certain individual rights.

[43] See generally R.P. George, *In Defense of Natural Law* (Oxford University Press, 1999).

the people or basic interests at stake. The basic goods or interests are thought to include knowledge, life and health, aesthetic experience and skilful performances of various types, as well as several goods that inherently involve choice: personal integration or self-constitution, friendship, marriage and religion.[44]

Here we should pause to note an important implication. If morality requires reasonably pursuing some goods while maintaining due regard for all of them in everyone, and different people's goods are incommensurable, it will always be wrong to *intend* damage to any basic good even as a means to others' fulfilment. Doing so could be responsive to the human good overall (i.e. integrally) only if it realised *simply greater good* – if the targeted damage led to a net increase in value. But in such cases it could not, precisely because different people's realisations of the basic goods are incommensurable.[45]

On this framework, moreover, politics flows out of the same unfettered concern for the human good. Individuals cannot pursue the basic goods well (or in some cases, at all) without others. We need friendship and family – and the specialisation and divisions of labour that wider networks like neighbourhoods make possible. But even these communities typically fall short of self-sufficiency in ways that both justify and limit state power. Communities need, for instance, widely accepted resolutions to coordination problems, and second-order rules for fairly changing these with time; fair ways of providing for those unable to help themselves or to find other help; defence against aggressors from within or without; and fair punishment for wrongs. The widest community capable of meeting these farthest-reaching requirements of the human good is the 'complete community', the polity. Its rules are the positive law; its institutional apparatus, the state.[46]

And it exists to play the supporting role just described: to protect just those interests that justify having a state. Call its proper aim the political common good: the conditions in which people and their communities can adequately and even richly pursue their all-around good.[47] Civil rights and liberties, for their part, must be grounded in the moral norms that govern

[44] Finnis, *Natural Law*, 81–133, 448; *Fundamentals*, 66–78. One of us has explained and defended the claim that religion is a basic human good. See R.P. George, *Conscience and Its Enemies* (Intercollegiate Studies Institute, 2013), ch. 11 (esp. 118–19).

[45] For an elaboration of this point, see Finnis, *Fundamentals*, 124–7.

[46] Finnis, *Natural Law*, 147–50.

[47] Ibid., 155.

state action, which specify the requirements of serving this same common good.

Note, however, that on this thoroughgoing pluralist perfectionism, the same is true of all political institutions. The moral limits on *all* law and policy have a common ground in the common good. Yes, these institutions depend for their existence on different social facts. But they are all meant to give effect to one or another dimension of the same common good.

So it is somewhat arbitrary how one draws the line between the common good-based norms for 'ordinary' state action (law and policy), and those that correspond to civil rights and liberties. They all have the same *ultimate* ground. But if any classification will be stipulative, it is also true that some ways of drawing the line are better for certain purposes. What, then, explains the line we *have* historically drawn? For what purpose is it especially useful to recognise a separate category of civil rights and liberties at all?

Perhaps it is the purpose of devising rules that express the most general moral limits on the legal system's ordinary activities – rules that thus apply to indefinitely many areas of state action, indefinitely into the future. Invoking the pluralist perfectionist framework, we can say that civil rights and liberties are meant to highlight the variety of basic interests to which a basically just state will always be paying heed. They fix officials' attention on the many basic facets of the common good, framing them from the beneficiaries' perspective to undercut temptations to attack some as a means to others.[48]

Sometimes they pick out a basic interest directly for respect and promotion. For illustration, consider religious liberty rights. As a natural human good, according to the pluralist moral theory that Finnis, George and others have developed, religion consists of harmony with whatever ultimate source(s) of meaning there might be. Like friendship, its realisations are inherently valuable for someone only when freely chosen.

So the state, in upholding the conditions under which individuals and communities can pursue their own well-being, must refrain from aiming at the coercion or prohibition of religious acts. Policies that require or forbid an act just because of its religious character[49] involve, after all, directly

[48] Ibid., 220–1.

[49] On the ground, say, that it is true or false in the state's view, or inexpedient because of the power it gives religious believers or believers in certain religions.

impeding a basic human interest. That is wrong when anyone does it, and wrong when it is done to anyone (citizen or not). So it is a wrong for the state, specifiable at a highly general level; so a civil liberty exists to rule it out.

What about incidental burdens on religion? Religious creeds, after all, typically call for a range of private and public performances meant to build up harmony with the divine. Some of these may conflict with state action aimed at promoting other parts of the common good. Here the basic interest or good of religion will require the state to avoid these burdens if it can reasonably achieve its ends in other ways. Not to do so would be to fail to take a basic interest into account – just what this pluralist perfectionism rules out.

But in addition to protecting basic interests against state action, civil rights and liberties can perform their ultimate function via the intermediate one of *protecting conditions instrumental to them.* Consider the case of speech. Communication of beliefs, desires, feelings and intentions is not one of the basic interests, but is crucial for all of them. Without the freedom to communicate, friendship never gets off the ground. Without new ideas and free dissent, knowledge shrinks and groupthink grows. Political authorities are cut off from the needs and aims of those they should be serving, and so on. So any state concerned with the many facets of the common good will respect a robust liberty of speech and expression.[50]

Since the basic interests are incommensurable, there will be many reasonable schemes of general rules for protecting them against state action and settling incidental trade-offs. What *is* ruled out is wilful or careless disregard of basic human interests, their general preconditions, or their potential beneficiaries.

So the intermediate and ultimate functions of civil rights and liberties are clear, even if incommensurability makes their edges fuzzy. But the same incommensurability, or thoroughgoing pluralism, also gives some rights an absolute *core*. Again, because instances of basic goods in different people are incommensurable, intending basic harm to one person cannot be justified as a means to simply greater good, an increase without basic loss.

Thus, the basic interest of personal integrity grounds an *absolute* right against state action aimed at breaking a person's will: this core of the right

[50] For extended defences of these civil liberties, see R.P. George, *Making Men Moral* (Oxford University Press, 1993), 192–208, 219–28.

against torture will be absolute.[51] And the basic interest of life will ground an absolute right not to 'be made the intended victims of a homicidal project'.[52] Alan Gewirth tries to derive both rights from the Kantian requirement to avoid treating others 'as if they had no rights or dignity', which he thinks always wrong because rights and dignity are the 'basic presuppositions of morality itself'.[53] But when the whole question is precisely whether the right not to be killed has exceptions – or whether human dignity requires *never* deliberately killing (innocents) – it is question-begging to appeal quite generally to the importance of rights and dignity. Our perfectionist account allows substantive basic interests to ground these substantive rights, and its incommensurability thesis explains their absoluteness.

5 Analyses – and Justifications – Revisited

Now we can revisit the analysis of civil rights and liberties. We saw in the introduction that in the focal case, they reflect the most general norms for the state's action and provision of its resources, toward all within its jurisdiction. But are they characteristically meant to protect rights-holders' interests, or choices? The answer is both – and neither.

The analysis of social institutions like rights and liberties must ultimately include their *ground*. But that ground is the common good, which is variegated. Some of its components – like friendship and religion – cannot be realised except by being freely chosen. Others, like knowledge, require as a precondition a wide range of choice within certain domains (like speech). So yes, several civil liberties protect choices in certain domains. But *pace* choice theorists like Hart, we cannot define the choices protected apart from human interests.

This pluralist perfectionism, then, captures the choice theory's appeal; it explains why choice often figures at the level of generality at which civil rights and liberties are cast. But unlike choice theory, it is discriminating

[51] For a defence, see P. Lee, 'Interrogational torture', *American Journal of Jurisprudence* 51 (2006), 131–47.

[52] We differ with Gewirth on just what the right in the vicinity excludes. He thinks Smith's intention is irrelevant to determining whether Smith has made someone 'the intended victim of a homicidal project'; we think it essential.

[53] A. Gewirth, 'Are there any absolute rights?', *Philosophical Quarterly* 31 (1981), 1–16, 9.

about *which* types of choices matter: namely, those most closely tied to a basic interest. Moreover, by so grounding the importance of choices in interests, *some* of which can be realised even *without* choice, it does not imperil children's rights, or unwaivable ones. And by basing rights and liberties on the human good, it is better positioned to answer someone who wonders why he should respect them at all.

At the same time, it implies that both sides in the long debate are wrong to focus just on *individual* choice or interest. The common good is that of individuals *and* the communities they form and maintain. Some civil rights and liberties serve shared conditions, for the sake of benefits to the whole community and not just the rights-holder. Freedom of the press gives the community a robust political culture; it is not for giving the journalist a hot story.

And so, by grounding and (relatedly!) defining civil rights and liberties in terms of the whole common good, individual and communal, our approach avoids counterexamples to the interest theory that exploit its focus on the rights-holder. At the same time, it preserves interest theorists' advantage over theories that appeal just to abstract ideals.

6 A Right to Do a Wrong?

But has it done so at an intolerable cost? Recall that Hart faulted interest theories for collapsing the distinction between rights and the rest of morality. We might now seem to have misheard that objection as advice. The approach we have sketched bases civil rights and liberties on the same human interests that (on our view) ground all of morality – and on the same common good that we think grounds *political* morality in particular.

As it happens, we regard this as no embarrassment. It even has a certain consonance with the historical development of discourse on justice and rights. In medieval thinkers like Aquinas, '*ius*' (from which is derived '*iura*' = rights) simply denoted *that which was due*: the requirements of justice. By the early modern period in which Suarez wrote, it had come to be specified as something *possessed* by individuals: a moral *power*. And from Grotius to Hobbes, precursors of contemporary choice theorists, it was increasingly identified with *freedoms* in particular.[54] This evolution

[54] Finnis, *Natural Law*, 206–8; cf. Griffin, *Human Rights*, 9–14.

suggests (but by no means proves) that the way we have carved out rights from other norms is a contingent response to historical concerns – reviewed in the introduction – to limit official power. It represents *one* legitimate way of dividing up the space of what morality requires, one that highlights the *beneficiaries* of certain norms, and especially their *freedom*. At least this history undermines the Hartian sense that there is a deep and intrinsic difference between rights and other political–moral principles.

Nevertheless, it is worth addressing the concern that so closely linking rights with the rest of morality and the human good will somehow rob them of their independence and value. We'll focus on one expression of this worry in philosophical debates on civil liberties in particular: that the value of civil liberties depends partly on their protecting a right to do certain moral wrongs – a right that perfectionist accounts might seem to threaten.

On Dworkin's 'political' view of human rights, the latter give individuals 'trumps' over policies otherwise justified as promoting the collective interest. They are grounded not in the human interests or autonomy, but in a right to 'equal concern and respect'.[55] Equal concern requires not discounting people's interests just because of who they are, or torturing them just for fun. And equal respect requires honouring their ability and responsibility to define what makes their own life good and worthy. Dworkin takes it to ground freedoms of religion, speech and press – and what he has called a 'right to moral independence'.[56]

In a piece on the alleged right to do wrong, 'Is there a right to pornography?', he spelled this out as people's right not 'to suffer disadvantage in the distribution of social goods and opportunities ... just on the ground that their officials or fellow citizens think that their opinions about the right way for them to lead their own lives are ignoble or wrong'.[57]

But a judgement that someone has chosen ill for himself needn't express contempt or even the slightest disregard. On the contrary, it could be motivated by a sense of his great worth and dignity, which (one believes) is besmirched by his life choices. Dworkin does not deny that such a belief could be true; he grants, in fact, that pornography is wrong and

[55] Dworkin, *Justice*, 329ff.
[56] R.M. Dworkin, *A Matter of Principle* (Harvard University Press, 1985), 353.
[57] R.M. Dworkin, 'Is there a right to pornography?', *Oxford Journal of Legal Studies* 1 (1981), 177–212, 194.

degrading – damaging to societies in which it flourishes and not only to its consumers' character. What he denies is that such judgements are proper grounds for legal bans.

Nor can his objection be just to citizens acting on opinions *regarding other people's lives*, as Hart once read Dworkin to imply. '*That* position', Dworkin agrees, would prove too much. It would rule out 'vot[ing] for social welfare programmes, or foreign aid'.[58] Indeed. But if we can act on our honest value or moral judgements about what would make others' lives go *better*, why not about what makes them go *worse*?

Pressed on this point, Dworkin subtly shifts emphasis. His objection to bans on pornography and similar 'morals' laws, in this clarification, is not that such laws are based on what would make another's life go well or ill. No, what he 'condemn[s]' is 'any political process that assumes that the fact that people have such [moral views] is itself part of the case in political morality for what they favor'.[59]

We agree that it demeans others to think that the sheer fact of your having an opinion is a reason to enshrine your opinion in law. That supposes that apart from their *merits*, some views count for more just because they are *yours*. Yet morals laws *needn't (and typically do not) rest on that idea at all.* People supporting them would promote certain values on the ground that they are *worthy*, not that they are *theirs*. So Dworkin's right to moral independence is no requirement of equal respect.[60] The latter ideal does not require our account of civil liberties to make special room for a right to do moral wrongs.

Waldron has argued that something else does: the importance of 'personal integrity', of having 'choices' to be able to 'decide what person one is to be', at least regarding politics, intimate relationships, expression of opinions, professional choices and the like.[61] Why? Because if we could (even in principle) limit people's freedom to do wrong in these realms, he thinks, they would have choices only over 'the banalities and trivia of human life'. They would have to forge their identity through 'the decision

[58] Ibid., 209.
[59] Ibid.
[60] For a detailed presentation of the argument we have here summarised against Dworkin's derivation of an alleged 'right to moral independence', see George, *Making Men Moral*, ch. 3.
[61] Waldron, 'A right to do wrong', 34. On Waldron's view, see George, *Making Men Moral*, ch. 4.

to begin shaving on chin rather than cheek, the choice between strawberry and banana ice cream'.[62] After all, it is 'completely implausible' to expect morality to have nothing to say about the more important realms of life mentioned above.

Our approach allows, again, that choice is essential to realising certain goods. The state cannot force you to marry someone, even on the honest belief that your marrying that person is, under the circumstances, morally best, for the result would be a sham. Forcing a 'marriage' violates a precondition of this basic interest, which our approach excludes.

The same does not hold of every basic interest, of course. Respiratory health would remain good for you, part of your basic interest in life and health, even if the state left you no choice to smoke. Yet we agree that there is value in people's forging their own identities – by their choice of profession, political expression, etc.

What we deny is that if morality has any say, it will choke off all meaningful choice. It might if utilitarianism were true. But on the foundation we have sketched for civil rights and liberties, the human good is variegated and marked by deep incommensurabilities.

Yes, morality excludes unfairness, direct harm to basic goods, etc. But professional self-constitution never depended on being free to become a pornographer or a poacher anyway; political self-determination does not hinge on the freedom to campaign for the National Socialists. What morality fences off is barren ground. The fields it leaves open for constituting ourselves are fertile and inexhaustible: capable of infinitely varied growth.

Of course, in the real world, the law must always leave open *countless* immoral options – because of the costs of enforcement, the threat of political abuse, or something else. Perhaps a particular community is so puritanical that enabling its officials to prosecute the production and use of pornography would send real artists into hiding. Or pornography might be so pervasive and intractable that banning it would breed contempt for law. Then Dworkin's right to consume pornography would exist, but in a watered-down sense on our framework. It would not be a general norm, or grounded in the individual's interest or even *directly* in the community's. It would be a local, contingent, indirect implication of the latter.

[62] Ibid., 36.

But even with this unsteady status for any alleged right to do moral wrong, the approach we have sketched is in no danger of limiting the freedom or diversity that on any sensible view will be essential for people and their communities to flourish. Its thoroughgoing value pluralism puts these values on firm ground indeed.

Conclusion

The plurality and incommensurability of human goods on this view is thus its backbone. It gives our approach evident advantages over attempts to pull a rich array of rights out of one abstract ideal of respect. It allows for a basis of rights in goods that can motivate adherence, without licensing a consequentialism that would unravel them all. It accounts for the absoluteness of some rights while accommodating their observed variety at the edges across basically just regimes. It explains the pivotal importance of choice to some foundational goods without blindness to all the others. And it allays an anxiety that has motivated its choice theory rivals and champions of a right to do wrong: the fear that without autonomy from the rest of morality and from the human good, civil rights will offer scant protection against the harsh pressures of common life on individual identity.

Criminal Law 16

R.A. Duff

Introduction

Philosophical (as distinct from sociological or historical) theories of criminal law display both analytical and normative dimensions. Analytically, they investigate the defining features of criminal law, as a distinctive kind of law. Normatively, they examine the proper structure and aims of criminal law: what principles should govern it? Toward what goals should it be oriented? Why should we maintain a system of criminal law?

To say that philosophical inquiries are distinct from sociological or historical inquiries is not to say that there is no significant connection between them: philosophical accounts must draw on these other disciplines. First, analytical theories of criminal law must be recognisable as accounts of this institution: an institution with a history (indeed with different histories in different places), and a distinctive place in the political structure. Second, normative theories must say something about the relationship between theory and existing practice. A normative theory offers a picture of what criminal law ought to be, and provides a model against which we can assess our existing laws. Actual practice doubtless falls far short of what it ought, according to the theory, to be: while that fact does not undermine the theory, it requires the theorist to say something about how to get from here to there, and how we should deal with our existing actualities.

There are deeper questions about the bearing of such other disciplines on philosophical theorising.[1] Can we aspire to a universal theory, whether analytical or normative, of 'criminal law' as such, at all times and places? Or, given the historical contingencies and the political and sociological

[1] See N. Lacey, 'Institutionalising responsibility: implications for jurisprudence', *Jurisprudence* 4:1 (2013); L. Farmer, *Making the Modern Criminal Law. Criminalization and Civil Order* (Oxford University Press, 2016).

particularities of different legal systems, can we only aspire, analytically, to give a more modest, local account of criminal law in this kind of polity; or, normatively, to make sense of our own system of criminal law and other systems that sufficiently resemble it? The discussion here will be relatively modest and local – an account of criminal law in modern liberal democracies: it will leave open the question of how far such an account could be extended to other kinds of polity.[2]

Philosophical accounts of criminal law must also draw on other branches of philosophy. They must draw on political philosophy: since criminal law is part of the political structure of a community, an account of criminal law must depend on an account of political community, and of the relationship between state and citizen.[3] They must draw on moral philosophy: for the criminal law aims to define, and attribute responsibility for, certain kinds of wrong.[4] They must draw on philosophy of action, since criminal law is centrally concerned with actions and our culpable responsibility for them.[5]

We will explore both analytical and normative questions here. The two kinds of question inevitably overlap. For criminal law is a normative institution, which claims the authority to guide and judge our conduct: any analysis of criminal law must deal with its normative claims. Nor can this be a simple analysis of what is already present to us: since any existing system of criminal law is the messy product of the shifting forces that determined its historical development, analysis must be an exercise in 'rational reconstruction'.[6] It must try to make normative sense of the array of doctrines, statutes and practices that constitute the criminal law, to fit them into a rationally ordered normative whole that expresses coherent

[2] See R.A. Duff and S.P. Green, 'Introduction: searching for foundations' in Duff and Green (eds.), *Philosophical Foundations of Criminal Law* (Oxford University Press, 2011), 1.

[3] See P. Pettit. 'Criminalization in Republican theory' in R.A. Duff, L. Farmer, S.E. Marshall, M. Renzo and V. Tadros (eds.), *Criminalization: The Political Morality of the Criminal Law* (Oxford University Press, 2014), 132; S. Dimock, 'Contractarian criminal law theory and *mala prohibita* offences' in Duff et al., *Criminalization*, 151; M. Matravers, 'Political theory and the criminal law' in Duff and Green, *Philosophical Foundations*, 67; V. Chiao, *Criminal Law in the Age of the Administrative State* (Oxford University Press, 2019).

[4] See e.g. S.P. Green, *Lying, Cheating, and Stealing: A Moral Theory of White-Collar Crime* (Oxford University Press, 2005).

[5] See e.g. M.S. Moore, *Act and Crime* (Oxford University Press, 1993); R.A. Duff, *Answering for Crime* (Hart Publishing, 2007).

[6] See D.N. MacCormick, 'Reconstruction after deconstruction: a response to CLS', *Oxford Journal of Legal Studies* 10 (1990), 539.

aims and values and that is adapted to the pursuit of identifiable ends; but in doing so it must reconstruct rather than simply describe, and recognise ways in which our actual systems fail to conform to the values that supposedly structure them.

Some theorists argue that such attempts at rational reconstruction must fail. Criminal law is not a rational practice; the principles by which it is supposedly structured serve not to order it, but to conceal the political forces that determine its actual workings, and the conflicts that undermine its pretensions to rationality.[7] Such criticisms are best rebutted by showing how a process of rational reconstruction can be carried through – while recognising that a coherent criminal law can include conflicts among its aims and principles.

1 What is Criminal Law?

The analytical enterprise might begin by asking 'What is criminal law?', in the hope of an answer that at least identifies the salient features of paradigm examples of criminal law.

Systems of criminal law typically have three dimensions. First, the substantive criminal law defines a range of crimes: it specifies the kinds of conduct that are to count as criminal, the conditions given which a person counts as committing a crime, and the defences through which one who commits a crime can avoid conviction. Second, the procedural dimension of criminal law defines the processes through which the substantive law is applied: these include the activities of the police in investigating crime, of prosecutors in bringing cases to court (or otherwise disposing of them), and of courts in trying defendants. Third, its penal dimension specifies the punishments to be imposed on those convicted of crimes, and the processes by which such punishments are administered.

We will not discuss punishment here, since it is discussed elsewhere in this *Companion*.[8] It is worth asking, however, whether punishment is an essential feature of criminal law: could a system lacking this dimension count as one of criminal law? Some theorists see punishment as the most

[7] See e.g. M. Kelman, 'Interpretive construction in the substantive criminal law', *Stanford Law Review* 33 (1981), 591; A.W. Norrie, *Crime, Reason and History*, 3rd ed. (Cambridge University Press, 2014).

[8] See Bennett and Brownlee, 'Punishment', in this volume.

salient feature of criminal law: they posit punishment as the aim of criminal law;[9] or they think that given the burdensomeness of punishment, in asking what kinds of conduct should be criminal we must be asking about the kinds of conduct for which people should be rendered liable to punishment.[10] Now when a system attaches (often onerous) punishment to criminal convictions, we must ask about the justification of such punishments, and remember that criminal liability is likely to lead to punishment. But we should not become obsessed by punishment as *the* focal point of criminal law. Suppose that a legal system defines crimes in the same way as do other systems of criminal law, and provides for a trial process that leads, as others do, to the formal conviction of those proved guilty of crimes, but does not provide for their punishment: perhaps what follows conviction is therapy, or a requirement to undertake a process of 'restorative justice'. We might argue about whether these would really constitute 'punishments', whether they would be normatively adequate responses, and whether such a system should 'strictly' count as a system of *criminal* law. But it would share significant features of criminal law; and we will see that we can offer a plausible account of some of the proper purposes of criminal law without referring to punishment as the inevitable result of conviction.

Focusing on the first two dimensions of criminal law, substantive and procedural, we can ask what distinguishes *criminal* law from other kinds of law.

We can get clearer about the concept of crime (as what substantive criminal law defines) by contrasting criminal law with other kinds of regulation. Some legal systems distinguish criminal law from non-criminal regulations whose breaches do not constitute crimes: German law distinguishes crimes (*Straftaten*) from 'regulatory' violations (*Ordnungswidrigkeiten*).[11] Even when no such distinction is formally drawn, courts and theorists sometimes distinguish 'real' crimes from 'quasi-crimes' or 'regulatory offences'.[12] Such distinctions are neither clear

[9] See e.g. M.S. Moore, *Placing Blame: A Theory of Criminal Law* (Oxford University Press, 1997), ch. 1.

[10] See e.g. D.N. Husak, *Overcriminalization: The Limits of the Criminal Law* (Oxford University Press, 2008).

[11] See M.D. Dubber and T. Hörnle, *Criminal Law: A Comparative Approach* (Oxford University Press, 2014), 96–7.

[12] See the judicial dicta cited in Simester, 'Is strict liability always wrong?' in A.P. Simester (ed.), *Appraising Strict Liability* (Oxford University Press, 2005), 21, 23–4.

nor uncontroversial, but the way in which they are drawn reveals something important about criminal law. A key feature of non-criminal (or 'quasi-criminal') violations is that they are not taken to merit the censure that a criminal conviction involves: the agent has broken a rule, and is penalised; but the finding that she broke the rule, and the administration of the penalty, do not censure her as a wrongdoer.[13] We can therefore say that the criminal law is concerned with wrongs: to define a type of conduct as criminal is to portray it as a wrong that merits formal censure or condemnation.

It might seem that while this is true of such core crimes as attacks on persons or property, it is not true of many contemporary criminal offences. It might be true of '*mala in se*', crimes that consist in conduct that is wrongful independently of its criminalisation (wrongful '*in se*', in itself); but it is not true of '*mala prohibita*', crimes consisting in conduct that is wrongful only (if at all) because it violates a legal regulation (is '*prohibitum*'). But many offences in contemporary legal systems are *mala prohibita*, not *mala in se*:[14] so it might seem misleading to say that criminal law is concerned with wrongdoing.

However, first, we must ask whether criminal law (rather than non-criminal regulation) is appropriately used for such a wide range of *mala prohibita*: perhaps this is one way in which its scope has been over-extended. Second, an account of criminal law as dealing with wrongs can capture *mala prohibita*, if they consist in the breach of a legal regulation which we have an obligation to obey, and thus do wrong in disobeying. There may be nothing in itself wrong about not paying a certain percentage of my income to my government – it is not a *malum in se*. But if we introduce a (just) regime of taxation, with regulations about how much citizens should contribute to fund the polity's civic enterprises, we have an obligation to obey those regulations; we commit wrongs if we violate them, and such violations can be made criminal.

We will return to this feature of the criminal law shortly, but must first note that it is not unique in being concerned with wrongs: tort law, for

[13] On 'punishments' and mere 'penalties', see J. Feinberg, 'The expressive function of punishment' in *Doing and Deserving* (Princeton University Press, 1970) 95, 96–8.

[14] See J. Horder, 'Bureaucratic "criminal" law: too much of a bad thing?' in Duff et al. (eds.), *Criminalization*, 101; on *mala prohibita* as wrongs, see D.N. Husak, '*Malum prohibitum* and retributivism' in D.N. Husak, *The Philosophy of Criminal Law* (Oxford University Press, 2010), 410; Duff, *Answering for Crime*, 89–93, 166–74.

instance, is also sometimes concerned with wrongs.[15] It might be tempting to draw a sharp distinction between tort law and criminal law by saying that whereas criminal law is concerned with wrongs and who should be held liable to censure (and punishment) for them, tort law is concerned with harm and who should be held liable to pay for it: the point of tort law is not to censure a wrongdoer, but to allocate the cost of harms that have been caused. But that would be too simple: sometimes, the point of a tort case is to seek redress for a wrong rather than compensation for a harm; to call to account the person who wronged me, rather than to shift onto another the cost of a harm that I have suffered.[16] To distinguish criminal law from tort law, we should look to the different legal processes that each involves.

A tort case is brought by a plaintiff, who sues another for a wrong or harm. The plaintiff decides whether to bring a case; whether to pursue it or settle it; and, if she goes to court and wins, whether to enforce the remedy awarded by the court. The case is listed as *P [Plaintiff]* v. *D [defendant]*' – it is *her* case. By contrast, a criminal case is investigated and controlled not by the individual victim (when there is one), but by a public prosecuting authority. It is for the prosecuting authority to decide whether to pursue the case, whether to take it to court; the case is listed as, for instance, *People* v. *D*; if the defendant is convicted, the sentence is administered by public officials – it is not for the victim to decide not to exact punishment.[17]

Thus whereas torts are 'private' wrongs, crimes are 'public' wrongs.[18] A tort belongs to the wronged plaintiff. She can use a public process to pursue her case; the polity will take public notice of her wrong at her request: but it is for her to pursue it or not, and the remedy is for her as the wronged party. By contrast, a crime belongs to the public – to the polity rather than to the individual victim. Although more must be said about this

[15] On tort law, see Gardner, 'Tort law', in this volume.

[16] For a nice example, see *Ashley* v. *Chief Constable of Sussex Police* [2008] 1 AC 962; see further J. Goldberg and B. Zipursky, 'Torts as wrongs', *Texas Law Review* 88 (2010), 917; M. Dyson (ed.), *Unravelling Tort and Crime* (Cambridge University Press, 2014).

[17] This picture is oversimplified: it ignores the various ways in which victims can have a formal or informal say in what happens; but the core point still holds.

[18] See, classically, W. Blackstone, *Commentaries on the Laws of England* (Clarendon Press, originally published 1765–9), https://avalon.law.yale.edu/subject_menus/blackstone.asp Bk IV, ch. 1.

idea of a 'public' wrong, in particular to meet the accusation that in treating crimes as public wrongs we 'steal' them from their victims,[19] we need say here only that crimes are public wrongs in that they properly concern 'the public' – the polity as a whole. Even if the wrong was done directly to an individual victim, we make it our collective business, as a wrong to which we should collectively respond.

What is distinctive about criminal law is thus that it is focused on 'public' wrongs. In its substantive dimension, it defines a set of wrongs that are 'public' in that they are wrongs to which the polity will make a formal public response; in its procedural dimension it provides for that response, which culminates in the criminal trial. The central normative question now is why we should maintain such an institution; and, if we do, what its scope and structure should be. Before we tackle that question, however, more should be said analytically about the internal structure of the substantive criminal law, and about the criminal process.

2 The Internal Structures of Substantive Criminal Law

An analytical account of substantive criminal law might hope to do more than say that it defines a set of public wrongs: to say something about its logical structure (although we must remember the danger that we will be analysing only our local criminal law).

The structure of the – or our – criminal law can be clarified by attending to a number of distinctions. In each case we must ask whether the distinction is just a matter of expository convenience, or reveals something deeper: does it simply offer a neater way of describing the law or does it show us something significant about the logic of criminal law?

The first distinction is between the 'general part' and the 'special part' of criminal law. The special part is that in which all the specific crimes are defined. The general part contains general principles and doctrines that apply, if not to all crimes, at least to a range of crimes.[20] The general part

[19] See N. Christie, 'Conflicts as property', *British Journal of Criminology* 17 (1977), 1; in response, see S.E. Marshall and R.A. Duff, 'Criminalization and sharing wrongs', *Canadian Journal of Law & Jurisprudence* 11 (1998), 7; for complications, see A.Y. Lee, 'Public wrongs and the criminal law', *Criminal Law & Philosophy* 9 (2015), 155.

[20] See G. Fletcher, *Rethinking Criminal Law* (Little, Brown & Co., 1978), 393–408; N. Lacey, 'Philosophy, history and criminal law theory', *Buffalo Criminal Law Review* 1 (1998), 295;

includes, inter alia, principles about the conditions of liability – for instance that criminal liability requires 'an act';[21] definitions of key liability terms – of such 'fault' terms as 'intention', for instance;[22] specifications of defences that apply to many offences;[23] and of secondary modes of liability (such as doctrines of attempt and conspiracy).[24]

The second distinction is between 'offences' and 'defences'. The offence of 'wounding with intent', for instance, is partly defined as deliberately wounding another.[25] Even if it is proved that I committed that offence, I can avoid conviction by offering a defence – that, for instance, I acted in self-defence, or under duress. Some argue that this is just an expository convenience: instead of having to list, for each offence, every element that bears on liability, we can specify the particular features of the offence in the special part, and then define in the general part those conditions that apply to all or most offences; instead of specifying, in each offence definition, that the defendant must not have acted under exculpatory duress, we can specify duress as a general defence in the general part.[26] Others argue that the distinction has substantive significance.[27] The definition of an offence specifies a (presumptive) wrong, for which the perpetrator must answer: if the prosecution proves that I committed the offence, I must answer for that commission. But I can answer for it in a way that averts conviction, by offering a defence.

Further distinctions might be drawn both between the different aspects of offences, and between different kinds of defence.

Common law textbooks often distinguish '*actus reus*' from '*mens rea*' as the two aspects of any offence, drawing on the old slogan that '*actus non facit reum nisi mens sit rea*' (an act does not make the person guilty unless his mind be guilty); any crime, it is said, involves (or should

J. Gardner, 'On the general part of the criminal law' in R.A. Duff (ed.), *Philosophy and the Criminal Law* (Cambridge University Press, 1998), 20; V. Tadros, 'The system of criminal law', *Legal Studies* 22 (2002), 448.

[21] E.g. the American Model Penal Code § 2.01 (but see at n. 30 below).

[22] E.g. Model Penal Code § 2.02.

[23] E.g. Model Penal Code Articles 3, 4; M. Bohlander, *The German Criminal Code: A Modern English Translation* (Hart Publishing, 2008), §§ 20–21, 32–35.

[24] E.g. Model Penal Code Article 5; German Criminal Code §§ 22–31.

[25] Offences Against the Person Act 1861, s. 18.

[26] See G. Williams, 'Offences and defences', *Legal Studies* 2 (1982), 233.

[27] See J. Gardner, *Offences and Defences* (Oxford University Press, 2007) papers 4, 7; Duff, *Answering for Crime*, ch. 9.

involve – here again the analytical rapidly leads into the normative) both an *actus reus* and a *mens rea*.[28] What is true in this slogan is that a criminal offence typically involves (and should involve) an active engagement in the world (the *actus reus*) by an agent who displays an appropriate kind of fault (the *mens rea*) in thus engaging.[29] Confusions arise, however, if the distinction is taken to be between two separate 'elements' of the offence, one consisting in an 'act' plus its relevant circumstances and consequences, the other in some 'mental state' associated with that act. This leads to controversies and confusions about what can be taken to constitute an 'act', and whether criminal liability does or should always involve an act;[30] and about how we can identify, and prove, the relevant mental states.

As for defences, it is now common to distinguish justifications from excuses.[31] Simply put, a justification claims that the commission of the offence was, in the circumstances, right or at least permissible; an excuse admits that the commission of the offence was wrong, but claims that given the special features of the situation or the agent it would be unfair to condemn him for it. Thus self-defence is a justification: I am permitted to use necessary, even fatal, force to defend myself against attack although this involves committing an offence of wounding or homicide. By contrast, duress is often an excuse: I should not have committed the offence, even to avoid the harm threatened against me; but I should not be condemned for giving in to that threat.[32] Thus in providing a justificatory defence, the law tells us that in the specified circumstances we may, or should, commit the offence; in providing for an excuse, it does not qualify the claim that we

[28] See A.T. Smith, 'On *actus reus* and *mens rea*' in P.R. Glazebrook (ed.), *Reshaping the Criminal Law* (Stevens, 1978) 95; Duff, *Answering for Crime*, 202–7.

[29] This raises the question of whether 'strict liability' – criminal liability without proof of fault – can ever be justified: see Simester (ed.), *Appraising Strict Liability*.

[30] See D.N. Husak, 'Does criminal liability require an act?' in *The Philosophy of Criminal Law*, 17; Duff, *Answering for Crime*, ch. 5.

[31] See J.L. Austin, 'A plea for excuses' in Austin, *Philosophical Papers* (Oxford University Press, 1961) 123, 125; Fletcher, *Rethinking Criminal Law*, ch. 10; V. Tadros, *Criminal Responsibility* (Oxford University Press, 2005) chs. 10–12; Duff, *Answering for Crime*, ch. 11; Gardner, *Offences and Defences*, papers 5–6. For sceptical discussion, see K. Greenawalt, 'The perplexing borders of justification and excuse', *Columbia Law Review* 84 (1984), 1897.

[32] See J. Dressler, 'Exegesis of the law of duress', *Southern California Law Review* 62 (1989), 1331.

ought not to commit the crime, but tells us that we will not be condemned if we do commit it under the specified circumstances.[33]

Some theorists go beyond this two-part schema of justification and excuse, to distinguish excuses from exemptions.[34] On this view, an excuse admits responsibility for the crime, as a wrong for which I must answer, and offers an exculpatory answer that appeals to my reasons for action. Exemptions, by contrast, negate responsibility: someone who pleads insanity, for instance, is not answering for his crime in a way that rationally exculpates it; he claims that given his disordered condition at the time, he was not a responsible agent who could answer for his conduct.

These distinctions are matters of structure rather than of substantive content. They do not tell us what the content of the law should be – what kind of 'act' (if any) criminal liability should require; or what kinds of 'fault' or *mens rea* should be required either generally or for particular kinds of offence; or what defences the law should recognise.[35] They are intended to help us understand the structure, the logic, of the criminal law – and thus to identify the range of normative questions that must be asked about its content.

Nor indeed do they tell us what kinds of conduct should be criminalised. Before we turn to that topic, however, we must attend briefly to the criminal trial.

3 The Criminal Trial

It might be tempting to understand the criminal trial in purely instrumental terms, as the process that connects crime to punishment. The point of the trial is to identify those who are to be punished, by identifying those who have committed crimes. If we care whether a penal system meets the minimal requirement of justice that it punish only the guilty, the point of the trial will be 'accurate decision-making':[36] to identify the guilty, and

[33] For further ramifications, see P. Alldridge, 'Rules for courts and rules for citizens', *Oxford Journal of Legal Studies* 10 (1990), 487.

[34] See Gardner, *Offences and Defences*, paper 6; Tadros, *Criminal Responsibility*, 124–9; Duff, *Answering for Crime*, 284–91.

[35] On which see A.J. Ashworth and J. Horder, *Principles of Criminal Law*, 7th ed. (Oxford University Press, 2013); Tadros, *Criminal Responsibility*.

[36] A.J. Ashworth and M. Redmayne, *The Criminal Process*, 4th ed. (Oxford University Press, 2010) 321: they describe this only as '*a* primary function'.

acquit the innocent. Of course, many features of our existing criminal process, especially in systems that preserve an 'adversarial' process that pits prosecution against defence (as distinct from 'inquisitorial' systems in which the process is one of investigation by a judge),[37] seem ill-suited to this aim. Quite apart from the stringent demand that the defendant must be acquitted if the prosecution cannot prove her guilt 'beyond reasonable doubt', many procedural rules, in particular those allowing or requiring the exclusion of certain kinds of evidence, cannot be plausibly justified as truth-serving: evidence that was illegally acquired, for instance, may be excluded from the trial even if it would contribute significantly to proof of the defendant's guilt.[38] Such features of the trial can be explained, from an instrumentalist perspective, as side-constraints on the pursuit of truth: constraints that aim to ensure that the trial is fair, that the defendant's rights are respected. It might then be said that the trial has two purposes: 'accurately to determine whether or not a person has committed a particular criminal offence and to do so fairly'.[39]

There are alternative views of the trial which do not tie it so closely to punishment, but give it more intrinsic significance as a response to (alleged) crimes. One such view is that the trial is best seen as a process of calling to account.[40] A citizen who is accused of committing a criminal wrong is called to answer to his fellow citizens through the criminal court. He is called to answer *to* the charge, by pleading 'Guilty' or 'Not Guilty'. If he pleads 'Guilty', he admits his culpable responsibility, and answers *for* the wrong that he admits.[41] If he pleads 'Not Guilty', and the prosecution cannot prove the offence, he has nothing to answer for; he is acquitted. If, however, the prosecution proves that he committed the offence, he is called

[37] See M. Damaška, 'Evidentiary barriers to conviction and two models of criminal procedure', *University of Pennsylvania Law Review* 21 (1973), 506.

[38] See further P. Roberts and A. Zuckerman, *Criminal Evidence* (Oxford University Press, 2004), especially chs. 1–4, 9, 11.

[39] Ashworth and Redmayne, *The Criminal Process*, 23.

[40] See R.A. Duff, L. Farmer, S.E. Marshall and V. Tadros, *The Trial on Trial (3): Towards a Normative Theory of the Criminal Trial* (Hart Publishing, 2007); on which see M. Redmayne, 'Theorizing the criminal trial', *New Criminal Law Review* 12 (2009), 287 . See also A.W. Dzur, *Punishment, Participatory Democracy, and the Jury* (Oxford University Press, 2012).

[41] In our existing systems, in which most defendants plead 'Guilty', many guilty pleas are bargained, and may be far from honest confessions of guilt: see further R.L. Lippke, *The Ethics of Plea Bargaining* (Oxford University Press, 2011).

to answer for that commission. He might answer by offering a defence, which if successful will lead to an acquittal. But if he offers no successful defence, he will be convicted: he will be held to account as a culpable wrongdoer. The main rationale for such a view of the trial is that it reflects a plausible conception of how a democratic polity should treat its members: it should treat them as responsible citizens; and to treat someone as a responsible agent is, inter alia, to treat her as someone who can be expected to answer for her own conduct. By calling alleged offenders to account, we thus respect them as citizens.

We cannot discuss the trial further here, but must turn instead to two large questions: why should we maintain a system of criminal law, and what should its scope be?

4 The Aims and Scope of the Criminal Law[42]

The criminal law's characteristic role is, first, to define a set of 'public' wrongs that merit a distinctive public response (and to specify the principles of liability for the commission of such wrongs); and second, to provide for that public response, through a criminal process that culminates in a criminal trial, as the result of which the person accused of a crime is either to be acquitted as one who is still presumed innocent, or to be convicted (and rendered liable to punishment) as a culpable wrongdoer. But why should a polity maintain such an institution? And what should its scope be: what kinds of conduct should it define as criminal?

Any answer to the second of these questions will depend on an answer to the first: until we determine the proper aims of the criminal law, we have no idea of what its scope should be. But any answer to the first question must be grounded in a political theory of the state: for the criminal law is part of the apparatus of the state; an account of its proper aims must be an account of how it contributes to the aims of the state, or of the polity of which the state is the institutional apparatus. We cannot embark on that task here, but should note three ways in which the aims of the criminal law might be articulated.

The first is purely instrumental: the institution of criminal law is justified insofar as it is an efficient means toward some further good that a state

[42] See also Stanton-Ife, 'The ends and limits of law', in this volume.

should pursue. Different theories offer different accounts of that further good:[43] but the distinctive contribution of criminal law to any such good is likely to lie in its efficiency as a way of preventing conduct that injures it. On this view, criminal law is one among other available techniques for controlling conduct (and punishment is no doubt crucial to that technique); we should therefore decide what kinds of conduct to criminalise by asking which it would be useful to criminalise in order to protect the specified good(s). This approach fits Mill's harm principle, which has dominated recent debates about the scope of the criminal law: if a primary aim of the state should be to prevent harm to its members, we might agree that 'the only purpose for which power can rightfully be exercised over any member of a civilised community against his will is to prevent harm to others';[44] and we might apply this principle to the criminal law, to hold that the only proper reason for criminalising conduct is to prevent harm to others.[45]

For pure instrumentalists, whether and when we should use criminal law depends wholly on its instrumental efficiency. Like any pure consequentialist, they then face the familiar objection that they fail to attend seriously enough to the legitimacy of the means that they use to their ends – for instance that they would be ready to criminalise conduct that did not merit such treatment if doing so would efficiently serve the aims of harm prevention or civil peace. A familiar response to such objections is to offer a side-constrained instrumentalist account.

The use of criminal law is now to be justified when, first, it is an efficient means toward the specified ends; and, second, its use would not violate any legitimate non-consequentialist side-constraints – constraints grounded in, for instance, the rights of those to whom the law is to be applied. Various constraints might be suggested, including those captured by the idea of the rule of law,[46] but we can focus here on one that will also lead us toward a different kind of account.

[43] For an ambitious consequentialist account, see J. Braithwaite and P. Pettit, *Not Just Deserts: A Republican Theory of Criminal Justice* (Oxford University Press, 1990).

[44] J.S. Mill, *On Liberty* (Parker, 1859), ch. 1, para. 9.

[45] See J. Feinberg, *The Moral Limits of the Criminal Law* (4 volumes: *Harm to Others*, 1984; *Offense to Others*, 1985; *Harm to Self*, 1986; *Harmless Wrongdoing*, 1988) (Oxford University Press, 1984 and subsequent years). Once we recognise that harms can be to collective as well as to individual interests we can connect this idea to the older idea that criminal law's main function is to protect 'civil peace': see A.E. Bottoms, 'Civil peace and criminalization' in Duff et al. (eds.), *Criminalization*, 232.

[46] See Tasioulas, 'The rule of law', in this volume.

This is the 'wrongfulness constraint', that we must not criminalise conduct that does not deserve to be condemned as wrongful: for criminalising conduct renders those who engage in it liable not just to punishment, but to the condemnation expressed in a criminal conviction, and marks the conduct as blameworthily wrongful.[47] This then gives us a negative version of 'legal moralism': the thesis that non-wrongful conduct ought not to be criminalised.[48] It might also lead us toward a different version of the harm principle.

Mill's formulation of the principle, like others,[49] focuses on the harm-preventive effects of criminalising (or otherwise coercing) a type of conduct: it does not require that the conduct to be criminalised should itself be harmful. Many theorists who discuss 'the Harm Principle', however, take it that what the principle rules out is the criminalisation of conduct that is not itself harmful, and this version might seem more attractive if we are concerned to preclude criminalising conduct that does not merit such a coercive state response. The mere fact that criminalising a type of conduct would help to prevent harm does not seem like a good reason to criminalise it, unless the conduct itself is harmful or at least dangerous as a likely source of harm; if we add the wrongfulness constraint, we arrive at the familiar position that we may legitimately criminalise a type of conduct only if that conduct is itself wrongfully harmful (or dangerous).[50]

This view raises several questions. Just what it allows us to criminalise depends on how we are to understand 'harm', as the evil or mischief against which all criminal law is to be aimed,[51] and on how close the connection must be between conduct and harm if the conduct is to be criminalised. But whatever account is given of harm, such views face two kinds of objection, which constitute a dilemma. On the one hand, if a reasonably determinate account of harm is given, it will be argued that the harm principle is too narrow to serve as *the* single principle of

[47] See D.N. Husak, *Overcriminalization: The Limits of the Criminal Law* (Oxford University Press, 2008), 72–6; A.P. Simester and A. von Hirsch, *Crimes, Harms, and Wrongs: On the Principles of Criminalisation* (Hart Publishing, 2011), 19–30.

[48] See R.A. Duff, *The Realm of Criminal Law* (Oxford University Press, 2018), 55–8.

[49] See e.g. Feinberg, *Harm to Others*, 26.

[50] On these two versions of the Harm Principle, see R.A. Duff and S.E. Marshall, '"Abstract endangerment", two harm principles, and two routes to criminalization', *Bergen Journal of Criminal Law and Criminal Justice* 3 (2015).

[51] See Feinberg, *Harm to Others*, chs. 1–3; Simester and von Hirsch, *Crimes, Harms, and Wrongs*, ch. 3.

criminalisation: we have good reason to criminalise kinds of wrongful conduct that neither cause nor threaten harm – harmless violations of others' dignity, for instance, or sovereignty, or rights.[52] But if we then expand the idea of harm to cover such cases, perhaps by counting violations of dignity as harms, we risk making the idea of harm so expansive as to become vacuous, so that we can count as 'harmful' any kind of conduct we think we have reason to criminalise.[53] (A similar problem faces any attempt to identify a single principle as *the* principle by which we are to decide what to criminalise: if it is determinate enough to do substantial work in guiding criminalisation decisions, it is too narrow; if it is given a broad enough meaning to avoid that charge, it becomes too indeterminate to do substantive work.)

It is also worth noting that even if we take harm as our focus, we can see good reason to criminalise some conduct that is not itself harmful or dangerous. We can sometimes prevent harm most efficiently by creating strict regulations, which prohibit some conduct that is quite safe as well as conduct that is dangerous: this is true, for instance, of speed limits, and drink-driving regulations specifying a maximum proportion of alcohol in a driver's blood. If such regulations are justified, as efficiently serving public safety without imposing unreasonable burdens on those bound by them, we can say that we all have a civic duty to obey them, even when we could breach them without causing harm; that one who breaks them therefore acts wrongfully, even if her conduct is not dangerous; and that we therefore have good reason to criminalise her conduct as a wrongful breach of a regulation that she ought to obey.[54]

We have been focusing so far on instrumental accounts (either pure or side-constrained) of the proper aims and scope of the criminal law. It is hard to deny that such instrumental considerations are relevant to

[52] See e.g. A. Ripstein, 'Beyond the harm principle', *Philosophy and Public Affairs* 34 (2006), 215 (on sovereignty); M. Dan-Cohen, 'Defending dignity', ch. 5, *Harmful Thoughts: Essays on Law, Self and Morality* (Princeton University Press, 2002), 150 (on dignity); H. Stewart, 'The limits of the harm principle', *Criminal Law & Philosophy* 4 (2010), 17 (on rights).

[53] For a related line of criticism, see B.E. Harcourt, 'The collapse of the harm principle', *Journal of Criminal Law and Criminology* 90 (1999), 109.

[54] See further Duff and Marshall, 'Abstract endangerment'; and text preceding n. 15 above. Note that we are talking here of what can give us good reason to criminalise. Good reasons might not be conclusive, and there is a large step from 'We have good reason to criminalise *X*' to 'We ought to criminalise *X* all things considered': see J. Schonsheck, *On Criminalization* (Kluwer, 1994); Duff, *The Realm of Criminal Law*, ch. 7.

questions about criminalisation: surely an institution as costly, and oppressive, as the criminal law can be justified only if it brings some significant goods or wards off some significant evil. Some theorists, however, deny just that. Or, more modestly, they might argue that such instrumental considerations specify not the aims of criminal law, but only side-constraints: its positive justification lies not in its consequential benefits, but in some non-instrumental value that it serves; but we may use it in the service of that value only if by doing so we can also achieve significant consequential good, or at least will not cause significant consequential harm.

What could that value be? One familiar answer takes us to a view classically seen as the main opponent of the harm principle – legal moralism: not a negative legal moralism that merely forbids us to criminalise conduct that is not wrongful, but a positive legal moralism according to which the wrongfulness of a type of conduct constitutes our positive reason to criminalise it. If we ask how this can be, a further familiar answer appeals to a retributivist theory of punishment. The function of criminal law is to do retributive justice by punishing 'all and only those who are morally culpable in the doing of some morally wrongful action'. We should therefore criminalise all and only morally wrongful actions: not to achieve some consequential good beyond criminal law, but to instantiate the good of retributive justice that is internal to criminal law (understood as a system focused on punishment), or to discharge our duty to inflict such justice on those who deserve it.[55]

There are various problems with this view. It relies on a particular type of retributivism according to which culpable wrongdoers deserve to have some kind of suffering inflicted on them, and the further claim that it is a proper task for the state to inflict such suffering: even those who accept the first claim should hesitate before accepting the second.[56] What we could say, however, is that a primary purpose of a system of criminal law is to define, and provide an appropriate response to, a set of public wrongs: not because this will efficiently achieve further consequential goods, but because it is appropriate formally to recognise and respond to such wrongs in this way. Why is it appropriate? Because a political community should

[55] See Moore, *Placing Blame*, ch. 1 (the quote is from 35), and ch. 18.

[56] See Bennett and Brownlee, 'Punishment', in this volume; also D.N. Husak, 'Why punish the deserving?' in *Philosophy of Criminal Law* (2010), 393.

take its defining values seriously; to take one's values seriously is, inter alia, to be ready to respond appropriately to violations of them; and the criminal law is one way in which a polity marks and responds to such violations. Furthermore, if we are to treat each other as responsible agents, we must be ready to respond to our wrongdoings by holding each other to account for them; and this is what the criminal law does in providing a criminal process through which alleged offenders are called to answer. A system of criminal law thus does justice to the polity's values, by taking formal note of their violation; to victims of crime, since an appropriate way to recognise the wrongs that victims suffer (as wrongs, not just as harms) is to hold their perpetrators to account; and to offenders, since by calling them to account for their crimes we treat them as responsible members of the political community.

This still leaves a major question: what kinds of wrong do we have reason to criminalise? On an ambitious version of legal moralism like Moore's, we have reason to criminalise *every* kind of culpable moral wrongdoing, although it turns out that on balance, after taking account of relevant countervailing reasons, we should refrain from criminalising many wrongs.[57] But this looks implausible: there are serious wrongs that we can commit, such as betrayals of trust in our intimate relationships, that we surely have *no* reason to criminalise; they belong to a private sphere that is 'not the law's business'.[58]

One response to this problem is to revert to the idea of crimes as 'public' wrongs: meaning not that they must be wrongs that directly affect 'the public' (the polity as a whole), but that they must be wrongs that are our collective business as members of the polity.[59] This then shifts the question to that of what makes a wrong our collective business, which is where criminal law theory must appeal to political theory. Rather than looking within criminal law theory for some principle that can ground decisions about criminalisation, we should begin with an account of the public sphere – the '*res publica*': that sphere of aims, activities and institutions that constitutes the civic life of the polity, the life in which its members

[57] See Moore, *Placing Blame*, ch. 18.

[58] J. Wolfenden, *Report of the Committee on Homosexual Offences and Prostitution* (HMSO, 1957), para. 61. A similar problem arises for the Harm Principle: many 'private' harms are surely not the criminal law's business.

[59] Blackstone, *Commentaries on the Laws of England*; Duff, *The Realm of Criminal Law*, ch. 2.

share as citizens. The articulation of that account is a matter of political deliberation for the members of the polity: once it is articulated, we will also be able to identify a range of different kinds of wrong that count as 'public' in the sense that they fall within that public sphere (just as, once we have an account of the life of an academic institution, we can identify the kinds of wrong that count as academic wrongs, which are therefore the business of the institution). These will be wrongs that we have reason to criminalise.[60]

We cannot pursue this line of thought here, save to note that it is unlikely to produce any single principle of criminalisation: there are different kinds of wrong, implicating different values, that we have reason to criminalise. It should, however, reinforce a point made earlier: that philosophy of criminal law must rely heavily on political philosophy.

[60] Which is not to say that we should, all things considered, criminalise them; see n. 54 above.

Contract 17

Daniel Markovits

Introduction

Contracts characteristically involve agreements, and contract law is – both conventionally and properly – understood as the law of agreements.

The central role that agreements play in contract law may be read off the face of contracts that arise in the orthodox fashion, through offer, acceptance and consideration. According to the US American Restatement, an *offer* 'is the manifestation of willingness to enter into a bargain, so made as to justify another person in understanding that his assent to that bargain is invited and will conclude it'.[1] *Acceptance*, for its part, involves 'a manifestation of assent to the terms [of the offer] made by the offeree in a manner invited or required by the offer'.[2] All orthodox contracts – contracts that arise through offer and acceptance – thus contain agreements. But not all agreements establish contracts. Most notably,[3] the common law further requires all valid contracts to be supported by *consideration*, which means (on the modern version of the doctrine) that 'a performance or a return promise must be bargained for', which is to say that 'it is sought by the promisor in exchange for his promise and is given

[1] Restatement (Second) of Contracts § 24 (1981).

[2] Restatement (Second) of Contracts § 50 (1981).

[3] Two very different additional sets of doctrines further limit the class of agreements that might establish contracts.

On the one hand, doctrines concerning fraud, duress, and incapacity insist that the agreements behind valid contracts must be knowingly and freely made. And on the other hand, doctrines that deny contractual recognition to illegal agreements or, more broadly, to agreements that violate public policy, prevent contract law from lending its aid to projects that the broader legal order considers unacceptably undesirable.

The first set of doctrines might be explained as shoring the central role of agreements in contract law, by requiring that the agreements at the heart of valid contracts be, in some general sense, genuine or full-throated. The second set of doctrines, by contrast, subjects contract law to limits based on values that come from outside the morality of agreements.

by the promisee in exchange for that promise'.[4] It is therefore not enough, for establishing an orthodox contract, that the parties happen, or fall into, an agreement, as might occur when a promissor offers a gift and her promisee accepts (both the gift itself and the conditions under which she might take possession of it).[5] Rather, the parties to a contract must be motivated to agree, in the sense that each must seek the other's agreement to the contractual proposition. The consideration requirement thus redoubles or deepens the role that agreements play in the common law of contracts, by giving contract law's concern for agreements a nested structure.

The orthodox regime does not exhaust contract law, to be sure. In the United States, for example, contract doctrine has at least since the Restatement (First) of Contracts and more expansively in the Restatement (Second) included the rule that '[a] promise which the promisor should reasonably expect to induce action or forbearance on the part of the promisee or a third person and which does induce such action or forbearance is binding if injustice can be avoided only by enforcement of the promise'.[6]

But even this principle of promissory estoppel operates, in judicial practice, in a manner that places agreements near the contract's core. Early courts thus insisted that contract liability might arise, under the principle of promissory estoppel, only where there had been reliance on a completed promise (and indeed, almost always, in connection with an exchange of promises), so that an orthodox contract failed on account only of the technical niceties of the consideration doctrine. Reliance on a mere offer – even where the relying party enjoyed but did not exercise the power to accept the offer – was thus expressly held insufficient to sustain liability.[7] Moreover, when courts liberalised liability under promissory estoppel, they

[4] Restatement (Second) of Contracts § 71 (1981).

[5] This distinction is famously illustrated by the case of Williston's tramp, who is told by a benevolent passer-by that if he walks to a nearby clothier, he may select an overcoat on his benefactor's credit. See Williston and Jaeger, *A Treatise on the Law of Contracts*, 3rd ed., Vol. 1 (Baker, Voorhis, 1957), § 112. Whether or not this promise is supported by good consideration depends on the parties' intentions with respect to the tramp's walking to the store. If the benefactor intends the promise to induce the tramp to walk to collect the coat (perhaps to assuage her guilt on going to a warm home), and if the tramp intends the walk to induce the provision of the coat, then there is consideration. If, on the other hand, the benefactor is merely offering to buy the tramp a coat but not to get it for him, and the tramp is merely deciding whether or not to collect on the offer, then there is no consideration.

[6] *Restatement (Second) of Contracts* § 90 (1981).

[7] See, e.g. *James Baird Co.* v. *Gimbel Bros*, 64 F.2d 344 (2d. Cir. 1933).

did so through doctrinal arguments that implied fully consummated agreements to underwrite plaintiffs' claims (for example by implying secondary promises to grant options that made primary offers irrevocable).[8] Finally, although some courts have imposed reliance-based obligations in the absence of any completed agreement, and based simply on manipulative (but not tortious) representations made during pre-contractual negotiations,[9] these decisions have attracted no substantial following. The overwhelmingly dominant view continues to insist that pre-contractual understandings can underwrite contract obligations only where there is 'overall agreement ... to enter into the binding contract'.[10]

Thus, while there was a time when Grant Gilmore could reasonably worry that promissory estoppel constituted a kind of 'anti-contract',[11] which might swallow orthodox contract whole, the doctrine has not played out this way. Even departures from the orthodox model of offer, acceptance and consideration continue to place agreements front and centre in contract's constellation.

1 Understanding Contract Law as the Law of Agreements

The central place of agreements in the law makes it tempting to suppose that contract law simply and directly implements the morality of agreements, so that to understand this field of law, one must first and exclusively study that branch of morals. But such reasoning, although tempting, is mistaken.

To begin with, legal obligation is a creature of law, not morals; and so the grounds of every legal obligation must be found in considerations that reflect legal values. As one court has perceptively said, the

> obligation of the contract does not inhere or subsist in the agreement itself *proprio vigore*, but in the law applicable to the agreement, that is, in the act of the law in binding the promisor to perform his promise. When it is said that one who enters

[8] See, e.g. *Drennan* v. *Star Paving, Co.*, 333 P.2d 757 (Cal. 1958).

[9] See, e.g. *Hoffman* v. *Red Owl Stores, Inc.*, 133 N.W.2d 267 (Wisc. 1965).

[10] See, e.g. *Teachers Ins. & Annuity Assoc.* v. *Tribune Co.*, 670 F. Supp. 491, 497 (S.D.N.Y. 1987). For a systematic survey of the US American decisions, see A. Schwartz and R. Scott, 'Precontractual liability and preliminary agreements', *Harvard Law Review* 120 (2007), 661–707, 672.

[11] G. Gilmore, *The Death of Contract* (Ohio State University Press, 1974), 61.

> upon an undertaking assumes the legal duties relating to it, what is really meant is that the law imposes the duties on him. A contract is not a law, nor does it make law. It is the agreement plus the law that makes the ordinary contract an enforceable obligation.[12]

Thus, although contract law might refer to the morality of agreements in elaborating its doctrines, that is a choice for the law to make, and the law must present legal justifications for whatever doctrinal choices it does make.

Moreover, there are good reasons for contract law to hold the morality of agreements at a distance.

To begin with, one of the foundational tenets of the liberal political values that dominate states in which contract law flourishes holds that a society's laws may not enforce controversial moral ideals. This principle entails that controversial moral ideas about agreements – including, most particularly, familiar but disputed ideas about the moral obligation to keep promises – are not appropriate grounds for legal doctrine. As Joseph Raz has observed, the moral good of enforcing agreements 'is not itself a proper goal for contract law', because to adopt this goal would be 'to enforce morality through the legal imposition of duties on individuals'.[13] Indeed, as Raz also says, a contract law that directly imposes the morality of agreements does not, '[i]n this respect . . . differ from the legal proscription of pornography'.[14]

Moreover, even those who believe that a community's law might properly reflect or promote its moral commitments need not adopt the simple-minded view that the law should do so directly, by *implementing* them. Oliver Wendell Holmes forcefully illustrates this point. Holmes believed that '[t]he law is the witness and external deposit of our moral life',[15] and even that by attending to this feature of law, the student of law might 'connect [his] subject to the universe and catch an echo of the infinite, a glimpse of its unfathomable process, a hint of the universal law'.[16] But he also took a decidedly un-moralistic view of contract, observing that 'the

[12] *Groves* v. *John Wunder, Co.*, 286 N.W. 235 (Minn. 1939).

[13] J. Raz, 'Promises in morality and law', *Harvard Law Review* 95 (1982), 916, 937 (reviewing P. Atiyah, *Promises, Morals, and the Law*).

[14] Ibid.

[15] O.W. Holmes, 'The path of the law', *Harvard Law Review* 10 (1897), 457–78, 459.

[16] Ibid.

duty to keep a contract at common law means a prediction that you must pay damages if you do not keep it, – and nothing else'[17] and, in this connection, dismissing 'those who think it advantageous to get as much ethics into the law as they can'.[18] Contract law ought, that is, to hold the morality of agreements tightly, but at arm's length.

A theory of contract law cannot, therefore, mechanically adopt or mindlessly mimic one or another preferred account of the moral obligations associated with the agreements, or promises, through which contracts typically arise. Instead, explaining or justifying agreement's central place in contract law requires an independent inquiry into the distinctively political and even legal values that this area of doctrine promotes, including through enforcing agreements.

As it happens, the most prominent theories of contract law all proceed in just this fashion – they set out from distinct (sometimes overlapping, sometimes competing) accounts of the point of contract and indeed of the point of contract's emphasis on enforcing agreements. The theories may be loosely classified by reference to these accounts of contract's purpose. The classification is necessarily imperfect, as the theories must be interpreted before they may be assigned to categories and are in any event not so monolithic as the categories suppose. Nevertheless, even an imperfect organising frame helps for understanding contract law and theory, most notably because it reveals that the several most prominent approaches to contract differ not just at their margins but, instead, understand this body of law in fundamentally different ways.

One class of theories, which includes both economic accounts of contract and philosophical theories that seek to connect contract to the morality of harm, understands contract law in *allocative* terms – that is, as a technology for distributing benefits and burdens across persons. A second class of theories understands contract in *integrative* terms – that is, in virtue of the relations among persons that contracts engender. Intramural differences also exist within each class, of course, and attending to these reveals both the internal flexibility of the allocative and integrative approaches to contract and the deep structural differences that nevertheless separate them.

[17] Ibid.
[18] Ibid.

2 Allocative Theories of Contract

The two most prominent allocative theories of contract law are the *efficiency-based* account that has come to dominate the academic study of contract in the United States and the *harm-based* theory that seeks to assimilate contract to the broader morality of injury and, most narrowly within the law, to tort.

a Contract Law and Economic Efficiency

Begin by considering the efficiency-based account of contract law and with it the economic analysis of contract law that accounts for much of the efficiency-based account's success, especially in the United States.

As Hume observed, 'experience has taught us, that human affairs wou'd be conducted much more for mutual advantage, were there certain symbols or signs instituted, by which we might give each other security of our conduct in any particular incident'.[19] Contract, according to the economic view, establishes the requisite symbols or signs, perhaps borrowing some from the moral practice of promising, and adds formalisms and third-party enforcement. These additions, and especially enforcement, immensely increase the social good – over and above what promise *simpliciter* provides – that contract can accomplish. Because legal enforcement 'allows individuals to bind themselves to a future course of conduct', which is to say to make credible commitments, contract 'makes[s] it easier for others to arrange their lives in reliance on [a] promise'.[20] Contract should thus be understood as a technology for promoting efficient coordination. Indeed, lawyer–economists may be heard to argue that contracts should be enforced only to the extent and in the specific fashion that establishes optimal incentives for reliance on promises and thus maximises the joint gains from trade the contractual coordination produces.[21]

[19] D. Hume, *A Treatise of Human Nature*, at bk. III, pt. II, sec. V, 522, L.A. Selby-Bigge (ed.), (1978) (emphasis removed).

[20] R. Craswell, 'Contract law, default rules, and the philosophy of promising', *Michigan Law Review* 88 (1989), 489, 496.

[21] See, e.g. A. Schwartz and R. Scott, 'Contract theory and the limits of contract law', *Yale Law Journal* 113 (2003), 541, 556. Some theorists have developed analogous accounts according to which contract law maximises not efficiency but party choice or autonomy (the fact that the Kaldor–Hicks conception of efficiency at the root of the economic theory constructs efficiency out of party choice accounts for the closeness of the analogy). One example of such

A comprehensive and thoroughgoing economic reconstruction of contract law would thus make optimal coordination and joint-surplus-maximisation into contract's lodestar. And some economically inflected scholars of contract have taken this lesson to heart, especially in commercial law. Thus one prominent view, after limiting its range of application to contracts that have sophisticated commercial parties on both sides, seeks expressly to reconstruct contract doctrine with the single-minded purpose of 'facilitating the ability of firms to maximise welfare [which in this context means joint contractual surplus] when making commercial contracts'.[22] This single-minded pursuit of joint surplus is justified by the focus of the theory on commercial firms. Because firms are not natural persons, commercial contract law need not consider values like autonomy and recognition (even if these properly figure in the morality of promising). And because firms are – the economic approach assumes – all owned by perfectly diversified shareholders (who thus possess equal interests on both sides of every commercial contract), commercial contract law need not consider either corrective or distributive justice.

These observations reveal that the economic analysis of contract possesses a deep radicalism and aims (foundationally) less at reconstructing conventional legal doctrine and more at law reform. It is commonly noted that even where economic analysis recapitulates conventional doctrinal themes – as in economic defence of the expectation remedy associated with the theory of efficient breach[23] – the conventional categories of promissory morality (fidelity, for example, or the agreement-based idea of securing the promisee's benefit of her bargain) 'will not have played any [independent] role in the analysis leading up to [the] conclusion' that the law should enforce promises.[24] (And some scholars have thought, for this

a theory is J. Kraus, 'The correspondence of contract and promise', *Columbia Law Review* 109 (2009), 1603. Some have suggested that Charles Fried's view of contract law, elaborated in his book *Contract as Promise*, possesses this structure: C. Fried, *Contract as Promise: A Theory of Contractual Obligation* (Oxford University Press, 1981). See, e.g. E. Weinrib, *The Idea of Private Law*, revised ed. (Oxford University Press, 2012), 50–1. Another interpretation, pursued below, treats Fried's view as an integrative rather than an allocative theory.

[22] Schwartz and Scott, 'Contract theory and the limits of contract law' at 556.

[23] For an early statement of this theory aimed at academic lawyers, see R.L. Birmingham, 'Breach of contract, damage measures, and economic efficiency', *Rutgers Law Review* 24 (1970), 273.

[24] R. Craswell, 'Against Fuller and Perdue', *University of Chicago Law Review* 67 (2000), 99, 107.

reason, that the economic approach makes it 'puzzling, to put it mildly, that the law enforces promises more readily than other commitments'.[25]) In fact, the radicalism of the economic analysis of contract law goes deeper still. A bedrock principle of conventional contract law, understood as the law of agreements, is that contracts establish obligations between *two separate parties*. But the deep structure of the argument just rehearsed – the fact that economic analysis achieves its elegant simplicity by imagining that all contracts in the end redound to the benefit of a perfectly diversified shareholder – reveals that the economic approach to contract contemplates *just one party*.

Indeed, contract law on this allocative view is perhaps best understood not as a theory of obligation at all but as a department of transactions costs economics and, even more narrowly, of the theory of the firm. As Ronald Coase famously proposed, the scope of the firm – the boundary between coordinating economic activity within a firm through ownership and managerial control and coordinating economic activity across firms by contract – is fixed by the balance between the transaction costs of each coordinating mechanism.[26] The economic approach to contract may be interpreted as an effort to reduce the transactions costs of contractual coordination across the firm boundary, with the consequence of reducing the optimal size of firms and, finally, increasing the efficiency of economic coordination overall.

b Contract Law and Harm

A second class of allocative theories of contract also poses a radical, structural challenge to conventional doctrinal understandings of contract – this time by seeking to explain contract law in terms of the law and morals of harm. These theories thus reject the conventional understanding that contract fundamentally concerns voluntary or chosen obligations and instead seek to understand contract as, at root, a particular elaboration of the general and unchosen duty not to harm others. In their doctrinal expressions, such theories seek to assimilate contract to tort.

[25] J. Gordley, *The Philosophical Origins of Modern Contract Doctrine* (Oxford University Press, 1991), 235. A similar point is made in P. Atiyah, *Promises, Morals, and the Law* (Clarendon Press, 1981), 50–1.

[26] See R. Coase, 'The nature of the firm', *The Firm, The Market, and the Law* 33 (1988), 43–4.

Some versions of such harm-based accounts of contract again have economic roots and thus approach the law's basic doctrinal categories with an openly reformist attitude. There exist economic accounts of contract law that propose mitigating losses – an immediately tort-like notion – as the root of a comprehensive theory of contract.[27] Contract law, according to these approaches, is just a special case of the broader tort duty not to impose unreasonable costs on others, adapted to the special circumstances in which the mechanisms of imposing costs involve inducing expectations and reliance concerning future conduct and the technologies of loss avoidance centrally include information exchanged between parties who are already in communication.[28] These arguments constitute a special case of the economic analysis of law's general disregard for doctrinal categories, which is itself a natural and direct consequence of a methodological commitment to directing legal theory toward explaining case outcomes and treating law's rule-based and hence doctrinal pronouncements as epiphenomenal.[29]

But other harm-based accounts of contract – including those proposed by genealogical thinkers as different as Patrick Atiyah and Margaret Jane Radin and by philosophical thinkers such as T.M. Scanlon – have sought to assimilate contract to tort while, and even through, respecting conventional doctrinal and moral categories.[30] These reconstructive approaches do not reject doctrinal distinctions out of hand, as the economic view does. Instead, they propose that the best and deepest reconstructions of legal

[27] See C. Goetz and R. Scott, 'The mitigation principle: toward a general theory of contractual obligation', *Virginia Law Review* 69 (1983), 967.

[28] For a judicial application of this approach, per Judge Richard Posner, see *Evra Corp.* v. *Swiss Bank Corp.*, 672 F.2d 951 (7th Cir. 1982).

[29] See J. Kraus, 'Philosophy of contract law' in J. Coleman and S. Shapiro (eds.), *The Oxford Handbook of Jurisprudence and Philosophy of Law* (Oxford University Press, 2002), 687. Kraus argues that the economic analysis of law 'rejects the significance of traditional distinctions between apparently different bodies of law' (699), such as contract and tort, and, moreover, 'does not take the doctrinal invocations and restatements as legal data to be explained' (692), but instead focuses its attention on explaining case outcomes. Earnest Weinrib has made a similar point. See E. Weinrib, *The Idea of Private Law*, revised ed. (Oxford University Press, 2012).

[30] For genealogical arguments, see, e.g. P. Atiyah, *The Rise and Fall of Freedom of Contract* (1979) and M.J. Radin, 'Market inalienability', *Harvard Law Review* 100 (1987), 1849. For philosophical arguments, see, e.g. T.M. Scanlon, *What We Owe to Each Other* (Harvard University Press, 1998), 295–327 and 'Promises and contracts' in P. Benson (ed.), *The Theory of Contract Law: New Essays* (Cambridge University Press, 2001), 86, 93–4.

practice require re-evaluating doctrinal categories that, even though they loom large in the unreflective dogmas of the legal profession, in fact merely skim the surface of the phenomena they purport to describe.

These efforts to assimilate contract to tort – precisely because they seek to explain rather than to abandon familiar doctrinal and legal principles – immediately confront two formidable doctrinal and structural hurdles.

First, contract law imposes strict liability rather than fault-based obligations: a contractual promisor might have exercised reasonable care both in making her promise and in attempting to keep it and yet remain liable in case she breaches. By contrast, the misrepresentation torts generally require that defendants have failed to exercise reasonable care in making their false statements and, additionally, require justifiable reliance as an element of a plaintiff's claim.[31] Indeed, certain doctrines – for example, concerning fraudulent misrepresentation – expressly add that tort liability requires that the party asserting liability has relied specifically *on the truth of the representation* upon which the claimed liability is based, rather than just 'upon the expectation that the maker [of the false statement] will be held liable in damages for its falsity'.[32] Once again, the bootstrapping that tort law refuses is of the essence of contract.

And second, contract law establishes forward- rather than backward-looking obligations: contract remedies thus expressly vindicate a promisee's expectation interest, 'by attempting to put him in as good a position as he would have been in had the contract been performed';[33] that is, by securing the promisee's 'benefit of the bargain'.[34] Tort, once again, takes a contrasting tack. The misrepresentation torts generally limit a plaintiff's recovery to losses sustained on account of the misrepresentation, that is, to the amount required to put the plaintiff in the position that she would have occupied had the misrepresentation never been made.[35]

[31] See, e.g. Restatement (Second) of Torts § 552, Information Negligently Supplied for the Guidance of Others ('One who, in the course of his business, profession or employment, or in any other transaction in which he has a pecuniary interest, supplies false information for the guidance of others in their business transactions, is subject to liability for pecuniary loss caused to them by their justifiable reliance upon the information, if he fails to exercise reasonable care or competence in obtaining or communicating the information.').

[32] See Restatement (Second) of Torts § 548 (1977).

[33] Restatement (Second) of Contracts §344 (1981).

[34] Restatement (Second) of Contracts §344 (1981).

[35] See Restatement (Second) of Torts § 552B (1977). An exception to this principle exists for certain frauds, established (in part) to prevent promisors from being able reduce the extent

Some reconstructive thinkers address their interpretive and theoretical energies directly to explaining these legal doctrines, or at least to explaining them away. These thinkers argue, in various ways, that nominal distinctions between contract and tort just rehearsed are illusions, even on a doctrinal level. They argue, that is, that the best purely doctrinal account of contract law directly assimilates contract to tort.

With respect to the first apparent distinction between contract and tort – concerning strict rather than fault-based liability – such thinkers emphasise that considerations of reasonableness run through contract doctrine and operate in ways that bend contract in the direction of fault-based liability.[36] For example, the doctrines governing orthodox contract formation make contractual obligations turn not on the parties' actual or subjective intentions but rather on so-called objective understandings of promissory utterances: the US American Restatement, once again, defines an offer as 'the manifestation of willingness to enter into a bargain, so made as *to justify another person* in understanding that his assent to that bargain is invited and will conclude it'.[37] Similarly, doctrines concerning contract interpretation and mistake connect the content of contractual obligations to the reasonable understandings of the parties: the Restatement, for example, allocates the risk of mistake as to the assumptions underlying a contract or the meaning of its terms based on a decidedly tort-like accounting of the parties' relative costs of mistake-avoidance.[38]

of their liability by arguing that their breaches are not innocent but fraudulent. Compare *Reno* v. *Bull*, 124 N.E. 144 (N.Y. 1919) with *Morse* v. *Hutchins*, 102 Mass. 439 (1869) and see, e.g. Restatement (Second) of Torts § 549(2).

[36] For a recent general argument assimilating contract and tort, see M. Gergen, 'Negligent misrepresentation as contract', *California Law Review* 101 (2013), 953.

[37] Restatement (Second) of Contracts § 24 (1981) (emphasis added). Note that although this definition of offer invokes intentions to assume obligations, the contemplated obligations need not, under US American law, be specifically legal. Thus the Restatement adds that 'Neither real not apparent intention that a promise be legally binding is essential to the formation of a contract, but a manifestation of intention that a promise shall not affect legal relations may prevent the formation of a contract.' Restatement (Second) of Contracts § 21 (1981). English contract law takes a different view and includes intent to create legal relations among the elements required for establishing an enforceable contract. See e.g. *Balfour* v. *Balfour* [1919] 2 K.B. 571, 579. English law also acknowledges a strong presumption that, in contexts involving commercial agreements, the required intent exists. As Patrick Atiyah has observed, this presumption entails that in practice, in most commercial cases, 'no positive intention to enter into legal relations needs to be shown'. P.S. Atiyah, *An Introduction to the Law of Contract*, 5th ed. (Clarendon Press, 1995), 153.

[38] See Restatement (Second) of Contracts § 154 (1981).

With respect to the second apparent distinction between contract and tort – concerning the forward- rather than backward-looking content of contractual obligation – such thinkers argue that the distinction is less crisp in theory and less honoured in practice than those who trumpet contract's distinctiveness suppose. Where markets are thick, every contractual expectation may be recharacterised in terms of the lost opportunity of dealing with an alternative counterparty and thus as a reliance cost. And where markets are not thick, any number of doctrines – such as those that limit recovery to expectations that were foreseeable at contracting[39] or that subject plaintiffs to the burden of establishing the value of their expectations with certainty[40] – effectively limit damages for breach to something like the recovery of costs incurred in reliance on the breached contract.[41]

Finally, the rise of promissory estoppel as an unorthodox ground of contract obligation (unorthodox insofar as it dispenses not just with consideration but with offer and acceptance[42]) and the rise of the unconscionability doctrine as a means by which courts might inject substantive notions of fairness into bargains, invited those who would assimilate contract to tort's doctrinal logic of harm to treat lost reliance as not just necessary but also sufficient for contractual obligation. These and other developments went so far as to lead Atiyah to propose that the best

[39] See, e.g. *Hadley* v. *Baxendale*, 156 Eng. Rep. 145 (Court of Exchequer, 1854).

[40] See, e.g. *Rombola* v. *Cosindas*, 220 N.E.2d 919 (Mass. 1966). Some cases even make reliance an express element of a claim for breach of contract and refuse to award damages for lost expectations that cannot be recast as reliance. See, e.g. *Overstreet* v. *Norden Laboratories, Inc.* 229 F. 2d 1286 (6th Cir. 1982). But these cases are probably outliers, and other opinions take the opposite view. See, e.g. *Texaco, Inc.* v. *Pennzoil, Co.*, 729 S.W. 2d 768 (Tex. App. Hous. (1 Dist.) 1987).

[41] These points have been familiar for some time. See L.L. Fuller and W.R. Perdue Jr, 'The reliance interest in contract damages: 1', *Yale Law Journal* 46 (1936), 52.

[42] Once again, the doctrinal path by which this result was approached proceeded in stages. First, older holdings insisting that promissory estoppel might properly be applied only in the shadow of completed promises (involving both offer and acceptance and lacking only consideration), see, e.g. *James Baird Co.* v. *Gimbel Bros.*, 64 F.2d 344 (2nd Cir. 1933), were replaced with holdings that applied promissory estoppel in the absence of any express accepted promise, that is, to mere offers, see, e.g. *Drennan* v. *Star Paving Co.*, 333 P.2d 757 (Cal. 1958). And second, a few opinions went so far as to apply promissory estoppel even where there existed neither a promise nor even a completed offer, and based instead on manipulative (but not fraudulent or otherwise conventionally tortious) representations made during pre-contractual negotiations. See *Hoffman* v. *Red Owl Stores, Inc.*, 133 N.W.2d 267 (Wis. 1965).

reconstruction of contract law, in its full historical development, de-emphasises chosen obligation and the promissory or agreement form in favour of the thought that contract law coordinates conduct, and rationalises socially productive reliance on promises, based not on individual private wills but rather on shared public norms – in Atiyah's words, on 'the social and legal morality of a group of persons'.[43] Others took a less salutary view of the same doctrinal developments. Grant Gilmore[44] and Charles Fried,[45] for example, openly despaired that lawmakers were codifying the relevant public norms and legal morality, at least for consumer contracts and possibly beyond. Gilmore, recall, went so far as to call promissory estoppel 'anti-contract'[46] and worry that it opened up a class of reliance-based, essentially tort-like obligation that would one day swallow contract whole.

Other reconstructive thinkers address their arguments to deeper or more foundational matters. Such thinkers do not just reinterpret contract doctrines to show that, beneath a thin veil of editorialising about promises or agreements, tort-like notions explain contract law's actual operation. Instead, these thinkers seek to establish a fundamental unity between contract and tort at these practices' moral and political foundations. In particular, these thinkers seek to recast promise itself as a special case of the morality of harm.

The leading contemporary proponent of this view is T.M. Scanlon, who argues, first, that promissory obligation should be understood in terms of the duty to avoid harming others and, second, that contract should be understood to import the moral principles governing promising into law.[47] With respect to promising, Scanlon proposes to find the grounds of the duty to vindicate promissory assurances in pre-promissory moral principles that forbid certain forms of manipulating others and, moreover, require that persons exercise due care in leading others to form certain expectations.[48] These pre-promissory principles, Scanlon proposes, explain the wrongfulness of making lying or careless promises. Scanlon

[43] Atiyah, *Promises, Morals, and the Law*, 121.
[44] See Gilmore, *The Death of Contract*.
[45] See Fried, *Contract as Promise*.
[46] Gilmore, *The Death of Contract*, 61.
[47] See T.M. Scanlon, *What We Owe to Each Other*, 295–327 and T.M. Scanlon, 'Promises and contracts' in *The Theory of Contract Law: New Essays*, 93–4.
[48] See T.M. Scanlon, *What We Owe to Each Other*, 298–300.

then defends a broader principle of promissory fidelity[49] by reference to the fact that promisees might reasonably trust promisors to avoid these narrower wrongs.[50]

Scanlon acknowledges that his view must account for the ways in which promise and contract depart from the tort-like norms that generally govern the morality and law of harm: including in particular the strict liability and forward-looking character of promissory and contractual obligations.[51] Scanlon defends these principles for promise and contract through the

[49] This is Scanlon's principle F, which states:

> If (1) A voluntarily and intentionally leads B to expect that A will do X (unless B consents to A's not doing so); (2) A knows that B wants to be assured of this; (3) A acts with the aim of providing this assurance, and has good reason to believe that he or she has done so; (4) B knows that A has the beliefs and intentions just described; (5) A intends for B to know this, and knows that B does know it; and (6) B knows that A has this knowledge and intent; then, in the absence of special justification, A must do X unless B consents to X's not being done.

Ibid. at 304.

[50] See ibid. at 308–9.

[51] Scanlon says:

> [I]t is reasonable to want a principle of fidelity that requires performance rather than compensation and that, once an expectation has been created, does not always recognize a warning that it will not be fulfilled as adequate protection against loss, even if the warning is given before any further decision has been made on the basis of the expectation.

Scanlon, ibid. at 304. Furthermore, Scanlon defends a principle for contract law, which he calls EF (for enforcing fidelity) which holds:

> It is permissible legally to enforce remedies for breach of contract that go beyond compensation for reliance losses, provided that these remedies are not excessive and that they apply only in cases in which the following conditions hold: (1) A, the party against whom the remedy is enforced, has, in the absence of objectionable constraint and with adequate understanding (or the ability to acquire such understanding) of his or her situation, intentionally led B to expect that A would do X unless B consented to A's not doing so; (2) A had reason to believe that B wanted to be assured of this; (3) A acted with the aim of providing this assurance, by indicating to B that he or she was undertaking a legal obligation to do X; (4) B indicated that he or she understood A to have undertaken such an obligation; (5) A and B knew, or could easily determine, what kind of remedy B would be legally entitled to if A breached this obligation; and (6) A failed to do X without being released from this obligation by B, and without special justification for doing so.

Scanlon, 'Promises and contracts', at 105. Scanlon believes that his argument shows only that such legal enforcement of contracts is permitted, not that it is required. See Scanlon, ibid. at 106.

methods of the broader moral theory that he calls 'contractualism':[52] he compares the benefits that the rules confer to the burdens that they impose and argues that, given the balance between these, it would be unreasonable for promisors who must bear the burdens to reject the rules and that promisees may justifiably insist on the benefits of the rules. For example, Scanlon argues that the benefits to promisees of protecting promissory expectations are substantial and that, given the conditions of mutual knowledge, etc. that are built into the general account of promising, the burdens that this rule imposes on promisors are slight.[53] And similarly, with respect to contract, Scanlon argues that the benefits of legal enforcement of contractual expectations are substantial,[54] while the costs of enforceability are much less weighty.[55] Given the balance, Scanlon concludes, promisees have reason to insist on a moral regime that protects promissory expectations and to prefer a legal regime that enforces contractual expectations, and promisors cannot reasonably reject either the moral or the legal regime.[56]

[52] According to contractualism, '[a]n act is wrong if its performance under the circumstances would be disallowed by any system of rules for the general regulation of behaviour which no one could reasonably reject as a basis for informed, unforced general agreement'. T.M. Scanlon, 'Contractualism and utilitarianism' in A. Sen and B. Williams (eds.), *Utilitarianism and Beyond* (Cambridge University Press, 1982) 103, 110.

[53] These include the psychological benefit of the confidence such protection promotes as well as the more direct benefit of increasing the likelihood that promisors will perform as promised. Scanlon, *What We Owe to Each Other* at 302–3. Here Scanlon might have added the benefits associated with encouraging reliance that figure so prominently in utilitarian and economic accounts of promise and contract.

Scanlon believes the burdens slight because a person can always avoid the obligation to satisfy expectations simply by warning that she is not making any promises.

[54] These benefits accrue, moreover, not just to the promisees who receive them directly but also to promisors who desire to be able to give firm assurances in order to increase the value of their promises and hence of what they can demand in exchange for them. See Scanlon, 'Promises and contracts', at 108.

[55] The error costs that accrue when legal enforcement is ordered against a person who has not in fact made an enforceable contract are kept small, Scanlon asserts, by the strict and fairly formal requirements for entering into a contract. See ibid. And the compliance costs that accrue when a promisor must make good the expectations created by a promise she has come to regret command little respect in the contractualist calculus, because they can be avoided ex ante at a low cost by refraining from making contractual promises and can be avoided ex post only by neglecting a moral obligation imposed by the moral principle of promise-keeping, and this is not a cost that promisors can reasonably cite as a ground for rejecting the legal enforcement of contractual expectations. Ibid.

[56] Scanlon, ibid., at 304–5.

In this way, Scanlon's theory seeks to reconstruct contract in terms of principles that concern the allocation of benefits and burdens – the morality of harm – through arguments that penetrate the surface of legal doctrine and go right down to the deepest roots through which contract and promise draw their vitality and appeal. Scanlon's theory of contract might thus be harm-based in its roots even as it also accepts, and indeed encourages, more superficial doctrinal distinctions between contract and tort.

3 Integrative Theories of Contract

A second class of theories seeks to understand contract not – or at least not fundamentally – in terms of the manner in which contract law allocates individual benefits and burdens across persons but rather in terms of the relations among persons that contracts establish and that contract law sustains. Such integrative theories of contract once again come in two principal varieties. The first variety understands contract as a site of *thick* relations modelled on ideals of fidelity and trust. The second variety of integrative theory takes a *thin* view of the contract relation, which it understands as an arm's length relation constituted by good faith.

a Thick Integrative Theories

Thick integrative theories share with harm-based theories an inclination to assimilate contract to a neighbouring body of law – in this case not to tort but rather to fiduciary law. These theorists elaborate what they sometimes call 'robust notions of contractual duty',[57] according to which contracting parties establish relations of mutual trust, fidelity and affirmative other-regard. Thick integrative theories typically begin from accounts of promissory obligation that propose that promises establish faithfulness and even egalitarian intimacy among the parties who make and receive them.[58] The theories then import their notions of promissory fidelity into contract law, to argue that the law should acknowledge and enforce fidelity and associated ideals of other-regard – constructed to resemble ideals of

[57] R.R.W. Brooks, 'The efficient performance hypothesis', *Yale Law Journal* 116 (2006), 568, 573.

[58] See, e.g. S.V. Shiffrin, 'Promising, intimate relationships, and conventionalism', *Philosophical Review* 117 (2008), 481.

fiduciary-like loyalty – as between contracting parties. Insofar as current doctrine departs from principles of promissory fidelity and requires contracting parties to display not fiduciary loyalty but only contractual good faith, these theories lament what they have called 'the divergence of contract and promise'.[59] Thick integrative theories thus tend (as did economically inflected allocative theories) toward recommending law reform.

The thick integrative theories' reformist agenda proceeds along several fronts. Perhaps most famously, those who understand contractual obligations to involve fidelity or quasi-fiduciary loyalty object to the common law's provision of expectation damages for breach of contract[60] and prefer specific performance, restitution (and other gain-based damages), or even punitive damages. The expectation remedy, these critics observe, does not sanction but merely prices breach; and it sets the price of breach sufficiently low (at a level that enables a breaching promisor to profit from her breach) to encourage breaches of the very promissory obligations that contract law purports to recognise and enforce. (The well-known theory of efficient breach of contract openly acknowledges and even celebrates this alleged moral defect in the doctrine.) By pricing and encouraging breach, the critics say, the law undermines the immanent normativity of contract obligation and introduces a demoralising and destructive tension between law and morality.[61] Other doctrines (which often interact with the expectation remedy in contractual practice) exacerbate the problem. The mitigation doctrine, for example, supports the expectation remedy by requiring promisees to respond to breach by taking steps to minimise their contractual disappointments. This requirement, thick integrative theories worry, empowers breaching promisors to draft their promisees involuntarily into their service, specifically by requiring promisees to exercise initiative in order to reduce the damages that breaching promisors owe.[62]

A single ideal animates and unifies these several complaints. This is the principle – which comprises the thickness of the thick integrative

[59] S.V. Shiffrin, 'The divergence of contract and promise', *Harvard Law Review* 120 (2007), 708.

[60] See, e.g. Restatement (Second) of Contracts § 344 (1981).

[61] Various of these claims appear in, for example, D. Friedman, 'The efficient breach fallacy', *The Journal of Legal Studies* 18 (1989), 1; S.V. Shiffrin, 'Could breach of contract be immoral?', *Michigan Law Review* 107 (2009), 1551; S.V. Shiffrin, 'The divergence of contract and promise', 708; R.R.W. Brooks, 'The efficient performance hypothesis', 568.

[62] S.V. Shiffrin, 'Must I mean what you think I *should* have said?', *Virginia Law Review* 98 (2012), 159.

view – that promises and contracts fundamentally re-orient the attitudes with which the parties to them approach one another. Before contracting, the parties hold each other at arm's length and may thus pursue their narrowly private interests, subject only to the side-constraint that they do not abuse each other through force or fraud. But a contractual promise transforms this relation into one of mutual trust and affirmative other-regard, which promisors who remained narrowly self-interested would wrongfully exploit (including even if they constrained their self-interest according to the terms set out in the contracts).

Contractual fidelity, according to the thick integrative view, cannot be vindicated by merely honouring the ex ante division of surplus established by a contract; instead, contractual fidelity requires an additional, affirmative inclination to share ex post, including in ways that the contract did not anticipate. The supracompensatory remedies that thick integrative theories prefer enforce precisely such ex post sharing: these remedies require, in their implementation, that the parties to contracts renegotiate in the face of temptations to breach. Whereas defenders of the conventional doctrine understand the renegotiation as imposing transactions costs that the parties, and the law, have reason to avoid,[63] thick integrative theories view renegotiation in terms of a sort of transactions benefit, concomitant to bringing contract law into alignment with the morality of promise and the affirmative other-regard between promisor and promisee that morality requires. Champions of thick contractual integration would achieve these moral ends by inserting fiduciary norms into contract law.[64]

b Thin Integrative Theories

A second class of integrative theories of contract retains the thought that contracts should be understood in terms of the relations that they establish between the parties to them but insists that these relations take a thin form, in which the parties recognise and respect each other not as intimates but rather while remaining at arm's length. As Charles Fried has observed, even as contracts involve and invoke trust between the parties, contractual

[63] Cf. D. Markovits and A. Schwartz, 'The myth of efficient breach: new defenses of the expectation interest', *Virginia Law Review* 97 (2011), 1939.

[64] Cf. D. Markovits, 'Sharing ex ante and sharing ex post' in A.S. Gold and P. Miller (eds.), *The Philosophical Foundations of Fiduciary Law* (Oxford University Press, 2014), 209–24.

trust does not establish intimacy but rather serves 'humdrum ends: We make appointments, buy and sell.'[65]

Some thin integrative theories of contract law associate themselves with moral views that understand even personal promises as establishing thin relations among parties who remain, within and indeed through their promises, at arm's length.[66] Other thin integrative theories propose that contract law, by replacing the trust that lies at the heart of personal promises with external enforcement, sustains constructive relationships among parties who remain impersonally detached.[67] Regardless of their internal differences, all thin integrative theories share that contractual sharing is cabined, ex ante, by the agreement of the parties and thus differs – structurally and qualitatively – from the open-ended sharing ex post contemplated by fiduciary obligations.

Thin integrative theories set their trajectory by the observation that '[o]ne of the hallmarks of [the] common law is that it does not have a doctrine of abuse of rights: if one has a right to do an act then, one can, in general, do it for whatever reason one wishes'.[68] This entails that '[e]xcept where the contracting parties are also in a fiduciary relationship, self-interest is permissible, and indeed is the norm in the exercise of contractual rights'.[69] Thin integrative theories thus embrace the contract doctrines – the expectation remedy, for example, and the mitigation requirement – that thick integrative theories condemn. With respect to remedies, for example, thin integrative theories celebrate the ways in which expectation damages encourage promisors to avoid the trades that their contracts describe when the gains from doing so exceed the costs. The thin theories applaud this practice of 'efficient breach' not only, and indeed not principally, because it increases the contractual surplus available for the parties to share. More fundamentally, a legal regime that permits efficient breach of contract permits promisors (and promisees) to fix the limits of their contractual relations at contract formation and thus to coordinate their

[65] Cf. Fried, *Contract as Promise*, 8.

[66] See, e.g. D. Markovits, 'Promise as an arm's length relation' in H. Sheinman (ed.), *Promises and Agreements: Philosophical Essays* (Oxford University Press, 2010) and D. Markovits, 'Contract and collaboration', *Yale Law Journal* 113 (2004), 1417.

[67] See, e.g. D. Kimel, *From Promise to Contract: Towards a Liberal Theory of Contract* (Hart, 2003).

[68] J. Beatson, 'Public law influences in contract law' in J. Beatson and D. Friedmann (eds.) *Good Faith and Fault in Contract Law* (Clarendon Press, 1995), 263–88, 266–7.

[69] Ibid. at 267.

conduct, ex ante, free from any concern that they will be required to make additional adjustments, or show additional concern, toward each other ex post. The thin conception of contract thus supports coordination among parties who take each other's contractual intentions at face value and neither ask nor worry about the interests and motives that lie behind them. This renders contract especially well suited to sustaining private orderings in open, cosmopolitan societies, in which traders share little outside a joint commitment to honour the agreed terms of their trades.

Thin integrative theories thus propose that contract's foundational value is not trust, fidelity, loyalty or some other fiduciary ideal but rather good faith. A fiduciary is 'required to treat his principal as if the principal were he'.[70] But good faith, by contrast, 'does not mean that a party vested with a clear right is obligated to exercise that right to its own detriment for the purpose of benefiting another party to the contract'.[71] Rather, in place of 'loyalty to the contractual counterparty', good faith requires 'faithfulness to the scope, purpose, and terms of the parties' contract',[72] which is to say 'honesty in fact and the observance of reasonable commercial standards of fair dealing'.[73] Thus, as one prominent judge has more colourfully explained, 'even after you have signed a contract, you are not obliged to become an altruist toward the other party'.[74] Nor does good faith require contracting parties to adopt even an attitude of substantive impartiality between their contractual interests and the interests of their contracting partners. The law does not seek, 'in the name of good faith, to make every contract signatory his brother's keeper'.[75]

Indeed, the duty of good faith in performance 'does not create a separate duty of fairness and reasonableness which can be independently breached'.[76] Instead, good faith characterises contract obligations' (thin) form and

[70] *Mkt. St. Assocs. Ltd. P'ship* v. *Frey*, 941 F.2d 588, 593 (7th Cir. 1991).

[71] *Rio Algom Corp.* v. *Jimco Ltd.*, 618 P.2d 497, 505 (Utah 1980).

[72] *ASB Allegiance Real Estate Fund* v. *Scion Breckenridge Managing Member, L.L.C.*, 50 A.3d 434, 440–1 (Del. Ch. 2012) *aff'd in part, rev'd in part on other grounds*, 68 A.3d 665 (Del. 2013). I owe this reference to Andrew Gold.

[73] Uniform Commercial Code §§ 1–201, 2–103.

[74] *Mkt. St. Assocs. Ltd. P'ship* v. *Frey*, at 594 (7th Cir. 1991) (Posner, J.). Not every court has always adopted this approach. See, e.g. *Parev Prods. Co.* v. *I. Rokeach & Sons, Inc.*, 124 F.2d 147 (2d Cir. 1941), which comes close to taking a fiduciary duty view of contractual obligations, seeking 'the really equitable solution' as opposed to 'a limited rule of good faith' (at 150).

[75] *Mkt. St. Assocs. Ltd. P'ship* v. *Frey*, at 593.

[76] Uniform Commercial Code § 1–304 [cmt. 1] (2003).

identifies an attitude toward contractual obligations: good faith supports the parties' contractual settlement, working to 'effectuate the intentions of the parties, or to protect their reasonable expectations'.[77] It is thus, fundamentally, an attitude of respect for the contract relation, and the measure of good faith is the contract itself. In particular, good faith precludes using the inevitable room to manoeuvre that arises within every contract, and the strategic vulnerabilities that a contract itself thus creates, 'to recapture [during performance] opportunities forgone upon contracting'.[78]

The duty of good faith in performance thus permits the parties to remain as self-interested within their contracts as they were without them, save that they must respect the terms of their contractual settlements as side-constraints on their self-interest. Taking this duty as capturing contract's core value is what makes thin integrative theories thin.

Conclusion

The recognition that contract law is the law of agreements thus frames understandings of contract law; but it does not fill the frame with specific content. Instead, the law's enforcement of agreements might serve very different kinds of purposes; and it might serve very different particular purposes within each kind.

Contract law has thus been thought, variously, to promote the efficient allocation of economic resources or to protect against harms incurred when promisees rely on promises. And contract law has been thought to establish intimate and loyal relations between the contracting parties or to establish respectful coordination among parties who hold one another at arm's length.

Contract theory has thus developed a flexibility that mimics the variety of contractual practice.

[77] S.J. Burton, 'Breach of contract and the common law duty to perform in good faith', *Harvard Law Review* 94 (1980), 369, 371. For cases see, e.g. *Sessions, Inc.* v. *Morton*, 491 F.2d 854, 857 (9th Cir. 1974); *Ryder Truck Rental, Inc.* v. *Cent. Packing Co.*, 341 F.2d 321, 323–4 (10th Cir. 1965); *Perkins* v. *Standard Oil Co.*, 383 P.2d 107, 111–12 (Or. 1963) (en banc).

[78] Burton, 'Breach of contract and the common law duty to perform in good faith', 373.

18 Tort Law and Its Theory

John Gardner

For the best part of fifty years, theoretical reflection on the law of torts has been afflicted by a schism between 'economic' and 'moral' approaches. More than an affliction, the schism has become an obsession among many who place themselves on the 'moral' side. On the 'moral' side, many write with embarrassing defensiveness as if their main task were to see off the economistic threat. Those on the 'economic' side who react at all tend to react condescendingly. As this cartoon suggests, the economists hold greater cultural sway, and this lends them a certain swagger in their work that their adversaries generally lack.

In saying this, I am thinking mainly of the United States and in particular of the intellectually impatient climate of many US law schools. In the rest of the common law world, economic analyses of law, including tort law, enjoy less attention and less prestige. That is not, however, because of any greater cachet attaching to the 'moral' approach. It is because, elsewhere in the common law world, the whole idea of a unified explanation of tort law, or of any other area of law, tends to be regarded with greater suspicion. Where I come from, the famous put-down 'it takes a theory to beat a theory', usually attributed to Richard Epstein,[1] has little resonance; theories are disposed of a lot more easily than that. No, the main reason why the great schism in theoretical reflection on tort law matters for the rest of us is that the US law school is where modern 'tort theory' was born, and where the most important theoretical puzzles of the subject were first laid bare. Works by Guido Calabresi,[2] Richard Posner,[3] Richard Epstein,[4]

[1] Its first appearance in print seems to be in Epstein, 'Common law, labor law, and reality: a rejoinder to Professors Getman and Kohler', *Yale Law Journal* 92 (1983), 1435 at 1435.

[2] *The Costs of Accidents: A Legal and Economic Analysis* (New Haven, 1970); with A.D. Melamed, 'Property rules, liability rules and inalienability: one view of the cathedral', *Harvard Law Review* 85 (1972), 1089.

[3] 'A theory of negligence', *Journal of Legal Studies* 1 (1972), 29.

[4] 'A theory of strict liability', *Journal of Legal Studies* 2 (1973), 151.

George Fletcher,[5] Jules Coleman,[6] Stephen Perry,[7] and (just over the northern border) Ernest Weinrib[8] are among the major *ur*-writings of the subject, and in all of them the schism is already evident, not to say conspicuous. It could be said that the subject was polarised at birth. And while much the same polarisation now afflicts the theoretical treatment of other areas of law, or at least of private law, it was here in the great 'tort theory' essays of the 1970s and 1980s that it first took hold.

I am talking of the polarisation as an affliction because, in spite of the great service that the original schismatics provided by helping to isolate puzzles and animate discussions, they also encouraged fundamentalist patterns of thought that were destined to become the enemies of open-minded reflection. Today the original schism often plays out in straw men, equivocations, excluded middles, red herrings and other argumentative fallacies. It has also led, predictably, to sub-factionalisation within each of the two factions. Rival orthodoxies have divided the moralists in particular. My own view, alas far from an orthodoxy, is that all sides in these rivalries, be they economistic or moralistic, capture some important truths about tort law, and that refusing to countenance this possibility has been the main enemy of progress with the subject. It is with some apprehension, therefore, that I set myself the task here of exploring, with a sceptical eye, some of the key points that have divided economists from moralists in their thinking about tort law. I risk making things even worse by doing so. Alas I see no way to show how much has gone wrong without explaining how it came to go wrong, and hence without giving yet further prominence to some debilitating pathologies of thought that we should all be working, in my view, to shake off.

1 Explanation

Writers in the economics-of-law tradition sometimes come over all innocent in the face of their 'moral' critics. Unlike you we have no normative ambitions, they say. We are only trying to *explain* the law of

5 'Fairness and utility in tort theory', *Harvard Law Review* 85 (1972), 537.

6 'The morality of strict tort liability', *William and Mary Law Review* 18 (1976), 259; 'Corrective justice and wrongful gain', *Journal of Legal Studies* 11 (1982), 421.

7 'The moral foundations of tort law', *Iowa Law Review* 77 (1982), 449.

8 'Toward a moral theory of negligence law', *Law and Philosophy* 2 (1983), 37.

torts.[9] The contrast being drawn here is vague. 'Normative' in this context is a technical term. It does not mean 'dealing with norms' or 'using norms', which is what it literally means. It means something more like 'justificatory'. Economists who deny normative ambitions are claiming not to be engaged in showing tort law, or any aspect of tort law, to be either justified or unjustified. What is less clear is what kind of explanation they claim to be offering instead. Is it historical (how tort law came to be like this) or psychological (what is motivating the judges and policymakers) or doctrinal (how the legal rules interrelate) or what? The obvious though rather unhelpful answer is that economists are offering an economic explanation. Can this answer be made more helpful? Closer inspection reveals that an economic explanation is universally taken by its practitioners to be a kind of rational explanation, viz. an explanation of the law of torts in terms of the reasons that, economically speaking, militate in favour of it and against it. That already means, however, that the ambition cannot but be justificatory. The aim can only be to show what if anything the law of torts has going for it, so far as economic considerations are concerned.

Yet the words 'so far as economic considerations are concerned' do provide a certain latitude for economists to distance themselves from the conclusions that they reach. They may reasonably say that they are not personally committed to those conclusions, or to the considerations offered in support of them. They are offering them only in a detached way, for whatever they are worth. For as economists, they may say, they are merely dispassionate scientists showing what *would be* justified in tort law *if* certain axioms of their system of thought were true. This differentiates them, they might add, from moralists, who cannot be similarly dispassionate. To make a moral case for anything is to give that case one's personal endorsement. It is part of the very idea of morality that coming to believe that something is morally justified is coming to believe that it is *ceteris paribus* justified. Whereas coming to believe that something is economically justified – like coming to believe that it is legally justified or astrologically justified or shamanically justified – is consistent with believing that it has nothing going for it, even *ceteris paribus*. For quite possibly, in these cases, the justification

[9] E.g. Posner, *Economic Analysis of Law*, 2nd ed. (Little, Brown & Co., 1977), 17–19; Coleman, 'Efficiency, utility, and wealth maximisation' *Hofstra Law Review* 8 (1980), 509 at 547; D. Friedman, 'A positive account of property rights', *Social Philosophy and Policy* 11 (1994), 1 at 15.

rests on the false presuppositions of a corrupt system of thought. If such an irredeemable thing as tort law is economically justified, a daring economist might even say, then so much the worse for economics. By contrast, a daring moralist in an analogous predicament could not intelligibly say 'so much the worse for morality'. If one concludes that tort law is morally justified, then one concludes that tort law is not after all irredeemable.

There is genuine space here for economists of tort law to distance themselves from the committed project of the moralists. It is another matter whether many economists of tort law actually occupy that space. Many who write in the economics-of-law tradition give away that they are indeed personally committed to the truth of their axioms. They regard what is economically justified as at least *ceteris paribus* justified, if not justified full stop, and they regard economics as a sensible guide, at least *ceteris paribus*, for legal doctrine and policy.[10] True, different economists of law endorse different axioms, and hence make different recommendations. Writers in today's 'behavioural' law and economics school, for example, reject the picture of human beings as bearers and pursuers of a transitively ordered set of valuings (or 'preferences'), a picture which was and remains axiomatic in what is often called 'classical' law and economics.[11] Nevertheless some axioms are more entrenched than others. It is hard to imagine someone being counted as an economist of law, for example, if she did not treat it as axiomatic that *value answers to valuings*: the value of anything, including the value of anything that the law can provide, is a function of people's valuations of that thing. To that account of the value to be pursued by tort law we will be returning in due course.

2 The Explanandum

I spoke of those who have theories about tort law with justificatory ambitions as those who are engaged in showing tort law, or any aspect

[10] See e.g. Calabresi, 'About law and economics: a letter to Ronald Dworkin', *Hofstra Law Review* 8 (1980), 553; Posner, 'Utilitarianism, economics, and legal theory', *Journal of Legal Studies* 8 (1979), 103, softened a bit in 'Wealth maximization and tort law: a philosophical inquiry' in D. Owen (ed.), *Philosophical Foundations of Tort Law* (Clarendon Press, 1995); B. Johnsen, 'Wealth *is* value', *Journal of Legal Studies* 15 (1986), 263; L. Kaplow and S. Shavell, 'Fairness versus welfare', *Harvard Law Review* 114 (2001), 961.

[11] C. Jolls, C. Sunstein and R. Thaler, 'A behavioral approach to law and economics' in Sunstein (ed.), *Behavioral Law and Economics* (Cambridge University Press, 2000).

of tort law, to be *either* justified *or* unjustified. But in fact theorists of tort law, 'economic' and 'moral' alike, tend to be strongly drawn to the first option, to showing tort law, or at least some major aspects of it, to be justified *as opposed to* unjustified. In other words, they treat fit with existing law as a badge of honour for their work. This is *prima facie* peculiar. It is surely not a prerequisite of decent theoretical reflection on tort law that one ends up finding anything to be said in favour of it.[12] Surely finding that tort law is worthless is equally a possibility. After all, anarchists do not fail to qualify as theorists of law just because they hold that all law is bad and wrong. On the other hand, anarchists may find themselves at a severe dialectical disadvantage because many of their readers do not already share the dim view they take of law. So one natural explanation for why fit with the law of torts is regarded as a desideratum by tort theorists of many different stripes is that they imagine a group of likely readers who already take tort law to be broadly justified. Thus, if any line of thought can be shown to be capable of justifying tort law then that will speak well for that line of thought.

In itself, this is not such a crazy idea. Moral philosophers routinely treat it as a desideratum of success in moral theorising that they come out on (what they imagine their readers will take to be) the right side in concrete applications. Most utilitarians in moral philosophy, for example, aim to show that their views do not force them to arrive at repugnant verdicts in hypothetical cases. One might imagine that, if they are serious utilitarians, they would think that the repugnance of a verdict would depend solely on whether it can be defended using the principle of utility.[13] But in fact, and understandably given what would otherwise be a severe dialectical disadvantage, utilitarians often take the opposite tack in argument: they proceed as if whether the principle of utility is acceptable depends on whether it is capable of avoiding certain verdicts already granted to be repugnant quite apart from the principle of utility. In much the same vein, tort theorists presumably take it to be a repugnant verdict – at least among their likely readership – that tort law is total junk. Therefore they treat it as lending

[12] For discussion see A. Slavny, 'Nonreciprocity and the moral basis of liability to compensate', *Oxford Journal of Legal Studies* 34 (2014), 417.

[13] Known in the trade as 'outsmarting', after utilitarian philosopher J.J.C. Smart who preferred simply to embrace the apparently repugnant conclusions. See D. Dennett and A. Steglich-Petersen, *The Philosopher's Lexicon*, 9th ed. (Aarhus, 2008), www.philosophicallexicon.com/.

credibility to their own theoretical stance that it is capable of saving tort law as we already know it, that is, that it has a good fit with tort law.

But what does that mean exactly? What counts as 'tort law' for these purposes? Many in the economics-of-law tradition are interested literally in *verdicts*. They regard tort law, in the relevant sense, as a long list of case outcomes binarily represented as 'wins' or 'loses' – as more or less unpatterned thumbs-ups and thumbs-downs that call for patterning. The patterning that the courts and black-letter lawyers already gave to these verdicts (in terms of clusters of legal rules and arcs of legal reasoning and lines of legal authority) is regarded, for these purposes, as a sideshow, or perhaps more often a smokescreen – less to be explained than to be explained away. Doctrinal explanation provided by legal officials themselves and their apologists does not belong to the explanandum but to the obscurantist folklore within which the true explanandum, *true* tort law, has been concealed.

In this the economists of law inherit the 'Legal Realist' mantle of O.W. Holmes.[14] Why does this threadbare mantle appeal? Partly because the economist combines her justificatory aims (this is rational, that is irrational) with an experimental scientist self-image (known to some outsiders as 'physics envy').[15] The experimental scientist, it is thought, looks for predictive power in her hypotheses. Notoriously, the ostensible rules of any legal system have patchy predictive power regarding the court verdicts to which they are ostensibly relevant. All are such that competent lawyers can (and do) disagree over which verdicts these rules yield in a wide range of cases. So – thinks the economist – we had better look for something that has greater predictive power than the ostensible rules. In the explanation with the greatest predictive power we will find what Karl Llewellyn called the 'real' rules.[16] This move, however, begs the question against the ostensible legal rules by assuming that they are *meant* to be good predictors of court verdicts. Why should we want or expect them to be that? Instead of good predictors, why should we not want or expect them to be, say, reliable guides in simpler cases but flexible tools that leave

[14] From his 'The path of the law', *Harvard Law Review* 10 (1897), 457.

[15] D. Farber, 'Toward a new legal realism', *University of Chicago Law Review* 68 (2001), 279 at 295.

[16] Llewellyn, 'A realistic jurisprudence – the next step', *Columbia Law Review* 30 (1930), 432 at 448.

our verdictive options open in more complex ones? Why could there not be value, perhaps, in some measure of *bad* predictive power in legal norms? Indeed, why could there not sometimes be *economic* value in some measure of bad predictive power? Legal determinacy has its costs and an economist of law needs to ask whether the costs are worth incurring. Here the economist of law's aim to hold everything about the law up to rational scrutiny threatens to collide with her self-image as an experimental scientist of law for whom court cases are the relevant experiments and the court verdicts in those cases are the relevant data-points.

Be that as it may, 'cases' and 'verdicts' are themselves artefacts of law. They exist only under the legal rules that constitute and individuate them. So the economist of tort law does not, in spite of first appearances, avoid a doctrinal pre-patterning of her data. She does not consistently treat the ostensible legal rules as a sideshow or a smokescreen. She does this for some legal rules but not for others. Why, we may wonder, is 'the verdict' or 'the court' not subjected to the same existential doubts as are 'the tort', 'the duty', 'the breach', 'the cause', and so on? Even these, on closer inspection, tend to be only very selectively placed under suspicion of non-existence. In general the cases clustered together for economic analysis are kept in their recognisable legal families, with tort cases distinguished from breach of contract cases, nuisance cases from trespass cases, and so on.[17] It is merely that the features in virtue of which these cases were officially clustered together by the law – their legally relevant features – are often replaced with other features, often in ways which make an economic analysis more alluring from the start.

Perhaps the most important move of this kind in modern tort theory is the substitution of *activities* (running trains, grazing cattle, growing crops, smelting iron) for *acts* (injuring someone's horse, damaging someone's fence, triggering someone's asthma attack, contaminating someone's ginger beer) as the focus of tort law's attention. In legal doctrine, a tort is conceptualised as an act done by one person to another. Sending out sparks from the chimney of his locomotive as he passes, for example, the steam-train driver sets fire to the farmer's cornfield. Following a seminal article by R.H. Coase,[18] economists of tort law have typically rejected this

[17] See e.g. Kaplow and Shavell, 'Economic analysis of law' in A. Auerbach and M. Feldstein (eds.), *Handbook of Public Economics* (Elsevier, 2002).

[18] 'The problem of social cost', *Journal of Law and Economics* 3 (1960), 1.

asymmetrical conceptualisation (in which a defendant acts and a plaintiff is acted upon) in favour of a symmetrical one (in which plaintiff and defendant alike are engaged in activities that interfere with and potentially inhibit each other). The railway operation creates risks of loss for the corn-farming business, but simply by reallocating the costs (via tort law or otherwise) we can equally regard the corn-farming operation as creating risks of loss for the railway operation. The effect of this reconceptualisation is not to eliminate the law of torts but to eliminate the idea that the law of torts is 'really' about torts. It is 'really' about the allocation of costs as between competing uses (and competing users) of resources. Labelling something 'a tort' is merely a fancy way of declaring the verdict that the costs are to be allocated to one activity rather than the other. So the situation is not, as the doctrinal understanding of tort law suggests, that one is liable to bear certain costs on the ground that one has committed a tort. Rather, one is *said* to have 'committed a tort' because one is chosen, *on other grounds*, to be the one who will be liable to bear certain costs.

Although the idea that torts occur at the interface of two activities may seem at first sight to preserve the legal idea that torts are things that are done by persons (human or corporate), that is an illusion. On the strictly Coasean view, torts are things that *happen* while *other* things are being done. That explains the temptation among economists of law to rebrand the law of torts as 'the law of accidents'. Accidents are things that happen. Torts, as they are legally conceptualised, cannot be accidents. True, as they are legally conceptualised, torts can be the *causing* or *occasioning* of accidents, but that is another idea altogether. Causings and occasionings, unlike accidents, are clearly the kinds of things that people do. Consider an analogy. An explosion is something that happens. Causing an explosion, however, is an action, something that is done with the result that an explosion happens. (A 'result' is the technical term among philosophers for an outcome that is a constituent of the completed action, as death is of a killing; an outcome that is not a constituent of the action is described, by contrast, as a 'consequence'.)

Since not all torts, as legally conceptualised, involve the causing or occasioning of accidents (many torts have no constituent outcomes at all; other torts involve the causing or occasioning of non-accidental outcomes), opponents of economic analysis are quick to jump on the economic recharacterisation of the law of torts as 'the law of accidents' as a simple scoping error, a mistaking of part of the law of torts for the whole. The law of negligence is treated as if it were more or less the whole of the law of torts, the critics say, while the torts of trespass, deceit, misrepresentation, defamation, conversion, inducing breach of contract, false imprisonment, malicious prosecution and many others are ignored.[19] This objection, however, underestimates the radical ambition of the economists' proposal. Their proposal – we may think of it as their signature proposal – is that even when conceptualised by the law as intentional these torts should still be reconceptualised, in a sound theoretical analysis, as accidents. The illusion-busting way to think about all of them – even when they extend to vandalism, torture, massacre and kidnap – is as things that happen when different activities are competing for the same resources. Whether they are, or necessarily involve, things done by somebody is irrelevant to whether they throw up the kind of cost-allocation problem that makes them suitable for the attentions of tort law.

If this is the signature proposal of the economists of law, then its rejection is surely what first animated, and still unites, their 'moral' opponents.[20] In saying this I am revealing a bit more about what the word 'moral' should be taken to mean in this context. Moral assessment, as the expression is used here, is assessment of things we do to each other, where the very fact that they are things that we do to each other, as opposed to things that just happen between us, is taken to be of the essence. The main moral critique of economistic writings ostensibly justifying the law of torts proceeds from the thought that economists are surreptitiously changing the subject by reconceptualising the law of torts as the law of accidents. They are not justifying the law of torts at all. They are justifying a wholesale replacement for the law of torts in which there are, on closer inspection, no torts. True, the court verdicts in the new system tend to come out much the same way as they did in the old system. Is this, wonder the moralists, just a piece of typical economistic trickery? Doesn't everything and its opposite have a surefire economic rationale if you know how to twiddle the dials right? Even if there is no trickery, however, there is a

[19] J. Goldberg and B. Zipursky, 'Torts as wrongs', *Texas Law Review* 88 (2010), 917.

[20] Including the works of Epstein, Coleman, Perry and Weinrib cited in notes 4, 6, 7 and 8 above; also Coleman's later *Risks and Wrongs* (Cambridge University Press, 1992), T. Honoré, *Responsibility and Fault* (Hart Publishing, 1999), A. Ripstein, 'Philosophy of tort law' in J. Coleman and S. Shapiro (eds.), *The Oxford Handbook of Jurisprudence and Philosophy of Law* (Oxford University Press, 2002), and the recent work of Goldberg and Zipursky, such as 'Torts as wrongs'.

more fundamental problem. The *reasons* for the verdicts in the new system are completely different from those in the old system. The law of torts is not a set of court verdicts, say the moralists, nor even a set of norms that pattern these verdicts. It is a body of case law, augmented by statute, in which the resident norms are used and shaped and reused and reshaped in argument, iteratively revealing the reasons why, in law, the norms are as they are. An explanation of tort law is only an explanation of tort law, according to the moralists, if it is true to the law's self-explanation delivered in this way.

In particular, the explanation must reveal how the typical arguments of tort lawyers work as arguments. One may of course reveal in the process that many of these arguments are deficient. Yet that is quite different from claiming that they are unintelligible and therefore should not, or cannot, be assessed in their own terms. And in the case of tort law, assessing them in their own terms means assessing them morally. For they are principally arguments oriented toward the identification and assessment of what the defendant did to the plaintiff – whether he caused her any relevant loss, whether he breached his duty in doing so, whether his breach of duty also violated her rights, whether he already paid all that he should have paid for the loss, whether the breach is ongoing, etc. – and arguments about these matters are all, in the relevant sense, moral arguments.[21]

A different case can be made for the same conclusion, one that makes more concessions to the economist. Suppose we grant, *arguendo*, that the law of torts is simply a list of court verdicts in tort cases. And let these verdicts be pre-patterned to suit any economistic taste you care to mention. And suppose we lift all suspicion of trickery and agree that a good economic analysis shows the verdicts, complete with their patterning, to be amply justifiable. Still the economist is not where she needs to be. Showing the verdicts to be justifi*able* is not the same as showing them to be justifi*ed*. To be justified a verdict must not only be rationally reachable; it must also have been rationally reached. It is not enough that the reasons advanced in support of it did indeed support it if it was not arrived at *for* (one or more of) those reasons. An analogy: if I am under lethal attack, it is justifiable for me to kill my lethal attacker. But what if I kill her not because she is

[21] I am here distilling common themes from E. Weinrib, *The Idea of Private Law* (Harvard University Press, 1995) and J. Coleman, *The Practice of Principle* (Oxford University Press, 2001), also echoed by several other writers.

attacking me (I have no idea that she is), but rather because, say, I don't like her politics? Then the justifiable killing is unjustified.[22] Noticing this enables us to see more clearly in what sense a justification qualifies as a kind of explanation: it gives a sufficient reason for doing something that is also the sufficient reason why it was done.

The same point also enables us to see more clearly why economic analysts of tort law are so keen to show a measure of economic influence upon, as well as good economic predictability of, court verdicts. Many take comfort[23] in Learned Hand's 'calculus of negligence' in *Carroll Towing*,[24] for example, even though Hand's words plainly do not peg the gravity of an injury to its economic cost, and so could equally be claimed on behalf of many rival moral views. The point of claiming them for law and economics is to establish that, in spite of the alleged smokescreen of received legal wisdom that usually blocks them from view, the economic reasons are the 'real' reasons for which judges in tort litigation act, such that their verdicts are not only economically justifiable, but economically justified as well. For anyone interested in the justification of judicial verdicts the pressure to examine the supporting judicial arguments – and to assess them in their own terms – is huge. In that task the economists find themselves at an equally huge disadvantage; for the normal terms of judicial argumentation are clearly moral terms. Even Learned Hand, it is often forgotten, was explaining which factors bear on whether a defendant *breached* his *duty of care* toward the plaintiff. His was a moral conceptualisation.

3 Instrumentality

At this point the economists have a natural fallback position, into which they sometimes slip unnoticed. There are duties in tort law after all, they may say, and they are, just as the law says they are, duties to take care, duties not to cause losses, duties to pay damages, etc. These duties are owed by defendants to plaintiffs, who therefore hold associated rights. So

[22] At this point I am drawing on ideas presented at greater length in my book *Offences and Defences* (Oxford University Press, 2007), especially ch. 5.

[23] E.g. R. Posner, *The Economics of Justice* (Harvard University Press, 1981), 5; J. Macey, 'The pervasive influence of economic analysis on legal decisionmaking', *Harvard Journal of Law & Public Policy* 17 (1994), 107.

[24] 159 F 2d 169 (1947) at 173.

the law of torts really is what is set out in the textbooks and what is used and developed by lawyers and judges in their legal arguments. These arguments are accordingly intelligible in their own terms and capable of being assessed *qua* arguments. The point is only that all of the rights and duties that figure in these arguments have sound economic justifications. The economic justifications may even extend to the bigger ideas sometimes favoured by lawyers and their moralising friends for connecting the various rights and duties into a tort law scheme. Corrective justice? Civil recourse? These are more abstract characterisations of the normative arrangements found in tort law, or of certain conspicuous aspects of them. Responsibility, redress, reasonableness? These are concepts invoked in many norms of tort law. Like everything else about the norms of tort law, says the fallback script of the legal economist, they are amenable to economic defence. They are part of what needs to be defended by any 'tort theory'. Economists are there to provide the defence.[25]

Economists who defend tort law in this way have taken their fight with the moralists to the moralists' backyard. Now they are rule-utilitarians (utilitarians who believe in the utility of having and using rules). Naturally, they face the usual catalogue of challenges that rule-utilitarians face in moral philosophy. However, in the context of tort theory they do not face the most familiar challenge to rule-utilitarianism. They do not face the challenge that even the rule with the greatest utility must eventually come up against the extreme case in which there would be more utility in bending it. In my view this is anyway an unconvincing line of attack on rule-utilitarianism. That it allows for the diminishing hold of rules at their limits is a virtue, rather than a vice, of any explanation of the place of rules in practical thought. But be that as it may the law of torts is not a good testbed for the objection, since the law of torts is rife with rules well suited to being adapted to novel and unforeseen circumstances. Whatever else they may do, qualifications like 'reasonable', 'ordinary' and 'due' that are used in formulating many tort law rules invite the rule-user to refer back the underlying merits of the case.[26] And even when the rules are not already set up like this, familiar common law techniques such as

[25] This is the line taken by Posner in 'The concept of corrective justice in recent theories of tort law', *Journal of Legal Studies* 10 (1981), 187.

[26] I have discussed this point at length in 'The many faces of the reasonable person', *Law Quarterly Review* 131 (2015), 563.

'distinguishing' the earlier cases or creating an 'equitable' qualification to the rule can be used to bend them ad hoc into conformity with the underlying merits. Tort law is nothing if not pliable, as systems of rules go. So those offering a rule-utilitarian defence of tort law have nothing much to fear from the charge – if they really want to treat it as a charge – that their ethics cannot but license a great deal of pliability in rules.

One might think that something similar would be true of another challenge to rule-utilitarianism, namely the challenge that it instrumentalises all rules, that is, judges them only by the consequences of having them and using them. What should the rules of tort law be if not instruments to improve what people do, namely by getting them to conform to those very rules? It might seem that, even if the rule-utilitarian defence of some *moral* rules could be criticised for excessive instrumentalisation, that critique should not extend to the rule-utilitarian defence of legal rules. Indeed it might be thought that a principal vice of rule-utilitarianism as a moral doctrine is precisely that it models moral rules, in this respect, too much on legal ones. Yet the best-known moral critique of the economic defence of the rules of tort law takes aim principally against its instrumentalisation of them. This is the Kantian critique, most often associated with Ernest Weinrib[27] and developed by Arthur Ripstein,[28] in which tort law falls to be defended as a system of correlative rights and duties that constitutes the parties to tort cases as equals in and before the law. Personally I do not share the taste for constituting people as juridical equals that lies at the heart of this view. But be that as it may, it is not clear why defending tort law as something that constitutes us as juridical equals should be thought inconsistent with defending tort law's rules as instruments for getting people to act better. Why should the rules of tort law not be instruments for getting judges and other officials to comply with the rules of tort law, *thereby* constituting the parties before them as juridical equals? And once we have got that far, why should the rules of tort law not also be instruments for getting would-be parties to avoid committing torts in the first place, thereby (presumably) acting just as juridical equals would? So long as torts have the appropriately Kantian content (so long as the primary rights and duties of tort law are such that their correct application constitutes the parties as equals) why is

[27] Weinrib, *The Idea of Private Law*, 80–3, 132–3.
[28] *Equality, Responsibility, and the Law* (Cambridge University Press, 1999), esp. ch. 3.

tort-deterrence not even better, so far as Kantian considerations are concerned, than tort-correction? It is hard to see how even Kant could exempt himself from the analytical truth that, *ceteris paribus*, prevention is better than cure. So it is puzzling that the Kantians of the tort theory world should set their faces so strongly against an instrumental defence of the rules of tort law.

Possibly the solution to the puzzle lies in the fact that, in the Kantian story, law in general, including private law, is conceived as an apparatus of coercion. Since coercion entails compliance (without compliance, it is only attempted coercion), perhaps the importance of tort law as an instrument of compliance with its own rules is not being denied in Kant's name so much as taken for granted. Being built into the very idea of tort law, compliance is another part of the object to be defended and not, as the economists would have it, part of the defence. If this is the idea then the correct response is to stand with the economists and deny that tort law works to change what people do primarily by coercion. Coercion may be used on occasions, but the law of torts more often secures compliance with its rules, when it does, by other means. On the other hand, however, one should stand with the Kantians, against the economists (or many of them), in denying that the means used can be reduced to providing incentives for compliance by putting the shifting of costs in prospect. That story drops the distinctiveness of law completely out of the picture. The law of torts, like other areas of law, indeed like any other body of rules, works by providing guidance (albeit not always highly determinate guidance) on what to do. In the case of law it purports to be the guidance of a morally legitimate authority. In this way, as Hart says, both the coercive mechanisms and the incentivising effect of their being in prospect 'are secondary provisions for a breakdown in case the primary intended peremptory reasons [here, the rules and rulings specifying which acts are torts, and which acts count as suitably remedial of torts] are not accepted [or used] as such'.[29]

Probably it is uncharitable to portray the Kantians as whitewashing the instrumentality of tort law in this contrived way. More charitable would be

[29] H.L.A. Hart, 'Commands and authoritative legal reasons' in his *Essays on Bentham* (Oxford University Press, 1982), 254. In tort law we might prefer to say that the coercive mechanisms are 'tertiary provisions' since the remedial rules and rulings may already be thought of as the 'secondary' ones.

to read them as objecting, not to all instrumental defences of tort law, but rather only to those that portray tort law as an instrument of *independent* goods, where securing compliance with tort law's own rules does not count as independent in the relevant sense.[30] But what is the relevant sense? Return to the thought, central to the Kantian picture, that tort law *constitutes* some aspect of our moral relations. Bracketing the special Kantian emphasis on equality, let's consider the proposal that tort law constitutes some of our moral relations, in particular the moral duties that we owe to each other. This seems entirely right to me. Part of the moral case for having law at all is to help us cope with moral indeterminacy by providing morally authoritative guidance on what to do. When successfully provided, and hence morally binding, this guidance makes the moral rules more determinate than they would be without the law. We already noted that in the law of torts, many of the rules leave significant moral indeterminacy unresolved. Sometimes deliberately. They include many qualifications, such as 'reasonable' and 'due', which deliberately refer us back to the underlying moral considerations. Nevertheless the rules of tort law are rules of law: they are not completely devoid of authoritative guidance. If nothing else, the law of torts takes various classes of actions that we have moral reasons not to perform but that apart from the law would defy determinate classification as breaches of duty, and it determinately classifies them as breaches of duty. That remains an important injection of authoritative determinacy even when the classes of actions affected are still quite indeterminately specified.

When is such an injection important enough to be morally legitimate?[31] The classic scenario (I do not say it is the only one) is the coordination scenario. This is the scenario in which, given the underlying moral indeterminacies, people with good moral judgement may differ among themselves in how they would react to a given situation, left to their own devices. The problem is that their different reactions will tend to be at odds with each other, creating extra problems for themselves and/or for others: extra delay, extra risk, extra damage, extra confusion and anxiety,

[30] Thus Weinrib objects only to seeing tort law as the servant of 'purposes external to itself': *The Idea of Private Law*, 50.

[31] In this paragraph and the next I sketch an argument developed at greater length in my 'What is tort law for? Part 1. The place of corrective justice', *Law and Philosophy* 30 (2011), 1.

extra escalation of conflict, extra burden on others to help, extra temptation for others to take sides, etc. It is *ceteris paribus* better, in this scenario, that all are bound and judged by a common standard, whichever of the morally eligible standards that may be. In that way all may have common expectations of each other's behaviour, such that incipient problems of the kinds just listed may be avoided or nipped in the bud. The law of torts does a great deal of this kind of coordination. Even when it does a relatively light-touch job of coordinating the actions of potential plaintiffs and defendants at the time of their original interaction (as in the law of negligence) it still does a great deal to coordinate expectations of what comes next, once a tort is committed. When it does this well, it part-constitutes (by lending extra determinacy to) the moral duties involved, in particular by determining that they are indeed duties.

It is fairly easy to see how the thought that the standard must be a common standard could mutate into the thought that it must be, in some sense, an equalising one, as the Kantians say. But that, to repeat, is not the lesson we are interested in. The lesson we are interested in is that recognising the moral-relations-constituting role of rules of tort law is not inconsistent with making an at least partly instrumental case for their existence. Indeed, in the coordination scenario, if not in all scenarios, the former positively *depends upon* the latter. It is only because and to the extent that the law of torts is a good tool for securing better actions that it succeeds in adding to, or giving shape to, the moral rights and duties of those who are subject to it. Here the good that tort law instrumentally serves is not independent of tort law in the relevant sense. It is a good that tort law also helps to constitute, namely the good of people doing their duty toward each other. Tort law helps to constitute this good by determining, when it is also a good instrument of conformity with duty, what counts as doing one's duty.

It is not clear, however, how this line of thought is going to be of any use in dispatching the rule-utilitarians, including the economists of law who make rule-utilitarian moves. For it is not clear why rule-utilitarians, any more than their Kantian critics, would need to present tort law as an instrument of a good that is, in the relevant sense, independent of tort law. Many torts, recall, are actions that come complete with constituent outcomes. More specifically, they are actions of causing or occasioning loss to another. Even those that are not outcome-constituted are nevertheless remedied, normally, by measuring the consequential loss, or some of it, that was done to another by the commission of the tort. Why should not a rule-utilitarian help herself to the natural thought that tort law is interested in these losses, and in particular in assigning different losses to different people as part of an authoritative scheme for coordinating people's loss-causing and loss-occasioning actions, as well as the loss-ameliorating actions that follow? When it coordinates well, this scheme too helps to determine what counts as doing one's duty to another (in respect of a range of loss-affecting actions) and so helps to constitute our moral relations with each another. Naturally there are big debates to be had about how exactly to cash out the 'when it coordinates well' condition. Does coordinating loss-affecting actions well equate, or even somehow approximate, to minimising the losses themselves? And are the losses themselves to be analysed in economic terms, or are they to be analysed in some other terms (e.g. in terms of freedom or pleasure or security foregone) for which economic value stands as a mere proxy at the regrettable moment at which tort damages come to be calculated in money amounts? These represent deep and difficult issues in moral mathematics. They concern, respectively, the calculus and the metric of moral success, be it the success of tort law or of anything else. But any disagreement that one might have with a rule-utilitarian about the calculus or the metric of moral success does not seem to be well-captured in the claim that rule-utilitarians are wrong to instrumentalise tort law. One may be a total instrumentalist about tort law (as indeed I am proud to be myself) while insisting that what tort law is an instrument *of* is – to take just a few examples – the avoidance of injustice, the performance of moral duty, the correction of wrongs, the maintenance of reciprocity, or the upholding of juridical equality, or indeed all of these at once (and more).

These remarks help to expose what may be regarded as a strategic error in the way that moral critiques of the economic analysis of tort law first got off the ground, and continue even now to present themselves. It was and remains common to contrast 'efficiency' with 'justice' in considering possible objectives for tort law.[32] But efficiency is not a possible objective for tort law unless tort law also has some *other* objective that it is supposed to be efficiently *serving*. Efficiency is none other than the avoidance of waste. Nobody, I hope, is in favour of waste. The disagreements are all about

[32] See e.g. G. Stigler, 'Law or economics?', *Journal of Law & Economics* 35 (1992), 455 at 461; G. Fletcher, 'Corrective justice for moderns', *Harvard Law Review* 106 (1993), 1658 at 1659.

which goods it is most important not to waste, because they are the most important goods. The economists narrow the list of important goods down to goods that are cast in exclusively economic terms. Naturally enough they prioritise efficiency in the service of those specialised goods. The sensible response is not to say that one does not favour efficiency, thereby allowing the economists proudly to claim a monopoly on the avoidance of waste. The sensible response is to reject the identification of goods in exclusively economic terms, or, to put it more tersely, to reject the idea that all value is economic value. The point is not to reject efficiency but to reject the preoccupation with merely *economic* efficiency, efficiency relative only to economic goods. What the law should be efficient *at*, the moral critic should say, is not, or not only, increasing wealth or allocating resources but (also) doing justice, preventing wrongs, protecting rights, mitigating insecurity, enabling recourse, guaranteeing freedom, aiding reconciliation, or . . . you can insert any imaginable good here.

4 Value

I said earlier that we would be 'returning in due course' to the economist's view that *value answers to valuings*: that the value of anything is a function of people's valuations of that thing. It goes beyond my brief for this paper, alas, to show how much is wrong with this view when it is fully generalised, and why adhering to it provides a terrible (and in particular obnoxiously illiberal) basis for public policy and legal doctrine.[33] But I hope to have said enough to persuade you that it is here, in the general philosophy of value, that the theoretical study of tort law inevitably ends up. The question, I have argued, is not whether tort law should be efficient, but which values it should efficiently serve. The question is not whether there is utility in having and using tort law's rules, but what exactly their utility is, that is, what goods they are capable of protecting and yielding. The question is not whether tort law is an instrument, but what it is an instrument of. Our valuings of the law of torts, as of everything else, answer to value that it has apart from anyone's valuings of it, and there is no escaping the ultimate question of what exactly that value is.

[33] Although overstated in places, R.M. Dworkin's critique in 'Is wealth a value?', *Journal of Legal Studies* 9 (1980), 191 hits many home runs.

I already suggested that the 'moral' critics of the economic analysis of tort law got off on the wrong foot in the 1970s and 1980s in allowing the economists to parade themselves as the only true guardians of efficiency, utility and instrumentality in the law of torts. We could well add 'rationality' and 'welfare' to the list. Failing to engage head-on with the economist's theory of value meant failing to stand up for the truth that one's welfare (or well-being) depends first on one's valuing things for value they have quite independently of anyone's valuing of them, including our own. And it also meant failing to uphold the truth that our capacity to detect such independent value and *thereby* to pursue it – not just accidentally to pursue it under the heading of preference – is what makes us rational creatures. Rejecting both of these truths makes the economists, classical and behavioural alike, the arch-parodists of our rationality and, very often, the archenemies of our welfare. So why were these not the first battle lines of tort theory? It is hardly surprising that the early 'moral' critics, already on the cultural defensive, tried to keep their fight with the economic analysis of tort law on what they took to be easier terrain, less rife with philosophical pitfalls. In the process, however, they created multiple new disadvantages for themselves and for their intellectual heirs. They targeted their offensive largely on the strongest points of the economic analysis while allowing the weakest points, defended mainly by flimsy newspeak, to go virtually unassailed. Tort theory today continues to suffer from the many consequences of these understandable errors. Critics too often concede the powerful concepts of efficiency, rationality, utility and welfare to the economists, even though the economists have no special claim on them (and indeed bear a special guilt for tendentious meddling with them). Meanwhile, as we saw, critics continue to mount the ill-starred critique that tort law is not, or not mainly, an instrument of sound public policy and so is not, or not mainly, to be judged as if it were one. One wishes that they would focus instead on explaining what sound public policy would be like, and what contribution tort law would make to it, in a world in which the economists, mistaking price for value, held less cultural sway.

Property Law 19

Larissa Katz[*]

Is property in some way basic to our moral lives? Many have thought so. For Aristotle, moral virtues, like liberality, presuppose some idea of property, for one can display liberality only with respect to what is one's own. For Kant, property is a requirement of freedom in the external world. For Locke, property, allocated according to principles of labour and desert, is basic to the very idea of justice that our political institutions are meant to secure. Others have denied that property is foundational in this way, suggesting rather that property is one strategy available to us in meeting the demands of our general theories of justice but is not itself morally basic.[1]

In this chapter, I want to unpack what contemporary writers have to say about property's moral salience. Philosophical inquiry of this sort, I will suggest, proceeds on three levels. On the *first* level, we ask what property is, as a conceptual matter. Property relations, we will see, are relations mediated by particular things.[2] A mediated relation is not just a relation between a person and a thing; rather, it is a relation among people with respect to specific things. Of the many ways that people might relate with respect to things, the idea of ownership is conceptually basic. Ownership is the foundation for the many other forms of property relations that we find in modern liberal societies, where owners can carve out subordinate interests in things for others: easements, security interests, profits, fisheries, leases, bailments, trusts, licences, etc. But all this is itself possible only within the framework that ownership sets down.

[*] I am especially grateful to Chris Essert, Hanoch Dagan, Avihay Dorfman, Arthur Ripstein, John Tasioulas and Malcolm Thorburn for comments.

[1] Rawls for instance was non-committal about property's place in the basic structure. See J. Rawls, *A Theory of Justice* (Harvard University Press, 1971).

[2] It is a 'bedrock' idea in law that property rights exist not 'in the air' but only with respect to specifically identified things. See Lord Mustill in *In Re Goldcorp Exchange Ltd* [1995] 1 AC 74.

The conceptual core of property, then, is ownership, and the conceptual core of ownership is the idea that someone is in charge with respect to that thing in relation to others. This kind of 'in charge of' position connotes at least exclusivity and the separability of thing from the owner. So fugitive resources, like air or flowing water or ideas, cannot be owned because we cannot relate to others through them in the way that is characteristic of ownership: these are resources over which no one is capable of exclusive control. Parts of our bodies, even parts that might be valuable to others, like our kidneys, cannot be owned because ownership is possible only with respect to things that are separate from us.

Much beyond this basic core is a matter of political choice about how to shape the position of ownership and the normative powers, privileges and responsibilities associated with it. There is, then, a *second* level of philosophical inquiry, concerning the place of property in our general theories of justice. Property is so often at the centre of revolutionary thinking about the social order because it organises a basic and unavoidable mode of human interaction: how we relate with respect to things. There is always a need for political philosophy to think and rethink the ways that people could possibly relate with respect to things. We can imagine a society that for reasons of freedom or utility leaves owners plenary power to profit and to advance their plans for life any way they can through their position. A utility-maximising system of property might grant owners wide latitude to use their position as owner just as a bargaining chip, to draw others into utility-enhancing transactions. We can also imagine a society that has theological or ideological commitments that lead to other-regarding restrictions on the agendas that owners can set with respect to a thing and that attach extensive duties to ownership.

There is yet a third level of philosophical thinking about property, which concerns the distribution of rights to hold property. At this level of inquiry, we engage a much larger set of questions about how justly to distribute basic goods in society. It is in this context, in resolving questions of distributive justice, that we may have doubts that property is itself an organising moral category. We can be concerned with a just distribution of the basic goods that people require, whatever their purposes in life, without being concerned to bring about this distribution *as* property. We might agree on the value of equal access to basic goods without being on board with the idea that these basic goods take the form of property. Many have argued plausibly enough that other levers of social justice, such as tax and transfer schemes or a system of public accommodations or use-rights, are better suited to redressing this kind of distributive injustice.

This chapter focuses on the first two modes of philosophical inquiry, those most directly concerned with the conceptual and normative contours of property in law. I will begin with some basic agreements and disagreements among contemporary property theorists about how to make sense of property as a conceptual matter. I will go on to frame the dominant accounts of property today in terms of what each has to say about the place of property within our larger institutional arrangements.

1 What Is Property?

Conceptual analysis of property begins with the idea of ownership. Ownership is structured as a position of authority in relation to others: what it means for me to own something is that I, not you, am in charge of setting the agenda for it. We need not invoke the idea of ownership to explain our being in charge of ourselves: ideas of personhood, rather than ownership, do the work there.[3] Ownership describes the kind of 'in charge' relation we might have with respect to things that have no necessary connection to any one of us. We can assume ownership only of things that are separable from us such that anyone at all could stand as owner in our stead without any normative change to the position itself.[4] We should understand this point formally: of course it might make all the difference in the world to my well-being, my sense of self, etc., that I, not you, own my beloved house. Nonetheless, the formal structure of ownership is the same whether it is you or I that stands as owner. It is in this sense then that houses are separable things capable of ownership. The position of ownership has the same normative components to it – the same exclusive authority to make decisions about the thing with respect to others – no matter who holds that position. By contrast, a person cannot take charge of another person in quite the same way as a person can be in charge of herself simply in virtue of being herself. As a moral and a legal matter, people can of course

[3] Lockean property theorists, who derive justifiability of property from self-ownership, do not see things this way.

[4] See J.E. Penner, *The Idea of Property in Law* (Oxford University Press, 1997). We find the idea of separability in Aristotle's treatment of property (in *Politics*).

assume positions of trust and responsibility in relation to others who lack the capacity to care for themselves. Think of parents or guardians of mentally incapacitated people. But when we move from a situation where one person is in charge of herself to a situation where another is in charge of her, there is a conceptual and normative difference too in the normative position of the person in charge.

The separability criterion sorts the world into *things*, which can be the object of property, and *persons*, who cannot. The person–thing distinction establishes the outer limits of property. The point I make here is a basic one: we, as embodied beings, cannot enter into the external relation of owner–owned thing with ourselves. The person–thing distinction leaves no room to consult other considerations, like our preferences or utility, for treating body parts as property so long as they remain part of us.[5] Body parts, while they remain part of the person, fall outside the limits of property. Even if my leg means less to me than the teacup my grandma left me, I may transfer property in my teacup, but not my leg, in my hour of need. By contrast, body parts already severed from the person are at least candidates for inclusion within our system of property. The conceptual obstacles to property are not present with respect to already severed body parts (e.g. my shorn hair). Whether body parts are ownable after severance is decided on public policy grounds, beyond anything the idea of property itself can sort out for us in conceptual terms.

Even if we believe on grounds of freedom that we are justified in treating body parts as property in the context of voluntary interactions, these intuitions surely falter when we consider how property in body parts would play out in other contexts. It is a mistake to think that property is defined with an eye just to its role in our voluntary transactions with others. Property by its very nature allows for many forms of succession, some voluntary as when we sell things or leave to others by will but some involuntarily too as when someone else adversely possesses our thing or is appointed owner by operation of law, as in a bankruptcy or a forfeiture.[6] If my leg could be an object of property, then we would have to allow that it could also work as property in circumstances in which the things that belong to me are made available, like it or not, to satisfy the claims of my

[5] See M. Radin, *Contested Commodities* (Harvard University Press, 1996).

[6] We may have public law reasons to allow debtors to shield some assets from creditors notwithstanding the logic of property.

creditors.[7] The person–thing distinction, which the separability requirement preserves, is important to guard against involuntary losses of our very persons.

The separability criterion offers a modest conceptual supplement to the ethical case against slavery: slavery is abhorrent as an ethical matter; slave-holding is also defective as a form of property.[8] The conceptual point is this: the master–slave relation is a status relationship that might be occupied without normative change by a great number of people, but not by anyone at all. The normative position of a master with respect to the slave is not a position that the slave herself could occupy. There is always someone for whom *A* is always and only a person and never a thing: *A* herself. Even those who find the idea of self-ownership compelling surely do not assert a normative equivalence between self-ownership and another's dominion over oneself.[9] The practice of slavery does not establish the possibility of property in persons.[10] Those who enslave people commit themselves to a category mistake – treating people as things – that is at the same time deeply unethical.

Property concerns things not persons. But does separability fully account for the thingness of property? Is there something else, like materiality, that is in play when it comes to allowing that some things are objects of property, others not? As we will see later, some of the normative reasons to have property at all are particularly compelling with respect to material resources, like land, which unavoidably form the setting for human life and activity. Materiality is not, however, conceptually required for property. What is crucial is that a thing, material or otherwise, is independent of persons such that anyone at all could take ownership without any normative change to the position itself. Take, for instance, a creditor's right to

[7] Think here of Shylock's claim to a pound of flesh from Antonio, in the *Merchant of Venice*.

[8] Cf. J. Waldron, *The Right to Private Property* (Oxford University Press, 1988) 33 n. 15 (making the case that there are ethical, not conceptual, problems with slavery. See Aristotle, in *Politics*, 1253b1 (concerning slave as 'an instrument of action, separable from the possessor').

[9] Cf. A. Ryan, *Property* (University of Minnesota Press, 1987) at 58–9.

[10] Slavery is conceptually intelligible not as property in human form but as a claim to dominion over another's *liberty*. In the natural law tradition, liberty and property were both thought to be capable of human dominion, in contrast to life, which was thought not to be as a matter of natural law. See e.g. Suarez, Disp XIII, 'On war' in *Selections from Three Works of Suarez* (Liberty Fund, orig. trans. 1944) at 845. Slavery is obviously ethically abhorrent whatever conceptual form it takes.

recover a debt obligation. This is a right to sue for the repayment of a sum of money. In fact, debt actions are treated in law as a kind of intangible property. On the basic view of property as an exclusive right to a separable thing, we can see why that is properly so. A debt action is separable from me, the original creditor, in just the same way that an apple is separable from me: neither resource constitutes me as a person (at least not until I eat the apple), and anyone else could stand in my place as owner of the apple or the debt without any normative alteration to the position. Because a debt action is separable, it can be a 'thing' assignable as property to others.

Now, contrast a debt action with an action in tort to recover compensation for a negligently inflicted injury. Say you were driving at a recklessly high speed and ran me over in an intersection, breaking my leg. I have a right of action against you for negligence. The separability requirement explains why personal tort actions are not assignable like debt actions can be: there is a special connection between my personhood and an action the purpose of which is to make me whole again. The inalienability of a right of action the purpose of which is to make me whole again can be understood as analogous to the inalienability of my leg or the licence to injure it.[11]

a Exclusivity

Ownership, as a position of being in charge of things in the world, also implies the *exclusivity* of the position itself. Most property theorists today take exclusivity to refer to a right to exclude others from a thing. Clearly, there are some things that are incapable of exclusivity in this basic sense. Take an idea, like the idea for a story. An idea, once it is shared publicly, is separable from me: it does not exist just in my mind anymore and others may think on it without interfering with my person. And yet ideas cannot be owned because, upon meeting the requirement of separability, they are at once no longer capable of exclusivity. If I tell you my idea for a story, at best all I can do is ask you not to repeat it or to use it for profit or copy the particular way I have expressed it. I cannot very well dislodge the idea itself from your thoughts so as to hold it exclusively for myself. So there are conceptual problems with thinking about ideas as ownable 'things'.

[11] We see precisely this reluctance to allow the propertisation of legal actions in historical legal rules against champerty and maintenance.

Other resources are separable from us but incapable of exclusivity because they lack boundaries along which another might be excluded. I can exclude you from a column of space filled with air. But I cannot exclude you from the air itself, which moves around and is not contained. Air is one of the things Blackstone called 'fugitive resources', which defy containment within fixed boundaries. Similarly, I cannot exclude you from running water, although I might be able to exclude you from a vessel that contains water or a column of space above submerged land across which water flows.

b Ownership as an Office

Is there anything more to the basic concept of ownership than the right to exclude and the separability of the thing? I think so: there is the normative power with respect to that separable thing, to which the idea of exclusivity refers. We cannot make sense of the idea of ownership without making sense of the nature and structure of the position owners exclusively occupy *within* the boundaries of the thing.[12] Take the case of land. Land clearly admits both of separability and excludability. While we must always stand somewhere, we can yet see how a particular space on Earth is separable from any one of us: there is no reason of personhood why a particular tract of land might not just as well be yours as mine. I can own land and exclude others insofar as they have somewhere to move upon being excluded.

But ownership of land seems to imply something more about the nature of the position I exclusively occupy as owner, something that does not cash out just in terms of exclusion. A sovereign, a private owner, a squatter, a tenant and a licensee may all have rights to exclude with respect to the same tract of land. In exercising their rights of exclusion, they might act in very similar ways, for example, building fences, refusing entry, etc. Yet, we invoke different kinds of decision-making power when we describe one holder of a right to exclude as an owner, another as a state, and yet another as a mere licensee. Owners are in charge of regulating private activity with respect to things for reasons of their own; states exercising territorial authority over that same land are in charge of making decisions on behalf of everyone subject to public justification

[12] See L. Katz, 'Exclusion and exclusivity in property law', *University of Toronto Law Journal*, 8 (2008), 275.

requirements.[13] We can similarly distinguish between owners and others who have private rights to exclude with respect to a thing, like the guest for the night or the finder of a thing. Owners are in charge in a way that a licensee, or a finder, is not. A licence is by its very nature a limited jurisdiction to make some particular use of a thing. A person licensed to occupy a house for the night has a right to exclude all comers for that night but she does not have the power to determine more generally the mode of occupation of that property or to vacate her position and appoint a successor or to carve out other lesser property rights for others, like a right of way for the neighbour or a mortgage for the bank. Similarly, someone who finds my necklace has a right to exclude other non-owners. But what we mean by a finder, in contrast to a thief, is someone who takes possession of a thing with the intention to return it to its owner, not someone who sets out to usurp the owner's role.

What then distinguishes the position of the owner from the position of the licensee or the finder or even the political sovereign, all of whom might have rights to exclude with respect to that same thing? It is the distinctive nature of the normative power that each has. The position of owner is defined by the kind of authority she has to set the agenda for the thing. What it is for a thing to be mine, in the sense that I own it, is that my decision-making authority is supreme among private actors. Seen in terms of its exclusive authority and the role it carves out for owners, ownership is perhaps best thought of as a kind of office: an impersonal, stable and enduring position of authority tasked at least with agenda-setting for things, allowing for a succession of officeholders by grant, usurpation or appointment by the state.[14]

Thinking about ownership as an office also accounts for another feature of ownership: the variety of ways we can conceive of *holding* ownership without changing the way ownership as an office functions in relation to third parties,

[13] See L. Katz, 'Property's sovereignty', *Theoretical Inquiries in Law* 18 (2017) 299, and A. Ripstein, 'Property and sovereignty: how to tell the difference', *Theoretical Inquiries in Law* 18 (2017) 243, on differences in the kinds of authority that states and owners have. See J. Waldron, 'Settlement, return, and the supersession thesis', *Theoretical Inquiries In Law* 5 (2004), questioning the state's right to exclude outsiders.

[14] L. Katz, 'Moral paradox of adverse possession: sovereignty and revolution in property law', *McGill Law Journal* 55 (2010), 47; L. Katz, 'Governing through owners', *University of Pennsylvania Law Review* 160 (2012), 2029; C. Essert, 'The office of ownership', *University of Toronto Law Journal* 63 (2013), 418.

that is, non-owners. The office of ownership may be highly individualised, as in the case of private property, or it may be collectively held, as in the case of communal ownership, according to which a group of people share in the decision-making. We can make the same basic point about the variety of ways that owners can arrange for the distribution of the benefits and burdens that accede to the office of ownership, for example, among present and future interest-holders, corporations and shareholders, trustees and beneficiaries. The basic idea of ownership as an office allows owners to make a variety of distributive choices within the office without any normative change to the basic 'in charge' relation of owners vis-à-vis others. The office of ownership sets out the framework for the kinds of things the rest of us can do as private actors with respect to that thing and from this standpoint it does not matter what internal governance structure is in place to run that office or who stands to receive whatever value happens to flows from it.

Even public ownership, as when the state owns things, makes use of the same basic idea of ownership as an office. The possibility of public ownership does not undermine the distinction I drew above between ownership and state sovereignty. When the state acts *qua* owner, it makes decisions that are attributable not to its distinctive public authority but to its ownership authority. There is a distinction then between ownership authority and other kinds of public authority, notwithstanding that a state, like a trustee, will have super-added constraints to exercise its ownership authority in the public interest. A state might fail to observe the distinction, of course. In failing to observe the distinction between ownership and public authority, the state simply acts ultra vires. I take it that this was Lord Mance's concern in a case against the British Secretary of State, following the forced removal of the Chagos Islanders, prior to the leasing of their island to the United States military.[15] In that case, the government claimed to be exercising its prerogative power in relation to the British Indian Ocean Territory but acted, according to Lord Mance, as though it were exercising a power to make decisions about the bare land. From the standpoint of an owner, as agenda-setter for the land, the state viewed the inhabitants as a mere inconvenience. That, it turned out, was the wrong standpoint to take.

One way to distinguish between public ownership and territorial authority is by applying the separability thesis in the context of public

[15] *Bancoult* v. *Secretary of State for Foreign and Commonwealth Affairs*, [2008] UKHL 61.

ownership. A state cannot act as owner with respect to things that are wrapped up in its very identity, such as its territory. It must be the kind of decision-making authority that the state in principle could convey to someone else without making that person, or entity, the state in its stead. Those things that a state owns it may transfer to another without undermining its status as a state. Those things that make the state a state, for instance, its territory, cannot be severed and transferred to another in the same way.[16]

2 Property's Place in the Legal Order

The idea of ownership at the core of property law is generally understood to be a way of attaching exclusive rights to scarce resources. Considerations of political justifiability yield different views of how property might operate within our legal order and lead theorists to develop subtly different conceptions of property.

Property theory today falls roughly into three ways of thinking about how to arrange property within the legal order. The first sees property as incidental to contract: property rights are just the bargaining chips we each start with as we contemplate contracting with one another.[17] This arrangement, according to which we go through property to get to contract, reflects broadly utilitarian considerations. A second view sees property primarily through the lens of tort: here it is claimed that the rights of ownership are plenary with respect to the thing, yielding an absolute right to exclude for any reason at all, reined in at a later stage by public law considerations. Thus, it is always a wrong for others to use or damage a thing in any way without the owner's consent. This view typically is motivated by an understanding of individual freedom that its proponents take to be conceptually basic to the idea of property: each person should be entitled to do as she likes with her thing, limited only by overriding public law considerations.[18]

[16] When the state grants private property rights, it is not giving up its political authority over lands privately owned. It is merely yielding private agenda-setting authority for those lands to owners, subject always to its public authority to regulate and even to expropriate for public purposes.

[17] See H.E. Smith and T.W. Merrill, 'What happened to property in law and economics?', *Yale Law Journal* 111 (2001) at 357.

[18] A. Ripstein, *Force and Freedom: Kant's Legal and Political Philosophy* (Harvard University Press, 2009).

Property is important insofar as it sets out additional ways in which others might wrong us. Here too property seems to occupy a place within our legal order that is on the way to somewhere else, viz., the law of torts. On these views, property law is liminal to the law of contract or torts, and itself has a very small normative footprint within the legal order.

A third view takes property relations to concern a broader slice of human interaction than our consensual or contractual relations. On this view, property is not liminal to these other modes of interaction; rather, it makes possible a distinctive kind of human interaction shaped by ownership authority itself.[19] I have characterised this normative power in terms of the owner's authority to set the agenda for a thing. There are other, much older, accounts of the normative position of owners in terms of stewardship, the power and the responsibility to care for things.[20] On this third view, it is in setting out a purposive idea of ownership that property law stakes out a distinctive place in our legal order.

Now let's take each view in turn, with an eye to explaining the political motivations for each.

a Property as Liminal to Contract

I will start with the idea that property just sets the stage for contract law, the idea that property is liminal to contract. Private ordering, on this view, is a matter of small-scale cooperation, or voluntary agreement between private actors. Property is simply the initial (and so provisional, if the market is working properly) allocation of veto-rights with respect to the use of scarce resources about which we then bargain toward an optimally efficient allocation of rights.[21] Many economists do not think there is a general principle that would establish who ought to have the

[19] This view lies somewhere between O.W. Holmes' view of property law as mostly technical and philosophically uninteresting, and Maitland's, who wrote that our whole legal order seems at times to be just an appendage to the law of real property. See Maitland, *The Constitutional History of England* (Cambridge University Press, 1920) at 538; O.W. Holmes, *The Common Law* (Little, Brown & Co., 1881).

[20] For a contemporary treatment, see J. Finnis, *Natural Law and Natural Rights*, 2nd ed. (Oxford University Press, 2011).

[21] For R. Coase and his followers, private ordering is primarily about voluntary transactions. See G. Calabresi and A.D. Melamed, 'Property rules, liability rules, and inalienability: one view of the cathedral', *Harvard Law Review* 85 (1972), 1089.

right to exclude, prior to any conflict about use. In a world of no transaction costs, the right could be allocated on either side of a conflict and we would still arrive at efficient outcomes. Take a conflict between factory owner A, who discharges pollution that drifts downstream onto the land of farmer B, and B over the right to pollute or to repel pollution. While a pollution-generating factory owner and a neighbouring farmer might themselves care very much who starts with the right to exclude, from the vantage point of efficiency it does not matter at all so long as there is no obstacle to bargaining. Through contract, the right moves to the highest-value user.

The corollary to the idea of property liminal to contract is a view of property as a bundle of rights: where transaction costs inhibit free market exchange, judges ought to arrange entitlements as between A and B so as to bring about our preferred outcomes, typically enhanced social utility or efficiency. From this standpoint, ownership does not take any particular form, such as a general right to exclude, but rather is a malleable bundle of rights. Each stick in the bundle represents a right to use or to exclude another from use with respect to something. The bundle itself may be tailored to meet the demands of social utility or efficiency in individual cases.

b Property as Liminal to Tort

Recall now the second idea, that property sets the stage for tort. Property, on this view, sets out a category of wrongdoing characterised by unauthorised boundary-crossings. From this viewpoint, owners have a plenary power to exclude others with respect to a thing, such that it is always a wrong for a person to enter another's property without her consent. Ownership is simply what results from a general right against unauthorised boundary-crossings, waivable by consent.

Those who position property at the threshold of tort insist that the right to exclude is a fixed input to judicial reasoning about property. In the dispute between the farmer and the factory owner, the farmer's right to exclude structures the analysis of tort liability: it is *prima facie* wrongful, on this account, to send substances over the boundary-line of another's property without her consent.

Kantian exemplars of this approach start with the idea of freedom as non-domination, according to which no one is subject to the choices of another. Property is an extension of this idea of freedom to things in the world. Through property, we are in charge of things in just the same way that we are in charge of ourselves more generally. The institution of private property as a plenary right with respect to things is taken to be a necessary condition for individual freedom.

More recently, others have developed instrumental accounts of property as liminal to tort. On these accounts, too, property is a right to exclude concerned primarily with the wrong of unauthorised boundary-crossings. One such account is an application of Joseph Raz's concept of authority to property as a discrete area of law, individuated by our valuable interest in using things.[22] Our interest in use thus justifies a duty on the part of others to exclude themselves and so yields the idea of property as a right against unauthorised boundary-crossings. At its core, this interest-based view of property rests on an empirical claim that it is a contingent but stable feature of human lives that we cannot effectively use scarce resources without excluding others.

Other instrumentalist accounts place property on the threshold of tort as a part of an indirect strategy to enhance the efficiency of the system.[23] The aim is to enable small-scale cooperation at optimally low social cost, and a commitment to a general right to exclude is cast as the best way overall to enable property to do that job within the private law order. By employing bright-line rules, such as 'keep off things belonging to others', we achieve greater efficiency: unauthorised boundary-crossing sets out a wrong that imposes lower information costs than defining rights and their correlating duties case by case. This indirect utilitarian approach is offered as a corrective to conventional economic accounts that take the 'liminal to contract' approach, according to which property is a bundle of rights assembled ad hoc.

c The Internal Domain of Property

This brings me to a third cluster of property theories, which explain property in terms of the normative power owners have and not merely in terms of a right to exclude over which *other* normative powers, such as power to contract or consent, can be exercised. Stewardship accounts of

[22] See Penner, *The Idea of Property in Law.*

[23] Henry Smith and Thomas Merrill are prominent exponents of this view.

property offer the most ambitious and extensive claims for ownership as a normative position defined in terms of its own internal mandate or purpose. Many such accounts of private property emerge from the biblical idea that the Earth is given to us in common.[24] Owners have private authority over particular resources as stewards for humankind. The basic justification of private property is its value in coordinating our care of the Earth: we are better able to care for things through highly individualised positions of stewardship. There are, relatedly, virtue-theories of property, according to which ownership decisions are meant to aim at and foster virtues such as humility, industry and justice.[25]

How else might we conceive of property as a purposive institution? There is a great distance between stewardship accounts of property, which claim a rich internal purpose for property, and accounts of property as just a right to exclude others, which tell us what property does (i.e. setting up gatekeepers with rights of exclusion) but that deny that property law aims at anything else in doing so. In this space, I have found room for a conception of property as a private office charged with setting the agenda for things in relation to others.

Ownership as an office of agenda-setting authority solves a basic moral problem about the standing to determine what ought to be done with things we all have an interest in using productively and without conflict. There is a problem of standing because none of us has the inherent moral imprimatur to impose our own views on others about what ought to be done with a thing (as we do with our bodies). Nor do we have standing to make decisions about things just in virtue of something like expertise or desert. Need, as we have seen, may justify a lesser right to use or consume something but not the greater power to set the agenda in relation to others. To see why that is so, consider our moral positions in relation to one another prior to anyone's having charge of things. The very first move – to take something up as my own – encounters a problem of standing: why me? I cannot justify taking charge of things just on the grounds that I thereby carve out a sphere for myself in which I am not subject to the

[24] Some readings of Locke suggest that through the sufficiency provision and the constraint on waste, we arrive at stewardship constraints on the normative powers of owners. See e.g. G. Sreenivasan, *The Limits of Lockean Rights in Property* (Oxford University Press, 1995).

[25] E. Penalver and G. Alexander, 'Properties of community', *Theoretical Inquiries in Law* 10 (2008); E. Penalver, 'Land virtues', *Cornell Law Review* 94 (2009) 821.

choices of another. Nor can I take charge on the grounds that I know best about what ought to be done. That is because, in taking charge of that thing, I displace a state of affairs in which others are not subject to my choices and in which others' views about what ought to be done with that thing have the same moral weight as my own.[26] We do not encounter this problem of standing with respect to our rights to our person: your views and my views about what ought to be done with my body are not on equal footing from the get-go.

Ownership solves the problem of standing by designating impersonal, individualised private offices, through which people have authority to take charge of things. Seen as a solution to one kind of moral problem, ownership does not entail a much larger authority to govern other aspects of human affairs or to conscript others in service of our agendas. For this reason, ownership regulates the activities of others only negatively, by enabling owners to establish the terms on which others may use her thing but not to conscript them to advance her agenda.

By focusing on the normative power of owners, we also focus on the sense in which ownership concerns our dealings with others, with respect to a thing. E.M. Forster made this point, tongue-in-cheek, when he described his attempts to find solitude and seclusion within 'his woods'. He found instead that ownership meant constant and complex dealings with others: stone-throwing boys, neighbours, ramblers, even birds presented themselves and required him to make more, rather than fewer, social decisions.[27]

The idea of ownership is less obviously important (and less intuitively at work) with respect to things that do not invite the same intensity of dealings by others – my single-use Kleenex, my apple, my disposable pen. Property with respect to these sorts of things is important if at all to work out a problem of scarce resources, or competing interests in use: one Kleenex, two runny noses, all that we could do is allocate a right to exclude to one or the other person. Of course exclusion sometimes matters to sort out rival claims to consume things in the context of scarce goods. But we can see how that concern is ably resolved simply by assigning rights to consume or use, protected by mere rights to exclude. Full-blown

[26] See L. Katz, 'Spite and extortion: a jurisdictional principle of abuse of property right', *Yale Law Journal* 122 (2013) at 1444.

[27] E.M. Forster, 'My wood', *The New Leader* (1926).

ownership matters where owners have work to do in harmonising the many ways that people might use things over time. Owners do this by setting the agenda for the thing and establishing a framework of lesser property rights and privileges.

It is not then, as Hume thought, scarcity that makes ownership so important – mere rights to possess can deal with the allocation of scarce resources as among competitors – but the complexity of human activity with respect to a thing over a period of time or space that requires someone in charge to draw up plans for that thing.

This turn from scarcity to complexity as the motivator for ownership fits our everyday intuitions about what is both attractive – and dangerous – about property today: an exclusive right to possess some space with a roof overhead is responsive to my need for shelter in conditions of scarcity. Full-blown ownership however puts me into a position to do a great deal more than just to satisfy my personhood interest in shelter or even my individual interest in possessing more than I need. It allows me to determine the relations others might have with respect to that thing on a much broader scale.

C.B. Macpherson famously drew our attention to the possessive individual, whose interest in property was based on consumption. I mean to draw attention to how ownership gratifies a very different human interest, our interest in being in charge. Ownership introduces a new capacity for self-seeking activity, not limited to consumptions or marked by possessive individualism. There is obviously a limit to our lives as consumers: there comes a point in my lifetime when I could not put on another garment, wear another pair of shoes, occupy another bed in yet another of my houses. I simply cannot stretch myself over that much stuff. And yet there is always scope for setting larger and more ambitious agendas for private activity with respect to the things we own.

This view of ownership as a private office carves out a constitutionally basic role for private actors without, however, eliminating a role for the state acting through public officials.[28] The office of ownership is charged

[28] But note that a network of private offices is liable to be repurposed to perform other tasks of public administration, too, a phenomenon I call 'governing through owners'. See L. Katz, 'Governing through owners', *University of Pennsylvania Law Review* 160 (2012), 2029. See R. Elllickson, 'The affirmative duties of owners' (Yale Law & Economics Research Paper No. 499, 10 July 2014).

with regulating one aspect of our shared lives while public offices are charged with regulating other arenas of human interaction. Being in charge of one aspect of a plan means not only making the decisions you are charged with but also leaving it to others to make those decisions charged to them. To do away with this aspect of private office-holding – to allow that property is merely a right to exclude, rather than a normative power of agenda-setting – would be, perhaps counter-intuitively, to relegate private actors to a much more trivially private sphere, one in which they are taken to concern themselves just with their own ends-setting, free to act strategically at every turn, to 'blow hot and cold' as their private interests dictate.

Property, seen this way, forms part of the constitutional order, the 'master plan' that allocates authority in society to private and public decision-makers.[29] (To quote Barbara Wootton out of context, it is never a question of whether to plan but only a question of who plans.[30]) A confederation of owners brings about a state of affairs in which there are no agenda-less things: all ownable things are subject to human agency if not to actual human use. What Holmes calls 'the general tendency of our law ... to favour appropriation, to abhor the absence of proprietary or possessory rights as a kind of vacuum' reflects I think a concern with vacancy in the office of ownership.[31] So too does a general restriction on abandonment that makes it very hard to vacate the office without having first someone ready to stand in your stead.[32] From the standpoint of property's internal mandate, we can see why the law abhors a vacancy: the office of ownership is *responsible* for agenda-setting for things. We can similarly make sense of other basic and otherwise puzzling aspects of property law, like adverse possession, from the standpoint of property's mandate. A person's hold on the office of ownership cannot survive a loss of de facto authority to another simply because de facto authority is essential to the fulfilment of the most basic role of owners actually to make plans for things.

[29] S.J. Shapiro, *Legality* (Harvard University Press, 2011), ch. 6.

[30] See B. Wootton, *Freedom under Planning* (University of North Carolina Press, 1945) (responding to Hayek).

[31] O. Holmes, *The Common Law* (Harvard University Press, 1991) at 237. This idea is, I think, a modern descendant of what Maitland called the ancient common law doctrine entitling the Crown to the service of its subjects.

[32] See E. Penalver, 'The illusory right to abandon', *Michigan Law Review* (2010).

Conclusion

So is property law morally salient? This chapter suggests ways that through our political choices we might make it so. Property is a flexible institution that history has shown capable of insinuating itself into more or less of our moral, social, economic and political lives. The work of the legal theorist is just to expose what property is in law, and how and on what terms it might be justified in organising our relations as they concern things in the world.

International Law 20

Guglielmo Verdirame

International law was a subject of interest for philosophers from the early modern period to the Enlightenment – from the Spanish Scholastics and Grotius to Christian Wolff and Immanuel Kant. With a few exceptions (most notably Jeremy Bentham and Hans Kelsen), however, it has not been a principal object of philosophical inquiry for much of the last two centuries. Why?

One reason for the paucity of philosophical interest in international law may have to do with the sequencing of inquiry in political philosophy. Political philosophers usually begin with questions about the domestic order, moving on to questions about the international order only later – if ever. This sequencing has been followed by the most disparate thinkers. Jean-Jacques Rousseau concluded the *Social Contract* with the observation that, having established foundations for the state, he could consider strengthening them by looking at 'the law of peoples, commerce, the right of war and conquest, public right, leagues, negotiations, treaties', but thought this subject too vast to explore in the *Social Contract* and never properly returned to it.[1] Hegel touched on international law in the concluding sections of *Philosophy of Right*, leaving a lot unanswered or ambiguously answered.[2] Even Kant, who wrote one of the most famous and lasting essays on international legal and political theory, came to this topic only at the end of his life.[3] As did John Rawls, who in this respect too

[1] J.J. Rousseau, 'Of the social contract' in V. Gourevitch (ed.), *The Social Contract and Other Later Political Writings* (Cambridge University Press, 1997), Book IV, ch. 9.

[2] G.W.F. Hegel, 'Elements of the philosophy of right' in A.W. Wood (ed.), *Elements of the Philosophy of Right* (Cambridge University Press, 1991), §§320–41.

[3] I. Kant, 'Toward perpetual peace' in M.J. Gregor (ed.), *Practical Philosophy* (Cambridge University Press, 1996), 311–51; I. Kant, 'Idea for a universal history with a cosmopolitan aim' in G. Zoller and R.B. Louden (eds.), *Anthropology, History and Education* (Cambridge University Press, 2007), 107–20.

followed 'Kant's lead',[4] and Ronald Dworkin, who died shortly before completing the final revision of his main contribution to the philosophy of international law.[5]

Coming to questions about the international order after others have been addressed seems to entail, or in any event produce, a normative preference for the domestic order: once basic political values – such as individual and political liberty or equality – are embedded in the legal and political order of the state, international law ends up being conceived exclusively as inter-state law. Such domestic-to-international sequencing would be rejected by cosmopolitans who would rather ground fundamental political and moral values in a cosmopolitan order, and identify the political units of that order subsequently and in a manner that is subservient to both those values and to the overarching cosmopolitan nature of the political order they advocate.[6] In this chapter, I will deal with explanatory and normative philosophical accounts of international law that accept the state as the principal political unit in the international system, and I will therefore exclude cosmopolitan theories. This acceptance of the state may be empirical for some, normative for others. Here it is merely a reflection of how the field of the philosophy of international law is generally demarcated.

I will focus on three strands of questions in this field. First, there are 'conceptual questions' about the nature of international law as law and 'the existence and content of its norms'.[7] The second strand concerns 'the formulation of moral standards for the evaluation of public international law'.[8] The third strand, which analytically can be viewed as a subset of the second, focuses on normative argument about the relationship between international law and national law – or, put in other terms, between the sovereign state and the international (or supranational) order(s). The first strand of questions is sometimes seen as the preserve of legal philosophy, while moral and political philosophers have tended to focus, respectively,

4 J. Rawls, *The Law of Peoples: With the Idea of Public Reason Revisited* (Harvard University Press, 1999), 10.

5 R. Dworkin, 'A new philosophy for international law', *Philosophy and Public Affairs* 41 (Winter, 2013), 3–30.

6 This seems to be the approach adopted by P. Allott, 'The concept of international law', *European Journal of International Law* 10 (1999), 31–50.

7 S. Besson and J. Tasioulas, 'Introduction' in S. Besson and J. Tasioulas (eds.), *The Philosophy of International Law* (Oxford University Press, 2010), 2.

8 Ibid., 13.

on the second and third strands. These distinctions should not however be taken rigidly, as philosophical investigation into international law will often involve conceptual, political and moral elements.

1 The Concept of International Law

Does international law possess the character of law? The answer to this question depends on what we understand the nature of law to be. Those who subscribe to John Austin's view that law exists only where there is a sovereign authority capable of issuing commands backed by sanctions will conclude that international law, as currently structured, should not be thought of as law.[9]

In the post-war tradition, the argument that international law is somehow incomplete, that it is law at best only in a primitive sense, is associated principally with H.L.A. Hart's *The Concept of Law*.[10] At the outset, Hart criticises Austin's theory of law as flawed and narrow, for it takes no account of rules, such as power-conferring rules, which are not formulated as commands but are nonetheless an important part of the phenomenon of law. Hart also rejects the view that law is somehow premised on the idea of sovereignty as ultimate authority. So far so good for international law: as long as notions such as ruler-command or sovereignty are considered necessary elements of the idea of law, the conclusion that international law is not law seems virtually inescapable.

The problem for international law resurfaces because of Hart's well-known conception of law as the union of two sets of rules: primary rules which impose obligations or create powers, and secondary rules which relate to the way in which those primary rules are identified, changed and adjudicated upon.[11] Hart discusses how international law fits into this conception in Chapter X of *The Concept of Law*. He concludes that international law possesses primary rules, and that these are for the most part observed in practice and perceived by states as binding. According to Hart, however, international law lacks secondary rules. In particular, he argued

[9] J. Austin, *The Province of Jurisprudence Determined* (Weidenfeld & Nicolson, 1954).

[10] H.L.A. Hart, *The Concept of Law*, 3rd ed. (Oxford University Press, 2012).

[11] Secondary rules are rules about rules which 'specify the ways in which the primary rules may be conclusively ascertained, introduced, eliminated, varied and the fact of their violation conclusively determined' (ibid., 94).

that international law lacks the secondary rule that provides the ultimate foundation for a legal system – the rule of recognition. International law is not therefore law in the modern, more advanced sense of a legal system defined by the union of primary and secondary rules; it is instead, according to Hart, law only in a primitive or incomplete sense.

A common response to Hart's criticism is to ask whether these conceptual issues matter. To put it bluntly: why should we care? A proposition can of course be true even if we choose not to care about it because, for example, we regard it as inconsequential. But, as Hart himself understood, a failure to conceptualise the social phenomenon that we normally describe as international law *does* matter, for it hinders both '*theoretical enquiries* . . . [and] *moral deliberation*'.[12] We need to understand what it is that we are talking about if we want to advance moral and political arguments about international law. International law scholarship nowadays has no shortage of 'theorists' with purportedly 'critical agendas', but an agenda that is truly critical, and not merely 'critical' in the self-congratulatory sense in which fuzzy postmodernist theorists have appropriated this word, necessitates conceptual inquiry.

Similarly misplaced is the retort that Hart's argument comes down to nothing more than a fruitless disagreement over definitions. This misses the point that there is a difference between terminological and conceptual disagreement. We can decide to expand the meaning of the word 'table' to include the objects we commonly describe as 'chairs', but conceptual differences between tables and chairs would survive this new-fangled linguistic sloppiness. Hart's conceptual critique of international law is not an arid terminological dispute about the meaning of the word 'law'. It forces us to confront crucial questions about the legal character of international law. But was he right to think of international law as possessing at best a primitive legal character?

What is odd about this characterisation is that a defining feature of primitive law is, as Hart himself put it, that it operates successfully only for 'a small community closely knit by ties of kinship, common sentiment, and belief, and placed in a stable environment'.[13] The context in which international law operates could not be more different. So how can international law function as merely primitive law? Hart did not address this

[12] Ibid., 214.
[13] Hart, *The Concept of Law*, 92.

question. His reservations about international law may help us pin down some important concerns about the legal character of international law, but the assimilation of international law to primitive law seems to miss out something important.

It is helpful to take a step back and reflect on the *doctrinal* account of international law on which Hart's conceptual analysis rests. Doctrinal accounts inform conceptual inquiry (and more generally philosophical inquiry). If we are to assess whether international law fits into a broader idea of law, we must appreciate the nature and functioning of international law as understood by those (governments, judges, academics, practising lawyers, and so on) who make it. In other words, the analysis of the legal character of international law must necessarily move on from a series of understandings about how international law functions. Central to those understandings in Hart's case was the notion that international law depends on the consent of states. He was not the only legal philosopher to proceed on this basis. In his posthumous contribution to international law, Dworkin, while displaying some ambivalence toward this consent-based doctrinal account of international law, also endorsed its doctrinal credentials, writing that the idea that a state is subject to international law only insofar as it has consented to be bound by it reflects a 'firmly positivist view of international law ... [which] seems to be now generally accepted by practitioners and scholars of international law'.[14]

Is this voluntarist doctrinal account of international law correct? It would be difficult to deny that it is a typical, and quite possibly *the* typical, account of how the formation and functioning of international law is explained – including by many international lawyers. But for all its success this account has flaws. One, as noted by Hart too,[15] is that consent cannot provide the basis for legal obligation for newly independent states, which become bound by rules of general international law to which they never had an opportunity to consent.

Even more fundamentally, voluntarism fails to explain key aspects of the sources of international law. Treaties are of course based on the voluntary consent of state parties. As the Vienna Convention on the Law of Treaties states, treaties cannot create 'obligations or rights for a third

[14] Dworkin, 'A new philosophy for international law', 5.
[15] Hart, *The Concept of Law*, 226.

State without its consent'.[16] But other sources of international law operate in a manner that can be described as consent-based only by stretching the meaning of consent beyond breaking-point. There is, first, the notion of *jus cogens*, that is, peremptory norms of international law. Dworkin, purportedly on the basis of the Vienna Convention, maintains that *jus cogens* too comes 'under the umbrella of consent',[17] but there is nothing in the definition of *jus cogens* in the Vienna Convention that points toward consent.[18] Moreover, consent does not feature in the standard definition of customary international law as 'general practice *accepted* as law'.[19] Acceptance and consent are different notions.

Positive evidence of *dissent* from a particular rule of custom can be relied upon by the dissenting state on the basis of the (not entirely uncontroversial) doctrine of persistent objection. Positive evidence of *consent* is not however required as a condition for a rule of custom to be formed and take effect vis-à-vis a state against which it is invoked. The International Court of Justice may itself have paid lip service to the idea that consent is a foundation of international law, in one case describing it alongside sovereignty as 'the very basis of international law',[20] but its method of ascertaining custom shows no evidence of adherence to strict voluntarism. The Court has regularly established the existence of a rule of custom even in the absence of any specific consent to it from the states concerned.

A consent-based account of international law also fails doctrinally, because it cannot provide a plausible explanation for change in customary international law that does not compromise its legal character. The replacement of a rule of custom with a contrary one (for example, of an obligation with permission) would have to be explained as a consequence of states openly withdrawing their consent, or perhaps of states acting in bad faith or error. As observed by John Tasioulas, such an account

[16] Vienna Convention on the Law of Treaties, Vienna, 23 May 1969, in force 27 January 1980, 1155 UNTS 331; (1969) 8 ILM 679; UKTS (1980) 58, Article 34.

[17] Dworkin, 'A new philosophy for international law', 6.

[18] The definition of peremptory norms of international law in Article 53 of the Vienna Convention is: '. . . a peremptory norm of general international law is a norm accepted and recognized by the international community of States as a whole as a norm from which no derogation is permitted and which can be modified only by a subsequent norm of general international law having the same character'.

[19] Statute of the International Court of Justice, Ch. II Competence of the Court, Article 38(1).

[20] *Legality of the Threat or Use of Nuclear Weapons*, Advisory Opinion, I.C.J. Reports 1996, 226 at para. 21.

'tarnishes the legitimacy of customary international law',[21] and undermines both the moral and systemic credentials of international law.

More could be said on whether an inadequate doctrinal account of international law may have informed – or rather misinformed – Hart's conceptual critique of international law.[22] In fairness to Hart, it must be emphasised that many an international lawyer embraced this doctrinaire voluntarism, notwithstanding its failure to provide a sound account of how international law functions in reality. The best that can be said of this voluntarism is that it offers a reductionist and crude way of thinking about international legal obligation. This is not to say, however, that consent is irrelevant – this too would be a gross misstatement. Consent does matter in the formation of rules of international law, yet it is not the only way in which international legal obligation emerges and it cannot provide a credible foundation to the system (if such it is) of international law.

If we move away from strict voluntarism, is there some way in which international law could be thought of as law in the modern sense? As mentioned, Hart's main reservations had to do with the absence of secondary rules, and in particular the rule of recognition. Hart was not prescriptive about the form of the rule of recognition: '[i]t may, as in the early law of many societies, be no more than that an authoritative list or text of the rules is to be found in a written document or carved on some public monument'.[23]

Is there a body of rules of international law that can be said to act as a basic norm or rule of recognition for the entire system? Hart and others were rightly dismissive of the possibility that *pacta sunt servanda* or consent could be such a basic norm: to say 'international law is what

[21] J. Tasioulas, 'Customary international law: a moral judgment-based account', *American Journal of International Law* 108 (2014), 331. See also by the same author: 'Custom, jus cogens, and human rights' in C. Bradley (ed.), *Custom's Future: International Law in a Changing World* (Cambridge University Press, 2016), 95–116.

[22] See, for example, M. Payandeh, 'The concept of international law in the jurisprudence of H.L.A. Hart', *European Journal of International Law* 21 (2010), who argues that changes in '*international legislation*' and '*international adjudication*' that have taken place since the publication of *Concept of Law* have superseded Hart's concluding assessment. It seems to me however still somewhat misleading to speak of '*international legislation*'. Custom and treaties, the main sources of international law, are different from statutes but these differences do not preclude the characterisation of international law as a system of law.

[23] Hart, *The Concept of Law*, 94.

states have consented to' or 'international law obligations must be performed' adds hardly anything of substance. A more serious candidate could perhaps be the Vienna Convention on the Law of Treaties. It is arguable that, as a treaty about treaties, the Convention has come to perform a systemic function as far as rules governing the adoption, entry into force, amendment and interpretation of treaties are concerned. But treaties are only one source of international law. Sceptics will rejoin that the Vienna Convention does no more for treaties than the Uniform Commercial Code in the US or the Code Civil in France does for contracts. It is, in other words, a set of *primary* rules that enables certain promises to have legal effect. The Uniform Commercial Code and the Code Civil have other rules behind them that explain how *they* have legal effect, but the same cannot be said of the Vienna Convention.

Another candidate for the position of basic norm or secondary rule is Article 38 of the Statute of the International Court of Justice (ICJ). Article 38 is a treaty provision which, on first inspection, does no more than identify the applicable law in disputes brought before the Court. Applicable law clauses are far from infrequent in treaties that provide for judicial settlement of disputes,[24] and their very existence may seem to support the non-systemic and episodic nature of international law. So in what way can Article 38 be said to be a basic norm?

Article 38 has taken on a life of its own, and grown well beyond the confines of the form which contains it. The main commentary on the Statute of the ICJ observes that, since its adoption in the Statute of the ICJ's predecessor (the Permanent Court of International Justice) in 1920, this rule has had 'an unquestionable influence on the development of international law and the law of international adjudication'.[25] It has been repeated or referred to in other treaties on dispute settlement,[26] and it is recited in full or in part in countless judgments of both international and national courts, as well as in the awards of international tribunals. There can be little doubt that Article 38 is viewed as an authoritative statement on the sources of international law.

[24] E.g. International Centre for Settlement of Investment Disputes Convention, Regulations and Rules Article, Section 3 Powers and Functions of the Tribunal, Article 42.

[25] A. Zimmermann, K. Oellers-Frahm, C. Tomuschat and C.J. Tams (eds.), *The Statute of the International Court of Justice: A Commentary*, 2nd ed. (Oxford University Press, 2012), 691.

[26] Ibid.

Even so, Article 38 may be foundational in an *explanatory* sense but not in a *constitutive* sense. If one looks for secondary rules more generally, that is, rules that tell us how 'primary rules may be conclusively ascertained, introduced, eliminated, varied', the results are more promising, certainly as far as treaties are concerned. As regards custom, the main obstacle is the persistence of a voluntarist doctrine which fails to provide a morally and systematically credible account of this source. As we have seen, moreover, the notion that consent is the overarching basis of legal obligation fails doctrinally, even before it founders philosophically.

Even if we were to overcome these obstacles, we would still need to accept that, while international law has matured into a system of law, it remains different in important ways from municipal legal systems. The main difference is not the absence of authoritative rules of identification and change. Nor is it one that can be aptly rendered by assimilating international law to primitive law. The main difference is in the field of adjudication. Notwithstanding the proliferation of international courts and tribunals, there is still no general system of compulsory adjudication. Various treaty regimes – for example, the World Trade Organization or bilateral investment treaties – have adopted complex and sophisticated dispute settlement mechanisms and procedures, which are however sporadic rather than systemic, and are subject to the consent of states. States can (and do) opt out of them. Exiting jurisdiction is a privilege not accorded to natural or legal persons in a municipal legal system. Some seek to downplay these differences arguing that '[n]ot every case that arises under constitutional law can be adjudicated in a judicial forum'.[27] In the United States, for example, 'the political questions doctrine will prevent an authoritative judicial decision' in the event of a dispute between branches of government.[28] But there is a difference between a doctrine of judicial restraint in the exercise of an existing jurisdiction, and the absence of jurisdiction in the first place.

Whether these differences in adjudication between municipal law and international law should be described as a weakness is a matter of normative assessment. As we shall see below, there may be good reasons for international law not to develop into a system of law in the municipal sense.

[27] Payandeh, 'The concept of international law in the jurisprudence of H.L.A. Hart', 986.
[28] Ibid.

2 The Morality of International Law

I will focus here on the morality of the idea of international law rather than the morality of specific principles (e.g. sovereign equality or self-determination), legal institutions (e.g. the legal regime on state responsibility), or subject areas (e.g. law of armed conflict, human rights, investment protection, and so on),[29] bearing of course in mind that the morality of the system (if such it is) of international law also depends on the morality of its component parts.

A crude way of assessing the systemic morality of international law is to ascribe to it *one* general moral purpose and purport to resolve conflicts between values by reference to it. An example is Antonio Cassese's argument that the legality of humanitarian intervention depends on *which* set of moral values – international peace or human rights and justice – international law prioritises.[30] This is a question-begging approach that is of no use to either legal doctrine or morality. International law, like domestic law, should not be thought of as founded upon one moral purpose to the exclusion of others. It is one thing to say that international law is one of the principal ways in which human societies promote a particular moral value, for example, the preservation of international peace and the prevention of war. It is another to claim that this functional relationship, with the value of peace or other values, generates a *moral* justification for international law to override other moral concerns. On the contrary, insofar as this relationship is used as a trump card in support of certain legal outcomes, it may constitute a moral defect in that it would render the system blind or insufficiently attentive to other moral concerns.

Even more fundamentally flawed is the approach of those who deny that moral values and purposes ever conflict *in practice*. An example is the sweeping claim that there can be no peace without justice. This has become almost an article of faith in the literature on international criminal law and transitional justice. It helps many conveniently to avoid and dismiss difficult moral and legal questions involving a conflict between peace

[29] See, for example, the various chapters in S. Besson and J. Tasioulas (eds.), *The Philosophy of International Law* (Oxford University Press, 2010).

[30] A. Cassese, '*Ex iniuria ius oritur*: are we moving towards international legitimation of forcible humanitarian countermeasures in the world community?', *European Journal of International Law* 10 (1999), 23.

and justice, for example on the desirability of amnesties in post-conflict situations.

A central question of systemic morality concerns the legitimacy of international law. Legitimacy is generally understood as the quality that an authority possesses when it has the right to rule.[31] It is important to distinguish the sociological sense of legitimacy from the normative one.[32] Sociological enquiries into legitimacy focus on the nature of the social beliefs that particular institutions or individuals have the right to rule. There is a small but growing body of academic literature on the sociological legitimacy of international law or some of its areas,[33] but many of the conceptual questions underlying even enquiries that purport to be empirical are still little explored. Whose beliefs should matter? Those of states? Or those of the international community? And, if so, how is this community constituted and who are its members?

As for normative enquiries into legitimacy, they concern themselves with the standards and conditions that must be met for such a right to rule to be justifiable. The sociological dimension of legitimacy need not be irrelevant to the normative one, but the relationship between the two must be properly theorised. Whether social considerations matter, and if so to what extent, will depend on the particular standards of legitimacy that we are adopting. Providing an account of what those standards ought to be – that is, a new theory of legitimacy – is beyond the scope of this chapter, and I will instead focus on problems with legitimacy that are more specific to international law.

A prior question is whether we should be talking about the legitimacy of international law or of the institutions that make it. In the words of Allen Buchanan, '[i]nternational laws are legitimate only if the institutions that make them are legitimate'.[34] This view seems entirely plausible but the

[31] See e.g. A. Buchanan's definition of political legitimacy: 'An entity has political legitimacy if and only if it is morally justifying in exercising political power' in *Justice, Legitimacy and Self-Determination: Moral Foundations of International Law* (Oxford University Press, 2004) 233.

[32] A. Buchanan, 'The legitimacy of international law' and J. Tasioulas, 'The legitimacy in international law' in S. Besson and J. Tasioulas (eds.), *The Philosophy of International Law* (Oxford University Press, 2010), 79–80 and 97–116.

[33] Two examples are: M. Finnemore and M.N. Barnett, *Rules for the World: International Organisations in Global Politics* (Cornell University Press, 2004); Simmons, *Mobilising for Human Rights: International Law in Domestic Politics* (Harvard University Press, 2009).

[34] Buchanan, 'The legitimacy of international law', 80.

relationship between ruling institutions and law is complicated by two critical factors. First, a lot of the law in force today – international or domestic – is the creation of institutions of the past: should the illegitimacy of past institutions continue to taint the laws they enacted?

Secondly, and this is a concern for international law, not all law is enacted by institutions. International institutions, in particular, play a very limited role in the formation of rules of international law. Those institutions are themselves the creation of rules of international law; they seldom make them. States remain the makers, albeit not by means of enactment, of international law. Does that mean that only international law emanating from legitimate states is to be viewed as legitimate? If so, vast swathes of international law – from the UN Charter to the International Covenant on Economic, Social and Cultural Rights and the UN Convention on the Law of the Sea – would need to be morally disowned as illegitimate because they were (or are) the product of states that fail certain standards of legitimacy.

Thirdly, and perhaps most importantly, there is the issue of consent. If the legitimacy of international law depends on the consent of states, does that not take us back to the arid voluntarist view discussed in the previous section which fails doctrinally even before it is tested philosophically? To say that the concept of international law does not entail consent but that its legitimacy does would still leave us with a flawed and ultimately non-viable idea of international law.

An attempt to obviate these difficulties and, in particular, the issue of consent is to apply Joseph Raz's service conception of legitimate authority to international law.[35] On this approach, international law would be legitimate with respect to a state if that state is more likely to comply with the reasons that independently apply to it by taking the law as its guide, rather than by making its own judgement on the balance of reasons. By way of example, in the event of a worldwide epidemic the legitimacy of the WHO might be justified as follows: there are objective WHO-independent and international law-independent reasons to contain a worldwide

[35] See Tasioulas, 'Human rights, legitimacy and international law'; S. Besson, 'The authority of international law – lifting the state veil', *Sydney Law Review* 31 (2009), 343–80. On the service conception see: J. Raz, *Morality of Freedom* (Oxford University Press, 1986) 23ff. and, by the same author, 'The problem of authority: revisiting the service conception', *Minnesota Law Review* 90 (2006), 1003–44.

epidemic – reasons which evidently apply to decent states too. States can better pursue compliance with those reasons by following the directives of a central coordinating authority like the WHO rather than seeking to generate similar directives through, for example, a series of necessarily more chaotic acts of bilateral coordination.

As Raz himself accepted,[36] this is a thin account of legitimacy. Its '*piecemeal nature*' might not for example justify the systemic legitimacy of international law as a whole.[37] On this account, some international laws and institutions could be legitimate, but others not; legitimacy, moreover, may be a transient quality. Think, for example, of the International Sea-Bed Authority under the UN Convention on the Law of the Sea. The exploitation of marine minerals in the sea-bed is subject to the authorisation and regulation of this Sea-Bed Authority. There may be good law-independent reasons to comply with the directives of the Sea-Bed Authority now, but imagine the case of a state that discovers a process for exploiting sea-bed resources so efficient that it could resolve its energy problems without any of the negative consequences, for marine life for example, associated with these activities, and yet is still denied a mining permit – why should that state follow the directives of the Authority at that point? Far from baulking at this example, a supporter of the service conception would argue that this is precisely the sort of situation where an institution may deserve to lose its legitimacy. If its directives are irrational and unjustifiable, why should we continue to view the International Sea-Bed Authority as legitimate?

A problem with the service conception may be that it does not take much notice of the nexus between individuals and societies on the one hand, and institutions and authority on the other. People may prefer to be subject to the less-than-rational directives of an institution that they perceive as *theirs* rather than the entirely rational directives of an institution which they perceive as distant or, worse, as imposed on them by others. One of the flaws with supranational projects is precisely to assume that their rational/technocratic credentials will generate sufficient legitimacy. You could argue that undeserving institutions that are nonetheless readily accepted by a particular society may have earned the right to rule in a sociological sense, but not in a normative

[36] Raz, 'Problem of authority', 1003.
[37] Besson, 'The authority of international law', 352.

one. But, whether we consider it under the umbrella of legitimacy or under some other category, the relationship between the ruled and the rulers has profound repercussions for the philosophy of international law – and indeed for the future of international law. These questions are explored in the following section.

3 The Problem of Sovereignty

I will refer to the problem that I began to outline at the end of the previous section as the problem of sovereignty. It is not my intention here to explore the conceptual difficulties with the idea of sovereignty (a task I have attempted elsewhere[38]), but I focus instead on normative arguments about the weakening of state sovereignty, and the expansion of international law and institutions. Is the weakening of the state a good thing? What principles should govern the transfer of powers and functions from states to the international sphere?

It may help to begin with a few observations on the development of international law in recent decades. It is no exaggeration to describe the rapid process of decolonisation that followed the end of the Second World War as a global political revolution which, surprisingly however, did not subvert the international order created by the UN Charter but somehow took place under it. The key principle that allowed this revolution to happen within international law rather than against it is self-determination. It had featured prominently in President Wilson's Fourteen Points but did not crystallise as a principle of international law in the interwar years. With its inclusion in Article 1 of the UN Charter as one of the purposes of the UN, its legal status could no longer be in dispute, but what gave self-determination legal content and purpose was decolonisation. Self-determination may have provided initially little more than a political vocabulary, but soon developed into an international legal framework on which colonised peoples relied to advance their political aspiration to self-government and independent statehood. International law, which had enabled the creation of colonial empires in decades past, presided over their demise in the 1950s and 1960s.

[38] G. Verdirame, 'Sovereignty' in J. D'Aspremont and J. Sahib (eds.), *Concepts for International Law – Contributions to Disciplinary Thought* (Edward Elgar Publishing, 2019).

With self-determination, international law also adopted a particular sense of the idea of sovereignty – popular sovereignty – which had played a central role in Western politics for centuries before.[39] International law continued to be state-centric, but it was no longer the bearer of an idea of sovereignty exclusively centred on states. It instead accepted, not unqualifiedly but in an important measure, that peoples are in some sense sovereign too.

It is no surprise that, with the end of the Cold War, some international lawyers, most notably Thomas Franck,[40] expected international law to take a further step in this direction and fully embrace the idea of popular sovereignty by developing self-determination into a general principle of democratic governance. Why didn't this happen? One reason may be the little enthusiasm that international lawyers themselves displayed for this argument and, indeed more generally, for normative arguments, as normative scepticism and arid postmodernism have tightened their grip on theoretical discussions in the field for at least two decades.

But the more important reason is a subtle but profound transformation in the role of international law in the last thirty years or so. International law is now seen as the main vehicle for the regulation of globalisation. Accompanied by the narrative of the ineluctable decline of the state, international law and its institutions have thus come to be viewed by many as institutions of government, destined to ultimately replace states. In Europe this process has not even been subtle or covert: member states of the European Union, especially those who joined the monetary union, have all but surrendered their ability to regulate the internal market through a massive transfer of powers traditionally thought of as quintessentially sovereign to the organs of the European Union. That EU-style supranationalism has then led to the hegemony of one country, Germany, is an important part of the story but one that will need to be told another time.[41]

While most realise that globalisation is obviously a threat to the state, few seem to appreciate that the *Kulturkampf* is not, or at least not only, between nationalism and the unstoppable forces of economic and

[39] Ibid. On the origins of popular sovereignty see E. Morgan, *Inventing the People: The Rise of Popular Sovereignty in England and America* (W.W. Norton & Company, 1988).

[40] T. Franck, 'The emerging right to democratic governance', *The American Journal of International Law* 86 (Jan. 1992), 46–91.

[41] But see: P. Lever, *Berlin Rules: Europe and the German Way* (I.B. Tauris, 2017); H. Kundnani, *The Paradox of German Power* (Hurst and Co., 2016).

technological progress. As the principal unit of self-government and political liberty, the state is an extraordinary achievement – one that international law too, as we saw before, recognised through the principle of self-determination. The question thus is this: can we protect this moral and political achievement while, at the same time, entrusting a greater governmental role to international law as globalisation continues to make strides?

While the so-called populists are often accused of offering easy solutions, the commonest reply to this question – to assert the purported inevitability of globalisation – does not even rise to the level of a solution. It is a lazy cliché that fails to engage with the basic problem of political morality that we are confronted with. Dani Rodrik argues that what we have before us is a trilemma: of globalisation, the state and democracy we can have only two at most – but not all three at the same time.[42] If this is right, is perhaps the best answer to make democracy global? To preserve the benefits of globalisation while addressing the democratic deficit of international institutions?

Possibly, but the idea of global democracy has no easy life either. Thomas Christiano, for example, argues that '[g]lobal democracy is highly unlikely to succeed given the weakness of global civil society and it is highly unlikely to be legitimate given the unevenness of stakes in its decisions and given the high chance of permanent minorities'.[43] Give it time, you might say. Let social media and new technologies work their magic, civil society and identities will be progressively reshaped, and we will overcome what are, after all, empirical obstacles to the realisation of the ideal of global democracy. But the obstacles may not all be empirical. There are two, in particular, that have a distinct moral dimension.

First, as noted at the end of the previous section, people tend to prefer *their* rulers to other people's rulers – and not necessarily because they think their rulers better. Most Italians would probably agree that Germany is better ruled than Italy but, if you then ask them whether they would want to be ruled by those supposedly better German rulers, they are very

[42] D. Rodrik, *The Globalisation Paradox: Why Global Markets, States and Democracy Can't Coexist* (Oxford University Press, 2011), esp. 184–206.

[43] See, for example, T. Christiano, 'Democratic legitimacy and international institutions' in S. Besson and J. Tasioulas (eds.), *The Philosophy of International Law* (Oxford University Press, 2010), 119 at 137.

likely to say no. It would be wrong to dismiss this preference as an expression of nationalistic bigotry. There is a moral value to it that we should not discount. For it is part of the moral ideas of self-respect and self-ownership, which apply to individuals as well as to political communities. A wrong decision taken by us has a moral quality that the right decision taken by others for us lacks: it is an act of self-government and makes self-improvement possible. The reason why partisans in Europe and liberation movements in former European colonies are so central to the national histories and iconographies is because, however limited their concrete military role, they helped restore a sense of collective self-respect after national humiliations.

The second obstacle was described by Kant in an important passage in his essay on 'perpetual peace':

> The idea of the right of nations presupposes the separation of many neighbouring states independent of one another; and though such a condition is of itself a condition of war (unless a federative union of them prevents the outbreak of hostilities), this is nevertheless better, in accordance with the idea of reason, than the fusion of them by one power overgrowing the rest and passing into a universal monarchy, since as the range of government expands laws progressively lose their vigour, and a soulless despotism, after it has destroyed the seed of good, finally deteriorates into anarchy.[44]

One can think of this as a contingent and empirical problem but, even if it is, we may need more time to develop a solution than the pace of globalisation allows. It may not be an argument against attempting global democracy *ever*, but it may be a good one against rushing into it *now*.

All of this morally justifies great restraint in the transfer of sovereign functions from states to regional or global institutions. Two principles must govern these transfers: one to do with individual liberty and the other with political liberty. First, in the exercise of those functions, international organisations must be capable of respecting fundamental human rights to the same degree as the transferring state. A state should not empower institutions that cannot guarantee human rights, at a minimum, to the same degree that it is committed to. Secondly, states should retain

[44] I. Kant, 'Toward perpetual peace' in M.J. Gregor (ed.), *The Cambridge Edition of the Works of Immanuel Kant in Translation: Practical Philosophy* (Cambridge University Press, 1999), 311–51 at 336.

sovereign control over functions the transfer of which would weaken political liberty, or the potential therefor, by engendering among the members of its political community a sense of alienation and self-diminishment. What about states that do not protect liberty? Shouldn't we encourage them at least to surrender all of their sovereign functions to more benign international rule? Quite aside from the fact that authoritarian states are, if anything, more reluctant to strengthen international law and to transfer powers to international institutions, the second principle still acts as a limit.

Conclusion

One area of discussion that this chapter has not touched on is the rule of law. The jurisprudential difficulties with extending the rule of law to international law derive, principally, from conceptual confusion about the rule of law itself and from the absence of the state. There is a rich and growing literature on these problems.[45] What I will note here is that an international law practice on the rule of law is developing, which may add an explanatory challenge to the conceptual and normative challenges that the rule of law already offers. In 2012 the UN General Assembly adopted a Resolution on the Rule of Law at the National and International Levels, which recognises a number of basic features of the rule of law (e.g. predictability, legality, equal subjection to and protection under the law) alongside more contested ones (e.g. the laws being 'fair and equitable').[46]

By contrast, twenty years earlier, in one of its first rulings in the *Tadić* case, the Appeals Chambers of the International Criminal Tribunal for the Former Yugoslavia had not helped the case for the rule of international law by holding that 'the principle that a tribunal must be established by law . . . is a general principle of law imposing an international obligation which only applies to the administration of criminal justice in a municipal setting'.[47]

[45] See for example: S. Beaulac, 'The rule of law in international law today' in G. Palombella and N. Walker (eds.), *Relocating the Rule of Law* (Hart Publishing, 2009) 197–223; J. Crawford, 'International law and the rule of law', *Adelaide Law Review* 24 (Jan. 2003) 3–12; J. Waldron, 'Are sovereigns entitled to the benefits of the international rule of law?', *European Journal of International Law* 22 (May, 2011) 315–43.

[46] UN General Assembly Resolution 67/1, 30 November 2012.

[47] *Prosecutor* v. *Tadić* (Jurisdiction), Appeals Chamber, 2 October 1995, International Law Reports 105 (1997) 472–3.

If pronouncements like this one, rather than being excoriated, had come to define the generally accepted practice of international law, the task of the philosopher would have been limited to exploring whether the rule of international law is conceivable conceptually and desirable as a moral aspiration, but it would have been difficult to escape the conclusion that it did not form any part of the phenomenon of international law. We have, fortunately, moved on from that first step and the *Tadić* ruling is viewed as a kind of faux pas. As Judge Crawford has written, a commitment to the rule of law must be a 'profession of values' and a 'fundamental goal' for international lawyers.[48] How it operates in practice, and how it differs from and relates to the rule of law at the national level are important questions. But it is difficult to see how any of the inquiries we examined before – on the concept of international law, its legitimacy, and the relationship with the state – can progress without a shared belief that international law must comprehend, at a minimum, basic ideas of non-arbitrariness, legality and equal subjection to law.

[48] J. Crawford, 'The rule of law', 12.

Index